Cloud Computing for Smart Education and Collaborative Learning

The book presents next-generation education technology and the pedagogy of the Education Cloud. It covers technological developments, case studies, innovative research approaches, and solutions for advanced learning paradigms using Internet of Things (IoT), cloud computing, and machine learning to handle various challenges of the smart education system. It discusses cloud architecture, management, and framework for education from virtual classrooms and labs. It shows how cloud computing framework can be integrated with fog computing, edge computing, deep learning, and IoT.

- Illustrates from fundamental theories to practical and sophisticated applications of cloud technology for the education domain
- Explores e-learning applications through location-independent cloud services to reduce cost
- Covers result-oriented, real-time solutions for smart, accessible education and its real-time application support
- Discusses accessible cloud services for people with special needs
- Presents flexible and scalable cost-effective e-learning architecture and scenario for education technology

It serves as a valuable resource for academicians, researchers, and professionals interested in smart education and cloud technology.

Cloud Computing for Smart Education and Collaborative Learning

Edited by

Urmila Shrawankar and Prerna Mishra

CRC Press
Taylor & Francis Group
CHAPMAN & HALL

Designed cover image: ShutterStock

First edition published 2025
by CRC Press
2385 NW Executive Center Drive, Suite 320, Boca Raton, FL 33431

and by CRC Press
4 Park Square, Milton Park, Abingdon, Oxon, OX14 4RN

CRC Press is an imprint of Taylor & Francis Group, LLC

Library of Congress Cataloging-in-Publication Data
Names: Shrawankar, Urmila, editor. | Mishra, Prerna, editor.
Title: Cloud computing for smart education and collaborative learning /
Edited by Urmila Shrawankar and Prerna Mishra.
Description: First edition. | Boca Raton, FL : C&H/ CRC Press, 2025. |
Includes bibliographical references and index. |
Identifiers: LCCN 2024050057 (print) | LCCN 2024050058 (ebook) |
ISBN 9781032741154 (hardback) | ISBN 9781032751313 (paperback) |
ISBN 9781003472537 (ebook)
Subjects: LCSH: Educational technology. | Cloud computing. |
Group work in education. | Education–Computer network resources.
Classification: LCC LB1028.3 .C627 2025 (print) | LCC LB1028.3 (ebook) |
DDC 371.33/4–dc23/eng/20240102
LC record available at https://lccn.loc.gov/2024050057
LC ebook record available at https://lccn.loc.gov/2024050058

ISBN: 9781032741154 (hbk)
ISBN: 9781032751313 (pbk)
ISBN: 9781003472537 (ebk)

DOI: 10.1201/9781003472537

Typeset in Times
by Newgen Publishing UK

Contents

Preface ix
Editor Biographies xi
List of Contributors xiii

SECTION I Educational Clouds: A Prologue

Chapter 1 Smart Learning Environments: Enhancing E-Learning with Cloud-Based Infrastructures 3

Prerna Mishra and Urmila Shrawankar

Chapter 2 Cloud-Based Learning: Reconceptualizing Educational Excellences 14

Neetu Amlani, Swapnil Deshpande, Zohra Yasmeen, and Priyanka Samarth

Chapter 3 The Educational Cloud: A Landscape of Promise and Peril 30

Dileep Kumar Singh and Sameera Khan

Chapter 4 Envisioning Tomorrow: Educational Clouds in Future Education 44

Roshni Bhave, Vijaya Kamble, Amita Meshram, A. Venkata Mahesh, and Dhananjay Bhagat

Chapter 5 Unveiling E-Learning's Potential: A Cloud-Based Multidimensional Approach 60

Sameera Khan and Dileep Kumar Singh

Chapter 6 Scale of Advancements in Smart Education and E-Study Using Cloud Authoring Tools 78

Karunya S. and Stephen S. Raj

Chapter 7 Enhancing Virtual Learning with Cloud Computing Paradigm 91

Ketaki A. Bhosale, Sangram T. Patil, and Shubhangi Suryawanshi

SECTION II Pedagogical Changes and Multi-faceted Aspects of Clouds in E-Learning

Chapter 8 Transformative Pedagogy: Collaborative Learning with Cloud Architecture and Virtual Programming Labs.................................... 105

Zulfiya Usmonova and Mohamed Uvaze Ahamed Ayoobkhan

Chapter 9 Challenges and Solutions in Industrial IoT Education after Navigating the Cloud.. 123

Satyajeet Shinge and Urmila Shrawankar

Chapter 10 Cloud-Powered Distance Learning: Breaking Geographical Barriers in Education.. 133

Vinay Kumar Yandrapalli and Shubham Sharma

Chapter 11 The Comprehensive Study for Enhancing Security in Cloud-Based Learning Environments through Blockchain.............. 145

Jagdish Pimple, Arti Burghate, Shraddha Raut, and Anil Band

Chapter 12 Unveiling Synergy: Explainable AI's Role in Enhancing Cloud-Based Collaborative Learning in the Cloud Era.................... 159

Vinay Kumar Yandrapalli and Shubham Sharma

SECTION III Challenges and Solutions in Educational Clouds

Chapter 13 Optimizing Learning Environments: A Critical Review of Unified Cloud-Based Platforms for Educational Resource Management.. 173

Manoj Bramhe and Jagdish Pimple

Chapter 14 Navigating the Legal and Ethical Aspects of Cloud-Based Education... 188

Vinay Kumar Yandrapalli and Shubham Sharma

Chapter 15 Navigating Remote Learning: Cloud-Powered Tools Transforming Education 199

Uma Yadav and Shweta Bondre

Chapter 16 Leveraging Multicloud Technology for Seamless Education in Rural Areas 214

Shweta Barhate, Snehal Narale, and M. P. Dhore

Chapter 17 Framework for Bridging the Skill Gap between Higher Education Institutions and Industry: A Machine Learning Approach 222

Saleema J. S., Lakshmi Shankar Iyer, and Lakshmi Sankaran

SECTION IV Panoramic Applications of Educational Clouds

Chapter 18 E-Learning Recommender System for Deaf and Hard of Hearing Learners 247

Anisha Poly and P. K. Nizar Banu

Chapter 19 Unlocking the Potential of Educational Cloud Platforms for Differently Abled People 262

Sohini Banerjee, Shweta Barhate, and M. P. Dhore

Chapter 20 E-Interpretation System: Smart Document Learning System Using Educational Clouds 275

Prerna Mishra and Urmila Shrawankar

Chapter 21 Revolutionizing Education: The Multifaceted Role of Cloud in Modern e-Learning Environment 286

Josephine A. Anitha

Chapter 22 Cloud-Based Secured Examination System for Collaborative Learning 299

Shatakshi Kokate and Urmila Shrawankar

Chapter 23 Role of Educational Clouds in the Transformation of Higher Education....308

Bhargavi S. Chinchmalatpure and Swati S. Sherekar

Chapter 24 Leveraging Educational Clouds for Empowering Rural Education....321

Siddhivinayak Kulkarni and Sally Firmin

Chapter 25 Building an Interactive Programming Learning Platform with MEAN Stack: Integrating Chatter Bots and Best Programming Practices....337

Baby Vadlana, N Venkata Sailaja, and D. N. Vasundhara

Chapter 26 From Screens to Classrooms: A Comprehensive Study of E-Learning, M-Learning, and Face-to-Face Learning....345

Reena Thakur, Nishal Puri, and Parul Bhanarkar

Index....359

Preface

The rapid rise of cloud computing has fundamentally transformed education, offering unprecedented opportunities for accessibility, scalability, and personalised learning. Cloud-based platforms now break down geographical barriers, making education more inclusive and adaptive. These platforms provide real-time collaboration, data-driven insights, and tailored learning experiences that improve educational outcomes across e-learning, mobile learning, and distance education. Institutions benefit from cost efficiency, robust infrastructure, and enhanced security, while educators leverage cloud tools to explore innovative teaching strategies, such as gamification and adaptive learning. As education continues to evolve, cloud computing stands at the forefront, driving remote, inclusive, and customised learning environments while addressing challenges such as the digital divide and security concerns.

In this book, we explore how the integration of cloud computing and advanced digital tools is reshaping education, particularly in collaborative and distance learning. Virtual Programming Labs (VPLs), cloud architectures, and other innovative platforms facilitate the sharing of knowledge and expertise, overcoming traditional limitations like resource shortages and physical classroom boundaries. In industrial education, cloud systems designed for the Industrial Internet of Things (IIoT) address the growing demand for standardised curricula, interdisciplinary skills, and heightened security measures, encouraging deeper collaboration between academia and industry. These same cloud platforms also support remote learning by providing scalable, real-time interactive experiences, such as artificial intelligence (AI)-powered personalized learning systems and virtual labs.

Security, a critical concern for cloud-based systems, finds potential solutions in blockchain technology, which can protect data integrity, authentication, and intellectual property. Additionally, the advanced method improves transparency, trust, and user engagement, making AI-driven educational frameworks more accessible and reliable. The convergence of these technologies is leading to a more secure, flexible, and inclusive global education system.

This book also delves into how unified cloud platforms enhance learning by centralising educational resources, optimising search functions, and simplifying access through single sign-in systems. Legal and ethical challenges surrounding cloud adoption, such as data privacy and digital equity, are addressed with practical strategies and case studies. The rise of remote learning tools such as video-conferencing platforms and learning management systems has transformed education, improving collaboration, student outcomes, and addressing both pedagogical and security concerns.

For learners with disabilities, including the deaf and hard of hearing (DHH), cloud-based technologies are making a significant impact. Tag-based content recommender systems and educational cloud architectures specifically designed for learners with sensory impairments are helping shift the focus from disability to engagement, allowing for more interactive, inclusive learning environments. Smart learning systems that incorporate cloud-based e-interpretation tools for real-time text and image translation further enhance accessibility for students with special needs. The book also highlights the integration of blockchain, fog computing, and cloud computing to secure examination processes, ensuring the integrity of educational assessments.

Particularly in rural education, the integration of multicloud architectures offers scalable, cost-effective solutions to overcome infrastructure, connectivity, and resource challenges. This approach empowers rural learners and educators with access to high-quality educational tools, overcoming longstanding barriers. By embracing these cutting-edge technologies, this book demonstrates how cloud computing and related innovations are fostering a more inclusive, secure, and efficient educational landscape, bridging gaps and unlocking new opportunities for learners worldwide.

Editor Biographies

Urmila Shrawankar received her Ph.D. degree in computer science and engineering from SGB Amravati University and M.Tech. degree in computer science and engineering from RTM Nagpur University. At present, Dr. Urmila is working as a professor and director, School of Computer Science and Engineering, Ramdeobaba University Nagpur (MS), India. Her areas of interest include high-performance computing, advanced operating systems, distributed and parallel computing, cloud computing, real-time computing, algorithms, and assistive technology. She is a recipient of 5 research grants. She has 6 grants, 12 published patents, and 18 copyrights registered. She is author of 2 books, editor of 3 books, 25 book chapters, and around 200 research papers in international journals and conferences of high repute. She has served as a part of the editorial boards, advisory boards, and reviewer boards for many journals. She has participated in many international conferences worldwide as a Core Organizing Committee member, Technical Program Committee member, Special Session Chair, and Session Chair. Dr. Urmila is a member of IEEE (SM), ACM(SM), CSI (LM), ISTE (LM), IE (LM), IAENG, etc.

Prerna Mishra received her Ph.D. degree in computer science and engineering from IIIT Raipur and M.Tech. degree in computer sci and engineering from RTM Nagpur University. At present, Dr. Prerna is working as an assistant Professor, Department of Computer Science and Engineering, IIIT Nagpur, India. Her areas of interest include image interpretation, document processing and analysis, computer vision, human–computer interaction, activity recognition and description, image reconstruction, and assistive technology. She has edited 1 book, published more than 15 research papers in international journals and conferences of high repute, authored 3 book chapters, and 2 published patents. She is serving as reviewer for many refereed journals and reputed conferences. She is a member of IEEE, CSI (LM), ISTE (LM), IE (LM), IAENG, etc.

Contributors

Neetu Amlani
Assistant Professor, Computer Science Department, S.S. Maniar College of Computer and Management, RTMNU Nagpur, India

Josephine A. Anitha
Ethiraj College for Women (Autonomous), Egmore, Chennai, Tamil Nadu, India

Mohamed Uvaze Ahamed Ayoobkhan
Department of Computer Science, New Uzbekistan University, Tashkent, Uzbekistan

Anil Band
Assistant Professor, Department of Computer Science & Engineering, G H Raisoni College of Engineering, Amravati, Maharashtra, India

Sohini Banerjee
Research Scholar, Department of Electronics and Computer Science, Rashtrasant Tukadoji Maharaj Nagpur University, Mahatma Jotiba Phule University Campus, Amravati Road, Nagpur, India

P. K. Nizar Banu
Associate Professor, Department of Computer Science, CHRIST (Deemed to be University), Bangalore, India

Shweta Barhate
Assistant Professor, Department of Electronics & Computer Science, Rashtrasant Tukadoji Maharaj Nagpur University Nagpur, Maharasthra, India

Dhananjay Bhagat
Assistant Professor, Department of Artificial Intelligence, G H Raisoni College of Engineering, Nagpur, affiliated with RTMNU Nagpur University, India

Parul Bhanarkar
Assistant Professor, Department of Computer Science & Engineering, Jhulelal Institute of Technology, Nagpur, Maharashtra, India

Roshni Bhave
Assistant Professor, Department of Computer Science & Engineering, Yeshwantrao Chavan college of Engineering, Nagpur, India, affiliation of RTMNU Nagpur University

Ketaki A. Bhosale
Department of Computer Science & Engineering, D Y Patil College of Engineering & Technology, Kolhapur, Maharashtra, India

Shweta Bondre
Shri Ramdeobaba College of Engineering and Management, Ramdeobaba University, Nagpur

Manoj Bramhe
Professor, Department of Information Technology, St. Vincent Pallotti College of Engineering and Technology, Nagpur, Maharashtra, India.

Arti Burghate
Assistant Professor, Department of Information Technology, Nagpur Institute of Technology, Nagpur, Maharashtra, India.

Bhargavi S. Chinchmalatpure
Assistant Professor, Bharatiya Mahavidyalaya, Maharashtra, India

Swapnil Deshpande
Assistant Professor, Computer Science Department, S.S. Maniar College of Computer and Management, RTMNU Nagpur, India

D. N. Vasundhara
Assistant Professor, Computer Science and Engineering, VNR Vignana Jyothi Institute of Engineering and Technology, Bachupally, Hyderabad, Telangana, India.

M. P. Dhore
Professor(Pro.Vice Chancellor), Sant Gadge Baba Amravati University, Amravati, Maharasthra, India

Sally Firmin
Institute of Innovation Science and Sustainability (IISS), Federation University, Ballarat, Australia

Lakshmi Shankar Iyer
Associate Professor, School of Business and Management, CHRIST (Deemed to be University), Hosur Road, Bengaluru, India

Vijaya Kamble
Assistant Professor, Department of Computer Science & Engineering, S.B. Jain Institute of Technology Management & Research, Nagpur, India

Sameera Khan
Assistant Professor, Department of IT, Vardhaman College of Engineering, Hyderabad, India

Shatakshi Kokate
Research Scholar, Department of Computer Science and G H Raisoni College of Engineering, Nagpur, India

Siddhivinayak Kulkarni
Department of Computer Engineering and Technology, Dr. Vishwanath Karad MIT World Peace University, Pune, India

A. Venkata Mahesh
Assistant Professor, Department of Computer Science & Engineering, GIET University, India

Amita Meshram
Assistant Professor, Department of Computer Science & Engineering, Yeshwantrao Chavan College of Engineering, Nagpur, affiliated with RTMNU Nagpur University, India

Prerna Mishra
Department of CSE, IIIT Nagpur, Nagpur, India

N Venkata Sailaja
Assistant Professor, Computer Science and Engineering, VNR Vignana Jyothi Institute of Engineering and Technology, Bachupally, Hyderabad, Telangana, India.

Snehal Narale
Assistant Professor, Rashtrasant Tukadoji Maharaj Nagpur University, Nagpur, Maharashtra, India

Sangram T. Patil
Department of CSE, DYP-ATU, Talsande, Maharashtra, India

Jagdish Pimple
Assistant Professor, Department of Information Technology, St.Vincent Pallotti College of Engineering and Technology, Nagpur, Maharashtra, India.

Anisha Poly
Research scholar, (Department of Computer Science), CHRIST (Deemed to be University), Hosur Road, Bengaluru, India

Nishal Puri
Assistant Professor, Computer Science & Engineering, Jhulelal Institute of Technology, Nagpur, Maharashtra, India

Stephen S. Raj
Assistant Professor, Department of Computer Science, Government Arts and Science College, Thirukovilur, Tamil Nadu, India

Shraddha Raut
Assistant Professor, Department of Computer Science & Engineering, G H Raisoni College of Engineering, Amravati, Maharashtra, India

Karunya S.
Assistant Professor, PG Department of Information Technology and BCA, Dwaraka Doss Goverdhan Doss Vai shnav College, Chennai, Tamilnadu, India

Saleema J. S.
Associate Professor, Department of Statistics and Data Science, CHRIST (Deemed to be University), Hosur Road, Bengaluru, India.

Priyanka Samarth
Assistant Professor, Computer Science Department, S.S. Maniar College of Computer and Management, RTMNU Nagpur, India

Lakshmi Sankaran
Research scholar, Department of Computer Science, CHRIST (Deemed to be University),Hosur Road, Bengaluru, India

Shubham Sharma
Research Scholar, National Institute of Technology, Raipur, Chhattisgarh, India

Swati S. Sherekar
Professor, SGBAU, India

Satyajeet Shinge
Research Scholar, Department of Computer Science and Engineering, G. H. Raisoni College of Engineering, Nagpur (MH), India

Urmila Shrawankar
Professor, School of Computer Science and Engineering, Ramdeobaba University, Nagpur, Maharashtra, India

Dileep Kumar Singh
Assistant Professor, School of Business Management, Narsee Monjee Institute of Management Studies, Hyderabad, India

Shubhangi Suryawanshi
Department of Artificial Intelligence and Data Science, Dr. D. Y. Patil Institute of Technology, Pune, Maharashtra, India

Reena Thakur
Assistant Professor, Computer Science & Engineering, Jhulelal Institute of Technology, Nagpur, Maharashtra, India

Zulfiya Usmonova
Department of Computer Science, New Uzbekistan University, Tashkent, Uzbekistan

Baby Vadlana
Associate Professor, Computer Science and Engineering, VNR Vignana Jyothi Institute of Engineering and Technology, Bachupally, Hyderabad, Telangana, India.

Uma Yadav
Shri RamdeUma Yadavobaba College of Engineering and Management, Ramdeobaba University, Nagpur

Vinay Kumar Yandrapalli
MDM Developer, Worldwide Technology, USA

Zohra Yasmeen
Assistant Professor, Computer Science Department, S.S. Maniar College of Computer and Management, RTMNU Nagpur, India

Section I

Educational Clouds
A Prologue

1 Smart Learning Environments

Enhancing E-Learning with Cloud-Based Infrastructures

Prerna Mishra and Urmila Shrawankar

1.1 INTRODUCTION

E-learning has emerged with the widespread use of the internet and digital communication systems, enhancing distance education. This approach leverages various formats and functions like virtual instruction, emails, web links, discussion boards, and other learning platforms, facilitating better management of the learning experience through the online integration of students, content producers, and professionals. Key benefits of e-learning include consistency, adaptability, accessibility, and ease of access, which have gained popularity in information technology, especially post-COVID-19. Various educational efforts, such as MOOCs, Blackboard, Desire2Learn (D2L) online learning platforms, and university virtual learning centers, have adopted e-learning globally.

Compared to traditional in-person classes, virtual programs under the e-learning paradigm provide an optimal learning environment and increased accessibility. However, the infrastructure required to support concurrent service for many students exceeds the capacity of traditional web applications, with instructional resource needs fluctuating rapidly and dynamically (de Souza Rodrigues et al. 2021). To address this, advanced infrastructure is necessary to handle peak demands without affecting other system services. Cloud computing technology offers a solution by providing services based on usage and paying only for the resources used, reducing computational costs while enhancing reliability and availability.

Cloud computing aims to provide transparent mobility and various services without needing users to be familiar with the underlying infrastructure. Unlike computing grids, which focus on maximizing system performance, cloud computing supports diverse services, including hosting and word processing, and is foundational to Service-Oriented Architecture (SOA). It overcomes organizational computing barriers like application integration, concurrency control, and security protocols while hiding the technical aspects of the infrastructure from users (Swan and Shea 2023). The advantages of cloud computing are clear, as users do not need to invest in new hardware, and cloud vendors offer comparable or better capabilities than local applications.

DOI: 10.1201/9781003472537-2

Additionally, cloud computing allows businesses to operationalize software faster with fewer information technology (IT) services, aligning IT assets based on computational complexity in virtual environments. Massive e-learning environments generate extensive archives of student participation, storing significant data that can be leveraged for various educational insights.

1.1.1 Smart Learning and Cloud Computing

E-learning systems have expanded rapidly due to the suspension of on-campus classes and a surge in students, instructional content, and available services (Ali et al. 2023). Choosing a scalable platform that balances costs while optimizing resources is crucial. Cloud computing facilitates this by delivering and retrieving information efficiently. Unlike traditional learning environments, Software as a Service (SaaS) applications offer resilient and comprehensive distance learning, enhancing the technological and pedagogical benefits. This shift supports the migration to online tools and interactive services, including teaching materials, recordings, and peer instruction.

Many educational institutions now use cloud technology, indicating a promising future. Education SaaS, a cloud-based e-learning system, benefits users through swift deployment and maintenance-free operations, focusing on critical business areas while receiving automatic updates and Web 2.0 resources. E-learning system architecture and cloud computing ensure consistency, harmony, effective resource use, and long-term stability (Gairola and Kumar 2022). This approach saves costs by eliminating software, deployment, or server management expenses, making it ideal for scenarios like the COVID-19 pandemic.

Cloud computing offers scalability, ensuring consistent software performance regardless of student usage. SaaS providers must maintain high security, consolidating consumer data across various services, which increases the need for platforms and data integrators. The cloud's advantages include affordability, ease of data access, and no need for physical data backups, allowing students to retain and grow their information (Meiryani et al. 2023). Cloud-based systems facilitate easy recovery from crashes and enable access and modification of files from multiple locations, which has been crucial during the lockdown for e-learning implementation.

Data access monitoring is simplified as only one location needs control instead of numerous dispersed computers, and cybersecurity modifications can be efficiently managed. Despite the need for further research on cloud-related pedagogies, the cloud's ease of access promotes collaboration from anywhere, reaching more students outside traditional teaching environments and providing meaningful information across diverse contexts (Meiryani et al. 2023). The cloud e-learning techniques involve three fundamental layers: a virtualized platform, a cloud management system, and services. This architecture supports efficient resource allocation, preventing virtual machines from interfering with each other and enabling instructional coordinators to create and manage virtual PCs for specific course projects (Gairola and Kumar 2022; Meiryani et al. 2023).

The integration of cloud technology with e-learning has garnered attention due to its high demand for continuing education. Almost all educational institutions consider it an effective and suitable alternative for e-learning. However, there is a lack of research providing a theoretical foundation for developing methodologies. The flexibility of the cloud strategy could be a significant advantage in creating analytical frameworks and successful teaching techniques. Despite limited strategic studies, the cloud's characteristics support social engagement and collaborative learning. For instance, research on students' views of interaction within sharable documents highlights the potential of cloud-based instructional methods to enhance collective learning experiences (Parusheva et al. 2023).

1.2 COLLABORATIVE LEARNING AND ACADEMIC MOTIVATION

"Collaborative learning" is a broad term describing activities where students work together to achieve shared educational goals (Kwiatkowska and Wiśniewska-Nogaj 2022). Unlike traditional lecture-based instruction, which emphasizes the passive reception of information, collaborative learning engages students actively in the learning process. This method is widely regarded as more effective than passive learning approaches and is considered a promising pedagogical strategy in higher education. The literature discusses that collaborative tasks enhance student engagement and participation, making learning more potent than traditional methods. Extensive research links collaborative learning to numerous positive student outcomes. Additionally, it is positively associated with academic achievement, need for cognition, and critical thinking (Khan et al. 2022). Collaborative learning also improves attitudes toward instructors, self-esteem, social interdependence, peer support, and openness to diversity through increased interactions with diverse peers (Khan et al. 2022).

Motivation in educational contexts refers to the factors that stimulate an individual's desire to complete tasks or achieve goals (Qureshi et al. 2023). There are three types of motivation: intrinsic, extrinsic, and amotivation. Intrinsic motivation is driven by internal satisfaction, while extrinsic motivation is driven by external rewards. Amotivation reflects a lack of both intrinsic and extrinsic motivation (Berestova et al. 2022). Academic motivation can coexist with intrinsic or extrinsic motivation; students can be motivated to learn regardless of their interest in the content. Intrinsic motivation refers to an internal drive to achieve academic goals and the satisfaction derived from learning. In contrast, extrinsic motivation is driven by external factors, such as pleasing parents or earning money. Academic motivation is dynamic and changes throughout a student's university years, typically decreasing over time. It is linked to various important outcomes, including academic engagement, persistence, cognitive engagement, retention of material, depth of learning, and grades (Dierendonck et al. 2023).

Several studies also examine academic motivation as an outcome measure, exploring how social interactions influence motivation. Researchers emphasize the role of social environments in shaping motivation levels and goals. Collaborative learning, for example, fosters accountability among students working towards shared goals (Kwiatkowska and Wiśniewska-Nogaj 2022). Studies suggest that peer interactions significantly impact academic motivation at both secondary. Despite limited recent research, contemporary studies argue that social dynamics, such as those in collaborative learning settings, are crucial for student success, including openness to diversity, academic performance, and persistence.

1.3 CLOUD ARCHITECTURE FOR E-LEARNING

A generalized architecture of a cloud computing platform, as depicted in Figure 1.1, is typical for most e-learning approaches on the cloud. The first layer represents the interface with the cloud environment, consisting of various management subsystems. These include a planner for storage services, a management system for distributing the execution load among virtual machines, a system administrator to monitor and initiate activities in each layer, and a security component to ensure the privacy, recovery, integrity, and security of user data and transactions. The second layer consists of virtual machines implemented within the system, while the third layer includes all the physical architecture of the system. The components of the architecture are discussed below.

1. **Client Layer:** This layer consists of various user devices, including laptops, tablets, and smartphones, which are used by students, teachers, and administrators to access the e-learning platform. These devices serve as the primary means for users to interact with the platform, allowing them to participate in online classes, access educational content, and manage their learning activities.

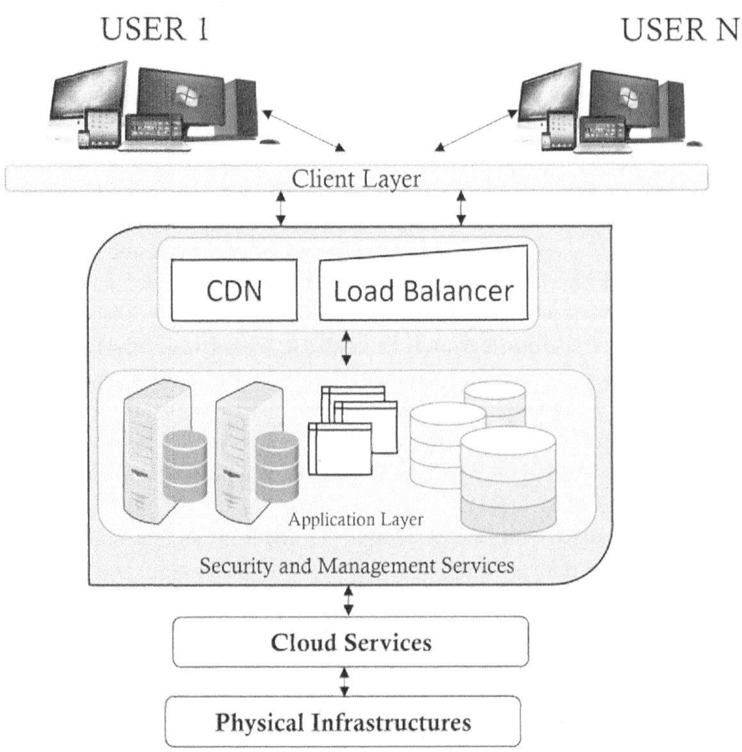

FIGURE 1.1 Cloud Architecture.

2. **Content Delivery Network (CDN):** The CDN is a network of geographically distributed servers that cache static content, such as images, videos, and text, close to the users. This proximity reduces latency, ensuring that content is delivered quickly and efficiently. By minimizing the distance data must travel, CDNs enhance the overall user experience, making it faster and more reliable.
3. **Load Balancer:** A load balancer distributes incoming traffic across multiple web servers in the application layer. This distribution ensures that no single server becomes overloaded, which can lead to slower response times or even server crashes. By managing the traffic flow, the load balancer helps maintain the platform's performance and scalability, allowing it to handle many simultaneous users.
4. **Application Layer:** The application layer hosts the e-learning application code responsible for essential functionalities. This includes user management for tasks such as login and registration, course creation and management, content delivery (lectures, assignments, quizzes), collaboration tools like forums and chat, and learning analytics and reporting. This layer is the core of the e-learning platform, providing the necessary tools and features for effective online education.
5. **Database:** A scalable cloud database stores all the application data, including user information, courses, content, learning progress, and assessment results. This centralized storage ensures that data is easily accessible and manageable, supporting the smooth operation of the e-learning platform. The database's scalability allows it to grow alongside the platform, accommodating increasing amounts of data as more users and courses are added.
6. **Cloud Storage:** Cloud storage is used to store large files, such as videos, audio lectures, and other learning materials. This type of storage is highly scalable and cost-effective, making it ideal for educational institutions that need to manage extensive multimedia content. By leveraging cloud storage, schools can ensure that their learning materials are always available to users, regardless of the file sizes or the number of resources stored.
7. **Security Services:** Security services provided by cloud providers include firewalls, intrusion detection/prevention systems (IDS/IPS), and data encryption. These services protect the e-learning platform from unauthorized access, cyberattacks, and data breaches. Ensuring the security of user data and transactions is crucial for maintaining trust and compliance with data protection regulations.
8. **Management Services:** Cloud providers offer tools for managing and monitoring the infrastructure, including virtual machines, databases, and storage resources. These management services help administrators provide resources, track performance, and ensure the smooth operation of the platform. By using these tools, schools can efficiently manage their IT resources without needing extensive in-house expertise.

The cloud architecture offers a scalable, secure, and cost-effective foundation for deploying an e-learning platform in a school environment. By leveraging cloud services, schools can focus on providing high-quality education without the complexities of managing IT infrastructure.

1.4 SMART EDUCATION FRAMEWORK

The framework for a smart education system integrates cloud architecture, physical devices, and collaborative environments to create an adaptive and personalized learning experience (Figure 1.2). This detailed framework ensures scalability, flexibility, and enhanced learning outcomes by leveraging various technological components.

1.4.1 Student-Centric Approach

Student: The student is the core component of the framework, around which all other components revolve. The system gathers comprehensive data on the student's behavior, emotions, and context to tailor the educational experience. This approach ensures that learning is personalized, addressing each student's unique needs and preferences.

Student Behavior: Understanding student behavior involves inferring complex behaviors and potential patterns associated with the learning process. This understanding is crucial as learning behaviors are directly related to knowledge construction.

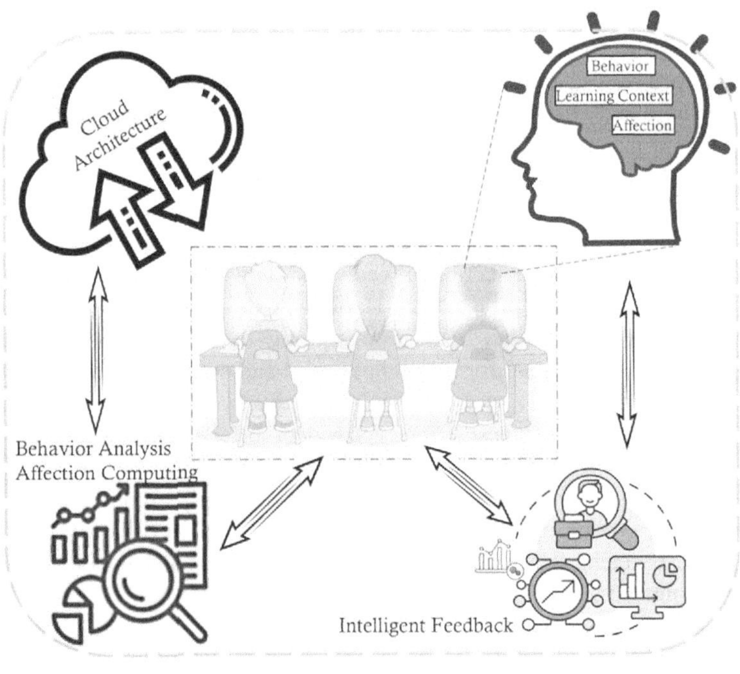

FIGURE 1.2 Smart Education Framework.

- **Data Collection:** The system captures data on the student's interactions with the learning platform, including the time spent on tasks, frequency of concept reviews, and types of mistakes made.
- **Analysis:** This data is analyzed to identify learning patterns and areas of difficulty, allowing for targeted interventions and support.

Student Affection: Student affections refer to the emotional and cognitive states of students, including emotions like boredom, anger, anxiety, enjoyment, and stress. It encompasses the study of how these affective states impact learning processes and outcomes.

- **Emotional Monitoring:** The system tracks the student's emotional state using various methods, such as surveys, facial recognition, and physiological sensors.
- **Impact Assessment:** Understanding the student's emotions helps in creating a supportive learning environment that can adapt to reduce stress and increase engagement.

Learning Context: Learning context is the environmental and situational factors that influence the learning experience. This includes considerations such as the physical environment (e.g., classroom conditions, ambient factors like light and temperature), temporal factors (e.g., time of day), social context (e.g., presence of peers), and technological context (e.g., devices and tools used for learning). Understanding learning context helps in designing adaptive learning environments that cater to diverse student needs and optimize learning outcomes.

- **Environmental Data:** The system collects contextual data about the student's environment, including location, time of day, and the presence of other students.
- **Adaptive Learning:** This data helps in adjusting the learning content and delivery method to suit the student's current context, making learning more relevant and effective.

Multimodal Learning: The framework integrates data from diverse sources such as IoT devices, learning management systems, and assessments to form a holistic view of the student's experience.

- **IoT Devices:** These devices, like wearables, gather data on physical activity, heart rate, and other environmental factors.
- **Group Collaboration:** The system supports collaborative learning through online forums, chat rooms, and other interactive tools, fostering peer-to-peer learning and communication.
- **Intelligent Feedback:** Based on collected data, the system provides tailored feedback in various formats, including text, audio, and video, to help students understand their progress and areas for improvement.
- **Learning Performance:** The framework measures student progress over time, using data analytics to identify strengths and weaknesses and to track the effectiveness of the learning system.

1.4.2 Understanding Students

Student Behavior Analysis: Utilizes data from embedded sensors in smartphones and wearables, Kinect sensors for body movement analysis, and eye-tracking combined with physiological data to assess learning behaviors.

- **Behavioral Patterns:** Analyzing these data sources helps in understanding how students engage with the material, allowing for the identification of active, semi-active, and passive learning states.
- **Personalized Interventions:** The insights gained enable the creation of personalized learning interventions that cater to the specific needs and learning styles of each student.

Student Affection Computing: Student affection computing involves understanding and analyzing students' affective states, which are critical for personalized instruction and interaction in smart education. This includes emotions, cognitive load, and stress, all of which are interconnected and impact learning outcomes.

- **Textual Data:** Sentiment analysis is performed on textual data from discussions and interactions to gauge emotional states.
- **Visual Data:** Facial recognition technology is used to detect emotions such as boredom, anger, anxiety, or enjoyment.
- **Vocal Data:** Speech analysis helps in identifying emotional nuances in the student's voice.
- **Physiological Data:** Measures such as electroencephalogram (EEG), electrooculogram (EOG), electromyogram (EMG), skin temperature, Galvanic Skin Response (GSR), Blood Volume Pulse (BVP), and respiration signals are used to assess cognitive load and emotional states, providing a comprehensive understanding of the student's affective state.

1.4.3 Smart Learning Environment

Intelligent Learning Spaces: The integration of ubiquitous computing and IoT infrastructure has enabled the creation of smart learning spaces, transforming traditional classrooms into student-centric intelligent tutoring environments. These spaces are designed to be adaptive and interactive, enhancing the learning experience.

- **Ubiquitous Computing and IoT Infrastructure:** These components create adaptive learning environments that respond to the student's needs.
- **Smart Classroom/Campus:** Prototypes of smart classrooms and campuses integrate various technologies and sensors to offer student-centric intelligent tutoring services.
- **Adaptive Environments:** Features like adjustable lighting, temperature, and air quality create a conducive learning environment.
- **Interactive Learning:** Gesture and speech recognition technologies facilitate interactive learning experiences.
- **Real-Time Adjustments:** The system analyzes student data in real time to provide immediate feedback to instructors, allowing them to adjust their teaching strategies based on student engagement and behavior.

1.4.4 Data-Driven Learning Analytics

Learning Performance Prediction: Predicting learning performance is essential for providing personalized tutoring services. This involves analyzing digital traces from online learning systems and integrating IoT data from physical learning environments to gain a comprehensive understanding of the learning process.

- **Data Utilization:** Student data, including digital traces from online learning systems and IoT data from physical learning environments, is used to predict learning performance and personalize learning paths.
- **Comprehensive Insights:** Combining digital and IoT data provides a thorough understanding of the learning process, enabling more accurate predictions and personalized interventions.

Intelligent Feedback: Intelligent feedback involves providing accurate and timely feedback to both instructors and students based on IoT multimodal data, enhancing the teaching process and learning activities.

- **Instructor Feedback:** Real-time analysis of group discussions and instructor activities (using audiovisual and accelerometer data) provides insights into student behavior and teaching effectiveness.
- **Student Feedback:** Automated feedback on oral presentations, mental effort, and learning progress helps students self-assess and improve their learning strategies.

1.4.5 Group Collaboration Modeling

Group collaboration modeling leverages multimodal learning analysis to understand collaborative learning in groups, improving both self-learning and group learning outcomes.

- **Multimodal Data Analysis:** This approach enhances collaborative learning by analyzing physiological synchrony (similarities in heart rate and skin conductance) and gaze similarity among students.
- **Collaboration Quality:** Understanding these factors helps in assessing the effectiveness of collaboration and identifying areas for improvement.

1.5 OVERCOMING PERSPECTIVE CHALLENGES OF E-LEARNING

E-learning today stands to gain significantly from advancements in cloud computing technologies and capabilities, marking a burgeoning industry. By leveraging cloud-based systems, there is potential to surpass the limitations of traditional physical labs and local computing setups. However, widespread adoption hinges on addressing critical challenges and barriers (Liu and Yu 2023).

To effectively integrate cloud computing into e-learning, instructors, and students must navigate a learning curve supported by robust IT infrastructure from academic institutions (Culduz 2024). This involves leveraging third-party solutions or existing cloud services tailored to educational needs. Instructors play a pivotal role by familiarizing themselves with cloud functionalities, consulting with IT departments, and configuring resources for optimal classroom use. Similarly, students need guidance on accessing and utilizing cloud-based learning materials tailored to the specific demands of their courses.

The benefits of cloud technology—such as cost-efficiency, fault tolerance, and enhanced accessibility—are pivotal in enhancing e-learning experiences (Culduz 2024). However, successful implementation requires meticulous pre-planning to maximize these advantages. Organizations transitioning from traditional e-learning setups to cloud-based systems must undertake feasibility studies that encompass user requirements, existing IT infrastructure, and cost–benefit analyses. Virtualization plays a crucial role in minimizing costs by optimizing resource allocation within the cloud architecture.

Despite global improvements in internet connectivity, slow speeds remain a hindrance, particularly when accessing non-regional cloud data centers. This latency issue can disrupt the user experience in cloud-based education. Additionally, disciplines reliant on specialized software or physical lab equipment—like digital forensics or robotics—may face limitations in cloud environments. In such cases, hybrid cloud solutions, combining on-premises resources with cloud capabilities, offer a viable approach.

Ultimately, the future of cloud-based e-learning hinges on addressing these complexities through strategic planning, technical adaptation, and hybrid solutions that blend the strengths of cloud and local infrastructure.

1.6 CONCLUSION

In conclusion, integrating cloud services into e-learning offers a compelling alternative, leveraging adaptability, flexibility, and security to support the foundational principles of accessible and anytime learning. By enhancing storage, computational capabilities, and network connectivity, cloud-based e-learning systems optimize educational resources while reducing costs associated with hardware and IT maintenance. Despite current limitations in personalization, advancements in cloud-based personalized learning hold promise for addressing individual student needs across diverse subjects. Moving forward, ongoing research is crucial to quantitatively assess the impact of cloud migration on educational quality, access speed, and overall return on investment, guiding the future development of robust cloud-based e-learning frameworks.

REFERENCES

Ali, Ashraf, Raja Muhammad Ishtiaq Khan, and Abdullah Alouraini. "A comparative study on the impact of online and blended learning." *SAGE Open* 13, no. 1 (2023): 21582440231154417.

Berestova, Anna, Gulnara Burdina, Liudmila Lobuteva, and Alisa Lobuteva. "Academic motivation of university students and the factors that influence it in an E-learning environment." *Electronic Journal of e-Learning* 20, no. 2 (2022): 201–210.

Culduz, Murat. "Benefits and Challenges of E-Learning, Online Education, and Distance Learning." In *Incorporating the Human Element in Online Teaching and Learning*, pp. 1–27. IGI Global, 2024.

de Souza Rodrigues, Marco Aurélio, Paula Chimenti, and Antonio Roberto Ramos Nogueira. "An exploration of eLearning adoption in the educational ecosystem." *Education and Information Technologies* 26, no. 1 (2021): 585–615.

Dierendonck, Christophe, István Tóth-Király, Alexandre J.S. Morin, Sylvie Kerger, Paul Milmeister, and Débora Poncelet. "Testing associations between global and specific levels of student academic motivation and engagement in the classroom." *The Journal of Experimental Education* 91, no. 1 (2023): 101–124.

Gairola, Ajay Krishan, and Vidit Kumar. "Role of Internet of Things and Cloud Computing in Education System: A Review." In *International Conference on Computational Intelligence and Smart Communication*, pp. 51–60. Cham: Springer Nature Switzerland, 2022.

Khan, Asif, Mohammad Kamrul Hasana, Taher M. Ghazal, Shayla Islam, Haitham M. Alzoubi, Umi Asma'Mokhtar, Rizwan Alam, and Munir Ahmad. "Collaborative learning assessment via information and communication technology." In *2022 RIVF International Conference on Computing and Communication Technologies (RIVF)*, pp. 311–316. IEEE, 2022.

Kwiatkowska, Wioletta, and Lidia Wiśniewska-Nogaj. "Digital skills and online collaborative learning: The study report." *Electronic Journal of E-Learning* 20, no. 5 (2022): 510–522.

Liu, Mengchi, and Dongmei Yu. "Towards intelligent E-learning systems." *Education and Information Technologies* 28, no. 7 (2023): 7845–7876.

Meiryani, Meiryani, Shinta Adiwijaya, Mochammad Fahlevi, and Holly Deviarti. "Effectiveness of E-Learning Cloud Computing and the Current Issues in Education." In *2023 8th International Conference on Business and Industrial Research (ICBIR)*, pp. 426–431. IEEE, 2023.

Parusheva, Silvia, Samo Bobek, and Simona Sternad Zabukovšek. "Sustainable higher education: From E-learning to smart education." *Sustainability* 15, no. 13 (2023): 10378.

Qureshi, Muhammad Asif, Asadullah Khaskheli, Jawaid Ahmed Qureshi, Syed Ali Raza, and Sara Qamar Yousufi. "Factors affecting students' learning performance through collaborative learning and engagement." *Interactive Learning Environments* 31, no. 4 (2023): 2371–2391.

Swan, Karen, and Peter Shea. "What eLearning Leaders Should Know about Online Teaching." In *Leading the eLearning Transformation of Higher Education*, pp. 96–115. Routledge, 2023.

2 Cloud-Based Learning
Reconceptualizing Educational Excellences

Neetu Amlani, Swapnil Deshpande, Zohra Yasmeen, and Priyanka Samarth

2.1 INTRODUCTION

Cloud computing (CC) has emerged as an optimal method for deploying solutions and enterprise applications to diverse businesses worldwide. The history of CC started in the early 1960s. Table 2.1 presents the outline of how CC evolved.

This chart provides an overview of the key developments in CC over the decades, highlighting the evolution from early concepts to mainstream adoption and ongoing innovation in the present day.

CC is frequently defined as a collection of resources and services typically provided via the Internet within a network setting. It represents the integration of computing capabilities for multi-user utilization through Internet technologies. While information sharing stands out as a notable feature of CC, it is important to recognize that CC encompasses more than just data exchange (Aldoayan et al. 2020).

CC has proliferated globally due to several contributing factors. Below is a tabular representation of the key factors driving the implementation of CC technology (Table 2.2).

In the above table,

- **Digital Transformation** represents the largest portion of the contribution, indicating that it is the most significant clause that drives the use and implementation of the CC technology.
- **Global Reach of Cloud Providers and Accessibility and Affordability** make up the next largest portions, highlighting their importance in enabling widespread access to cloud services.
- **Technological Advancements, Scalability, Flexibility, Diverse Range of Services, and Global Collaboration and Connectivity** each contribute smaller portions to the overall adoption of CC.

CC offers enhanced flexibility and speed by enabling access from anywhere without the necessity of being tied to a particular location or reliant on specific Internet connectivity methods. It operates on a framework that allows for swift adjustments in service scale, with the capability to rapidly expand or contract resources as needed.

DOI: 10.1201/9781003472537-3

TABLE 2.1
Evolution of Cloud Computing

Decade	Key Developments
1960s–1970s	Time-sharing systems lay the foundation for shared computing resources.
1980s–1990s	Client-server architecture and LANs enable distributed computing.
1990s	Emergence of Application Service Providers (ASPs) offers hosted software applications over the internet.
Early 2000s	AWS launches, offering Infrastructure as a Service (IaaS) with services like Amazon S3 and EC2.
	Google introduces Google Apps, providing cloud-based productivity tools.
	Salesforce.com popularizes the Software as a Service (SaaS) model with its CRM platform.
Mid-2000s	Mainstream adoption of cloud computing begins, with businesses recognizing its potential for IT transformation.
	Microsoft Azure launches, offering a comprehensive cloud platform for building, deploying, and managing apps.
Late 2000s	Cloud computing has become integral to the digital economy, driving innovation and digital transformation.
Present	Cloud providers expand their service portfolios to include a wide range of offerings, from Platform as a Service (PaaS) to AI and IoT.

TABLE 2.2
Adoption of Cloud Computing

Key Factors	Contribution (%)
Digital transformation	25
Global reach of cloud providers	20
Accessibility and affordability	15
Technological advancements	10
Scalability and flexibility	10
Diverse range of services	10
Global collaboration and connectivity	10

Additionally, monitoring, controlling, and reporting resource usage is simplified within this structure (Aldoayan et al. 2020).

The term "cloud computing" is now widely used in the IT industry and has applications in a variety of fields, including education. CC is being implemented quickly in higher education institutions and is quickly becoming a vital component of the campus environment. Higher education institutions have benefited considerably from CC, which may also be used to reduce IT expenses.

CC can be utilized to supply a range of cloud-based services and apps to help teachers and students with their daily tasks (Olaloye et al. 2019). Cloud tools are suitable for chatting, recording audio sessions, providing content, and emailing queries, and they may be essential in creating a positive learning environment for students.

In the education sector, teachers as well as students may use cloud-based services and apps for both formal and informal learning with free access to CC. CC ensures that staff, students, and trainers can access any type of data from anywhere, anytime, using any device. The implementation of CC in higher education institutions has produced several benefits for colleges and universities.

The Internet is a medium that can transform CC and provide highly advanced software along with learning materials, hardware resources, and services to learners, even in the poorest or remote schools in the state without advanced IT skills in these places (Nguyen et al. 2024).

In today's world, various cloud platforms, such as Microsoft and Google, offer different applications and services free of cost to employees and students from different educational institutions. A few examples of these free services are email, calendars, contact lists, document storage, website creation services, and document exchange services (Baharuddin et al. 2021). Several educational institutions use CC to provide scalability, reliability, and flexibility, as well as reduce IT costs.

CC also affects working in three crucial domains, namely integration, time value, and security (Zhao et al. 2020). Teachers have an excellent platform to improve their productivity and teaching methods with the help of CC. As multiple stakeholders use the infrastructure simultaneously for research, teaching, and learning, CC technology saves not only money but also energy (Baanqud et al. 2020).

Online learning allows students to learn anything on a smaller budget without expert instruction. The importance and need for cloud technology emphasize the practicality of its implementation and application in university education and the benefits of cloud technology in teaching (Aydin 2021).

Recently, a large number of users have access to an online education system that allows them to work together virtually using smart devices (mobile devices). Through the use of modern technologies in e-learning, students may communicate with instructors, complete online tests, and receive instant results. Teachers and students can upload and submit their assignments virtually on a cloud. Students may access learning resources from any location with the aid of e-learning (Mohsen et al. 2021).

Thus, education system development is a process that began with obsolete pattern-learning up to e-learning via multimedia, the Internet, e-books, and more (Sasikala and Nachimuthu 2022). Figure 2.1 shows the use of CC in the field of education.

Objectives

The present work entitled 'Impact of Cloud Computing on Education System' is an abstract which aims at the following:

1. To elaborate on the concept of CC with its key features in brief.
2. To elucidate the types of CC.
3. To gather knowledge of some notable existing works in CC field-based education.
4. To trace the CC impact on education, teaching, and learning.
5. To collect the challenges and issues of CC in educational accomplishments.

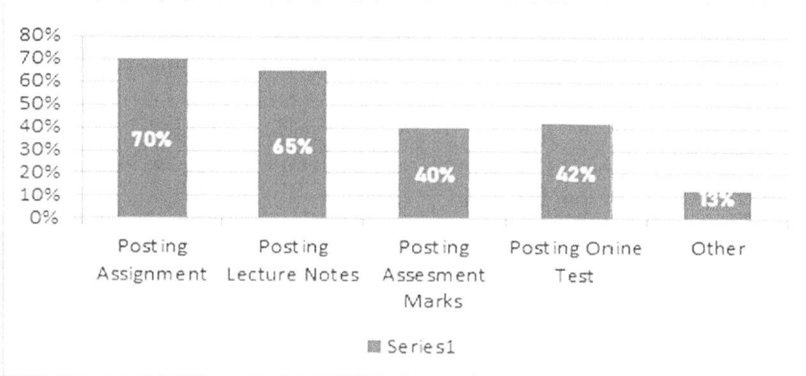

FIGURE 2.1 Cloud Computing in Education.

2.2 LITERATURE REVIEW

This literature review plays a crucial role in the understanding of the term CC. The work and achievements in the field of CC are analyzed and evaluated in the present study with the help of the available literature. CC is the most recent technology in today's world.

This paper presents a new perspective on dealing with intelligent learning processes based on the optimization model in the cloud environment that can help improve performance. Scientific research requires many large calculations, and many research institutions do not have such large calculation equipment. The design was tested in a smart study. The results will be applied to real-life situations.

This study explores the role by which cloud technology can be useful to students in critical thinking, knowledge sharing, as well as knowledge acquisition. The impact of experiences of CC on the cognitive abilities of the students for the creation of knowledge was studied. An interactive hierarchical model was designed to describe students' knowledge construction. The results revealed that knowledge integration, knowledge sharing, and reflective thinking had a positive impact on students' knowledge construction. This can be helpful for policymakers and researchers to understand the potential of using cloud technology to enhance personal information.

This paper provides an outline of the research, data collection, and use of interactivity in smart learning through bibliometrics and content analysis of the use of interactivity in smart learning in the last few years, as well as explore the application of interactivity in intelligent learning from the perspective of bibliometric analysis over the years. This study can also provide information on the successes of existing research in the field of collaboration and education in different contexts (Dehbi et al. 2022).

The present work proposes a novel CC e-learning solution. The solution precisely encompasses the learning content from the cloud. It improves data analysis performance, reduces the encryption burden of calculating the cost of users by transferring part of the encryption cost to cloud servers, and also provides access to learning content by encrypting classes and exams with different passwords.

Fine-grained access control technologies such as improved binary-block embedding (IBBE) and (Ciphertext Policy Attribute Based Encryption) CP-ABE also offer an integrated system that can help teachers find nearby colleagues efficiently and safely. Security analysis shows that our scheme can ensure confidentiality of data, effective access control, collision avoidance, and uninterruptibility. Performance measurement shows the effectiveness of solutions in terms of cryptographic expenses (Amor et al. 2020).

This paper provides a cloud-based collaborative scheduling algorithm for implementing resource scheduling as an intelligent learning model to improve educational performance. Experimental studies show that scheduling of intelligent learning (SES)-based cloud-sharing algorithms can improve CCERS results. To improve the resource SES, the cloud edge collaborative scheduling algorithm is combined with the resource scheduling of the intelligent learning model, and the standard closed-loop load model is proposed (Li and Shu 2023).

This paper introduces a new collaborative e-learning model called cloud collaboration, in which knowledge modeling and business economics are used to optimize collaboration in the use of e-learning, including teachers, students, and collaborative products. To follow this approach, CC and e-commerce are used to better connect students and collaborate with e-learning resources. Collaborative learning now focuses on collaboration or group discussion rather than providing adequate support to everyone throughout the learning process, which uses knowledge and business models to enhance collaboration between education, such as teachers, students, and collaborative objects in e-learning. To implement this approach, CC and e-commerce are used to connect students and collaborate more effectively with resources in e-learning (Nguyen et al. 2024).

This paper presents a model for educational institutions using CC. Establishing a private cloud for all universities and covering all universities will ensure that institutions in the private cloud have good operations and save money. By using this model, the state can invest in universities at low cost, and the quality of the education system will not need to be improved for anything. The main purpose of the application model is to use the least resources and be efficient. May Aldoayan et al. uncover some inefficiency in resource management due to the lack of centralized monitoring of resources across the organization. Additionally, by using a standard design, the widespread use of pirated software can be controlled (Aldoayan et al. 2020).

This paper develops the technology of the future cloud system as an intelligent learning environment and conducts research on intelligent learning based on N display. Therefore, based on the analysis of learning activities and characteristics in the smart media environment, the learning design is designed to make the most of smart learning. This paper introduces the use of technology as an intelligent learning environment to realize the design process of future CC and learn about intelligent learning based on N displays. For this reason, the use of the smart learning system was studied based on the evaluation of the learning functions and features in the smart media environment, and the development process was carried out at the maximum level. Therefore, education services, smart connections, and integration of technologies based on CC and N-screen technology are needed (Grover and Nandal 2024).

This technology helps reduce IT costs and services. Additionally, by adopting the educational climate model, multiple universities can share the same framework for teaching, learning, and research. The article also addresses the challenges that educational institutions, such as schools, colleges, and universities, may encounter when implementing climate models (Agrawal 2020).

These efforts determine the benefits related to the use of CC technology in schools. Cloud technology affects the quality of teaching–learning in schools by providing solutions that make R&D and teaching more efficient and effective. This has led many schools to adopt cloud technology to solve the many challenges they face every day.

The purpose of this work is to understand the importance of climate change in higher educational institutions. This work also highlights CC benefits that it can bring to higher education, examines the toughest challenges academics may face as a result of CC, and suggests some steps to be proactive in using CC while mitigating risk. This paper acknowledges the breadth of different organizations and the CC grant process by combining multiple perspectives on a single phenomenon from sources with diverse cultures and backgrounds. The differences and contributions are based on the integration of research studies found in various documents. The findings of this analysis show that adopting CC in universities can be understood by several factors that influence the acceptance of CC, like regulatory and government agencies, internal stakeholders, cloud providers, IT frameworks, etc. The world is working to better understand the variations in this field and change the importance of decisions. The current state of cloud-based pedagogy is also analyzed to highlight challenges and identify how to improve the e-learning environment in universities. Once limitations and issues are identified, this study shows that many of the problems in developing virtual learning environments (VLEs) can be overcome. Therefore, solutions can be implemented to support cloud services for schools, such as using Infrastructure as a Service (IaaS) to overcome limitations by adding useful discussion tools and using Software as a Service (SaaS) to improve the learning environment (Aydin 2021).

A cloud-based content-sharing system has been introduced that can update data in the cloud in a multi-user, multi-device environment based on a distributed model. The content-based cloud data logging system has the development of decentralized data history, automatic login and logout process, and automatic update management components, as well as fixing an issue by integrating cloud data transfer using content transfer. This system allows multiple users to use the First In-First Out-based (FIFO) spin-locking mechanism to access shared cloud data to avoid data conflicts. The proposed system can merge shared files without causing archive conflicts and compare results with the existing standard (Ullah Khan et al. 2022).

This paper discusses the significance of CC for the global education sector in the context of schools of the future; identifies some of the challenges that need to be solved; and shows that CC can provide part of the overall solution. It also shows a new vision of the implementation of the educational environment in the new generation of smart school environments. Regarding the Etisalat BT Innovation Cente (EBTIC) leader of the international iCampus initiative, the difference between the six central campuses, especially the use of mobile cloud education, is currently being examined. Many commitments are still in place and being implemented that will bring us closer to achieving the above goals (Olaloye et al. 2019).

This article examines whether CC will be present in education, especially in computer-oriented universities, and the efforts that can be taken to step up the use of such applications for learners as well as teachers (Kasumu et al. 2022).

This paper describes the learning environment and how colleges and universities can benefit from it, in terms of cost-efficacy, performance, quality, security, reliability, and mobility. Common examples of CC in the field of education are given, and research articles on applications are further illustrated and discussed. The success of implementing CC models in schools can only be measured as a limit. The present article takes the initial step in the above context by bringing together different concepts and implementations of CC in the educational sector. This paper shows the basic structure of cloud education service and use, such as the features of the education platform and the flexibility for all school levels, high school, and college. This paper also presents different types of training programs used in education. CC in education solves problems not only through education but especially in cost reduction, communication efficiency, security, privacy, convenience, and easy access (Baharuddin et al. 2021).

In this study, CC, its services, and its advantages in the context of electrical engineering are also elucidated. CC is a computing prototype model that solves problems like processors, storage, networks, as well as software and offers them as a service on one of the platforms. This effort aims to regulate if CC can be used for educational purposes and the different benefits provided by CC in education. In this study, a data collection process in the form of qualitative description and data analysis was adopted (Baharuddin et al. 2021).

This paper shows the power role of CC in the educational sector and its usage to provide quality education. The golden rule of making work accessible anywhere, anytime, and also sharing it with anybody makes it outstanding. It eliminates the need for a dedicated machine to access data or applications (such as word processors or spreadsheets). It also explains the learning environment and how it can benefit students, teachers, and schools in providing quality education.

This paper proposes a cloud-based intelligent teaching system for e-learners to provide and share educational information, including text, images, videos, three-dimensional (3D) objects, virtual reality, and extended augmented reality scenes. The proposed system offers new solutions for broadcast services that can be accessed through smart devices, cloud-based smart service environments, and overall integration (Maraou et al. 2021).

This paper provides a literature review on mobile-CC, specifically in the educational field along with its benefits and also how to use it to overcome security issues. This paper discusses the collaborative learning network model with MCC and identifies the need for the use of radio in education and its ability to improve the quality of teaching in school. Secure the connection between the server and the end system. Focus on using techniques to secure connections between end machines and servers.

2.3 METHODOLOGY

The proposed work aims to elaborate on the concept of CC, including the types, impact, and application to the field of education. The existing works of the last 10 to 12 years have been planned, scrutinized, and reported in this work.

2.3.1 Basics of Cloud Computing

One of the emergent constituents of IT is CC (Dehbi et al. 2022). The following are the types of CC. Figure 2.2 represents different types of CC.

1. **Public Cloud:** It indicates the cloud in which services are provided by third-party providers for general use. The data is further stored at the provider`s end. Basically, used for massive collaborative projects.
2. **Private Cloud:** As the name suggests, it is an internal model developed for an organization itself. Here, the server is maintained by a third party, but the hardware is managed in-house. This is used for close-end environments.

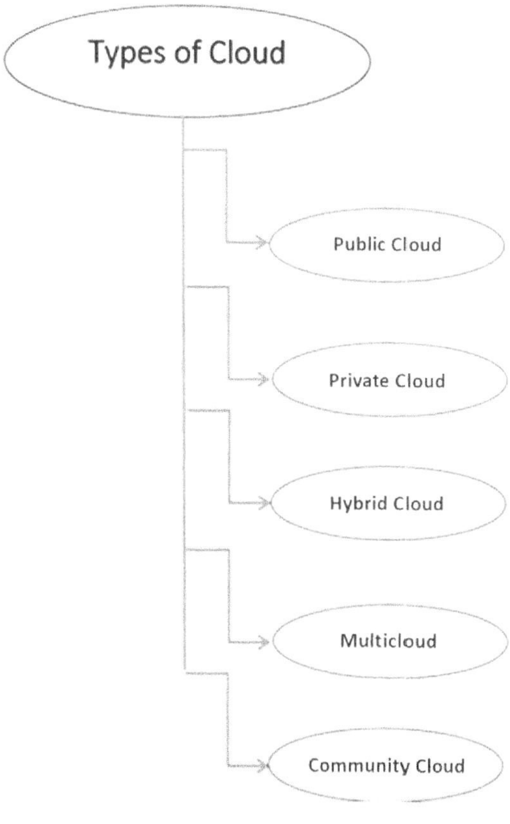

FIGURE 2.2 Types of Cloud Computing.

3. **Hybrid Cloud:** This model combines two or more cloud servers to generate a single architecture.
4. **Community Cloud:** This indicates many organizations with common backgrounds on the server. This model thus allows the sharing of common resources, business infrastructure, etc., with the community.
5. **Multi-Cloud:** This type uses multiple public clouds. It uses multiple IaaS vendors. This type is used for system backups.

2.3.2 Models of Cloud Service

Depending upon different types of situations, conditions, and types of CC, the following are the types of different models developed.

- **SaaS:** This is a method of delivering applications over the Internet.
- **Platform-as-a-Service:** It is an entire cloud environment that includes everything that a developer requires for building, running, and managing applications, from servers to networking, storage, and tools.
- **IaaS:** Through the use of this model, virtual computing resources can be made available on the Internet.
- **Storage-as-a-Service:** This model offers a service in which the provider gives access to a data storage platform to the customer.
- **Security-as-a-Service (SECaaS):** This is a cloud-delivered model for outsourcing cyber security services. The security service provided by SECaaS is on a subscription basis hosted by the providers.

2.3.3 Cloud Service Providers

CC services are the IT firms that offer computing resources for individuals as well as corporate users. Their services include physical servers and virtual servers, databases, messaging services, and Big Data analysis resources. Due to the competition among service providers, every year these companies come up with flexible functionality and reasonable pricing models. Based on the market share, cost/month, and free trial, the top cloud service providers are:

- The Amazon Web-Services
- The Google Cloud Platform
- The IBM Cloud
- The Microsoft Azure
- The Digital Ocean.

Table 2.3 shows a comparative summary of five cloud service providers.

2.3.4 Cloud Computing in Different Sub-Sectors in the Education System

In this digital era, along with business and other industries, education sector too has ominously enriched the learning process. This digital transformation in the

TABLE 2.3
Comparative Summary of the Top Five Cloud-Service Providers

Name	Amazon Web-Services	Google-Cloud-Platform	IBM Cloud	Digital Ocean	Microsoft Azure
Market Share	33.00%	08.00%	06.00%	1.50%	16%
Cost/Month	$0.025/hour	$0.047/hour	$0.04/hour	$0.015/hour	$0.043/hour
Trials (Free)	12 Months	12 Months	Lite Tier with 256 MB	50$ Free Credit	12 Months

educational sector has placed education within the reach of humans in remote regions too. CC benefits in the education sector are as follows.

1. CC in School and Higher Education.
2. CC in Health Education.
3. CC in Spiritual Education

2.3.4.1 Cloud Computing in Schools and Higher Education

The history of the education system in India started at Gurukul, where the disciples stayed in Guru's Ashram and acquired knowledge. It was for the holistic development of the disciples (students) where they studied in the lap of nature. Also, the qualities of kindness and sympathy were imbibed in the little minds.

Later on, the modern education system gave rise to schools where students went to school for 5 to 6 hours and learned different subjects, including English, Hindi, mathematics, and science. This was basic education, which worked as a ladder to college. The education system followed a 10 + 2 pattern. Today, the introduction of the National Education Policy (NEP), which follows 5 + 3 + 3 + 2 and further, makes higher education multidisciplinary. This makes the education system student-centric and technology-based. This aims to use online courses for training students in all fields. More emphasis is given to the use of the cloud for all advanced learners. NEP has also introduced an Open Elective group in the undergraduate courses, which aims for the students to learn at least two courses per semester through the cloud.

Since the last decade, there has been a notable surge in the popularity of cloud-based learning as people may acquire new skills through education over the cloud. One of the post-pandemic effects is the remarkable increase in online learning.

Table 2.4 shows the increase in course enrollments in Study Webs of Active Learning for Young Aspiring Minds (SWAYAM) post pandemic.

Table 2.5 shows growth in enrollment in the last 5 years in IGNOU.

Another example is from Courseera.org, which aims to provide the latest learning skills and save money on learning. Figure 2.3 graph shows the increase in number of enrollments from 2016 to 2021.

TABLE 2.4
Increase in Course Enrollments in SWAYAM Post Pandemic

Year	Semester	Course Enrollments
2024	January	3,471,948
2023	July	3,664,608
2023	January	3,543,422

TABLE 2.5
Growth in Enrollment in the Last Five Years in IGNOU

Description	2015–2016	2016–2017	2017–2018	2018–2019	2019–2020
Enrollment	796,127	917,117	1,072,578	1,148,956	1,348,948
Fresh	455,882	545,840	652,504	673,797	818,997
Re-registered	340,295	371,277	420,074	475,159	529,951
Annual growth in enrollment		120,990	155,461	76,378	199,992
% Growth		15.20%	16.95%	7.12%	17.41%

Source: Annual Report IGNOU 2019–2020, www.studocu.com/in/document/indira-gandhi-national-open-university/introduction-to-sociology-1/annual-report-2019-20-e/80632650.

The following are the benefits of CC:

1. **Personalized Learning:** Learning by choice is the feature provided by CC. Students can use the World Wide Web (Internet) to access all the resources and tools that are as per their interest.
2. **Promoting Women's Education:** With CC, the female gender cannot be restricted due to geographical regions. Easy access can also increase women's literacy ratio.
3. **Reduced Costs:** By using the latest technologies, the needs of the learners are met. Students need not purchase the application.
4. **Accessibility:** Since the data is available 24 × 7, anybody can log in and access the information from anywhere. This applies to people who are working. Without hampering their jobs or the working hours, they can learn and upgrade their knowledge and thereby their profiles.
5. **Extra Infrastructure Not Required:** No extra labs are required for learning through the cloud.
6. **Supporting Go Green Revolution:** The use of CC helps in reducing the carbon footprint.
7. **User-Friendly Environment:** The users do not have to worry about the complexity behind the cloud. They can easily operate and comprehend the data through the cloud.

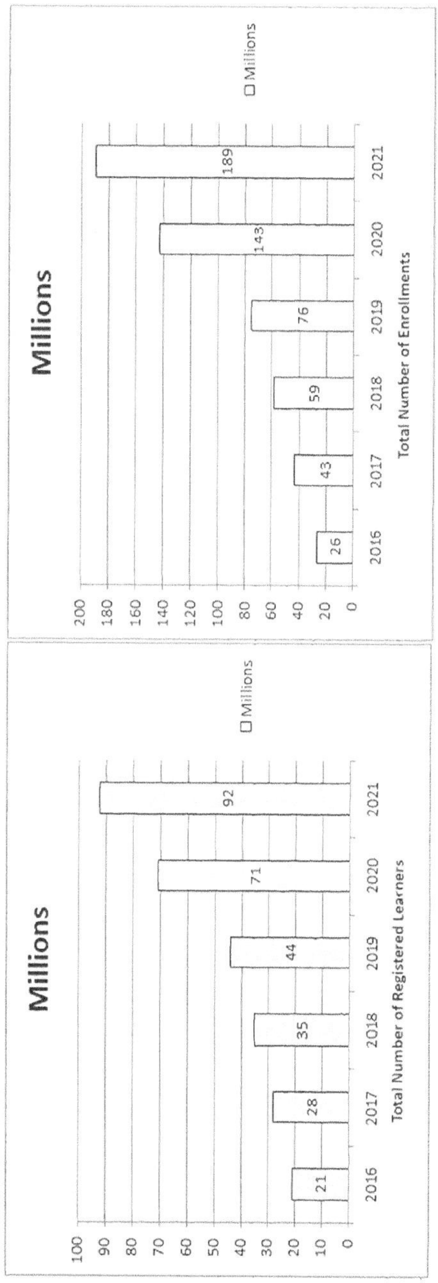

FIGURE 2.3 Growth in the Number of Learners Using Online Teaching.

FIGURE 2.4 Advantages of Cloud Computing in the Education Field.

Figure 2.4 shows the advantages of CC in the education sector, which include online education, workshops, training, blended as well as hybrid modes of education, examination, and evaluation processes, thereby avoiding the inadequacies of pen-and-paper-based tests. Also, e-library is booming these days. Campus education is also among one of the benefits of CC.

2.3.4.2 Cloud Computing in Health Education

Maintaining the record of patients for the best treatment as well as care and keeping a health history is difficult using traditional record keeping. The healthcare data is further used in decision-making and delivering appropriate treatment. With the advancement in technology, this became a little easier. However, with CC the task of keeping records in the field of healthcare sector has become easier and reliable. As per the National Institute of Standards and Technology (NIST), the CC model allows a set of computing resources that are configurable.

Figure 2.5 represents CC use in health education.

The data on the cloud is useful for doctors, families, authorities, as well as pharmacists through e-Health Cloud, shown in Figure 2.6. Due to the comfort of interoperability, saving cost, and ownership of patient data, the technology of CC is increasingly used by doctors. Additionally, moving from traditional data storage to present digitized storage saves space and makes the data easily available at any time, which is useful for patients and medical professionals. Moreover, the data is also useful for studying and further prediction of diseases. Thus, the use of advanced tools can help this industry in research and better treatment prospects.

CC thus helps in drug discoveries, keeping personal records of the patients, and maintaining Health Information Systems. Cloud-based digital libraries contribute to the analysis and prediction of diseases. This data can also be used for research purposes in the manufacture of drugs or medicines, potentially contributing to the cure of diseases and, thereby, reducing the mortality rate.

FIGURE 2.5 Use of Cloud Computing in Health Education.

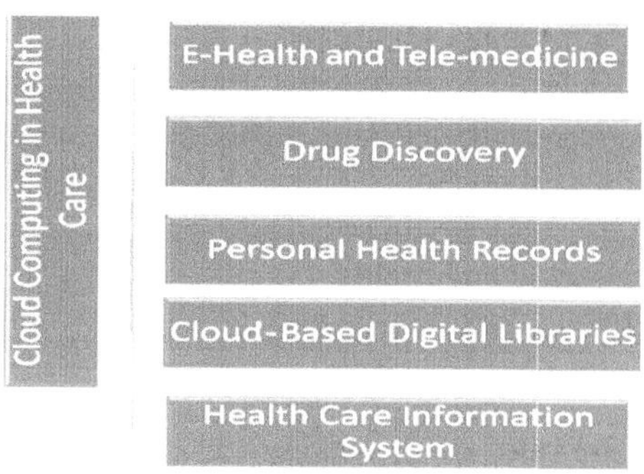

FIGURE 2.6 Cloud Computing in Healthcare.

2.3.4.3 Cloud Computing in Spiritual Education

Spiritual education is about pursuing a crucial connection with someone superior to oneself, which can affect positive emotions like mental peace, wonderment, serenity, and thankfulness. Spiritual health helps in reducing anxiety, anger, stress, and depression, too. To attain spiritual education, a person may connect to his/her religion or may not.

Following are a few ways to improve one's spiritual health.

1. Associate with your faith community**:** The worship place provides a sagacity of connection. By associating with a faith community, one can reach out to any spiritual leader and find ways to connect with compatible people within the community. Also, listening to the discourse of spiritual leaders adds to mental peace and inculcates positivity in oneself.

   Thus, CC has a significant role-play in catering to the spiritual needs of the people as the discourse or Satsang can be streamed live on different channels or can be saved on the cloud for the future. Table 2.6 shows how tech-savvy spiritual masters use the cloud to circulate their spiritual discourses.

TABLE 2.6
Use of Cloud for Circulating Spiritual Discourse by Spiritual Masters

Spiritual Master	Facebook	Instagram	YouTube
Sant Shri Asaramji Bapu	6.4 trillion	36.3 trillion	5.5 million
Pradeep Mishraji	1.6 million	123 K	4.42 million
Dhirendra Shastriji	57 K	316 K	4 million
Jaya Kishoriji	8.8 million	4.8 million	1.96 million
Anirudhacharya Maharaj	41.8 K	10.8 million	1.3 million

2. Practice Yoga: Yoga is an alternative therapy for medicine for stress management and mood maladies. It is rightly said that "Yoga Se Hoga" by Yog Guru Ramdev Baba. Yoga also supports in curing several diseases and helps to keep the body fit. CC also contributes in imparting yoga using the Intelligent Internet of Things (IioT), which helps in identifying and monitoring the body postures during yoga with the help of cameras and sensors embedded into the yoga mat. Training places for advice on the posture of the physician and independent guidance at home without the presence of a tutor are the outcomes of cloud in maintaining good health.

2.4 CONCLUSION AND FUTURE SCOPE

With the evolution of CC, the light of education is spreading all over. Cloud provides global access to data anywhere and anytime. It also enables collaborative learning and also contributes to cost-effective solutions. A new learning environment is created by which dynamic and technology-driven teaching–learning is possible.

With more advancements in technology, the impact of education will undoubtedly grow stronger and reach a global audience.

The data stored on the cloud is undoubtedly centralized and helps in contributing to all fields. However, there is a security question that arises regarding the data. Strong security tools can be further introduced to avoid data theft.

REFERENCES

Agrawal, Somya (2020, December), "A Survey on Recent Applications of Cloud Computing in Education: COVID-19 Perspective", *International Symposium on Automation, Information and Computing (ISAIC 2020)*, Beijing, China.

Aldoayan, May, Reza Sahandi, David John, & Deniz Cetinkaya (2020, February), "A Conceptual Framework for Cloud-Based Collaborative Online Course Provision", *9th International Conference on Educational and Information Technology*, Oxford, United Kingdom, pp. 27–31.

Amor, Arij Ben, Mohamed Abid, & Aref Meddeb (2020), "Secure Fog-Based E-Learning Scheme", *IEEE Access*, Vol. 8, pp. 31920–31933.

Aydin, Hakan (2021, September), "A Study of Cloud Computing Adoption in Universities as a Guideline to Cloud Migration", *SAGE Open Journal*, Vol. 11, No. 3.

Baanqud, N. S., H. Al-Samarraie, A. I. Alzahrani, & O. Alfarraj (2020), "Engagement in Cloud Supported Collaborative Learning and Student Knowledge Construction: A Modeling Study", *International Journal of Educational Technology in Higher Education*, Vol. 17.

Baharuddin, D. Ampera, Fibriasari, H., Sembiring, M. A. R., & Hamid, A. (2021), "Implementation of a Cloud Computing System in Learning System Development in Engineering Education Study Program", *International Journal of Education in Mathematics, Science, and Technology (IJEMST)*, Vol. 9, No. 4, pp. 728–740.

Dehbi, Amine, Rachid Dehbi, Abdellah Bakhouyi, & Mohamed Talea (2022, December), "Interoperability in Smart Education: A Systemic Review Based on Bibliometric and Content Analysis Methods", Vol. 100, No. 24.

Grover, Veena, & Manju Nandal (2024, January), "Education System Using Cloud Computing: A Proposed Model", *Educational Perspectives on Digital Technologies in Modeling and Management.*

Kasumu, Rebecca Oluwayimika, & Uduak Idoghor (2022 August), "Cloud Computing in Education and its Importance to University Students", *International Journal of Research and Innovation in Social Science (IJRISS)*, |Vol. VI, No. VIII, pp. 472–278.

Li, Guirong, & Lei Shu (2023), "Smart Education System Enhancing Collaborative Learning with Virtual Reality and Cloud-Edge Computing Task Scheduling Algorithm", *Computer-Aided Design and Applications*, Vol. 20, pp. 50–71.

Maraoui, Mohsen, Wei Wu, & Anastasiia Plakhtii (2021, May), "E-Learning Based on Cloud Computing", *International Journal of Emerging Technologies in Learning (iJET)*, Vol. 16, No. 10, p. 4.

Nguyen, Loan, Sarath Tomy, and Eric Pardede (2024), "Enhancing Collaborative Learning and E-Mentoring in a Smart Education System in Higher Education", *Computers*, Vol. 13, No. 1, pp. 1–29.

Olaloye, F. J., A. D. Adeyemo, E. Edikan, & C. O. Lawal (2019, March), "Cloud Computing in Education Sector: An Extensive Review", *International Journal of Civil Engineering and Technology (IJCIET)*, Vol. 10, No. 03.

Sasikala, P., & K. Nachimuthu (2022, February), "The Role of Cloud Computing in Education", *Computers and Society, International Journal of Innovative Research in Technology*, Vol. 8, No. 9, pp. 679–682.

Ullah Khan, Habib, Farhad Ali, & Shah Nazir (2022, June), "Systematic Analysis of Software Development in Cloud Computing Perceptions", *Software Evolution and Process*, Vol. 36, No. 2, pp. 1–26.

Zhao, Hui, Yu Jiang, & Xiying Zhao (2020, December), "Design and Research of University Intelligent Education Cloud Platform Based on Dubbo Microservice Framework", *5th International Conference on Mechanical, Control and Computer Engineering (ICMCCE)*, Harbin, China, pp. 870–874, doi: 10.1109/ICMCCE51767.2020.00191.

3 The Educational Cloud

A Landscape of Promise and Peril

Dileep Kumar Singh and Sameera Khan

3.1 INTRODUCTION

3.1.1 The Upsurge of the Educational Cloud

In the last decade, a significant transformation took place in the educational sector catalyzed by the upsurge of the educational cloud. Defining the key components of the educational cloud lays the foundation for understanding its importance. At the heart of the educational cloud lies a group of digital services and resources distributed over the internet, giving educators and learners exposure to a large variety of tools, data, and applications (Mittal et al. 2023). Thus, the learning management systems (LMSs) based on the cloud, content warehouses, collaboration platforms, and productivity tools are the major components of the educational cloud. All these components along with other tools form the spine of the educational cloud, resulting in easy access to resources anywhere anytime.

Observing the increasing need for cloud learning platforms inside educational institutions, a noteworthy shift has been registered to accept cloud technology in learning systems. Right from the beginning of school education at the K-12 level to the universities, cloud learning platforms have been adopted rapidly at all levels (Stein et al. 2013). In addition to learning platforms, the cloud has also been deployed for administrative tasks and collaboration among teachers, parents, and students. These utilities of the cloud in the educational setup have created a huge space and requirement for the educational cloud. Such e-learning platforms have a huge potential to revolutionize the conventional teaching–learning process and make it more suitable for the digital era (Zieliński et al. 2017).

The educational landscape can be significantly transformed by using the advantages of cloud platforms, as they are capable of reducing infrastructure costs and are highly scalable. In addition to these advantages, such platforms are also flexible and easily accessible (Jin et al. 2023). Ease of access and flexibility give the users a choice of time slots and devices in which they can learn according to their choice (Maaita, Muhsen, and Nsour 2013). Additionally, cloud learning platforms facilitate data-driven decision-making and personalized learning experiences, allowing teachers to define specific instructions for specific students according to their requirements.

 DOI: 10.1201/9781003472537-4

3.1.2 Landscape of Educational Cloud Technologies

Educational cloud platforms provide a vast range of tools as a solution to various teaching–learning problems. From industry giants like Google Workspace for Education and Microsoft 365 Education to specialized platforms such as Canvas and Schoology, the educational cloud provides a large spectrum of institutional requirements and preferences. Each platform has its unique qualities and features, which are reflected in content creation, evaluation techniques, analytics, report generation, etc. Such diversities give a unique experience while using any specific platform (Liu 2016; Wu and Mou 2015). Various technologies are merged to meet educational requirements and create a teaching–learning platform based on cloud technology. Such an ecosystem shows the versatility of cloud technology (Muniasamy and Ejalani 2014). Technologies like advanced learning algorithms of artificial intelligence (AI), virtual reality (VR), augmented reality (AR), and other additional technologies are used to expand the boundaries of classroom activities (Uehara 2013). It also helps in creating a personalized learning path that can be self-paced. Furthermore, it also provides immersive experience through simulation, experience-based learning, etc. in different subject areas (Takabe and Uehara 2013).

Like every other technology, the educational cloud has opportunities as well as challenges (Singh et al. 2023). Although such technologies have a vast potential to inculcate creativity, increase learner engagement, as well as improve learning outcomes, they also pose a serious threat to privacy and ethical concerns (Parveen and Chikhaoui 2017). As cloud technologies are rapidly entering the educational landscape, it is very important to strike the right balance between responsible implementation of new technology and innovation, to ensure such teaching–learning innovation results in positive outcomes only (Jamadar and Patankar 2013).

3.2 CHALLENGES IN IMPLEMENTING EDUCATIONAL CLOUD

3.2.1 Security and Privacy Concerns

While implementing the educational cloud, institutions go through the sensitive data collection of students, which encompasses personally identifiable information (PII). This PII has data like student names, addresses, telephone numbers, grades, health information, and, sometimes, intellectual property rights (Idrissa et al. 2016). In the implementation of the educational cloud storing and managing, this data is very sensitive. Careful handling of security and privacy concerns is required (Salvi et al. 2015).

To ensure the successful and safe implementation of the educational cloud, firstly categorizing the data is needed. Student PII, educational records, protected health information, and intellectual property all require strong safety measures. Implementing robust algorithms for security and privacy measures is significant for protecting such sensitive data from threats (Cappos et al. 2009). Data breaches, unauthorized access, and accidental data loss can pose adverse consequences, compromising student privacy, disrupting academic progress, and potentially leading to compliance fissures with regulations like Family Educational Rights and Privacy Act (FERPA) and General Data Protection Regulation (GDPR) (Slakmon 2017).

A crucial strategy is needed to enforce clear security rules and regulations. This set of rules defines a hierarchy of access levels to different users, data classification protocols, and incident response plans. Additionally, implementing hierarchical access controls with multifactor authentication and role-based access guarantees that only authorized people have access to certain types of data (Salvi et al. 2015). Furthermore, encrypting data in a repository and transaction with strong algorithms protects the data in case of a breach. Conducting timely penetration testing and vulnerability assessments help to identify and resolve any security issues before they can be exploited. In addition, educational institutes are required to collect only that information which is strictly necessary. Storing unnecessary information can use more space and also is more prone to breaches. Before collecting any information, consent should be taken from the parents and students. Also, if the need for the information collected is informed to them, the process will be more transparent and trustworthy. Policies regarding data retention, the period for which data will be saved, and safe disposal after its usage period has expired should be properly formulated and informed. Students and parents should also be informed about how this information is saved, where it is saved, and who has access to their information Such transparency strengthens the trust of the parents and students so that they can wholeheartedly participate in security practices (Idrissa et al. 2016).

By adopting a comprehensive approach encompassing robust security measures alongside data minimization, informed consent, clear data retention policies, and open communication, educational institutions can harness the power of cloud computing while prioritizing the security and privacy of their students' data. This comprehensive approach fosters trust within the educational community and allows institutions to leverage the benefits of cloud technology with confidence.

3.2.2 Digital Divide and Equity Issues

Digital divide and equity issues create a significant challenge in the deployment of educational cloud technologies. Socioeconomic disparities are the major challenge in the implementation of cloud technologies. The major problem is internet connectivity issues and access to technology (Kaihua et al. 2022) among different socioeconomic groups. Various research and surveys have been done, which reveal the fact that lower-income household groups and people of marginalized communities face barriers to reliable internet connections (Pietrzak 2016) and modern computing devices. This inequality intensifies the existing educational disparities among students of various socioeconomic backgrounds. Those who belong to the backward community remain untouched by this educational revolution, which is powered by technology, as they may lack the necessary resources to use cloud-based learning platforms (Ouahabi et al. 2014). Additionally, cloud technologies can potentially widen this gap as the privileged will benefit from more facilities and the underprivileged will be left behind, unable to take assistance from the educational opportunities provided by cloud-based resources (Huang et al. 2013). Thus, to solve this disparity, strategies to lessen this gap are required. A few steps that can be used in this path include providing free or subsidized internet facilities, making cheaper computing devices available to the underprivileged, and the overall infrastructural development (Kibe et al. 2013) to improve internet connectivity in rural and urban areas. Furthermore, to ensure the use of the educational cloud among all communities and socioeconomic groups alike, inclusivity should be there in content, design accessibility, etc. A user-centered design principle is needed to design such a platform that can be used in the same manner by a diverse set of people with different backgrounds and abilities (Liu 2016). Furthermore, content creation should be done and used in such in multiple formats to make it easy for students of different proficiency levels to use it. By prioritizing inclusivity and addressing the digital divide, educational institutions can harness the potential of cloud technologies to provide equitable educational opportunities for all students, regardless of their socioeconomic background.

3.2.3 Technological Challenges and Integration Hurdles

The present educational system has been designed with zero to little technological intervention. In such a scenario, integrating cloud learning platforms can pose various technological challenges and integration hurdles (Taheri, Zolfpour-Arokhlo, and Rad 2016). Identifying these obstacles and resolving them constitute the most significant part of cloud deployment in educational systems. The major concern lies in identifying potential technical problems associated with cloud deployment. Technological challenges can comprise outages, service disruption, toggle in bandwidth data rate, network infrastructure compatibility issues, etc. (Ceballos and Lopez Leyva 2015). In addition to all these, data migration and sync issues need careful planning and execution as the cloud environment and the on-premise systems should not generate data redundancy.

Data portability and interoperability across various platforms is another major concern (Czekierda et al. 2021). Educational institutions often utilize diverse software and applications and ensuring seamless data exchange between these platforms and the cloud environment is critical. This may involve implementing data format standardization or adopting cloud solutions that offer robust API (Application Programming Interface) integrations (Idrissa et al. 2016) with existing systems. Successful implementation of cloud technologies requires critical planning (Uehara 2013) and consideration of the present infrastructure. Seamless integration of the cloud in the present infrastructure can be achieved by using a phased implementation. It should start with piloting cloud services for certain applications or departments before migrating the whole system. Some cloud solutions (Mittal et al. 2023) provide open APIs and tools for integration. Use of such solutions can further facilitate a smooth transition. Additionally, using existing industry standards and protocols can help in avoiding any compatibility issues that may rise and ensure data flow between the cloud and existing systems to be smooth.

Training plays a significant role too. It is very important to impart proper training to teachers and students on how to use cloud-based learning platforms. Without such pieces of training, it is impossible to successfully implement cloud-based solutions for educational systems. Establishing readily available technical support is also important to address any technical glitch immediately.

By acknowledging potential technical challenges, addressing data portability and interoperability concerns, implementing a strategic integration plan (Wu and Peng 2014), and prioritizing user support and training, educational institutions can overcome the hurdles associated with cloud adoption. This proactive approach paves the way for a smooth and successful transition to a cloud-enabled learning environment, empowering both educators and students (Xia 2016) to leverage the full potential of this transformative technology.

3.2.4 Human Factors and Resistance to Change

As discussed earlier, the present educational system has zero to little technological intervention, which makes cloud learning platforms unfamiliar to both educators and learners. In such a scenario, the use of cloud technologies in education may face strong resistance. Frequently, various cultural and psychological influences act as roadblocks (Boyatt and Sinclair 2012) for administrators. Furthermore, teachers are hesitant to adopt the new revolutionary tools. It also raises identity crises among the educational workforce. One major concern is the fear of losing control. In schools, the conventional approach is to manage the data and resources in papers and files, unlike cloud platforms. The sense of autonomy provided by the conventional approach is absent in the cloud solutions, which makes the administration think twice about adopting new technology. It can also create anxiety about losing the data, or data security, accessibility, and other issues (Liu 2016). The fear of being over-reliant on technology and failure of technology after being reliant on it is the major issue among the teachers which is making it difficult for them to leave traditional approaches (Kibe, Uehara, and Yamagiwa 2011). Additionally, the fear of losing jobs and technology replacing them is prevailing among the educational workforce. Due to this, they dismiss the use and opportunities provided by cloud-based platforms.

To overcome such challenges raised by humans, proper training is required. Moreover, the setup of an innovative and inclusive culture with effective technology management that acts as an assistant to the existing workforce is rather the need. It also requires the formulation of proper strategies for use. This can be done by creating an environment that motivates experimentation, and innovation, and acknowledges the significance of technology in the digital era. (Ł. Czekierda, Zieliński, and Szreter 2017). Setting up a clear information dissemination system will benefit the deployment of cloud platforms deeply in the conventional education system.

In addition to all these, spending time and resources on training and development may help teachers to better accommodate themselves in the cloud-based environment. They can acquire new skill sets, which will make them more suitable for the digital era and also boost their self-confidence. Collaborative learning (Gandia, Zieliński, and Konieczny 2021) and the efforts of the team as a whole are also crucial, allowing teachers to share best practices, provide mutual support, and collectively navigate the transition process. By providing exposure to a culture of innovation, implementing effective change management strategies, investing in training and development, and encouraging collaboration, conventional educational systems can enable their staff to embrace cloud computing with confidence (Takabe and Uehara 2013). This will certainly reduce the resistance but will also empower teachers to join the full potential of this technology to create engaging and effective learning experiences for their students.

3.3 SOLUTIONS AND FUTURE DIRECTION

3.3.1 Designing Effective Cloud-Based Learning Environments

The conventional education system is going through a transformation, by implementing cloud-based platforms to provide engaging and immersive learning experiences. To navigate this new frontier effectively, educators need to explore the (Zygmunt, Konieczny, and Zielinski 2019) fundamentals of designing engaging online programs, leveraging cloud-based pedagogies, and harnessing cutting-edge instructional techniques.

3.3.2 Fundamentals of Effective Virtual Programs

- *Learner-Centric Design*: Cloud-based learning should prioritize the learner's needs and preferences. Interactive elements, gamification, (Ł. Czekierda, Zieliński, and Szreter 2017), and personalized learning paths are essential for maintaining engagement and motivation.
- *Accessibility and Flexibility*: Learners should be able to access learning materials anytime, anywhere, and on any device (Uehara 2013). Cloud platforms offer the flexibility to cater to diverse learning styles and schedules.
- *Collaboration and Community Building*: Foster a sense of community by creating opportunities for collaboration (Mittal et al. 2023) through online forums, discussion groups, and project-based learning.
- *Continuous Feedback and Assessment*: Utilize cloud-based tools for formative and summative assessments, providing real-time feedback (Boca et al. 2023) to learners and instructors for continuous improvement.

3.3.3 Cloud-Based Pedagogy Best Practices

- *Active Learning*: Promote active learning through interactive activities, simulations, case studies, and problem-solving exercises. Cloud platforms offer a rich (Kibe, Koyama, and Uehara 2012) repository of resources to facilitate these practices.
- *Microlearning and Blended Learning*: Break down complex concepts into bite-sized, easily digestible modules. Combine (Gil-Ortego et al. 2017) online learning with face-to-face interactions for a holistic learning experience.
- *Inquiry-Based Learning*: Encourage inquiry and critical thinking by posing open-ended questions, facilitating research projects, and fostering online discussions. Cloud platforms provide (Li 2017) access to vast information resources and collaboration tools to support this approach.

3.3.4 Cutting-Edge Instructional Techniques

- *VR and AR*: Immerse learners in virtual environments or overlay digital elements (Singh et al. 2023) onto the real world to enhance understanding and engagement.
- *AI*: Utilize AI-powered tutors and personalized learning recommendations to provide tailored learning paths (Uehara 2013) and support individual needs.
- *Big Data and Learning Analytics*: Analyze student data to identify learning gaps, personalize instruction, and monitor progress. Cloud platforms (Boyatt and Sinclair 2012) offer the infrastructure and tools to manage and analyze large datasets effectively.

3.3.5 Fostering Critical Thinking, Teamwork, and Communication

Cloud-based learning environments can be designed to actively promote critical thinking, teamwork, and communication skills through:

- *Collaborative Projects*: Assign collaborative projects requiring students to work together virtually, fostering teamwork (Buehrer, Wang, and Chien 2010) and communication.
- *Online Discussions and Debates*: Encourage critical thinking and communication through online forum discussions, debates, and presentations (L. Czekierda, Zieliński, and Zieliński 2021).
- *Peer Review and Feedback*: Implement peer review processes for student work to develop critical evaluation and communication skills (Tian et al. 2013).
- By embracing these design principles and incorporating innovative cloud-based tools, educational institutions can foster engaging, effective, and future-proof learning environments that empower students to develop critical thinking, teamwork, and communication skills critical for success in the 21st century.

3.4 ASSESSMENT AND EVALUATION IN THE EDUCATIONAL CLOUD

Evaluating student learning is an essential component of any educational program, and cloud-based learning environments present both challenges and opportunities in this realm. To navigate this landscape effectively, educators need to understand the fundamentals of assessment in virtual programs, address the unique challenges and opportunities presented by cloud-based learning, explore various evaluation tools, and leverage data-driven insights for continuous improvement.

3.4.1 Fundamentals of Assessment in Virtual Programs

- *Alignment with Learning Objectives*: Assessments should align directly with the learning objectives and curriculum of the virtual program, ensuring they measure the intended knowledge, skills, and competencies.

- *Variety of Assessment Methods*: Utilize a diverse range of assessment methods beyond traditional exams, such as online quizzes, portfolios, peer reviews, and self-reflection activities, to capture a more holistic picture of student learning.
- *Accessibility and Fairness*: Ensure all assessments are accessible and fair to students with diverse learning styles and needs.
- *Clear Feedback and Guidance*: Provide timely and specific feedback to students on their performance, guiding them toward improvement and learning from their mistakes.

3.4.2 Challenges and Opportunities in Cloud-Based Assessment

- *Academic Integrity*: Maintaining academic integrity in online environments can be challenging, and educators must employ strategies (Idrissa et al. 2016) like proctoring software, plagiarism detection tools, and clear guidelines on ethical behavior.
- *Standardized Testing*: Traditional standardized tests may not be well-suited for measuring the diverse learning outcomes and skills developed in cloud-based environments.
- *Data Security and Privacy*: Data security and student privacy are paramount concerns, and robust safeguards (Mittal et al. 2023) must be implemented to protect sensitive information collected during online assessments.

3.4.3 Despite these Challenges, Cloud-Based Learning also Presents Valuable Opportunities for Assessment

- *Real-time Feedback and Insights*: Cloud platforms offer tools for real-time feedback on student performance, enabling educators to intervene and adjust instruction as needed (Cappos et al. 2009).
- *Detailed Data Analysis*: Cloud-based tools can analyze vast amounts of assessment data, providing insights into individual (Ameen, Sanjay, and Patel 2012) student progress, identifying areas for improvement at the program level, and informing data-driven decision-making.
- *Scalability and Efficiency*: Cloud platforms can efficiently manage large-scale assessments and automate various aspects of the evaluation process, freeing up valuable educator time (Buehrer and Wang 2012).

3.4.4 Exploring Cloud-Based Evaluation Instruments

A variety of cloud-based tools can enhance the assessment process:

- *Online Quizzes and Exams*: Platforms offer secure, automated quiz and exam delivery with features like randomized question pools and immediate grading (Veni and Masillamani 2010).
- *Collaboration and Project Management Tools*: These tools facilitate collaborative projects and peer-review activities, allowing evaluation of teamwork (D. Wu and Peng 2014), communication, and problem-solving skills.

- *E-Portfolios*: Students can build online portfolios showcasing their learning journey, including assignments, reflections, and multimedia content (Brzozowska and Greblicki 2014), providing a holistic view of their progress.

3.4.5 Ensuring Accuracy and Consistency of Cloud-Based Assessments

- *Standardized Rubrics and Scoring Criteria*: Utilize well-defined rubrics and scoring criteria consistently applied by educators to ensure fairness and consistency in evaluation.
- *Regular Calibration Sessions*: Conduct regular calibration sessions where educators come together to compare their interpretations of rubrics and scoring criteria, minimizing inter-rater variability.
- *Pilot Testing and Validation*: Pilot test new assessments before large-scale deployment to identify any potential issues and ensure their validity and reliability.

3.4.6 Data-Driven Decision-Making and Continuous Improvement

Cloud-based learning generates a wealth of data, and harnessing this data through learning analytics is vital for continuous improvement. By analyzing assessment data, educators can identify areas of strength and weakness (Huang et al. 2013) in the curriculum, track individual student progress, and make data-driven decisions to personalize learning, improve instruction, and enhance the overall effectiveness of the educational program.

By embracing these principles and utilizing the unique capabilities of cloud-based learning environments, educators can develop robust assessment strategies that ensure accurate, consistent, and data-driven evaluations, ultimately leading to continuous improvement and enhanced student learning outcomes.

3.5 CONCLUSION AND FUTURE SCOPE

The educational landscape is undergoing a rapid transformation driven by the ever-evolving world of cloud computing. New developments and emerging trends are reshaping the way we learn and teach (Jin et al. 2023), opening doors to innovative possibilities for the future of education.

One of the most significant forces driving change is the rise of AI and machine learning (ML) (Mittal et al. 2023). These technologies have the potential to revolutionize cloud-based learning environments by:

- *Personalizing Learning*: AI can personalize the learning experience by analyzing individual student data, strengths, and weaknesses to tailor content, pacing, and support. This allows educators to cater to diverse learning styles (Kaihua et al. 2022) and needs more effectively.
- *Providing Intelligent Tutoring*: AI-powered virtual tutors can offer personalized guidance and feedback, answer student questions, provide targeted support, and offer additional resources based on their specific needs.

- *Creating Adaptive Learning Systems*: ML algorithms can analyze student performance and adjust the difficulty and content of (Supreeth and Patil 2022) learning materials in real time, ensuring students are challenged appropriately and continuously engaged.

However, with these advancements come critical ethical considerations and potential challenges that need to be addressed:

- *Bias and Fairness*: AI algorithms trained on biased data can perpetuate existing inequalities in education. Ensuring fairness and mitigating biases in AI-powered learning systems is crucial.
- *Data Privacy Concerns*: Collecting and utilizing student data for personalized learning raises concerns about privacy and data security (Almotiry et al. 2021). Ethical guidelines and robust data protection measures are essential to ensure student privacy is protected.
- *Teacher Displacement*: While AI can be a valuable tool, it should not replace the role of educators. Educators must adapt and evolve alongside technology (Englisch, Bergelt, and Hardt 2021), focusing on higher-order thinking skills, creativity, and fostering emotional intelligence in students.

This pivotal moment demands a collective call to action. Educators, educational institutions, policymakers, and technology developers must work together to harness the potential of the educational cloud responsibly and ethically. Some significant aspects to look after are discussed below:

- *Investing in Research and Development*: Further research is needed to explore the ethical implications of AI in education and develop (Czekierda, Zieliński, and Zieliński 2021) responsible and unbiased learning models.
- *Educating Educators*: Equipping educators with the necessary skills and knowledge to use cloud-based technologies (Ananthi Claral Mary and Arul Leena Rose 2020) effectively and adapt to the evolving educational landscape is crucial.
- *Developing regulatory frameworks*: Establishing clear guidelines and regulations around data privacy, security, and ethical AI development (Fangguo 2020) is essential to ensure responsible use of technology in education.

By embracing innovation, fostering collaboration, and addressing potential challenges ethically, we can unlock the immense potential of the educational cloud to create radically innovative learning opportunities, empower educators, and ultimately empower learners to thrive in the 21st century and beyond. As we move forward, let us remember that technology should serve as a tool to enhance learning, not replace the irreplaceable role of educators and the human connection at the heart of a truly enriching educational experience.

REFERENCES

Almotiry, O N, M Sha, M P Rahamathulla, and O S Dawood Omer. 2021. "Hybrid Cloud Architecture for Higher Education System." *Computer Systems Science and Engineering* 36 (1). doi:10.32604/csse.2021.014267.

Ameen, M N, H A Sanjay, and Y Patel. 2012. "A Service Provisioning and Managing Framework for Platform as a Service in Educational Cloud." In *Proceedings of 2012 2nd IEEE International Conference on Parallel, Distributed and Grid Computing*, PDGC 2012, 262–7. IEEE. doi:10.1109/PDGC.2012.6449829.

Ananthi Claral Mary, T, and P J Arul Leena Rose. 2020. "The Impact of Graduate Student's Perceptions towards Usage of Cloud Computing in Higher Education Sectors." *Universal Journal of Educational Research* 8 (11): 5463–78. doi:10.13189/ujer.2020.081150.

Boca, L, E M Ciortea, C Boghean, A Begov-Ungur, F Boghean, and V T Dădârlat. 2023. "An IoT System Proposed for Higher Education: Approaches and Challenges in Economics, Computational Linguistics, and Engineering." *Sensors* 23 (14). doi:10.3390/s23146272.

Boyatt, R, and J Sinclair. 2012. "Navigating the Educational Cloud." In *Advances in Intelligent Systems and Computing*, AISC 173, 179–91. Springer. doi:10.1007/978-3-642-30859-8_17.

Brzozowska, A, and J Greblicki. 2014. Mathematical Model of Task Scheduling in Educational Cloud. In *Advances in Intelligent Systems and Computing*, AISC 286, 115–22. Springer. doi:10.1007/978-3-319-07013-1_11.

Buehrer, D J, and C-Y Wang. 2012. CA-ABAC: Class Algebra Attribute-Based Access Control. In *Proceedings of the 2012 IEEE/WIC/ACM International Conference on Web Intelligence and Intelligent Agent Technology Workshops*, WI-IAT 2012, 220–5. IEEE. doi:10.1109/WI-IAT.2012.268.

Buehrer, D J, C-Y Wang, and L-R Chien. 2010. "The Cadabia Cloud." In *Proceedings – International Symposium on Parallel and Distributed Processing with Applications*, ISPA 2010, 631–8. IEEE. doi:10.1109/ISPA.2010.15.

Cappos, J, I Beschastnikh, A Krishnamurthy, and T Anderson. 2009. "Seattle: A Platform for Educational Cloud Computing." In *SIGCSE'09 – Proceedings of the 40th ACM Technical Symposium on Computer Science Education*, 111–5. ACM. doi:10.1145/1508865.1508905.

Ceballos, S S, and J A Lopez Leyva. 2015. "An Optimized Collaborative Platform for Educational Cloud Computing in Application and Presentation Layers of OSI Model." In *2015 International Conference on Computing Systems and Telematics*, ICCSAT 2015. IEEE. doi:10.1109/ICCSAT.2015.7362922.

Czekierda, Ł, F Malawski, R Straś, K Zieliński, and S Zieliński. 2021. "Leveraging Cloud Environment Flexibility to Smoothen the Transition to Remote Teaching during COVID-19 Pandemic – A Case Study." *Bulletin of the Polish Academy of Sciences: Technical Sciences* 69 (4). doi:10.24425/bpasts.2021.137934.

Czekierda, Ł, S Zieliński, and M Szreter. 2017. "Benefits of Extending Collaborative Educational Cloud with IoT." In *Proceedings – 2017 IEEE 26th International Conference on Enabling Technologies: Infrastructure for Collaborative Enterprises*, WETICE 2017, 80–5. IEEE. doi:10.1109/WETICE.2017.57.

Czekierda, L, K Zieliński, and Sł. Zieliński. 2021. "Automated Orchestration of Online Educational Collaboration in Cloud-Based Environments." *ACM Transactions on Multimedia Computing, Communications and Applications* 17 (1). doi:10.1145/3412381.

Englisch, N, R Bergelt, and W Hardt. 2021. "An AUTOSAR-Specific Static Testing Strategy for Educational Automotive Software Engineering." In *2021 10th Mediterranean Conference on Embedded Computing*, MECO 2021. IEEE. doi:10.1109/MECO52532.2021.9460273.

Fangguo, W. 2020. "Design of Teaching Model of Ideological and Political Education Network Course Based on Educational Cloud Platform." In *Proceedings – 2020 5th International Conference on Smart Grid and Electrical Automation*, ICSGEA 2020, 485–8. IEEE. doi:10.1109/ICSGEA51094.2020.00111.

Gandia, R L, S Zieliński, and M Konieczny. 2021. "Model-Based Approach to Automated Provisioning of Collaborative Educational Services." In *Lecture Notes in Computer Science (Including Subseries Lecture Notes in Artificial Intelligence and Lecture Notes in Bioinformatics)*, 12747 LNCS, 640–53. Springer. doi:10.1007/978-3-030-77980-1_48.

Gil-Ortego, R, M Castro-Gil, S Tzanova, and E Sicard. 2017. "Work in Progress: MicroElectronics Cloud Alliance: The Design of New Open Educational Resources for a Educational Cloud." In *2017 IEEE International Conference on Microelectronic Systems Education*, MSE 2017, 43–4. IEEE. doi:10.1109/MSE.2017.7945082.

Huang, C.-Q., Y Li, Y Tang, and R.-H. Huang. 2013. "A Research on Replica Management of Cloud Storage System for Educational Resources." *Beijing Youdian Daxue Xuebao/ Journal of Beijing University of Posts and Telecommunications* 36 (2): 93–7.

Idrissa, S M, K Djibo, S Bisso, and H Saliah-Hassane. 2016. "A Secured Resource Access Management in Educational Cloud Computing Environment." In *4th International Symposium on Digital Forensics and Security*, ISDFS 2016 – Proceeding, 14–9. IEEE. doi:10.1109/ISDFS.2016.7473510.

Jamadar, Z, and A Patankar. 2013. "Discovery of the Educational Cloud Services." In *Proceedings of the 2013 IEEE International Conference in MOOC, Innovation and Technology in Education*, MITE 2013, 228–33. IEEE. doi:10.1109/MITE.2013.6756340.

Jin, X, M Fan, Q Wang, and D Guo. 2023. "Research on Dynamic Learning Intervention Driven by Data." In *Lecture Notes in Computer Science (Including Subseries Lecture Notes in Artificial Intelligence and Lecture Notes in Bioinformatics)*, 13978 LNCS, 239–49. Springer. doi:10.1007/978-3-031-35731-2_21.

Kaihua, L, C Mei, W Dongying, and W Guoning. 2022. "Under the Mode of 'Internet Plus', Construction and Practice of Regional Intelligent Education Cloud Platform – Take E City's Smart Education Cloud Platform Construction as an Example." In *Lecture Notes in Electrical Engineering*, LNEE 791, 1485–91. Springer. doi:10.1007/978-981-16-4258-6_183.

Kibe, S, T Koyama, and M Uehara. 2012. "The Evaluations of Desktop as a Service in an Educational Cloud." In *Proceedings of the 2012 15th International Conference on Network-Based Information Systems*, NBIS 2012, 621–6. IEEE. doi:10.1109/NBiS.2012.43.

Kibe, S, M Uehara, and M Yamagiwa. 2011. "Evaluation of Bottlenecks in an Educational Cloud Environment." In *Proceedings – 3rd IEEE International Conference on Intelligent Networking and Collaborative Systems*, INCoS 2011, 520–5. IEEE. doi:10.1109/INCoS.2011.87.

Kibe, S, S Watanabe, K Kunishima, R Adachi, M Yamagiwa, and M Uehara. 2013. "PaaS on IaaS." In *Proceedings – International Conference on Advanced Information Networking and Applications*, AINA, 362–7. IEEE. doi:10.1109/AINA.2013.73.

Li, C. 2017. "An Architecture Design of Educational Cloud System and the Development of Resource Sharing Capability." *Boletin Tecnico/Technical Bulletin* 55 (13): 425–30.

Liu, C. 2016. "Design and Key Techniques in Education Cloud Platforms for Teaching." *International Journal of Simulation: Systems, Science and Technology* 17 (16): 6.1–6.10. doi:10.5013/IJSSST.a.17.16.06.

Maaita, A A, Z F Muhsen, and A J Nsour. 2013. "Cloud Computing Educational Environment." In *Proceedings of the European, Mediterranean and Middle Eastern Conference on Information Systems*, EMCIS 2013. Springer.

Mittal, N, M Saxena, P K Sarangi, N Phutela, and M Sharma. 2023. "Analysis of E-Learning Trends Using Educational Cloud in Cloud Computing." In *Artificial Intelligence, Blockchain, Computing and Security: Volume 2*, 2, 282–7. CRC Press. doi:10.1201/9781032684994-44.

Muniasamy, V, and I M Ejalani. 2014. "Moving towards Virtual Learning Clouds from Traditional Learning: Higher Educational Systems in India." *International Journal of Emerging Technologies in Learning* 9 (9): 70–6. doi:10.3991/ijet.v9i9.4183.

Ouahabi, S, A Eddaoui, E H Labriji, E Benlahmar, and K El Guemmat. 2014. "Educational Modelling in Cloud Computing Using IMS Learning Design." *Journal of Theoretical and Applied Information Technology* 66 (3): 654–60.

Parveen, R, and E Chikhaoui. 2017. "Legal Issues and Challenges in Educational Cloud Computing in the Kingdom of Saudi Arabia." *International Journal of Economic Research* 14 (20): 357–71.

Pietrzak, M. 2016. "Use of Information and Communication Technology and Resources of the Internet in Education Natural Sciences." In *Current Topics in Czech and Central European Geography Education*, 147–68. Springer. doi:10.1007/978-3-319-43614-2_9.

Salvi, S, H A Sanjay, K M Deepika, and S R Rangavittala. 2015. "An Encryption, Compression and Key (ECK) Management Based Data Security Framework for Infrastructure as a Service in Cloud." In *Souvenir of the 2015 IEEE International Advance Computing Conference*, IACC 2015, 872–6. IEEE. doi:10.1109/IADCC.2015.7154830.

Singh, L, S S Bisht, P Shukla, Y Singh, V M Kapse, and P Chandani. 2023. "Cloud Computing and Its Applications to E-Learning." In *Integration of Cloud Computing with Emerging Technologies Issues, Challenges, and Practices*, 227–38. CRC Press. doi:10.1201/9781003341437-20.

Slakmon, B. 2017. "Educational Technology Policy in Israel." *Pedagogy, Culture and Society* 25 (1): 137–49. doi:10.1080/14681366.2016.1231709.

Stein, S, J Ware, J Laboy, and H E Schaffer. 2013. "Improving K-12 Pedagogy via a Cloud Designed for Education." *International Journal of Information Management* 33 (1): 235–41. doi:10.1016/j.ijinfomgt.2012.07.009.

Supreeth, S, and K Patil. 2022. "Hybrid Genetic Algorithm and Modified-Particle Swarm Optimization Algorithm (GA-MPSO) for Predicting Scheduling Virtual Machines in Educational Cloud Platforms." *International Journal of Emerging Technologies in Learning* 17 (7): 208–25. doi:10.3991/ijet.v17i07.29223.

Taheri, A, M Zolfpour-Arokhlo, and F Rad. 2016. "Improve Educational Cloud Using Grid Capabilities." *Journal of Engineering and Applied Sciences* 11 (9): 2014–8. doi:10.3923/jeasci.2016.2014.2018.

Takabe, Y, and M Uehara. 2013. "Rapid Deployment for Machine Learning in the Educational Cloud." In *Proceedings – 16th International Conference on Network-Based Information Systems*, NBiS 2013, 372–6. IEEE. doi:10.1109/NBiS.2013.59.

Tian, W, X Sun, Y Jiang, and H Wang. 2013. "CRESS: A Platform of Infrastructure Resource Sharing for Educational Cloud Computing." *China Communications* 10 (9): 43–52. doi:10.1109/CC.2013.6623502.

Uehara, M. 2013. "Proposal for BYOD Based Virtual PC Classroom." In *Proceedings – 16th International Conference on Network-Based Information Systems*, NBiS 2013, 377–82. IEEE. doi:10.1109/NBiS.2013.60.

Veni, P, and R Masillamani. 2010. "Resource Sharing Cloud for University Clusters." In *Proceedings – 2010 IEEE/ACM International Conference on Green Computing and Communications, GreenCom 2010, 2010 IEEE/ACM International Conference on Cyber, Physical and Social Computing, CPSCom 2010*, 873–8. IEEE. doi:10.1109/GreenCom-CPSCom.2010.142.

Wu, D, and X Peng. 2014. "Research on Constructing the Standard Architecture of Educational Cloud Computing." In *Proceedings – 2014 International Conference on Intelligent Environments*, IE 2014, 326–9. IEEE. doi:10.1109/IE.2014.71.

Wu, F, and Z Mou. 2015. "The Design and Development of Electronic Schoolbag System Based on Educational Cloud Service Platform." In *Lecture Notes in Educational Technology*, no. 9783662441879, 313–9. doi:10.1007/978-3-662-44188-6_43.

Xia, J. 2016. "Theories and Methods of Using the Educational Technology in Teaching Chinese as a Second Language." In *Proceedings – 2015 International Conference of Educational Innovation through Technology*, EITT 2015, 279–82. IEEE. doi:10.1109/EITT.2015.64.

Zieliński, K, Ł Czekierda, F Malawski, R Straś, and S Zieliński. 2017. "Recognizing Value of Educational Collaboration between High Schools and Universities Facilitated by Modern ICT." *Journal of Computer Assisted Learning* 33 (6): 633–48. doi:10.1111/jcal.12207.

Zygmunt, M, M Konieczny, and S Zielinski. 2019. "Accuracy of Statistical Machine Learning Methods in Identifying Client Behavior Patterns at Network Edge." In *2019 42nd International Conference on Telecommunications and Signal Processing*, TSP 2019, 575–9. IEEE. doi:10.1109/TSP.2019.8768885.

4 Envisioning Tomorrow
Educational Clouds in Future Education

Roshni Bhave, Vijaya Kamble, Amita Meshram, A. Venkata Mahesh, and Dhananjay Bhagat

4.1 INTRODUCTION

The capacity of cloud computing to reduce information technology (IT) [ok]expenses is its main benefit. By utilizing cloud computing, businesses may rent resources and only pay for the services they use, avoiding the need to build their own IT infrastructure. Even with cloud computing's alluring advantages, poorer nations are still adopting it slowly for a variety of reasons. There has not been much research done on the use of technology in these areas, particularly as it relates to cloud computing in higher education. This intends to contribute to the literature on cloud computing acceptance in developing nations, as most previous studies have concentrated on technology adoption in rich countries and, to a lesser extent, in developing countries within non-educational contexts like e-government (Hussain & Abubakar, 2018).

Innovative technologies are driving a fundamental shift of traditional educational techniques in today's quickly expanding digital landscape. The creation of the Educational Cloud stands out among these innovations as a sign of optimism for future learning generations. This innovative platform transforms the educational process and breaks down geographical barriers by introducing a dynamic and simply accessible method to learning. This study offers a case study of a university that has embraced cloud computing to improve education through cloud-based learning. For other universities hoping to make the shift to education and attain academic greatness, it provides a useful blueprint (Zameer Bhat et al., 2022). The Educational Cloud, which uses cloud computing to provide an extensive range of educational resources and applications, represents a major change in the way education is provided. Institutions can overcome the limitations of traditional infrastructure by moving their educational services to the cloud, offering scalable solutions that cater to the various demands of students all over the world. The accessibility of the Educational Cloud is one of its main benefits. Students can access learning materials utilizing cloud-based systems on any internet-connected device, at any time, from any location. This flexibility allows students to engage with the material at their own speed and creates a customized learning environment based on their unique preferences and learning preference. Moreover, the Educational Cloud fosters worldwide cooperation and communication between educators and students. Through instantaneous

 DOI: 10.1201/9781003472537-5

communication and smooth resource exchange, this platform breaks down geographical boundaries and promotes intercultural communication and cooperation. Through project collaboration, virtual classroom participation, and discussions with peers and experts globally, students can expand their perspectives and enhance their learning experience.

Additionally, curriculum creation and teaching methodology innovation are fueled by the Educational Cloud. By utilizing data analytics and machine learning (ML) algorithms, educators can obtain valuable insights into student performance and tailor their instructional tactics to match individual needs. Through the utilization of data-driven insights, instructors can identify areas that require development, track students' progress, and provide tailored feedback, all of which contribute to the enhancement of learning outcomes and students' achievement. In the future, the Educational Cloud has enormous potential to transform education and provide the next generation of students more authority. This revolutionary platform has the power to influence education in the future by providing students with the information and abilities they need to succeed in the digital era. It does this by democratizing access to high-quality education and encouraging creativity and teamwork (Zameer Bhat et al., 2022).

An Educational Cloud serves as a catalyst for positive transformation, paving the way for a more promising and inclusive future in education. The global pandemic provided educators with a unique opportunity to revolutionize classrooms worldwide. Education must become more flexible, just as technology is shaping the jobs of the future. Cloud computing in higher education caters to a diverse student body by offering personalized attention, helping students instructors and within the confines of a classroom. This setup was particularly effective in the 20th century, when conventional teaching methods were integrated with scientific and technological advancements, leading to significant progress, such as the notable rise in life expectancy during that era.

Nevertheless, a great deal has changed in the first 20 years of this century. These days, our pupils are always connected via digital channels. Therefore, incorporating new technologies and creative methods is no longer just an option for organizations and teachers—rather, it is now a crucial precondition that cannot be disregarded.

The primary benefit of these new technologies is that they have the potential to achieve a goal in education that has never been achieved before: the fusion of quality and quantity. By making education more accessible to a wider audience, we can improve its quality in ways that have never been possible before. We are moving away from the idea that excellence in education is only available to a select few and toward a new paradigm that states that effective education requires large amounts of data, robust analytical skills, and widespread participation (Aljenaa et al., 2011). To put it another way, by having more information available, we can better understand each student and thus customize and personalize for effective learning experiences.

The main advantage of these new technologies is the unparalleled chance they give us to accomplish a goal in education that we have not fully succeeded in: combining quantity with quality. We can now realistically improve the quality of education as we can reach more children than ever before. In other words, when we gather more data, we have a deeper understanding of each student and are able to customize and provide more appropriate, individualized, and successful learning trajectories (Ashtari & Eydgahi, 2017). One of the most important resources in the pursuit of high-quality education that is universally available, flexible for any educational setting, and, most importantly, personalized is cloud computing. Gradually, education will fully integrate its "head" into the Cloud, with gains made for its particular objectives. The cloud is an advanced technology that shifts focus from traditional, location-specific computer networks to a completely virtual environment. This shift provides increased productivity, superior security, and almost infinite processing power. There are several cloud environments available, each with special benefits and features.

It is fully possible to construct learning environments that are accessible to educators, administrators, and students through intelligent and integrated platforms by utilizing cloud technology. This substitute frees educational establishments of all stripes, from preschool to university, from the burden of managing separate computer centers and other operational and administrative assets, allowing them to concentrate safely on instruction (Aljenaa et al., 2011). Tracking each student's progress requires integrating advanced learning environments, which include virtual classrooms backed by continuous learning analytics services, and digital resources, which include simulation laboratories and immersive experiences. This method gives teachers the ability to skillfully create individualized learning pathways (Vilela et al., 2017).

On a case-by-case basis, it can result in significant cost savings for both schools and students. The decisive element? Reimbursement solely for rendered services, ensuring the best possible ratio of value for all involved. Additionally, educational institutions no longer have to worry about having to update their gear and software on a regular basis, which saves money, effort, and time (Zameer Bhat et al., 2022; Hussain et al., 2017). Clearly, adopting cloud computing can benefit educational institutions, students, and teachers in a big way. The more we invest in the cloud now, the more these developments will allow everyone to learn continuously—everyone in their own unique and customized way (Mircea & Andreescu, 2011).

4.2 CHALLENGES IN EDUCATION BEFORE CLOUD

Schools and colleges function in highly controlled environments with clearly defined roles, stringent policies, physical locations, standardized curriculum, curricula, and bureaucratic settings where faculty members are frequently viewed as superior to students during the teaching and learning process. Before cloud computing became widely used, one of the main issues facing the educational system was the sudden disruption of classroom instruction brought on by unanticipated natural disasters like fires or cyclones (Hussain et al., 2017; Aljenaa et al., 2011). The incapacity to retrieve crucial records in the event of server malfunctions, fires in server rooms, or other man-made calamities such as deliberate file deletions constituted another difficulty. It was frequently impractical for the education sector to develop complete disaster recovery (DR) procedures due to its limited financial resources.

In the past, educational establishments developed independent DR plans, leading to different methods for recovering data. Storage area networks (SANs), tape backups, and outsourcing to outside contractors for off-site solutions were common examples of these strategies. Resources were few as most educational materials, such as research papers and textbooks, were only available in physical form. This made it difficult for teachers and students to acquire these materials, especially in rural or underdeveloped areas. Large volumes of data, including student records and administrative documents, were difficult for educational institutions to store, necessitating a large quantity of physical storage space and continuous upkeep.

Geographical restrictions made it difficult for some children to receive education—traditional classrooms were the main form of instruction; thus those with impairments or other impediments could not attend. Data security was a top priority because sensitive information needed to be protected from breaches and unwanted access on institution-owned servers hosting locally stored data. Therefore, strong security measures were needed. Outside of the classroom, student–teacher collaboration was difficult, because it relied on ineffective techniques like email correspondence or in-person meetings, which hampered real-time collaboration and feedback (Kaur & Singh, 2015).

All things considered, the pre-cloud period of education was marked by a number of difficulties that limited the efficiency, accessibility, and flexibility of educational programs.

4.3 SOLUTIONS FOR THE CHALLENGES IN EDUCATION BEFORE CLOUD

Using reliable systems and fast networks, cloud computing offers a flexible approach to providing information and communication technology (ICT) services in times of crisis. It achieves tremendous scalability by utilizing shared redundant platforms, distributed hardware, and software resources. While they do not directly enhance instructional pedagogy, cloud solutions for DR and business continuity planning (BCP) help to protect data and keep systems operational in times of emergency. To maintain data integrity during emergencies and adjust to organizational changes, effective backup strategies and procedures are crucial (Hussain et al., 2017).

Using cloud computing, which simply requires an internet connection that is often inexpensive, educational institutions can access cutting-edge computing resources at a significant savings. Cloud-based data retrieval is quick; therefore, downtime and resource limitations are reduced compared to traditional tape backup methods. For educational institutions, cloud solutions offer seamless continuity and data integrity because of the time-sensitive nature of data recovery, especially during crucial operations like result declaration and admissions (McCrea, 2009).

For research projects and educational goals, a multitude of cloud providers provide cutting-edge technology and high-performance computing with scalable and affordable solutions designed specifically for the education sector. One such example is that Amazon Web Services (AWS) offers Teaching Grants to educators globally, allowing them to use free AWS services, such as Amazon EC2, S3, SimpleDB, RDS, SQS, CloudFront, and Elastic MapReduce, for qualifying courses.

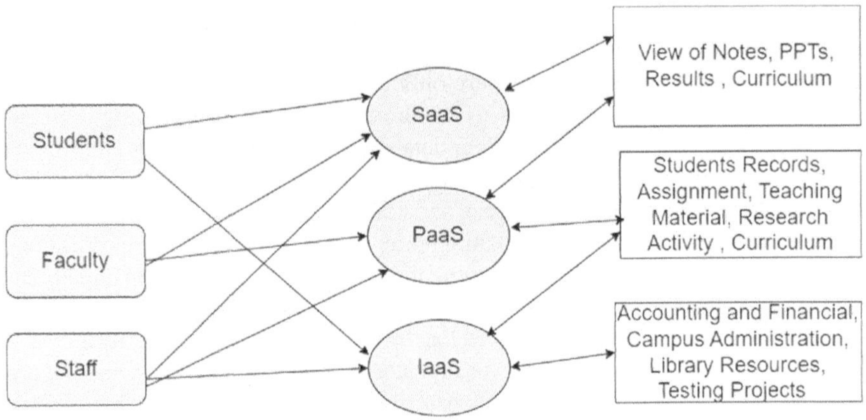

FIGURE 4.1 Cloud Users on Different Platforms.

4.4 CLOUD-BASED MODEL FOR EDUCATION

Students, instructors, and staff are important players in the educational system, and they possess vital information about student performance, cost plans, homework, curricula, and more (Figure 4.1). When needed, losing any records pertaining to these organizations is a serious problem. Documents were formerly kept on local servers, where their loss after a disaster may bring the system to a complete stop. Faculty members used to back up their documents using universal serial bus (USB) drives. By adopting USB drives, the faculty may be hoping to ensure that, in case of an emergency, laboratory manuals, notes, and student findings can be safely stored at home. However, the professors identified an undetectable harmful virus on the USB after inserting it into a private laptop. The virus spread quickly and, for lack of any warning, caused a laptop to crash in a matter of hours, corrupting or erasing most of the data (Zameer Bhat et al., 2022; Hussain et al., 2017).

Cloud technology benefits all user groups by enabling access to databases, emails, files, and applications from anywhere at any time, promoting efficient information use. It aims to meet the needs of staff, teachers, and students with cost-effective, advanced technologies that enhance document protection and accessibility. Cloud platforms like Platform as a Service (PaaS) and Software as a Service (SaaS) improve student learning through communication and teamwork, while also offering faculty secure storage for teaching and research materials. Infrastructure as a Service (IaaS) benefits employees, particularly developers, by allowing app creation, testing, and deployment directly from cloud servers, surpassing the limitations of local networks.

4.5 IMPLEMENTATION

Figure 4.2 makes it clear that educational institutions can use the cloud as a platform to create online learning environments for instructors and students. To host and manage an online learning platform, these institutions might make use of cloud

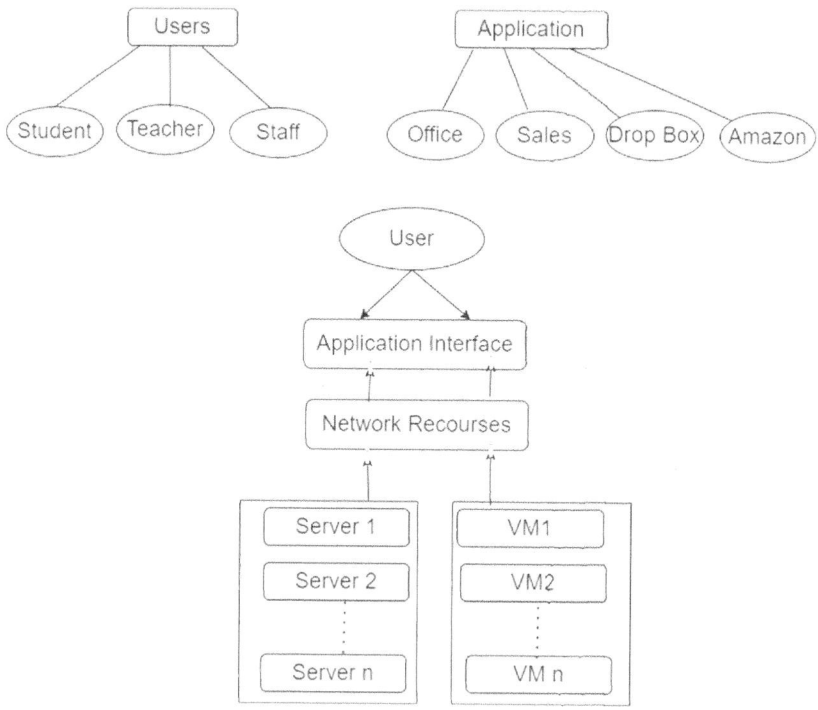

FIGURE 4.2 Cloud Architecture in Education.

infrastructures, which include servers, storage, communication tools, and e-learning applications. With this configuration, educational institutions can enable smooth communication between instructors and students, giving students access to the knowledge of world-class lecturers at a reasonable cost and from anywhere. Additionally, it creates a competitive environment among educators, which promotes creativity in the classroom.

The concept creates an efficient and convenient learning environment with a variety of features, such as online chat and audio/video sessions. Furthermore, there are resources for enriching educational content that enable content to be published, reviewed, and created, encouraging the development of new learning resources.

4.6 COMPONENT OF THE EDUCATIONAL CLOUD

The future of education for the coming generation is being shaped in large part by the Educational Cloud. By utilizing cloud computing technologies, it transforms conventional methods of instruction (Qasem et al., 2019). The following is a summary, along with an illustration (Figure 4.3) of the Educational Cloud functions:

Cloud Infrastructure: The Educational Cloud makes use of a strong cloud infrastructure that includes networking, storage, and servers. Because of these

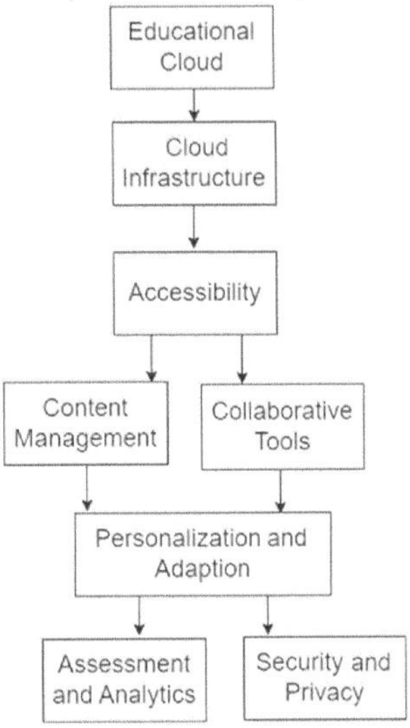

FIGURE 4.3 Components of Educational Cloud.

resources' scalability and flexibility, educational institutions can easily adjust to changing demands.

Accessibility: The Educational Cloud is available to teachers, administrators, and students from any location with internet access, creating a global learning environment. This accessibility guarantees inclusion and supports a range of learning preferences and styles.

Information Management: Textbooks, multimedia files, and interactive teaching aids are all housed in the Educational Cloud's enormous warehouses of educational information. Because of its logical organization, users can easily search for, access, and share this content with others.

Collaborative Tools: The Educational Cloud's collaborative tools enable smooth interaction and communication between teachers and students. In the context of a digital learning environment, features like virtual classrooms, discussion boards, and real-time messaging improve collaboration and build a sense of community.

Personalization and Adaptation: To tailor educational experiences, sophisticated algorithms examine user data and behavior (Qasem et al., 2019). The Educational Cloud's adaptive learning platforms maximize learning results by customizing instructional materials and activities to each student's requirements, preferences, and learning style.

Assessment and Analytics: To track student development and performance, the Educational Cloud has powerful assessment tools and analytics capabilities. Teachers are able to monitor students' progress, pinpoint areas that need work, and offer prompt feedback to facilitate individualized learning (Lazowska et al., 2008).

Security and Privacy: To ensure confidentiality, integrity, and availability of sensitive educational data stored in the cloud, strict security measures are in place.

Adherence to data protection laws and standards is crucial to preserving user confidence and trust.

Each element of the Educational Cloud ecosystem is represented in this diagram as being interrelated and contributing to a creative and productive learning environment for the coming generation (Qasem et al., 2019).

4.7 THE EDUCATION DOMAIN IS WITNESSING THE ASCENDANCY OF CLOUD COMPUTING DUE TO VARIOUS COMPELLING REASONS

In the education industry, cloud computing is becoming increasingly common; 50% of institutions are using cloud solutions (Baliga et al., 2018). There are several compelling reasons why cloud technology has gained such widespread adoption in education, which are discussed below.

4.7.1 Addressing the Needs of Virtual and Hybrid Learning Environments

Virtual classrooms revolutionize education by creating dynamic, accessible, and personalized learning experiences. They promote inclusivity and flexibility, preparing students for a digital world. Effective virtual learning requires adaptable teaching methods, robust tech infrastructure, and tailored support. Combining analog and digital techniques, cloud computing accelerates educational innovation and real-time collaboration. As virtual learning grows, demand for high-speed internet rises. According to Accenture, 96% of students now consider a high-quality digital experience essential, emphasizing the cloud's role in improving satisfaction and increasing enrollment. However, challenges persist: 1,356 schools still lack fiber connectivity, and 2.3 million children do not have internet access in their classrooms. As a result, organizations must ensure reliable connectivity (Baliga et al., 2018).

Regardless of where students and teachers are physically located, meeting the needs of virtual and hybrid learning environments requires putting strategies into place and making use of resources to guarantee effective teaching and learning experiences. Here are some important things to think about:

1. *Technology Integration*: Make use of the platforms and tools offered by technology to support virtual and hybrid learning. Examples of these include learning management systems (LMS) (like Moodle, Canvas), video conferencing apps (like Zoom, Google Meet), and teamwork applications (like Microsoft Teams, Google Workspace).
2. *Accessible Content*: Ascertain that all students, including those with impairments, have equal access to the learning resources. Providing content in alternate formats, including screen reader-friendly documents and video transcripts, may be one way to achieve this.
3. *Engagement Strategies*: Use breakout spaces, surveys, tests, and discussion boards to encourage involvement and teamwork among students during

virtual classes. Incorporate interactive activities and discussions to keep them interested.

4. *Clear Communication*: Clearly define expectations and channels of communication for teachers and students. Give instructions on proper online conduct, how to get help quickly, and how to get technical support.
5. *Flexible Assessments*: Create tests that can adapt to various classroom settings. Think about utilizing a variety of forms, including group projects, presentations, online tests, and written assignments.
6. *Equitable Access*: Regardless of where they attend school or their financial situation, make sure all children have equal access to resources and support services. This could entail giving students, who require them, laptops or internet access in addition to providing virtual office hours for extra help.
7. *Professional Development*: Educate and assist teachers in navigating hybrid and virtual learning environments. Provide training sessions on inclusive teaching methods, digital tools, and online pedagogy.
8. *Input and Reflection*: To determine areas for development and assess students' experiences in virtual and hybrid learning environments, solicit regular input from students. To improve the learning experience, consider the input and make any necessary modifications.
9. *Community Building*: Use online gatherings, group projects, and cooperative exercises to help students and teachers feel more like a community. To boost motivation and engagement, foster peer relationships and support systems.
10. *Continuous Improvement*: Assess the efficacy of hybrid and virtual learning tactics on an ongoing basis and adapt in response to user input and new best practices. To improve teaching and learning outcomes, stay up to date on new technologies and pedagogical approaches.

4.7.2 Minimizing Needless Spending on Expensive Textbooks

Reducing spending on expensive textbooks can greatly increase educational accessibility and affordability. The Educational Cloud offers discounted access to digital resources like Open Educational Resources (OER) and subscription-based textbooks, allowing students to rent, share, and customize materials, thus eliminating the need for costly printed textbooks and easing financial stress on students. Additionally, teachers can collaborate to create superior instructional materials, further lowering costs for educational institutions (Buyya & Ranjan, 2019).

4.7.3 Utilize Data to Enhance Results

The Educational Cloud leverages data to enhance results by examining student interactions, test scores, and curriculum performance. Using learning analytics, predictive analytics, and continuous monitoring, educators can identify children who are at risk, personalize learning experiences, and allocate resources as efficiently as possible. The use of a data-centric approach promotes ongoing enhancements in curriculum development, student support, and instructional practices, all of which lead to better educational outcomes. Data has a lot of potential for educational establishments. But keeping this data around can put further burden on already tight resources. Thoroughly assess your infrastructure before introducing Internet of Things (IoT) devices or investigating edge computing's real-time feedback capabilities (Buyya & Ranjan, 2019).

- To overcome this challenge, move some chores to the cloud. This enables you to take use of modern technology and investigate how to incorporate artificial intelligence (AI) and ML into your LMS.
- To monitor safety on playgrounds and to evaluate social interactions, educational institutions have incorporated sensors into toys. Additionally, edge computing provides real-time data, which allows learning systems to dynamically adjust to the individual learning preferences of every learner.
- Instead of making large investments in hardware and IT, educational institutions can work with managed cloud service providers to accomplish these goals. However, for any technology objective, cybersecurity and student data privacy should continue to be the top priorities.

4.7.4 Enable for Personalized Education

A needs-based approach supports students' communication, learning, and engagement styles. With the help of cloud technologies, students can review their content and make use of a variety of instructional resources, such as interactive tutorials and videos. This flexibility gives students a sense of agency, which is one of the main reasons that 82% of participants in the Houghton Mifflin Harcourt (HMH) Educator Confidence Report believe that in the years to come, instruction and education will undergo a revolution because of individualized learning for every student (Nicholson, 2009).

Cloud computing in education allows for customized learning experiences based on the requirements of each individual student. Through the use of cloud-based platforms and applications, educators can offer adaptable access to materials, promote teamwork, and establish adaptive learning systems. This method creates dynamic, inclusive learning environments, raises student involvement, and improves learning results (Baliga et al., 2018).

With regard to the benefits of educational technology (EdTech), it is undeniable that 81% of respondents had experienced "enhanced student engagement, tailored individualized instruction, and convenient access to instructional materials." Students are empowered to extend their learning beyond typical classroom settings by having access to transcripts, recordings, and additional resources via the cloud, which accommodates a variety of learning preferences (Buyya & Ranjan, 2019).

Reliable internet and networking infrastructure, coupled with scalable cloud services, are essential for the successful deployment of EdTech. Whether you choose managed cloud services or private cloud solutions, you can focus on modernizing your IT infrastructure and implementing student-centric upgrades instead of hiring and training IT specialists.

4.7.5 Permit to Access a Range of Learning Resources

Examining "The Future of Cloud in Education" calls for the use of strategies designed to make a wide range of educational resources easier to obtain. This entails creating frameworks and platforms that make it simple and efficient for instructors and students to access a range of cloud-based educational resources. By means of this procedure, people have access to a wide array of resources, including interactive simulations, academic journals, multimedia files, textbooks, and teamwork tools. By providing flexible, scalable, and anytime, anywhere access to instructional materials, this method enhances the educational process. Additionally, it promotes cooperation, creativity, and customized learning opportunities in the educational field (Buyya & Ranjan, 2019; Gai et al., 2018).

Cloud-based platforms, like Moodle, provide easy access to a variety of resources, including slides, videos, and notes.

4.7.6 Reduces Hardware Costs and Increases Scalability

The future of cloud computing in education depends on two key factors: lowering hardware costs and improving scalability. First, educational institutions can considerably reduce their need on expensive physical infrastructure by utilizing cloud-based solutions. To accommodate a variety of educational applications and services, traditional school setups frequently need to make large investments in servers, networking hardware, and storage devices. However, because of cloud technology, a large portion of this hardware load is reduced as cloud service providers host and operate computing resources off-site. Institutions can now reduce their expenditures for both initial hardware purchases and continuing maintenance and upgrades (Baliga et al., 2018).

Second, cloud computing provides unmatched scalability—a crucial feature for meeting the ever-changing demands of learning environments. Cloud-based solutions offer the flexibility to modify resources as needed, whether that means scaling down during low activity or up to meet increasing demand during peak periods. This scalability applies not only to processing resources but also to bandwidth, storage capacity, and other crucial elements of the IT infrastructure for educational institutions. Without being constrained by conventional hardware limitations, educational institutions can easily scale their cloud resources to meet changing requirements as they grow or change. Overall, the advantages of lower hardware costs and improved scalability will be the main drivers of cloud technology in education going forward (Gai et al., 2018). Educational institutions can increase operational efficiency, maximize their IT investments, and better meet the changing demands of administrators, teachers, and students by implementing cloud-based solutions.

4.7.7 Enabling Multi-Device Usage Is a Crucial Aspect of the Future of Cloud Technology in Education

Cloud technology's ability to support multiple devices is crucial for future education. With many students and teachers using smartphones, tablets, and computers, they expect flexible access to resources. Cloud technology provides this, enabling access to learning platforms and materials from any internet-connected device. This flexibility enhances educational experiences by accommodating different learning styles and preferences, allowing seamless switching between devices. It also promotes inclusivity and collaboration, as educators can create and share content across platforms, facilitating engagement and communication. Overall, multi-device support makes education more adaptable, accessible, and collaborative (Dutta & Borah, 2019).

4.7.8 Protect Student Data and Network

Ensuring the security of student data and networks is critical in the future educational landscape of cloud computing. As cloud-based systems are used increasingly for educational reasons, safeguarding sensitive student data becomes crucial. Strong security measures must be put in place by educational institutions to protect student data from misuse, illegal access, and breaches (Hussain et al., 2017). Encrypting data to prevent unauthorized access is one method of safeguarding student information. Strict access restrictions and user authentication procedures should also be put in place to guarantee that only people with permission can access sensitive data. To keep the network infrastructure resilient against cyberattacks, regular security audits and vulnerability assessments assist in locating and addressing possible gaps in the system. Furthermore, by keeping up with new developments in cybersecurity, educational institutions can proactively strengthen their security posture.

In addition, fostering a culture of security awareness within the educational community is achieved through teaching students, instructors, and administrative staff on cybersecurity best practices and the significance of securing sensitive data. In conclusion, securing student data and networks in the context of cloud computing in education will necessitate a multifaceted strategy that includes cybersecurity best practices education, encryption, access limits, and frequent assessments. By placing a high priority on security, educational institutions can guarantee the privacy, availability, and integrity of student data, which will increase users' trust and confidence in cloud-based learning environments (Hussain et al., 2017).

4.8 BENEFITS OF CLOUD TECHNOLOGY IN EDUCATION

Higher education has come to be understood as a key factor in the development of society over time. The adoption of cloud computing in educational institutions is favorably influenced by a number of factors. IaaS is provided by cloud computing, which has numerous benefits over conventional systems. Its centralized infrastructure is a major advantage as it eliminates the need for tedious operations at the local deployment level, saving money, time, and resources on infrastructure setup (Aljenaa et al., 2011). Furthermore, because cloud deployment is nimble, it may be quickly implemented throughout an enterprise, requiring less technical effort in individual departments or schools. As long as they can run a web browser, even the most basic machines can function as web-based platforms for interactive learning (Aljenaa et al., 2011). Moreover, educational establishments can employ pre-packaged SaaS, PaaS, and IaaS solutions without having to worry about infrastructure setup or maintenance (Hussain et al., 2017). Another benefit of cloud computing is that it allows standardized content delivery to multiple virtual classrooms from a central location. This guarantees uniformity and synchronization in learning and training across multiple locations, with students receiving the same study materials. Kaur and Singh (2015) emphasize that cloud technology supports small-group-maintained distance learning classrooms, which is advantageous in situations where staffing levels are low. Kaur and Singh (2015) also note that cloud computing offers robust backup for course content, reducing the risk of data loss during system crashes. You can store different types of content in the cloud, such as documents, applications, audio/video, and documents. Cloud computing enables multiple students to collaborate and automatically provides software updates, ensuring that users can access the latest versions without any manual intervention (Kaur & Singh, 2015). Administrative tasks are completed more quickly and effectively because of administrative staff and educators being able to concentrate more on the needs of the institution rather than on setting up IT infrastructure and applications. In conclusion, higher education institutions can gain considerably from cloud computing. By automating system maintenance and upgrades, it reduces the strain of a lack of IT staff and standardizes and refreshes educational content. It also makes it easier for students and teachers to collaborate. Furthermore, the impact of system failures is lessened by cloud computing's backup capability. Collaborations between academic institutions, governments, and businesses have highlighted the important roles that researchers and students play in transforming society and the global economy. Because cloud computing offers quick IT deployment, institutions can place more emphasis on teaching and research projects than complex IT configurations and software systems. Considering this, cloud computing improves e-learning solutions by providing platforms, infrastructure, and instructional services straight from cloud providers, utilizing virtualization, centralized data storage, and access control techniques. The following are some benefits of cloud computing for the education sector:

1. *Instantaneous Learning*: The main advantage of cloud computing is its ability to provide instant access to real-time information from anywhere in the world. As a result, an open learning atmosphere is promoted, allowing students to easily share their ideas, work, and knowledge (Bittman, 2008).
   - *Energy Conservation*: Documents, software, apps, and other resources are kept on remote servers instead of local networks under cloud computing systems. When storing such materials remotely as opposed to on personal systems, less energy is used. Thus, the education sector benefits considerably from energy saving.
   - *Cost Reduction*: Schools and colleges can cut costs related to equipment and operations by adopting cloud computing technologies like remote desktops and cloud-based IT support. By using the cloud to provide these services, the need for on-site technical support and maintenance services is reduced, and upgrades can be carried out automatically for every end user, saving a substantial amount of money.

2. *Content Expansion*: In the past, the majority of content came from a few select sources, like newspapers, television, encyclopedias, and textbooks. But a lot of content these days comes from comparatively “lesser-known” online sources. However, the internet is more than just a less trustworthy encyclopedias; it is a medium for content creation and interaction. One more drawback of the old system was that pupils were usually restricted to one class, one school, or even one small town. The main benefit of the cloud is that anyone may create information that can be quickly viewed by people all over the world and may even last forever. Updates, contact, and cooperation can all lead to a constant evolution of content. Every year, new tools for content creation, dissemination, and interaction are developed. People no longer only reference or repeat material; instead, they actively participate with it by altering and enhancing it. This is a habit that should be promoted (Qasem et al., 2019).
    - *Collaboration*: Technological developments are quickly improving our capacity for interpersonal communication and teamwork. In the past, we formed teams and collaborated in person by speaking with individuals over the phone or in person. The limited social circle was one major drawback, but cloud computing gets around these limitations by enabling connections through a variety of social platforms, such as Facebook, Twitter, and so on. These were initially largely personal tools, but they are finding their way into the professional sphere more and more. Finding and connecting with people is now easier because of a plethora of new and growing channels, including blogs, social and collaborative software, email, instant messaging, mobile phones, and instant messaging apps. In the past, collaboration was a sequential, one-time, and largely static procedure. However, cloud computing makes it possible for students to connect with one another virtually, whether they are in the same class or not.
    - *Storage*: There is reduced vulnerability to risks like laptop theft or loss because sensitive and important data can be centrally kept on cloud servers.
    - *Easy to Use*: Cloud technology is incredibly convenient for people to adopt due to its online capabilities. An internet connection is all that is needed. We have access to our data at all times and can make any necessary changes, no matter where we are in the world.
    - *Simplified Integration*: It is easier to combine apps running in private clouds with other internal apps, including identity management systems.

4.9 CONCLUSION

The future of cloud computing appears to be in educational cloud computing because of its cost-effectiveness, scalability, and flexibility. With features like disaster resilience, accessibility from anywhere, and collaborations with top providers like Microsoft and AWS, it transforms education. The future of education offers greater efficiency, cooperation, and creativity as institutions continue to adopt educational cloud solutions, creating a more impactful and inclusive learning environment for all. DR and BCP are two areas where cloud-based educational solutions truly excel in terms of flexibility and resilience. During times of crisis, educational institutions can maintain the integrity of their operations by utilizing robust technologies and networks to guarantee data protection and system functionality (Aljenaa et al., 2011).

Furthermore, cloud computing for education breaks down geographical boundaries by giving instructors and students access to cutting-edge computing resources and teamwork tools from any internet-connected location. Accessibility promotes inclusiveness and facilitates creative pedagogies that address a range of learning requirements (Qasem et al., 2019). Leading cloud providers like AWS and Microsoft collaborate with educational institutions to provide access to cutting-edge technology and high-performance computing resources, which enhances the educational experience even more (Baliga et al., 2018; Dutta & Borah, 2019). Teaching grants and cooperative projects make sure that teachers have access to the materials and instruments they need to equip students with employable, real-world skills.

REFERENCES

Aljenaa, E., Al-Anzi, F., & Alshayeji, M. (2011). *Towards an Efficient e-Learning System Based on Cloud Computing*. Paper Presented at the Proceedings of the Second Kuwait Conference on e-Services and e-Systems. https://doi.org/10.1145/2107556.2107569.

Ashtari, S., & Eydgahi, A. (2017). "Student perceptions of cloud applications effectiveness in higher education." *Journal of Computational Science*, 23, 173–180.

Baliga, J., Ayre, R. W., Hinton, K., & Tucker, R. S. (2018). "Green cloud computing: balancing energy in processing, storage, and transport." *Proceedings of the IEEE*, 99(1), 149–167.

Bittman, T. (2008). *Cloud Computing and K-12 Education*. http://blogs.gartner.com/ thomas_bittman/2008/11/26/cloud-computing-and-k-12-education/. Accessed October 2013.

Buyya, R., & Ranjan, R. (2019). "Special section on autonomic cloud computing: technologies, services, and applications." *IEEE Transactions on Cloud Computing*, 7(2), 285–290.

Dutta, P., & Borah, M. D. (2019). *Implementing e-Learning System in University Environment Using Service Oriented Architecture*. Proceedings of the IEEE International Conference on Technology Enhanced Education (ICTEE).

Gai, K., Qiu, M., & Sun, X. (2018). "A survey on FinTech." *Journal of Network and Computer Applications*, 103(2018), 262–273.

Hussain, F., & Abubakar, M. (2018). "Cloud computing as a solution for educational services in developing countries." *Information Technology for Development*, 24(3), 658–673. November 2017. *International Journal Social Sciences and Education* 7(2):45–54.

Kaur, R. & Singh, S. (2015). "Exploring the Benefits of Cloud Computing Paradigm in Education Sector." *International Journal of Computer Applications*, 115(7), 1–3. https://doi.org/10.5120/20160-2217

Lazowska E, Lee P, Elliott C, & Smarr L. (2008). *Infrastructure for eScience and eLearning in Higher Education*. Computing Community Consortium (Online). Retrieved 5 October 2010. www.cra.org/ccc/docs/init/Infrastructure.pdf

McCrea, B. (2009). *IT on Demand: The Pros and Cons of Cloud Computing in Higher Education*. Campus Technology (Online). Retrieved 5 October 2010. http://campustechnology.com/Articles/2009/08/20/IT-on-Demand-The-Pros-and-Consof-Cloud-Computing-in-Higher-Education.aspx

Mircea, M., & Andreescu, A. I. (2011). *Using Cloud Computing in Higher Education: A Strategy to Improve Agility in the Current Financial Crisis*. Communications of the IBIMA, pp. 1–15. doi: 10.5171/2011.875547. www.ibimapublishing.com/journals/CIBIMA/cibima.html

Nicholson, J. (2009). *Cloud Computing's Top Issues for Higher Education*. University Business Solution for Higher Education Management (Online).

Qasem, Y. A. M., Abdullah, R., Jusoh, Y. Y., Atan, R., & Asadi, S. (2019). "Cloud computing adoption in higher education institutions: a systematic review." *IEEE Access*, 7, 63722–63744. doi: 10.1109/ACCESS.2019.2916234.

Vilela, J., Castro, J., Martins, L. E. G., & Gorschek, T. (2017). "Integration between requirements engineering and safety analysis: a systematic literature review." *Journal of Systems and Software*, 125, 68–92.

Zameer Bhat, A., Dhibi, M., Pandey, J., & Vikram Singh, A. (2022). *Role of Cloud Computing in Facilitating Educational Excellence, A Case Study of Higher Education Institution in Oman*. 2022 10th International Conference on Reliability, Infocom Technologies and Optimization (Trends and Future Directions) (ICRITO), Noida, India, pp. 1–6. doi: 10.1109/ICRITO56286.2022.9964736.

5 Unveiling E-Learning's Potential

A Cloud-Based Multidimensional Approach

Sameera Khan and Dileep Kumar Singh

5.1 INTRODUCTION

The conventional education system is going through a transformation revolution with the addition of new-era technologies. To make the education system up to date with the digital era, this transformation is the need of the hour. Deployment of cloud-based learning platforms is one major breakthrough in this transformation. It gives the teaching–learning process a new avenue with immersive learning experiences and improvised teaching experiences. To investigate about the multifaceted aspects of clouds in e-learning (Al Manyi, Yusof, and Sadiq 2024), there are two crucial aspects. First, the definition of cloud in the context of e-learning and second its significance. Both aspects are discussed in detail as below.

5.1.1 Definition of Cloud Computing in the Context of E-Learning

Cloud computing, in the context of e-learning, refers to the on-demand delivery of educational resources (Eljak et al. 2024) and services through a network of remote servers. This eliminates the need for physical storage and software installations on individual devices, making learning materials readily accessible from anywhere with an internet connection.

5.1.2 Significance of Cloud Technology in Educational Settings

Cloud-based learning platforms have tremendously revolutionized the teaching–learning process. It offers various advantages as mentioned below:

- **Increased and Ease of Accessibility:** Cloud-based solutions for e-learning make it easy for students to access the content as per their requirements and schedule. It is available 24×7 and can be used from any location. The only requirement is an uninterrupted internet connection (Selviandro and Hasibuan 2013). Such accessibility endorses inclusivity and also provides solutions to diverse learning styles.

DOI: 10.1201/9781003472537-6

- **Scalability and Cost-Effectiveness:** Cloud-based platforms are easily scalable. They can be scaled up or scaled down as per the requirements of the educational institution. This scaling does not require any change in hardware or software which can incur extra cost. Thus, it makes cloud platforms cost-effective.
- **Collaboration and Communication:** Cloud platforms provide shared workspaces, document sharing, document editing, and communication tools. By using these tools, teachers and students may establish good communication. Additionally, it facilitates collaboration among peers and group activities much easier (Masharova et al. 2020).
- **Data Storage and Security:** All the information and data are saved in the cloud. Thus, cloud-based platforms provide a repository for educational data. This repository is safeguarded by encryption algorithms and also by hierarchical access permissions. Cloud storage also ensures disaster recovery. Using cloud storage is cost-effective too as compared to physical storage infrastructure.
- **Streamlined Learning Management:** Learning management systems (LMS) based on cloud technology (Dutta et al. 2021) provide a centralized platform for managing content for learning, student assessments, and student progress, restructuring administrative tasks for teachers.

5.2 FOUNDATIONS OF CLOUD COMPUTING: A CORNERSTONE FOR E-LEARNING

As the conventional educational system mitigates itself with cloud technologies, understanding the basic concepts and features of cloud computing is required. In the following section a foundational overview of cloud computing is discussed, setting the groundwork for its multifaceted applications in e-learning environments.

5.2.1 FEATURES OF CLOUD COMPUTING

- **On-demand Self-service:** Users do not need any intervention from the cloud service provider. They can set up and use their computing resources on their own as and when required. Instead of waiting for new servers to be delivered to a private data centre, developers can select the resources and tools they need typically through a cloud provider's self-service portal and build right away.
- **Broad Network Access:** An internet connection and a computing device are necessary for using cloud services. These are the bare minimum requirements with which anyone can use cloud services from anywhere anytime (Simoes et al. 2012). A significant part of the cloud's efficacy is its ubiquity. Data can be uploaded and accessed from anywhere with an internet connection.
- **Resource Pooling:** For optimal resource utilization, one of the basic techniques used is resource pooling. Resources from multiple servers are pooled to serve numerous users dynamically. Public cloud architectures are based on multi-tenant architectures to serve more users simultaneously.
- **Rapid Elasticity/Scalability:** Scaling up or scaling down, both horizontally and vertically, as per user requirement is very easy and convenient (Cucinotta et al. 2012). Resource pooling allows scalability to be achieved

for both cloud providers and users, letting them add or remove computing resources, make networks and share other assets as needed. IT helps to optimize the cloud-hosted workloads and avoid end-user bottlenecks.

- **Measured Service:** Cloud services are usually billed as per their usage. So, the bill is based on used resources. This model achieves economies of scale through reducing costs on a large scale and seeing an increase in efficiency. It is cost-effective as the users pay for what they use (El-Sofany et al. 2013).
- **Resilience and Availability:** The service providers of the cloud use various techniques to offer high availability and recovery solutions in case of disasters, safeguarding against downtime and data protection for e-learning solutions based on clouds. Minimizing regional dependency is one such technique that can be used to avoid single-point failures (Hu 2016).
- **Security:** Most cloud providers employ some of the best security experts in the world and are generally better equipped to handle threats. They implement strong security measures to protect user data and applications (Degambur, Armoogum, and Pudaruth 2022).

5.2.2 Types of Cloud Deployments

- **Public Cloud:** All the computing resources like hardware and software are shared among users and organizations on a subscription basis over the public internet. This cloud deployment model is cost-effective and scalable (Penney et al. 2023). As it uses public internet, it might not be suitable for sharing sensitive educational data.
- **Private Cloud:** Such models are used for a single organization and host resources on-site or in a secure data centre. It is the most secure model with maximum control over the resources (Jabbar and Bhaya 2022). It is comparatively expensive and needs management expertise.
- **Hybrid Cloud:** It is a mixed technique which combines both the models of public and private cloud deployments. It exploits the benefits of both models. Educational institutions can store sensitive data in the private cloud (Barbierato et al. 2021) while utilizing public cloud resources for non-critical tasks.

5.2.3 Cloud Service Models

- **Infrastructure as a Service (IaaS):** It is also known as hardware as a service. It provides the elementary blocks of computing required for cloud infrastructure which includes virtual servers, storage, and networking hardware (Wu, Loiseau, and Hyytia 2020). Users can access these services on the basis of pay-per-use policy. It eliminates the need for maintaining information technology (IT) infrastructure at the organizational level. This model offers high flexibility for e-learning environments requiring granular control over the infrastructure.
- **Platform as a Service (PaaS):** It provides a runtime environment to develop, deploy, and manage applications. It encompasses servers, storage, networking hardware as well as middleware, development tools, database management

systems, and business intelligence. It simplifies the development process of an e-learning platform by eradicating the infrastructure management overhead (Nasr and Ouf 2012).

- **Software as a Service (SaaS):** It is also known as on-demand software. It delivers services to the end users as complete software applications over the internet. It offers business services, document management, social networks, mailing services, etc. It can be used directly with minimal maintenance overhead (Fithri, Utomo, and Nugraha 2020).

5.3 INFRASTRUCTURE AND RESOURCES IN CLOUD-BASED E-LEARNING

The traditional education system has been revolutionized with the introduction of cloud technology. Using cloud in teaching learning process is based on strong infrastructure support and resource utilisation. These properties provide high scalability and elasticity to the integration of cloud computing into the educational landscape presenting a paradigm shift in e-learning. This transformation hinges on a robust infrastructure and resource allocation system, fostering scalability and elasticity to provide increasing support for education systems.

5.3.1 Cloud-Based Learning Management Systems

The basis of cloud-based e-learning is the LMS. A learning platform based on the cloud works on remote servers. Thus, it eradicates the need for high investment on expensive infrastructure. Use of cloud has provided various advantages like cost effectiveness, ease of accessibility, scalability, smooth administration and maintenance (Chao et al. 2015). As cloud technology is available in a pay-per-use billing pattern, it reduces the cost significantly. Additionally, the need to purchase specialized hardware and licences has also been reduced. Students and teachers are able to access and create content anywhere anytime which makes it suitable for a large group of users with diverse schedules and learning styles. In addition to these advantages, it is highly scalable as per requirement. Number of users can be easily increased or decreased. Maintenance overhead is taken care of by the cloud service providers. They manage updates, fix security issues, infrastructure maintenance, etc. Thus, organizational resources are freed up to perform academic activities. Some popular cloud-based LMS options include Moodle, Blackboard Learn Ultra, and Canvas. These platforms offer a comprehensive suite of features for content delivery, assessment creation, communication tools, and progress tracking.

5.3.2 Virtualization and Resource Allocation

Within the cloud environment, it is possible to augment resource allocation with the aid of virtualization technology. By using this approach, multiple computer systems can be allowed to process separate functions using their own software, thereby causing synergy to be achieved (Ariza et al. 2021). This technology plays an important role in resource allocation optimization within the cloud environment. Hardware utilization is maximized and the energy consumption is reduced by using fewer machines to deploy multiple physical servers. Cloud-based learning platform supports virtualization by dynamic resource allocation. Processing power and memory are allocated on the basis of real-time demand, providing smooth and uninterrupted functionalities of teaching and learning activities during periods of high activity of the users. Furthermore, virtualization also helps in disaster recovery. It creates frequent backups of the virtual machines, which enables the system to be quickly recovered on any other server. Finally, all these advantages lead to minimal downtime giving the users 24×7 access to the platform (Kim 2018).

5.4 DATA MANAGEMENT AND SECURITY IN E-LEARNING CLOUDS

The widespread adoption of cloud technologies in e-learning presents immense opportunities for educational institutions. However, effectively managing and securing the vast amount of data generated within these virtual environments is paramount (Durairaj and Manimaran 2015; Degambur, Armoogum, and Pudaruth 2022). This section delves into crucial aspects of data management and security in e-learning clouds.

5.4.1 Data Storage and Retrieval in the Cloud

Cloud storage is a mode of computer data storage in which digital data is stored on servers in off-site locations. The servers are maintained by a third-party provider who is responsible for hosting, managing, and securing data stored on its infrastructure. The provider ensures that data on its servers is always accessible via public or private internet connections. Cloud storage enables organizations to store, access, and maintain data so that they do not need to own and operate their own data centres, moving expenses from a capital expenditure model to operational. Cloud storage is scalable, allowing organizations to expand or reduce their data footprint depending on need. Use cases for cloud storage include data backup, archiving, disaster recovery, data processing, and serving media content. Organizations can choose from various cloud storage models, such as public cloud, private cloud, hybrid cloud, and multi-cloud, depending on their requirements. The benefits of cloud storage include cost efficiency, elasticity, scalability, flexibility, and global accessibility (Andreica and Belfo 2018; Gopinath and Geetha 2015).

5.4.2 Security Challenges in Cloud-Based E-Learning

While implementing the educational cloud, institutions go through the sensitive data collection of students, which encompasses personally identifiable information (PII). This PII has data like student names, their addresses, telephone numbers, grades, health information, and sometimes intellectual property rights too (Idrissa et al. 2016). In the implementation of the educational cloud storing and managing, this data is very sensitive. Careful handling of security and privacy concerns is required (Salvi et al. 2015).

The cloud-based platforms for education face numerous security challenges within the cloud setup. Data stored in the cloud is sensitive as student records and intellectual property are the main constituents. It makes them easy targets for cyberattacks and data breaches. People who are inside the system or those who have access to secure information can pose a potential threat to the information saved. Such attacks are known as insider attacks. To minimize these threats and risks, strong security algorithms must be employed. Data encryption can also be used to safeguard the data. Furthermore, it is important to employ strong disaster management recovery algorithms. It includes frequent and multiple backups and saving data on multiple servers so that, in case of accidental data loss, data can be recovered immediately without much downtime. Moreover, compliance with data privacy regulations such as Family Educational Rights and Privacy Act (FERPA) and General Data Protection Regulation (GDPR) is imperative for educational institutions, necessitating cloud providers to offer solutions that ensure regulatory compliance (Najm, Alsamaraee, and Jalal 2022; Al Manyi, Yusof, and Sadiq 2024).

5.4.3 Encryption and Data Privacy Measures

In safeguarding sensitive information within e-learning platforms, several security measures are crucial. Data encryption, both at rest and in transit, plays a pivotal role in protecting data integrity even in the event of a breach. By rendering data unreadable without the decryption key, encryption significantly mitigates the risk of unauthorized access. Implementing robust access controls and user authentication mechanisms, such as multi-factor authentication and role-based access controls, ensures that only authorized individuals can access specific data types, minimizing the likelihood of unauthorized data viewing, modification, or deletion. Moreover, adopting a data minimization strategy, where educational institutions only collect and store necessary data for legitimate educational purposes, reduces the potential impact of a breach and simplifies data management processes. Additionally, data anonymization techniques can further enhance privacy protection by anonymizing sensitive information like student names and addresses for research or analytical purposes, allowing valuable insights to be gleaned from the data while safeguarding individual privacy (Kumaresan and Gopalan 2018; Salvi et al. 2015).

5.4.4 Compliance with Data Protection Regulations

In the educational system, it is vital to emphasize various important factors while implementing cloud-based learning solutions. It is important to safeguard the student information and records. Data storage must be aligned with the regulations mandated by the local and regional national data privacy laws. This compliance must be ensured for data residency requirements too. Data collection, usage, and data-sharing processes must be transparent to all the stakeholders. Proper consent from the students and parents should be taken before data collection. In addition, strongly sticking to the regulations regarding data breach notification requirements is vital. It ensures that the institution promptly informs people affected by data breaches and lessens the associated risks. Further, scheduling regular audits related to the security of e-learning platforms is important to recognize and address any potential security threats proactively (Zhang and Zhu 2017).

Using proper strategies for data management and security, in addition to scheduling regular security checks, can significantly lessen the threats of data breaches and attacks. This can be taken up collectively by the administration, parents, and students.

5.5 COLLABORATIVE AND SOCIAL ASPECTS OF CLOUD-BASED E-LEARNING

The traditional educational system has transformed in this digital era giving rise to various advantages and disadvantages of the same. Certain social and collaborative aspects have been discussed below.

5.5.1 Social Learning Platforms in the Cloud

The learning platforms which are cloud-based act as virtual environments where teachers and students can connect and also with their peers. They can also interact, and participate in shared learning experiences (Anshari, Alas, and Guan 2015). Such cloud-based platforms provide a variety of features specifically designed to encourage socialization through learning. Features like discussion forums, leaderboards, etc. are among the most popular social aspects of e-learning platforms. These discussion forums provide an asynchronous communication platform where students and teachers can share ideas, ask questions, and offer support to other participants. Such participation nurtures a sense of community and encourages learning through various views (Hendradi, Khanapi, and Mahfuzah 2019). Implementing various social media elements like news feeds, group activities, messaging, etc. provides the extension of learning beyond the boundaries of the classroom, creating a more engaging and connected ecosystem. Furthermore, video chats and live sessions conducted on the cloud allow the participants to interact instantly, exploiting the benefits of collaborative learning. It creates a more immersive environment and significantly enhances the teaching-learning experiences (Masharova et al. 2020).

5.5.2 Real-time Collaboration Tools and Features

To allow users to experience collaborative learning following tools are provided by cloud-based learning platforms:

- **Collaborative Document Editing:** To enhance teamwork and group activities tools like Google Docs are used to enable simultaneous document editing. Also, collaborative whiteboards are introduced which allow learners to interact and present their ideas in a better way.
- **Shared Workspaces:** Teachers and learners can share their resources among their peers and also with each other. These virtual spaces allow users to control with whom they want to share their resources. It can help in idea sharing, working on team assignments, brainstorming ideas, etc.

- **Real-time Feedback and Annotations:** Peer-to-peer learning is encouraged by implementing real-time feedback where students can give instant feedback on each other's work. It also enhances critical thinking (Naveed et al. 2019).

5.5.3 Collaborative Learning Environments

Cloud technology empowers the creation of dynamic and interactive learning environments that promote collaboration. Cloud platforms offer diverse avenues for interactive and engaging learning experiences. Project-based learning allows learners to collaborate on real-world projects, promoting teamwork, problem-solving abilities, and effective communication skills. Through role-playing simulations facilitated by cloud platforms, learners can engage with simulated scenarios, applying their knowledge and collaborating within a safe and controlled environment, thereby enhancing their practical understanding of concepts. Additionally, platforms enable peer review and feedback mechanisms where learners can offer constructive critiques of each other's work, nurturing critical thinking skills and cultivating a culture of continuous improvement among participants. These features contribute to fostering a dynamic and enriching learning environment conducive to holistic skill development and knowledge acquisition (Rani, Nayak, and Vyas 2015; Togawa and Kanenishi 2013).

5.6 MOBILE LEARNING IN THE CLOUD

The integration of mobile technologies with cloud computing has opened new avenues for e-learning, particularly through Mobile Learning (M-Learning). This section delves into the key aspects of M-Learning in the cloud, exploring its advantages and potential challenges.

5.6.1 Accessibility and Ubiquity in Mobile Learning

One of the most significant advantages of M-Learning within a cloud environment is its inherent accessibility and ubiquity. Learners are no longer constrained by physical classrooms or fixed schedules. Cloud-based learning resources can be accessed anytime, anywhere, on any mobile device with an internet connection. This empowers learners to:

- **Fit Learning into Their Busy Schedules:** Short bursts of learning can be completed during commutes, waiting times, or breaks throughout the day.
- **Learn on the Go:** M-Learning allows individuals to access educational materials and complete coursework irrespective of their location. This is particularly beneficial for geographically dispersed learners or those with limited access to traditional learning environments.
- **Personalized Learning Pace:** Learners can revisit specific topics, review materials at their own pace, and reinforce their understanding through readily available resources. This flexibility fosters a learner-centric approach to education, catering to individual learning styles and preferences (Hou et al. 2022).

5.6.2 Responsive Design and Cross-Platform Compatibility

Cloud-based M-Learning platforms offer the advantage of responsive design and cross-platform compatibility. This ensures that learning materials and applications adapt automatically to different screen sizes and operating systems. Learners can access educational content seamlessly on smartphones, tablets, or any other mobile device, eliminating the need for device-specific applications (Hu 2016; Zubani et al. 2022).

- **Reduced Development Costs:** Responsive design eliminates the need to develop separate applications for various platforms, streamlining the development process and reducing costs.
- **Wider Reach:** Cross-platform compatibility ensures that learning materials are accessible to a broader audience regardless of the mobile device they possess.
- **Improved User Experience:** Responsive design provides an optimal viewing experience on any device, making learning materials easily readable and navigable.

This fosters inclusivity and ensures that learners with different devices can access educational content without technical barriers.

5.6.3 Cloud-Based Mobile Applications for E-Learning

Cloud computing empowers the development of robust and scalable mobile applications specifically designed for e-learning. These applications leverage the cloud's infrastructure to deliver various functionalities, including (Wang et al. 2019; Naveed et al. 2019):

- **Interactive Learning Content:** Gamification elements, quizzes, and multimedia resources can be integrated into mobile applications, making the learning process engaging and interactive.
- **Offline Access:** Certain applications allow learners to download learning materials for offline access, enabling them to continue learning even in areas with limited or no internet connectivity.
- **Push Notifications and Reminders:** Applications can send timely notifications and reminders to learners about upcoming deadlines, assignments, or new learning materials available.
- **Collaboration and Communication Tools:** Features like chat forums, discussion boards, and video-conferencing functionalities can be integrated within the applications, fostering collaboration and communication among learners and educators.

These functionalities enhance the overall learning experience by providing a dynamic and interactive environment accessible through mobile devices.

5.6.4 Challenges and Opportunities in Mobile Learning

While M-Learning in the cloud presents numerous advantages, some challenges need to be addressed (Cucinotta et al. 2012):

- **Data Security and Privacy:** Ensuring the security and privacy of student data stored in the cloud is paramount. Robust security measures and adherence to data privacy regulations are crucial.
- **Potential for Distractions:** The ubiquitous nature of mobile devices can lead to distractions during the learning process. Strategies to minimize distractions and promote focused learning need to be implemented.
- **Limited Screen Size:** Mobile devices have smaller screens compared to traditional computers, which can hinder the visibility of complex information or multimedia content.
- **Digital Divide:** Not all learners have access to reliable internet connectivity or mobile devices, potentially exacerbating existing educational inequalities.

Addressing these challenges requires a multifaceted approach. Therefore, institutions need to:

- Invest in robust security solutions and implement clear data privacy policies.
- Encourage learners to adopt responsible mobile learning practices and cultivate focused learning environments.
- Develop learning materials optimized for smaller screens and explore alternative content delivery methods like audio (Ahmed and Hussain 2018) lectures or podcasts.
- Bridge the digital divide by providing necessary infrastructure and affordable learning resources to ensure equitable access to education.

By acknowledging these challenges and implementing effective solutions, M-Learning in the cloud can be harnessed to its full potential, fostering a flexible, accessible, and engaging learning experience for all.

5.7 COST–BENEFIT ANALYSIS OF CLOUD ADOPTION IN E-LEARNING: MULTIFACETED ASPECTS OF CLOUDS IN E-LEARNING

Evolving technological landscapes present educational institutions with a crucial decision: adopting cloud-based solutions like e-learning platforms. While the benefits of enhanced accessibility, scalability, and collaboration are undeniable, a thorough cost–benefit analysis is essential to ensure a financially sound investment (Alajmi et al. 2018; Degambur, Armoogum, and Pudaruth 2022).

5.7.1 Economic Considerations for Educational Institutions

Educational institutions operate with constrained budgets, making cost-effectiveness a primary concern. Cloud adoption in e-learning presents both potential cost savings and additional considerations (Madjarov 2014):

- **Reduced Upfront Costs:** Cloud services eliminate the need for significant upfront investments in hardware, software licenses, and IT infrastructure. Institutions pay a subscription fee based on usage, reducing the initial financial burden.

- **Variable Costs:** Cloud services offer a pay-as-you-go model, allowing institutions to scale their resource utilization (storage, processing power) based on student enrolment and course requirements. This flexibility prevents overspending on underutilized resources.
- **Maintenance and Support:** Cloud providers handle server maintenance, software updates, and technical support, freeing up institutional IT staff to focus on core educational activities.
- **Subscription Fees:** Recurring monthly or annual fees for cloud services need to be incorporated into the budget.
- **Data Transfer Costs:** Moving large datasets (e.g., video lectures) to and from the cloud can incur additional charges depending on the chosen provider and data volume.
- **Vendor Lock-in:** Dependence on a single cloud provider might limit future flexibility and potentially result in higher costs when switching vendors.

5.7.2 Total Cost of Ownership in Cloud Environments

A comprehensive cost analysis requires considering the Total Cost of Ownership (TCO) in both traditional and cloud-based e-learning models. TCO factors in not just the upfront costs but also ongoing expenses associated with maintenance, support, and upgrades over the lifecycle of the system (Togawa and Kanenishi 2013).

- **Traditional Model TCO:** Includes upfront hardware and software acquisition costs, additional licensing fees, dedicated IT staff salaries for maintenance and support, electricity expenses for powering on-premise servers, and potential costs for software upgrades.
- **Cloud Model TCO:** Encompasses subscription fees, data transfer charges, potential vendor lock-in costs, and any additional cloud-based service fees.

While upfront costs might be lower in the traditional model, ongoing maintenance, staff salaries, and potential hardware upgrades can significantly increase the TCO over time. Cloud adoption often reduces these ongoing expenses, leading to a lower overall TCO in the long run.

5.7.3 Return on Investment in Cloud-Based E-Learning

Evaluating the return on investment (ROI) provides a broader perspective on the financial benefits of cloud adoption. Measuring ROI goes beyond just cost savings and considers the positive impact (Pireva et al. 2014; Ahmed 2015):

- **Improved Learning Outcomes:** Increased accessibility, personalized learning experiences, and readily available learning materials can lead to improved student engagement and academic performance.
- **Enhanced Operational Efficiency:** Reduced administrative burden due to automated tasks and centralized data management frees up valuable staff time for other key activities.

TABLE 5.1
Comparison of Traditional and Cloud-Based E-Learning Models

Feature	Traditional Model	Cloud-Based Model
Upfront costs	High (hardware, software, infrastructure)	Low (subscription fees)
Ongoing costs	High (maintenance, staff, upgrades)	Lower (reduced maintenance, potential staff reallocation)
Scalability	Limited (requires additional hardware)	High (easily scalable resources)
Accessibility	Limited by on-premise infrastructure	Accessible from anywhere with an internet connection
Security	Requires dedicated IT staff and security measures	Cloud providers offer robust security features
Data management	Requires in-house data storage and backup solutions	Centralized and secure data storage in the cloud
Feature	Traditional model	Cloud-based model

- **Greater Scalability and Flexibility:** Cloud-based platforms can easily adapt to accommodate fluctuating student enrolment or the addition of new courses without significant infrastructure upgrades.

While directly quantifying the impact on learning outcomes might be challenging, improved student performance and engagement can positively influence the institution's reputation and potentially attract a wider student base, leading to increased revenue streams.

5.7.4 Comparative Analysis of Traditional Versus Cloud E-Learning Models

A side-by-side comparison of traditional and cloud-based e-learning models highlights the cost-benefit trade-offs is highlighted in Table 5.1.

While the traditional model offers a sense of control over the infrastructure, the ongoing costs and limited scalability can hinder long-term financial sustainability. Cloud adoption, on the other hand, provides a cost-effective solution with inherent scalability, improved accessibility, and reduced administrative burden, leading to a potentially higher ROI over time.

5.8 ENABLED BY CLOUD TECHNOLOGY: MULTIFACETED ASPECTS OF CLOUDS IN E-LEARNING

The integration of cloud technology within the e-learning landscape presents a multitude of opportunities for pedagogical innovation. By leveraging the vast resources and functionalities offered by cloud platforms, educators can create dynamic and engaging learning environments that cater to individual student needs and promote deeper understanding. Here is a closer look at some key advancements facilitated by cloud technology (Kumar and Sharma 2021):

5.8.1 Adaptive Learning Systems in the Cloud

Cloud computing empowers the development and deployment of sophisticated adaptive learning systems. These systems utilize student data, including performance on assessments, learning pace, and areas of difficulty, to personalize the learning experience in real time.

- **Dynamic Content Delivery:** Cloud-based platforms can analyse student data and adjust the difficulty level, presentation format (e.g., text, video, audio), and recommended learning resources based on individual needs. This ensures students are challenged appropriately, without feeling overwhelmed or under-stimulated.
- **Personalized Learning Paths:** Algorithms can analyse student progress and suggest alternative learning pathways that address identified weaknesses or accelerate progress in mastered areas. This allows students to focus on areas requiring improvement and progress at their own pace.
- **Real-time Feedback and Intervention:** Cloud-based systems can provide immediate feedback on assessments and offer targeted support mechanisms based on student performance. This enables educators to intervene promptly and address any learning gaps before they become significant hurdles.

5.8.2 Personalized Learning Experiences

Cloud technology empowers educators to create truly personalized learning experiences that cater to diverse student needs, learning styles, and preferences (Nan, Jiang, and Li 2023).

- **Content Curation:** Educators can leverage cloud storage to curate a vast repository of learning materials, including multimedia resources, interactive simulations, and e-books. Students can then access and explore materials that align with their preferred learning styles and interests.
- **Collaborative Learning Activities:** Cloud-based platforms facilitate collaborative learning activities through online forums, group projects, and real-time communication tools. This fosters teamwork, communication skills development, and peer-to-peer learning.
- **Self-paced Learning:** Cloud-based learning environments allow students to learn at their own pace, revisiting challenging concepts, and accelerating through mastered topics. This caters to individual learning styles and accommodates students with varying schedules and learning abilities.

5.8.3 Gamification and Simulations

Cloud computing opens doors to the integration of gamification elements and immersive simulations into the learning experience (Ma and Wang 2021; Matchacheep, Chookaew, and Nilsuk 2019).

- **Engaging Learning Environment:** Gamification techniques, such as points, badges, and leaderboards, can be incorporated into online learning platforms to increase student motivation, and engagement, and encourage healthy competition.
- **Interactive Simulations:** Cloud-based platforms can host complex simulations that allow students to practice real-world scenarios in a safe and controlled virtual environment. This fosters practical application of knowledge, decision-making skills development, and problem-solving abilities.
- **Immersive Learning Experiences:** Cloud technology can facilitate the creation of virtual reality (VR) and augmented reality (AR) experiences, enabling students to virtually explore historical sites, conduct scientific experiments, or interact with complex data visualizations. This promotes deeper engagement with the learning material and enhances knowledge retention (Al Manyi, Yusof, and Sadiq 2024)

5.8.4 Analytics for Student Performance Assessment

Cloud platforms provide educators with a wealth of data-driven insights into student performance, learning progress, and areas requiring additional support (Skene, Winer, and Kustra 2024; Abed, Sultan, and Mohammed 2023).

- **Real-time Performance Monitoring:** Cloud-based LMS can track student activity, assessment results, and engagement levels in real time. This allows educators to identify potential learning difficulties early on and intervene proactively.
- **Data-driven Decision-making:** Educators can analyse student performance data to identify learning trends, gauge the effectiveness of different teaching methods, and tailor their instruction accordingly. This data-driven approach allows for continuous improvement of the learning experience and ensures learning objectives are effectively met.
- **Personalized Feedback and Support:** Analytics can be used to provide students with targeted feedback based on their performance. This allows educators to identify areas where students excel and offer specific support mechanisms to address identified weaknesses.

5.9 CONCLUSION

Cloud technology presents a paradigm shift in education, offering robust security measures to protect sensitive student data. By prioritizing learner-centric design, institutions can create captivating virtual environments with accessibility, flexibility, and a strong sense of community. Effective virtual assessment requires diverse tools, addressing challenges like academic integrity and data security. Cloud platforms empower educators with real-time data and analytics to personalize learning, fostering a dynamic and data-driven approach. The future holds immense potential with AI-powered advancements but necessitates addressing ethical concerns and responsible development. A collaborative effort from educators, institutions, and policymakers is crucial to harness the potential of the educational cloud and unlock a brighter future for learning, thus empowering educators and students alike.

REFERENCES

Abed, H.I., N.A. Sultan, and O.Y. Mohammed. 2023. "An Evaluation of Machine Learning and Big Data Analytics Performance in Cloud Computing and Computer Vision." *International Journal on Recent and Innovation Trends in Computing and Communication* 11 (6): 79–88. doi:10.17762/ijritcc.v11i6.7144.

Ahmed, F.F. 2015. "Comparative Analysis for Cloud Based E-Learning." *Procedia Computer Science* 65: 368–76. doi:10.1016/j.procs.2015.09.098.

Ahmed, I.A., and Z. Hussain. 2018. "A Proposed Model of Cloud Based E-Learning for Najran University." *International Journal of Advanced Computer Science and Applications* 9 (12): 577–82. doi:10.14569/IJACSA.2018.091281.

Alajmi, Q.A., A. Kamaludin, R.A. Arshah, and M.A. Al-Sharafi. 2018. "The Effectiveness of Cloud-Based E-Learning towards Quality of Academic Services: An Omanis' Expert View." *International Journal of Advanced Computer Science and Applications* 9 (4): 158–64. doi:10.14569/IJACSA.2018.090425.

Al Manyi, N.A., A.F. Yusof, and A.S. Sadiq. 2024. "Emerging Trends in Cloud-Based e-Learning: A Systematic Review of Predictors, Security and Themes." *KSII Transactions on Internet and Information Systems* 18 (1): 89–104. doi:10.3837/tiis.2024.01.006.

Andreica, A., and F.P. Belfo. 2018. "Building Cloud Data Interchange Services for E-Learning Systems: Applications on the Moodle System." In *CLOSER 2018 – Proceedings of the 8th International Conference on Cloud Computing and Services Science – Volume 1*, 565–72. doi:10.5220/0006783905650572.

Anshari, M., Y. Alas, and L.S. Guan. 2015. "Pervasive Knowledge, Social Networks, and Cloud Computing: E-Learning 2.0." *Eurasia Journal of Mathematics, Science and Technology Education* 11 (5): 909–21. doi:10.12973/eurasia.2015.1360a.

Ariza, J., M. Jimeno, R. Villanueva-Polanco, and J. Capacho. 2021. "Provisioning Computational Resources for Cloud-Based e-Learning Platforms Using Deep Learning Techniques." *IEEE Access* 9: 89798–811. doi:10.1109/ACCESS.2021.3090366.

Barbierato, E., L. Campanile, M. Gribaudo, M. Iacono, M. Mastroianni, and S. Nacchia. 2021. "Performance Evaluation for the Design of a Hybrid Cloud Based Distance Synchronous and Asynchronous Learning Architecture." *Simulation Modelling Practice and Theory* 109: 102303. doi:10.1016/j.simpat.2021.102303.

Chao, K.-M., A.E. James, A.G. Nanos, J.-H. Chen, S.-D. Stan, I. Muntean, G Figliolini, et al. 2015. "Cloud E-Learning for Mechatronics: CLEM." *Future Generation Computer Systems* 48: 46–59. doi:10.1016/j.future.2014.10.033.

Cucinotta, T., F. Checconi, G. Kousiouris, K. Konstanteli, S. Gogouvitis, D. Kyriazis, T. Varvarigou, et al. 2012. "Virtualised E-Learning on the IRMOS Real-Time Cloud." *Service Oriented Computing and Applications* 6 (2): 151–66. doi:10.1007/s11761-011-0089-4.

Degambur, L.-N., S. Armoogum, and S. Pudaruth. 2022. "A Study of Security Impacts and Cryptographic Techniques in Cloud-Based e-Learning Technologies." *International Journal of Advanced Computer Science and Applications* 13 (1): 58–66. doi:10.14569/IJACSA.2022.0130108.

Durairaj, M., and A. Manimaran. 2015. "A Study on Security Issues in Cloud Based E-Learning." *Indian Journal of Science and Technology* 8 (8): 757–65. doi:10.17485/ijst/2015/v8i8/69307.

Dutta, B., M.-H. Peng, C.-C. Chen, and S.-L. Sun. 2021. "Interpreting Usability Factors Predicting Sustainable Adoption of Cloud-Based e-Learning Environment during Covid-19 Pandemic." *Sustainability (Switzerland)* 13 (16): 9329. doi:10.3390/su13169329.

Eljak, H., A.O. Ibrahim, F. Saeed, I.A.T. Hashem, A. Abdelmaboud, H.J. Syed, A.W. Abulfaraj, M.A.B. Ismail, and A. Elsafi. 2024. "E-Learning-Based Cloud Computing Environment: A Systematic Review, Challenges, and Opportunities." *IEEE Access* 12: 7329–55. doi:10.1109/ACCESS.2023.3339250.

El-Sofany, H.F., A.A. Tayeb, K. Alghatani, and S.A. El-Seoud. 2013. "The Impact of Cloud Computing Technologies in E-Learning." *International Journal of Emerging Technologies in Learning* 8 (S1): 37–43. doi:10.3991/ijet.v8iS1.2344.

Fithri, D.L., A.P. Utomo, and F. Nugraha. 2020. "Implementation of SaaS Cloud Computing Services on E-Learning Applications (Case Study: PGRI Foundation School)." *Journal of Physics: Conference Series* 1430: 012049. doi:10.1088/1742-6596/1430/1/012049.

Gopinath, R., and B.G. Geetha. 2015. "Dynamic Block Level Error Recovery to Trust Multimedia Data for E-Learning Cloud Based Storage Services." *Research Journal of Applied Sciences, Engineering and Technology* 10 (5): 553–61. doi:10.19026/rjaset.10.2463.

Hendradi, P., M. Khanapi, and S.N. Mahfuzah. 2019. "Cloud Computing-Based e-Learning System Architecture in Education 4.0." *Journal of Physics: Conference Series* 1196: 012038. doi:10.1088/1742-6596/1196/1/012038.

Hou, L., Q. Liu, J. Nebhen, M. Uddin, and A. Chaudhary. 2022. "Implementation of Cloud Computing Protocol in E-Learning for Future Wireless Systems." *Wireless Communications and Mobile Computing*. doi:10.1155/2022/1954111.

Hu, C. 2016. "Application of E-Learning Assessment Based on AHP-BP Algorithm in the Cloud Computing Teaching Platform." *International Journal of Emerging Technologies in Learning* 11 (8): 27–32. doi:10.3991/ijet.v11i08.6039.

Idrissa, S.M., K. Djibo, S. Bisso, and H. Saliah-Hassane. 2016. "A Secured Resource Access Management in Educational Cloud Computing Environment." In *4th International Symposium on Digital Forensics and Security, ISDFS 2016 – Proceeding*, 14–19. doi:10.1109/ISDFS.2016.7473510.

Jabbar, A.A., and W.S. Bhaya. 2022. "Secure Private Cloud Using Machine Learning and Cryptography." *AIP Conference Proceedings* 2547: 060002. doi:10.1063/5.0112135.

Kim, Y. 2018. "A Design of Human Cloud Platform Framework for Human Resources Distribution of E-Learning Instructional Designer." *Journal of Distribution Science* 16 (7): 67–75. doi:10.15722/jds.16.7.201807.67.

Kumar, V., and D. Sharma. 2021. "E-Learning Theories, Components, and Cloud Computing-Based Learning Platforms." *International Journal of Web-Based Learning and Teaching Technologies* 16 (3): 1–16. doi:10.4018/IJWLTT.20210501.oa1.

Kumaresan, G., and N.P. Gopalan. 2018. "A Dynamic Four-Level Authentication Framework to Enhance Security in Public Cloud Using Hybrid Cellular Automata." In *Proceedings of the 2nd International Conference on Intelligent Computing and Control Systems, ICICCS 2018*, 1912–17. doi:10.1109/ICCONS.2018.8663078.

Ma, Y., and X. Wang. 2021. "To Enhance Learning Outcome: Cloud-Assisted Gamification in Higher Education Institutions." In *ACM International Conference Proceeding Series*, 1046–49. doi:10.1145/3482632.3483080.

Madjarov, I. 2014. "Cloud-Based Mash-up Authoring Tools for e-Learning." In *CSEDU 2014 – Proceedings of the 6th International Conference on Computer Supported Education* 1: 526–31. doi:10.5220/0004957105260531.

Masharova, T.V., E.A. Mikhlyakova, V.Y. Krukovskiy, and G. Yang. 2020. "The Use of Cloud Services to Enhance Information Interaction in E-Learning to Improve the Quality of

Educational Results." *Perspektivy Nauki i Obrazovania* 47 (5): 384–97. doi:10.32744/pse.2020.5.27.

Matchacheep, S., S. Chookaew, and P. Nilsuk. 2019. "A Gamification Digital Storytelling Learning Based on Cooperative Social Cloud to Promote Students' Teamwork Skill in Primary School." In *ACM International Conference Proceeding Series*, 132–35. doi:10.1145/3369199.3369211.

Najm, Y.A., S. Alsamaraee, and A.A. Jalal. 2022. "Cloud Computing Security for E-Learning during COVID-19 Pandemic." *Indonesian Journal of Electrical Engineering and Computer Science* 27 (3): 1610–18. doi:10.11591/ijeecs.v27.i3.

Nan, Y., S. Jiang, and M. Li. 2023. "Large-Scale Video Analytics with Cloud–Edge Collaborative Continuous Learning." *ACM Transactions on Sensor Networks* 20 (1): 1–23. doi:10.1145/3624478.

Nasr, M., and S. Ouf. 2012. "A Proposed Smart E-Learning System Using Cloud Computing Services: PAAS, IAAS and Web 3.0." *International Journal of Emerging Technologies in Learning* 7 (3): 19–24. doi:10.3991/ijet.v7i3.2066.

Naveed, Q.N., M.R.N. Mohamed Qureshi, A. Shaikh, A.O. Alsayed, S. Sanober, and K. Mohiuddin. 2019. "Evaluating and Ranking Cloud-Based E-Learning Critical Success Factors (CSFs) Using Combinatorial Approach." *IEEE Access* 7: 157145–57. doi:10.1109/ACCESS.2019.2949044.

Penney, D., B. Li, L. Chen, J.J. Sydir, A. Drewek-Ossowicka, R. Illikkal, C. Tai, R. Iyer, and A. Herdrich. 2023. "RAPID: Enabling Fast Online Policy Learning in Dynamic Public Cloud Environments." *Neurocomputing* 558. doi:10.1016/j.neucom.2023.126737.

Pireva, K., P. Kefalas, D. Dranidis, T. Hatziapostolou, and A. Cowling. 2014. "Cloud E-Learning: A New Challenge for Multi-Agent Systems." *Advances in Intelligent Systems and Computing*, 296: 277–87. doi:10.1007/978-3-319-07650-8_28.

Rani, M., R. Nayak, and O.P. Vyas. 2015. "An Ontology-Based Adaptive Personalized e-Learning System, Assisted by Software Agents on Cloud Storage." *Knowledge-Based Systems* 90: 33–48. doi:10.1016/j.knosys.2015.10.002.

Salvi, S., H.A. Sanjay, K.M. Deepika, and S.R. Rangavittala. 2015. "An Encryption, Compression and Key(ECK) Management Based Data Security Framework for Infrastructure as a Service in Cloud." In *Souvenir of the 2015 IEEE International Advance Computing Conference, IACC 2015*, 872–76. doi:10.1109/IADCC.2015.7154830.

Selviandro, N., and Z.A. Hasibuan. 2013. "Cloud-Based e-Learning: A Proposed Model and Benefits by Using e-Learning Based on Cloud Computing for Educational Institution." In *Lecture Notes in Computer Science (Including Subseries Lecture Notes in Artificial Intelligence and Lecture Notes in Bioinformatics)*, 7804 LNCS: 192–201. doi:10.1007/978-3-642-36818-9_20.

Simoes, T.M.C., J.J.P.C. Rodrigues, J.E.F. Costa, and M.L. Proenca. 2012. "E-Learning Solutions for Cloud Environments." In *Proceedings of the 2012 IEEE Latin America Conference on Cloud Computing and Communications, LatinCloud 2012*, 55–59. doi:10.1109/LatinCloud.2012.6508158.

Skene, A., L. Winer, and E. Kustra. 2024. "Clouds in the Silver Lining of Learning Analytics: Ethical Tensions for Educational Developers." *International Journal for Academic Development* 29 (1): 128–40. doi:10.1080/1360144X.2022.2099208.

Togawa, S., and K. Kanenishi. 2013. "Private Cloud Cooperation Framework for Reducing the Earthquake Damage on E-Learning Environment." In *Lecture Notes in Computer Science (Including Subseries Lecture Notes in Artificial Intelligence and Lecture Notes in Bioinformatics)*, 8005 LNCS: 503–10. doi:10.1007/978-3-642-39262-7_57.

Wang, L.-Y.-K., S.-L. Lew, S.-H. Lau, and M.-C. Leow. 2019. "Usability Factors Predicting Continuance of Intention to Use Cloud E-Learning Application." *Heliyon* 5 (6): e01788. doi:10.1016/j.heliyon.2019.e01788.

Wu, X., P. Loiseau, and E. Hyytia. 2020. "Toward Designing Cost-Optimal Policies to Utilize IaaS Clouds with Online Learning." *IEEE Transactions on Parallel and Distributed Systems* 31 (3): 501–14. doi:10.1109/TPDS.2019.2935199.

Zhang, W., and Y. Zhu. 2017. "A New E-Learning Model Based on Elastic Cloud Computing for Distance Education." *Eurasia Journal of Mathematics, Science and Technology Education* 13 (12): 8393–403. doi:10.12973/ejmste/80800.

Zubani, M., L. Sigalini, I. Serina, L. Putelli, A.E. Gerevini, and M. Chiari. 2022. "A Performance Comparison of Different Cloud-Based Natural Language Understanding Services for an Italian e-Learning Platform." *Future Internet* 14 (2): 62. doi:10.3390/fi14020062.

6 Scale of Advancements in Smart Education and E-Study Using Cloud Authoring Tools

Karunya S. and Stephen S. Raj

6.1 INTRODUCTION

The internet revolutionized teaching methods by making statistics more accessible and user-friendly, leading to cost-effective education. However, despite this significant shift and the surge of advancements around 2000, internet-based training seminars were still limited in American society for education and development. As a result, there is a growing trend of continuous access to online services, ensuring that access is never denied when needed. An e-learning organization for online education has been developing over the past decade. The person behind it has established some research – who maintains that semantic mesh has the ability to gear for structuring an E-studying scheme (Li et al. 2019).

E-studying could be electronic knowledge for all teachers within their organization, where you are not required to contact students physically (Talan 2020). All you have to do is just need to verify the E-studying websites. Whatever time you can resolve within a fraction of a second through these websites, your determination needs to be clear and clever to recognize your entity vividly. When you create your structure, you need a fundamental trainer who knows how to put forward or carry out things that help to educate life. This netting side is supposed to be liberally cultivated, and the presence of this website needs to be attractive for the learner, an assortment of the university's additional capability as a complement should be instructed in the socket, and video instructions ought to be incorporated. The trainer is well required to give a number of handovers on paperwork to the learner. The router and paperback must be uploaded to this website openly and free of charge.

E-studying is one of the inexpensive, progressive, and contemporary habits of any type of knowledge. As stated in Chandra et al. (2012), development is a prerequisite in the teaching organization of country areas, E-learning is incredibly imperative, and to supply an E-studying podium, this exploration is increasing the samples used for an E-studying connoisseur classification, mainly for elevated education. E-learning requires effective communication between students and teachers/lecturers, and

DOI: 10.1201/9781003472537-7

establishing it with traditional resources can be very costly. Therefore, transitioning to cloud-based solutions makes it more feasible.

Essential supplies for dark communications are deliberate so that its strength must be attuned to the financial plan of senior teaching. As reported by Moravčík et al. (2017), the senior teaching scheme involves several academic processes such as the design of course drawn around, route, and study fabric, which is very difficult to handle using the traditional means of the current educational system. As reported by Naveed et al. (2019), the investigation has been conducted to reply to the next question. Are educational institutions equipped with e-learning technologies and mechanisms? Is e-learning feasible in rural areas? Even in developing countries, there is an understanding of how this approach can be improved and implemented from the ground up in an e-learning context.

6.2 LITERATURE REVIEW

The fast advancement of Data and Communication Innovation (DCT) has covered all angles of human life, including individuals who work, learn, and instruct. As per Liu et al. (2020), distance instruction is an instruction attempted by understudies in a setting farther from the normal campus of the instructive institution. Joshi et al. (2019) propose a geological partition between the educator and the understudy. Previously, separate learning was conveyed by "online courses" such as radio broadcasts, but, by and large, this sort of learning did not give any sort of input or interaction among other persons of the instructive handle. These days, the learning materials may well be conveyed to learners through Web-based lessons or E-studying.

This type of separate instruction might be created within the present Web environment with the assistance of online-based course readings, mail records, chats, offbeat gatherings, laptops and generation programs, and others. Colman-Meixneret al. (2016) report that it could lead to better outcomes while reducing costs and improving performance. E-learning is expected to become a crucial component of various functions. Three worldwide bench-marking improvements are E-brilliance, the E-studying Bench-marking Work out 2010, and the Primary Double Mode Separate Learns Bench-marking Club. As per Nazir et al. (2020), a comparison of these models uncovers a maybe tall upper level accordingly. Based on the conclusions and the current discussions regarding e-learning, a conceptual framework has been developed, grounded in a set of key success factors for e-learning. Giannakis et al. (2019) report that utilized as an establishment for near E-studying and as a motivation to create, execute, assess, and internalize E-studying.

E-studying has more than final long time Hendradi et al. (2020), and its rising acknowledgment display teachers with a chance to convert instruction and get together the wants of a much broader, assorted gather of learns in contrast to the history. Understudies all over the world are winning diplomas, attractive courses in themes not previously accessible to them, interfacing with understudies in remote places and expanding their charge of greater than the technique and pace of their instruction (Ahmad 2017).

6.3 CLOUD AUTHORING TOOLS THROUGH FITTING INSTRUCTIVE

Cloud authoring tools for education have been increased in terms of question banks, questionnaires, and survey tools, which help students concentrate more on their education rather than the extra work given by the educator. If the educator provides any project works on any topic, these cloud authoring tools enable the answers to the questions provided by the students with their assignments, questionnaires, and survey works. In the cloud-based tool, a survey question has been asked, and the answers received from the authoring tool are as follows with the courses and measures inbuilt workflow of the survey,

Survey Questions: According to Galletta et al. (2017), a survey was conducted for this study and distributed to various educational institutions in rural areas, where the education system is particularly weak. The pandemic further exacerbated the challenge, making it even more difficult to deliver quality education. As stated by Hendradi et al. (2019), the instructive organizing is congested, and understudies have misplaced due to the inaccessibility of customary lessons. This cloud computing (CC) model, applied to the implementation of e-learning, was examined, and responses from the participants were collected after applying this model. The survey results can be found in Table 6.1. It is standing ahead of 15 topics (Kumar et al. 2016).

Course of action 1: The records have "15" questions data (Hussein et al. 2020).

Course of action 2: Data preprocessing in sequence and accusation implication (Sultana et al. 2017).

Course of action 3: Estimate modus operandi to obtain the finest parameters (Abdullahi et al. (2018).

Course of action 4: Classify the result.

Course of action 5: Meticulousness will be evaluated and presented (Buyya et al. 2018).

Course of action 6: Lastly, appraisal metrics and conclusion (El Mhouti et al. 2018).

In Figure 6.1, how the authoring tools in the cloud are giving outcomes are as follows with the overall outcome in methodology design starting from question to the accurate results being projected.

6.3.1 Computer Program-Based Cloud Authoring Tools

Once the authoring tools are used, there will be backend programming on the cloud tools. Here, the computer programming behind the tools is seen with the detailed description of the request and response payoff. The computer program would be the program permitting and conveyance demonstration that gives program items to clients by Ahmad et al. (2020). Its administrations are facilitated by a CC supplier of computer program requests (Masud et al. 2012). The computer program, as

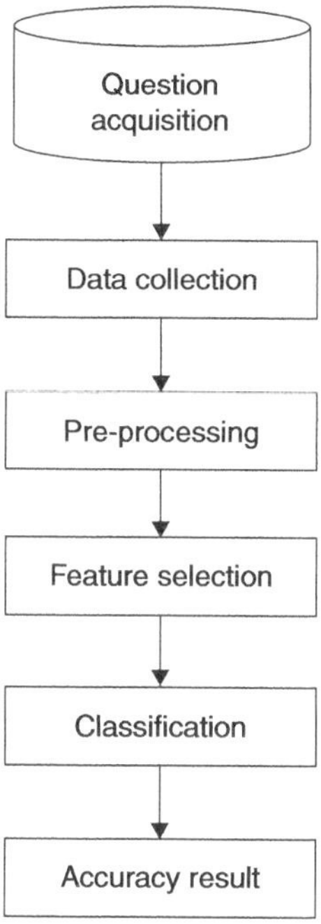

FIGURE 6.1 Methodology Design.

TABLE 6.1
Attribute and Description

Short form	Description
ST	Secondary-tier base
CM	Channel management
P	Primary tier
S	Secondary tier
N	num devices
S	Subscript
F	frame index
ETT	Estimated transmission
CS	Channel sense
S	Single strait
PT	Primary tier
ST	Single threshold
DT	Double threshold

a benefit, conveys such administrations as mail, conferencing computer programs, and different commerce requests like Endeavor Asset Arranging, Client association Administration, and Sequence Administration (Korepin et al. 2020). Table 6.1 shows the abbreviation of terms used in this research work.

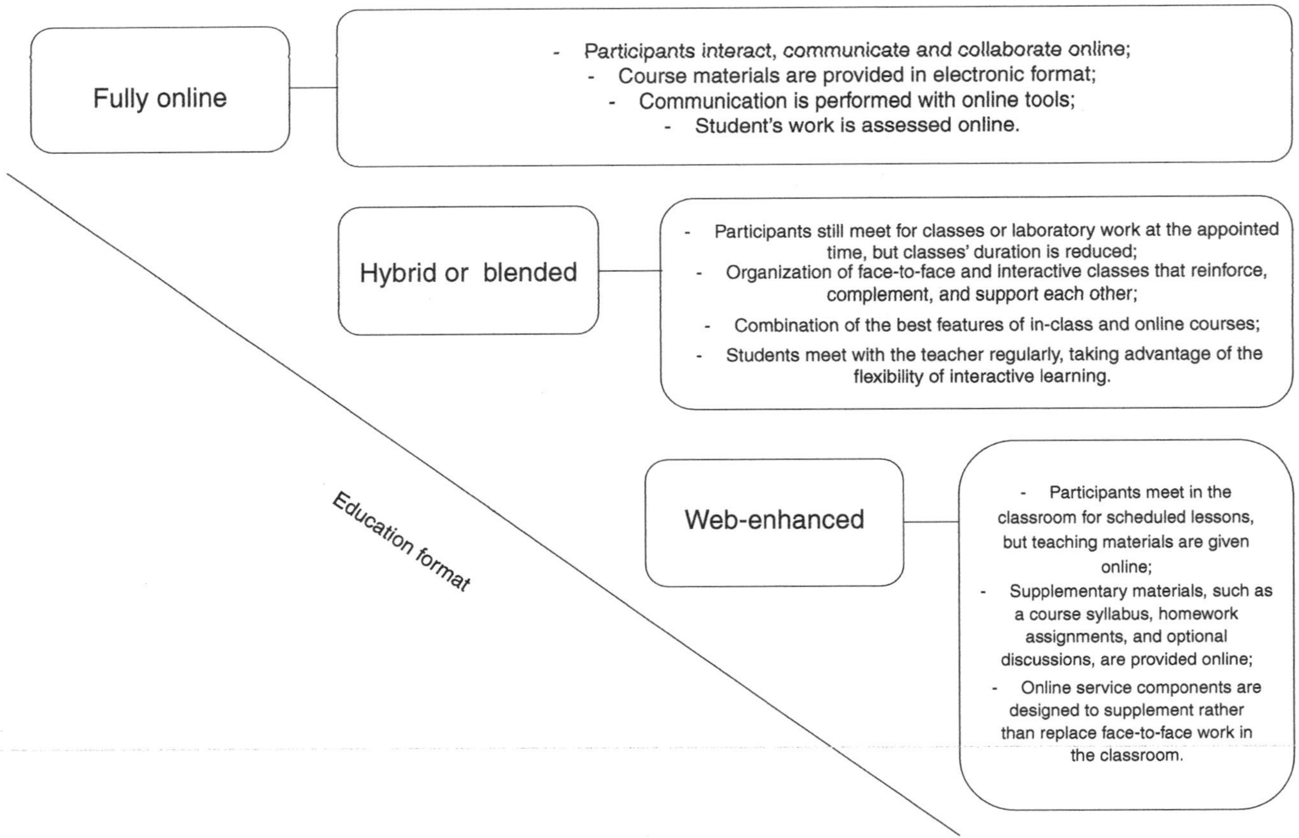

FIGURE 6.2 Category of On-Line Route in Blackboard Study.

A single request is a lope on the member of staff serving at the table side, gotten to via single or supplementary lope on the cloud services and frequent end-users or consumer association. The foremost broadly known computer program as a benefit case is Salesforce.in, Google Apps, Dropbox. Computer programs are additionally considered an essential benefit show utilized to get to the software through the cloud (Mell et al. 2011). Fake insights (artificial intelligence, AI) in computer programs as a benefit is represented within the frame of machine learning (ML), which is included in mechanism-to-person workflows (Shirzad et al. 2012). The nearness of AI in computer programs as a benefit takes the shape of overexcited personalization. It stands for a custom instructive substance that rises after the client works together with ML (Lee et al. 2018).

Figure 6.2 presents the CC clients that do not influence the quality, judgment, and accessibility of information.

They have to depend on safety measures and actions embraced by cloud suppliers (Tchernykh et al. 2019). In this way, cloud benefit vendors' notoriety primarily depends on the implementation of the assistance Level Assentation, which they achieve amid prepared exercises (Zaballos et al. 2018).

Measurable Difficult: When the connection occurs at every point in each graphic representation, it summarizes information such as mean, mode, and median. Chandra et al. (2012) discusses Total Cost of Ownership of cloud environment to be established in the premises (Tables I–IV).

$$c = f\left(Cx_C{}^c\right) \tag{6.1}$$

a number of these sensors act as most important users and others as minor users. To update the conduit in order of the primary user, each inferior user creates a conduit free list F_L. Major users will televise their company timestamps, ID, and position at ordinary period, and all inferior users within the prime user's reporting C_R will receive these notifications and modernize the sequence they have sent in their complementary list. [34][35]

$$D_{ist=}\sqrt{|f - x|^2 + |f_1 + x|^2} \tag{6.2}$$

Table 6.2 describes about function and equation of class function with different combination of value with x1 and x2.

6.4 METHODOLOGY

6.4.1 Effective Educational Process Organization

The proposed show coordinates cloud and CLOUD inside an Ed-cloud framework, which might give effective capability for instructive education, instructors, and understudies. Ed-cloud could be a future general CC foundation outlined particularly for instructive educators who look for adaptable cloud assets without having to depend

TABLE 6.2
Descriptive Statistics of (I), (II), (III), (IV) Answers

Class limit	f	Cf	X	Fx^1	$X^1 - X^2$
0.05–0.15	1	4	0.115	0.24	0.023706
0.15–0.25	2	4	0.15	0.01	0.010806
0.20–0.35	0	6	0.225	0.01	0.002906
0.25–0.40	0	5	0.255	0.265	0.000006
0.30–0.35	0	6	0.315	0.315	0.002106
0.35–0.50	1	7	0.365	0.365	0.009206
0.40–0.55	2	7	0.435	0.1	0.021306
0.45–0.60	3	11	0.445	1.7	0.038406
	ϵ 12			ϵ 3.34	ϵ 0.150044

Class limit	f	Cf	X	Fx^1	$X^1 - X^2$
0.05–0.15	1	4	0.115	0.24	0.023706
0.15–0.25	2	4	0.15	0.01	0.010806
0.20–0.35	0	6	0.225	0.01	0.002906
0.25–0.40	0	5	0.255	0.265	0.000006
0.30–0.35	0	6	0.315	0.315	0.002106
0.35–0.50	1	7	0.365	0.365	0.009206
0.40–0.55	2	7	0.435	0.1	0.021306
0.45–0.60	3	11	0.445	1.7	0.038406
	ϵ 12			ϵ 3.34	ϵ 0.150044

Class limit	f	Cf	X	Fx^1	$X^1 - X^2$
0.05–0.15	1	4	0.115	0.24	0.023706
0.15–0.25	2	4	0.15	0.01	0.010806
0.20–0.35	0	6	0.225	0.01	0.002906
0.25–0.40	0	5	0.255	0.265	0.000006
0.30–0.35	0	6	0.315	0.315	0.002106
0.35–0.50	1	7	0.365	0.365	0.009206
0.40–0.55	2	7	0.435	0.1	0.021306
0.45–0.60	3	11	0.445	1.7	0.038406
	ϵ 12			ϵ 3.34	ϵ 0.150044

Class limit	f	Cf	X	Fx^1	$X^1 - X^2$
0.05–0.15	1	4	0.115	0.24	0.023706
0.15–0.25	2	4	0.15	0.01	0.010806
0.20–0.35	0	6	0.225	0.01	0.002906
0.25–0.40	0	5	0.255	0.265	0.000006
0.30–0.35	0	6	0.315	0.315	0.002106
0.35–0.50	1	7	0.365	0.365	0.009206
0.40–0.55	2	7	0.435	0.1	0.021306
0.45–0.60	3	11	0.445	1.7	0.038406
	ϵ 12			ϵ 3.34	ϵ 0.150044

on nearby data. By consistently coordinating the foundation with its instruction database and AI methods, Ed-cloud makes a central store for all imperative instructive information that incorporates understudy data, lesson points of interest, and authoritative records (El Mhouti et al. 2018).

Ed-cloud utilizes a cluster of progressed CLOUD calculations through which strong experiences might be obtained from endless instructive information chronicles put away inside their Storage (Stephen et al. 2019).

These bits of knowledge control prescient analysis, which encourages personal learning suggestions empowering individuals' informational and versatile appraisals based on each person's one-of-a-kind capacities plus desires. Practical classrooms are enhanced with video conferencing options, which facilitate communication between students and instructors while promoting active engagement among them (Papadakis et al. 2017).

The reliable checking of understudy advances other than participation minutes are encouraged by cloud innovation consolidated inside Ed-cloud, encouraging educated choice creation based on investigation utilizing mechanized mediations to guarantee any subject or confront lift is settled pro-actively (Shahzad et al. 2016).

Safety measures must be maintained through regular upkeep and updates to best practices, ensuring optimal efficiency while adapting to ongoing technological changes. Simulated stress testing exercises play a crucial role in minimizing the impact during exceptional situations (Siddiqui et al. 2019).

The Ed-cloud gives the essential computational assets and capacity for preparing CLOUD models, whereas CLOUD calculations and methods might use the information put away within the Ed-cloud to provide modified and statistics-ambitious instructive encounters.

Manufacturing data is used in pre-designed simulations to develop courses that should be offered to groups of students. Their importance was restricted to route administration, but moreover displayed in recording participation, review assessment, and comes about era. There is a mechanized AI bottom application that might offer assistance and bolster in understanding issues in different courses that the understudies think about and back them anytime they require. In cutting-edge applications like meta poetry, the part of AI gets to be unavoidable.

Figures 6.3, 6.4, and 6.5 describe the efficiency of the classroom climate, lesson conveyance, understudy appointment, test, assessments, and evaluating framework that are totally rendered within the form. For such type of near framework, a colossal sum of preparing, difficulty-free displaying, and basic arrangement methods are, for the most part, favored. Hence, AI would engage in recreation as an input part of the cutting-edge classroom state of affairs. Therefore, AI would play a key role in enhancing the modern classroom environment. With its flexibility, portability, and ease of access to and sharing of information, AI presents both challenges and opportunities within the educational sector.

6.4.2 Cloud Computing Common Dialect Handling

E-study instruction has been altogether improved by the addition of different manufactured insights (CC) innovations. CC has changed the online knowledge

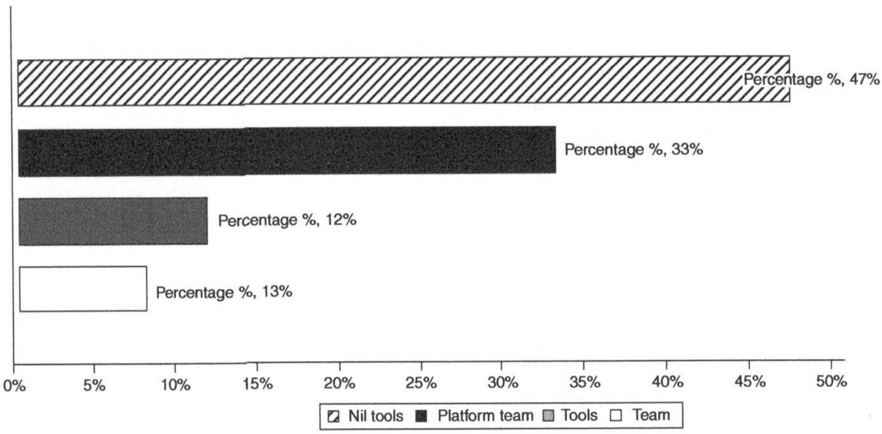

FIGURE 6.3 Efficiency of Content.

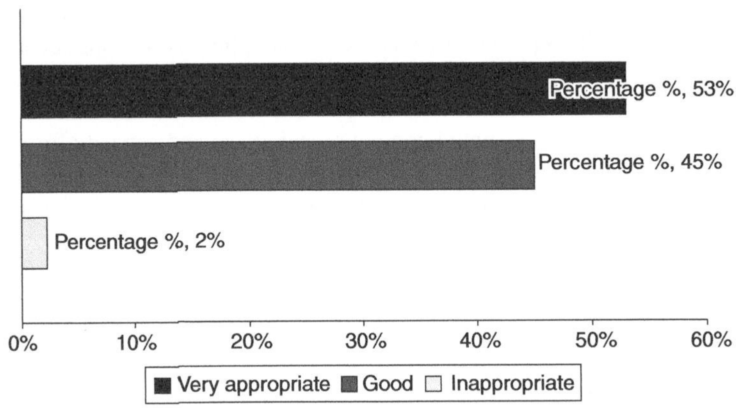

FIGURE 6.4 Proposal of Modified Prototype.

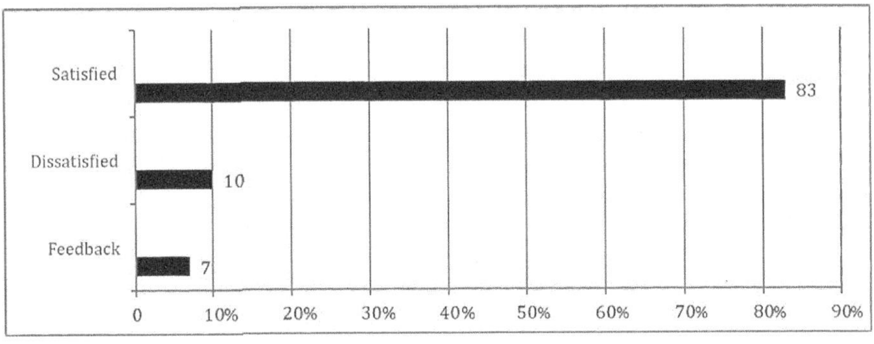

FIGURE 6.5 Proposal of Modified Prototype.

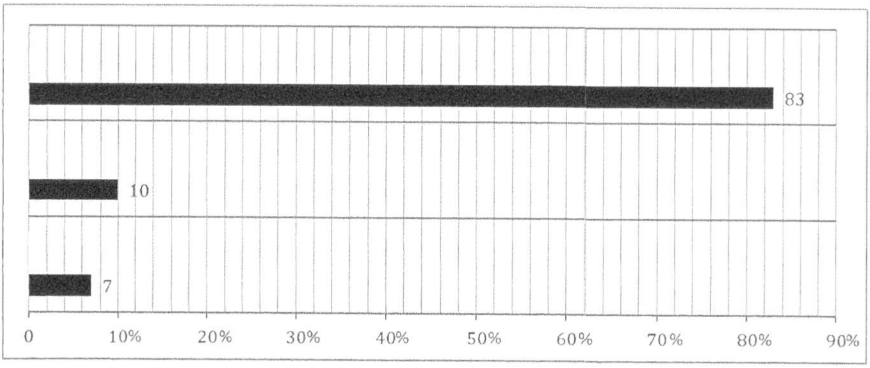

FIGURE 6.6 Alertness about E-Learning.

scene, making it additionally intelligent, versatile, and effective. CC calculations and common dialect handling, contain transfigure substance conveyance and appraisal. These advances empower e-education stages to study students' execution and fit education resources to personal needs, advertising a modified learning involvement. Conversation bots and effective associates have developed as advanced instructing and back devices, giving quick reactions to understudy questions and helping with authoritative assignments, in this manner progressing the general e-education involvement. Moreover, AI-powered information analytics offer assistance in instructive education, accumulating bits of knowledge into understudy behavior and learning designs and encouraging evidence-based decision-making to optimize educational program plans and instructing techniques.

Figure 6.6 presents the overall feedback on E-learning through a survey which provides the percentage of people who accept E-learning to the core. In this survey, a greater number of people agree that E-learning is essential for the individual in terms of education.

6.5 RESULT AND DISCUSSION

Chalkboard learning is a wide, CC-based instruction stage centered on improving the learner's experience by giving online preparation openings in asynchronous and offbeat situations. In an asynchronous space, understudies and instructors are known to have the capacity to connect on genuine occasions. A celebrated case of an asynchronous device is chalkboard work together, where one can organize ponder sessions, have offhand talks, and have a visitor speaker. In an offbeat environment, understudies can benefit from the hourly created plan of updates on almost up-and-coming occasions.

Figure 6.7 illustrates the chalkboard study which suggests that learners experience different sorts of paths: completely online, crossover or mixed, and a conventional with an included mesh mechanism. The Slate knowledge platform allows students to track their progress, complete coursework and exams, participate in discussions, initiate group sessions, and view grades. As per Siddiqui et al. (2019), the Slate

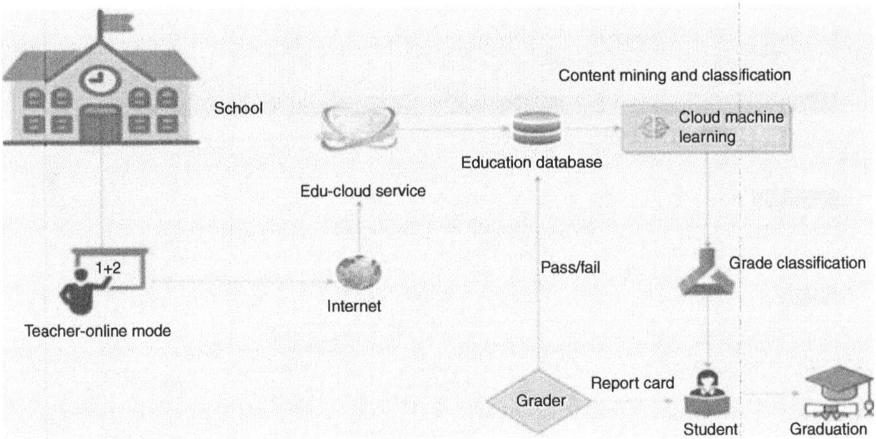

FIGURE 6.7 Structure Online Class Working.

Teachers versatile app permits instructors to see the route substance, review coursework, experience talks with understudies, and work with their understudy bunches.

6.6 CONCLUSION

These digital methods of instruction and the addition of counterfeit insights (AI) CC ideas have certainly transformed the instruction framework. Making unclear computing and unused mechanism innovations have been added essentially to this change. The display planned to demonstrate, joint Ed-cloud, and CC that empowers the advancement of brilliantly instructive frameworks, modified knowledge situations, and information ambitious verdict manufacture forms collectively help to progress instructive results and also to upgrade the general instruction involvement in online learning. This function of innovation improves the viability and thereby inculcates adaptability of online instruction, which in turn provokes through assembling the advanced needs of present-day beginners. In the future, education will be a practical and hands-on experience for any individual using these authoring tools.

REFERENCES

Abdullahi, M.S.I., Salleh, N., Nordin, A., Alwan, A.A. (2018), "Cloud-based learning system for improving students' programming skills and self-efficacy", *Journal of Information and Communication Technology*, 17(4): 629–651,. https://doi.org/10.32890/jict2018.17.4.6.

Ahmad, N. (2017), "Cloud computing: Technology, security issues and solutions", In *Proceedings of the 2017 2nd International Conference on Anti-Cyber Crimes (ICACC)*,. Abha, Saudi Arabia;, pp. 30–35,. https://doi.org/10.1109/anti-cybercrime.2017.7905258.

Ahmad, N., Hoda, N., Alahmari, F. (2020), "Developing a Ccloud-Bbased Mmobile Llearning Aadoption Mmodel to Ppromote Ssustainable Eeducation"., *Sustainability*", 12: 3126,. https://doi.org/10.3390/su12083126.

Buyya, R., Srirama, S. N., Casale, G., Calheiros, R., Simmhan, Y., Varghese, B., Gelenbe, E., Javadi, B., Vaquero, L.M., Netto, M.A.S., Toosi, A.N., Rodriguez, M.A., Llorentem I.M., De Vimercati, S., Samarati, P., Milojičić, D.S., Varela, C.A., Bahsoon, R., De Assunção, M.D., Rana, O.F., ZhouW., Jin, H., Gentzsch, W., Zomaya, A.Y., Shen, H. (2018), "A manifesto for future generation cloud computing: Research directions for the next decade", *ACM cComputing sSurveys (CSUR)*, 51(5): 1–38,. https://doi.org/10.1145/3241737.

Chandra, D.G., Borah, M.D. (2012), "Cost benefit analysis of cloud computing in education", In *2012 International Conference on Computing, Communication and Applications*. IEEE, pp. 1–6. https://doi.org/10.1109/iccca.2012.6179142.

Colman-Meixner, C., Develder, C., Tornatore, M., Mukherjee, B. (2016), "A survey on resiliency techniques in cloud computing infrastructures and applications", *IEEE Communications Surveys & Tutorials*, 18(3): 2244–2281. https://doi.org/10.1109/comst.2016.2531104.

El Mhouti, A., Erradi, M., Nasseh, A. (2018), "Using Ccloud Ccomputing Sservices in EeLearning Pprocess: Benefits and Cchallenges", *Education and Information Technologies*, 23(2): 893–909. https://doi.org/10.1007/s10639-017-9642-x.

Galletta, A., Carnevale, L., Celesti, A., Fazio, M., Villari, M. (2017), "A Ccloud-Bbased Ssystem for Iimproving Rretention Mmarketing Lloyalty Pprograms in Industry 4.0: A Sstudy on Bbig Ddata Sstorage Iimplications", *IEEE Access*, 6(c): 5485–5492. https://doi.org/10.1109/access. 2017.2776400.

Giannakis, M., Spanaki, K., Dubey, R. (2019), "A cloud-based supply chain management system: effects on supply chain responsiveness", *Journal of Enterprise Information Management*, 32(4): 585–607. https://doi.org/10.1108/jeim-05-2018-0106.

Hendradi, P., Abd Ghani, M.K., Mahfuzah, S.N., Yudatama, U., Prabowo, N.A., Widyanto, R A. (2020), "Artificial Iintelligence Iinfluence in Education 4.0 Tto Aarchitecture Ccloud Bbased Ee-Llearning Ssystem", *International Journal of Artificial Intelligence Research*, 4(1): 1–9,. https://doi.org/10.29099/ijair.v4i1.109.

Hendradi, P., Khanapi, M., Mahfuzah, S.M. (2019), "Cloud Ccomputing-Bbased Ee-Llearning Ssystem Aarchitecture in Education 4.0", In *Journal of Physics: Conference Series*. IOP Publishing, Vol. 1196, No. 1, p. 012038. https://doi.org/10.1088/1742-6596/1196/1/012038

Hussein, L.A., Hilmi, M.F. (2020), "Cloud Ccomputing Bbased E-learning in Malaysian Uuniversities", *International Journal of Emerging Technologies in Learning*, 15(08): 4–21. https://doi.org/10.3991/ijet. v15i08.11798.

Joshi, N., Shah, S. (2019), "A comprehensive survey of services provided by prevalent cloud computing environments", In *Smart Intelligent Computing and Applications*. Springer, Singapore, pp. 413–424. https://doi.org/10.1007/978-981-13-1921-1_41.

Korepin, V.N., Dorozhkin, E.M., Mikhaylova, A.V., Davydova, N.N. (2020), "Digital Eeconomy and Ddigital Llogistics as Nnew Aarea of Sstudy in Hhigher Eeducation", *International Journal of Emerging Technologies in Learning*, 15(13): 137–154. https://doi.org/10.3991/ijet.v15i13.14885.

Kumar, S., Vajpayee, A. (2016), "A survey on secure cloud: sSecurity and privacy in cloud computing", *American Journal of Systems and Software*, 4(1): 14–26.

Lee, K. (2018), "AI Pplatform to Aaccelerate API Eeconomy and Eecosystem", *Harvard Business Review*, 2012: 848–852.

Li, Y., Xia, S., Cao, B., Liu, Q. (2019), "Lyapunov optimization-based trade-off policy for mobile cloud offloading in heterogeneous wireless networks", *IEEE Transactions on Cloud Computing*, pp. 1–3. https://doi.org/10.1109/tcc.2019.2938504

Liu, Z.-Q., Dorozhkin, E., Davydova, N., Sadovnikova, N. (2020), "Effectiveness of the Ppartial Iimplementation of a Ccloud-Bbased Kknowledge Mmanagement Ssystem",

International Journal of Emerging Technologies in Learning, 15(13): 155–171. https://doi.org/10.3991/ ijet.v15i13.14919.

Masud, M.A.H., Huang, X. (2012), "An e-learning system architecture based on cloud computing", *System*, 10(11): 255–259.

Mell, P., Grance, T. (2011), "*The NIST dDefinition of cCloud cComputing*",. National Institute of Standards and Technology.

Moravčík, M., Segeč, P., Uramová, Y., Kontšek, M. (2017), "Teaching cloud computing in cloud computing", In *Conference: 2017 15th International Conference on Emerging eLearning Technologies and Applications (ICETA)*. IEEE, pp. 1–6. https://doi.org/10.1109/iceta. 2017.8102512.

Naveed, Q.N., Ahmad, N. (2019), "Critical Ssuccess Ffactors (CSFs) for Ccloud-based Ee-Llearning", *International Journal of Emerging Technologies in Learning*, 14(01): 140–149. https://doi.org/10.3991/ijet.v14i01.9170.

Nazir, R., Ahmed, Z., Ahmad, Z., Shaikh, N.N., Laghari, A.A., Kumar, K. (2020), "Cloud Ccomputing Aapplications: A Rreview", *EAI Endorsed Transactions on Cloud Systems*, 6(17): 5. https://doi.org/10.4108/eai.22-5-2020.164667.

Papadakis, S., Kalogiannakis, M., Sifaki, E., Vidakis, N. (2017), "Access moodle using smart mobile phones",: A case study in a Greek University". In *Interactivity, Game Creation, Design, Learning, and Innovation*. Springer, Cham, pp. 376–385. https://doi.org/10.1007/978-3-319-76908-0_36.

Shahzad, N., Ismail, A., Golamdin, A.G. (2016), "Opportunity and Cchallenges using the Ccloud Ccomputing in the Ccase of Malaysian Hhigher Eeducation Iinstitutions", *International Journal of Management Science and Information Technology*, 20(20): 1–18.

Shirzad, M., Ahmadipour, M., Hoseinpanah, A., Rahimi, H. (2012), "E-learning based on cloud computing", In *2012 International Conference on Cloud Computing Technologies, Applications and Management (ICCCTAM)*,. IEEE, pp. 214–218,. https://doi.org/10.1109/icectam.2012.6488101.

Siddiqui, S.T., Alam, S., Khan, Z.A., Gupta, A. (2019), "Cloud-based e-learning: Using cloud computing platform for an effective e-learning", In *Smart Innovations in Communication and Computational Sciences*, Springer, Singapore, pp. 335–346, https://doi.org/10.1007/978-981-13-2414-7_31.

Stephen, A., Benedict, S., Kumar, R.A. (2019), "Monitoring IaaS using various cloud monitors", *Cluster Computing*, 22(5): 12459–12471,. https://doi.org/10.1007/s10586-017-1657-y.

Sultana, J., Mazmum, M.F., Nipa, N.J. (2017), "Factors Aaffecting Ccloud Ccomputing Aadoption in Hhigher Eeducation in Bangladesh",: A Ccase of University of Dhaka", *Applied and Computational Mathematics*, 6(3): 129–136. https://doi.org/10.11648/j.acm.20170603.11.

Talan, T. (2020), "The effect of mobile learning on learning performance: A meta-analysis study", *Educational Sciences: Theory and Practice*, 20(1): 79–103. https://doi.org/10.12738/jestp.2020.1.006.

Tchernykh, A., Schwiegelsohn, U., Talbi, E.G., Babenko, M. (2019), "Towards understanding uncertainty in cloud computing with risks of confidentiality, integrity, and availability", *Journal of Computational Science*, 36: 100581. https://doi.org/10.1016/j.jocs.2016.11.011.

Zaballos, A.G., Rodríguez, E.I. (2018), "Cloud Ccomputing: Opportunities and Cchallenges for Ssustainable Eeconomic Ddevelopment in Latin America and the Caribbean", *Inter-American Development Bank*, https://doi.org/10.18235/0001083.

7 Enhancing Virtual Learning with Cloud Computing Paradigm

Ketaki A. Bhosale, Sangram T. Patil, and Shubhangi Suryawanshi

7.1 INTRODUCTION

The educational landscape has changed drastically in recent years due to the rapid advancement of technology. Cloud computing has evolved over time to take on a new role in the IT industry. A class of computer resources known as "cloud computing technology"takes advantage of the Internet to provide external services that are extremely ascendable. Because cloud computing has the ability to transcend physical classrooms and regional limitations, it has completely changed the way how education is delivered. Educational institutions may establish immersive digital environments that promote seamless collaboration, engagement, and information dissemination among students and educators alike by using the potential of cloud-based platforms and services [1]. The cloud offers learners everywhere previously unheard-of levels of flexibility and involvement, whether via live-streamed lectures, interactive virtual classrooms, or on-demand learning materials. Scalability and accessibility are two major benefits of using cloud computing in virtual learning. Cloud-based solutions, in contrast to traditional on-premises infrastructure, offer unmatched scalability, enabling educational institutions to adapt to changing demands and scale up their resources dynamically to suit expanding student populations. Furthermore, learners can use any Internet-enabled device anytime, anywhere to access instructional resources and engage in collaborative activities because of the cloud's ubiquitous accessibility [2][3].

On-demand access is given to shared pools of re-configurable computer resources such as servers, storage, networks, apps, and services [4]. Service providers and managers do not have to do much to set up and scale these tools quickly. Through pay-as-you-go models, cloud computing essentially abstracts the complexity of infrastructure management and enables consumers to utilize computing resources as a utility. This paradigm is a mainstay of contemporary IT infrastructure and is propelling digital transformation throughout asit provides advantages including scalability, flexibility, cost-effectiveness, accessibility, and innovation [5].

DOI: 10.1201/9781003472537-8

7.2 PERSPECTIVES ON FORMULATING CLOUD COMPUTING PLANS FOR REMOTE EDUCATION

Implementing cloud computing strategies for distance learning requires an integrated approach that considers factors such asinfrastructure, security, accessibility, scalability, and budget. Here are some perspectives to think about.

7.2.1 Incorporate Cloud Computing intoOne's IT Plan

Choose the kind of cloud solution that best suits the need to structure the institution's instructional activities. The public cloud's easy adoption could be the ideal strategy for tiny universities with a limited enrollment of distance learning students. For instance, some small colleges do not have the staff or specialized internal infrastructure needed to handle their online courses. After all, with the advantages that cloud computing can provide—like lower setup and maintenance costs and cost savings—it could be wiser for colleges to think about implementing a public cloud for their online courses.

Largedistance learning units that have made years of investments in their own IT systems ought to think about creating a hybrid cloud to make the most of their current resources. Administrators of such sizable distance learning units should first concentrate on creating an internal private cloud out of the current IT programmers and systems (such as learning management systems, customer relationship management systems, and instructional support systems). For initial testing, they could start by building a small-scale experimental cloud environment. For example, they could investigate ways to use internal user account databases to enable authenticated access to cloud-based IT applications and systems. They might also deal with issues like access control and data sharing that could arise during integration. After the employees engaged in remote learning have gained the requisite experience in cloud integration and execution, they can create internal private clouds for the entire unit. They might eventually go to hybrid cloud architecture. To provide better control, security, and privacy, sensitive student data may be stored in private clouds alongside other essential apps. However, whenever possible, non-core IT programs like customer relationship management (CRM) and learning management systems could be contracted out to the public cloud. This hybrid strategy combines the benefits of private and public clouds [6]. To aid in the cloud's development, a phased implementation approach is advised. Initially, the main focus may be Software as a Service (SaaS) initiatives, such as moving systems for creating syllabiand blackboards to the cloud. Subsequently, the focus may shift to Platform as a Service and,eventually, Infrastructure as a Service [7]. Larger remote learning units can profit from and gain organizational support over time by progressively progressing cloud services [8].

7.2.2 Variety of Factors to Consider While Assessing and Choosing Cloud Service Providers

The cloud platform maturity, technological alignment, operational alignment, and geographic alignment are the four main factors. Organizations need to evaluate how well a cloud solution fits with their application architecture, customer support requirements, and requirements for service level, security, privacy, and compliance, in addition to cost, operational stability, and scalability. Weighted evaluation criteria, such as ability to execute and completeness of vision, should also be considered. Furthermore, particular standards adapted to the needs of remote learning have to be created.

Considerations include licensing agreements, price structures, and support for platforms such as Sakai or Moodle. With so many cloud service providers on the market, selectingone that best suits the particular requirements of each distance learning unit requires careful consideration. Customization choices are available from many suppliers. There can be contractual issues such as defining service parameters, data ownership, security requirements, and audit rights. It is necessary for distance learning administrators and practitioners to have conversations to define specific selection and assessment standards; these conversations should ideally be aided by the field's current professional groups.

7.2.3 Adopt a Comprehensive Strategy

The responsibilities of individuals, particularly IT staff, and organizational dynamics are significantly altered by the integration of cloud computing. The cloud service providers are in charge of upholding system and application uptime. Moreover, the implementation of cloud computing has consequences for budgetary allocations, economic models, and institutional IT funding methods. Therefore, instead of focusingonly on moving particular applications to the cloud, administrators of remote learning programmers need to take a more comprehensive approach to cloud adoption. This includes giving top management support, careful planning, and extensive stakeholder education top priority.

7.2.4 Collaboration with Other Distance Learning Institutes

The establishment of a shared cloud for distance learning would facilitate the easy exchange of online learning resources and applications among members of the distance learning community. This inclusive strategy guarantees teachers and students equal access to educational resources, regardlessof the size or standing of their respective institutions. It is recommended that distant learning professional associations lead efforts to develop standards, guidelines, and policies for cloud adoption, deployment, and assessment in partnership with member schools. These initiatives should address important issues such asthe sharing of educational resources, copyright concerns, security precautions, and the protection of personal and financial data privacy.

Effective communication between administrators and practitioners of remote learning can be promoted by utilizing tools such as wikis and forums. In addition to simplifying the process of obtaining federal and state financing, the use of a community cloud in remote learning reducesdevelopment and operating expenses and avoids the waste of important resources.

7.3 E-LEARNING FOR SUSTAINABLE EDUCATION: AN ANALYSIS OF ILEARN2.0'S CASE STUDY

A blended learning program was offered from 2018 to 2020 by a university in central Taiwan. This method made use of an on-site classroom and the Moodle e-learning platform iLearn2.0. Data analysis, mobile learning, cloud services, and flipped classrooms are the four main components of iLearn2.0. From 2018 to 2020, the citizen participation course made use of the platformto help teachers and researchers create interactive course materials and help students complete tasks on their devices. Between 2018 and 2020, using a variety of instructional strategies, 127 students enrolled in citizen participation courses were instructed [9]. Figure 7.1 explains various aspects that are associated with the functionality of the i-Learning 2.0.

Three classes taught by one teacher (the current researcher) between 2018 and 2020 make up the case study under examination here to answer the following questions: A user-based platform, iLearn involves education.

First, can students' performance be improved by e-learning and online technology?

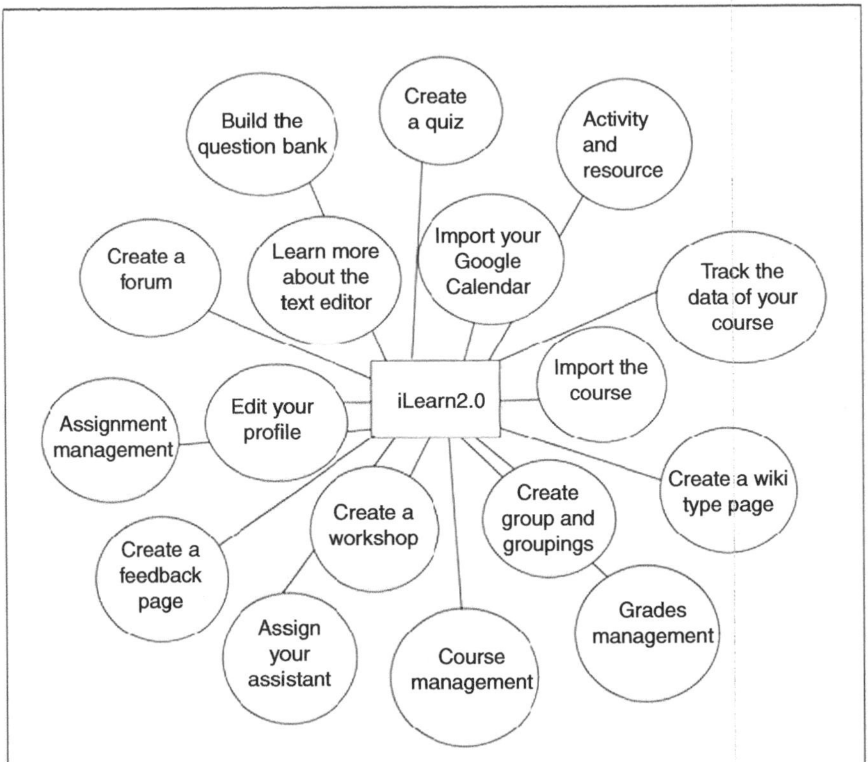

FIGURE 7.1 iLearn2.0 Functionality.

Second, in an online learning environment, such as iLearn2.0, how might the teaching methodology support students' sustainable learning?

And finally, what challenges do students face with iLearn2.0?

7.3.1 Limitations of Traditional Education

In the field of education, Taiwan encountered several obstacles, such as:

- **Limitations on Resources:** In isolated and rural locations, there is inadequate access to high-quality educational materials and technology.
- **Challenges with Scalability:**An increasingly diversified and expanding student body poses challenges for educational resource scalability.

  Heavy use of tangible resources such as paper and textbooks has an adverse effect on the environment.

  Ensuring that all kids, regardless of location or socioeconomic background, receive an interesting and accessible education is imperative.
- **Technology Integration:** Using contemporary technology to improve learning results by incorporating it into conventional teaching approaches.

7.3.2 Goals of i-Learn 2.0

The goals of i-Learn 2.0 are listed as follows:

- **Encourage Sustainable Education:** By using fewer physical resources, education can have a smaller negative impact on the environment.
- **Boost Accessibility:** Give every student fair access to top-notch learning materials.
- **Enhance Learning Outcomes:** Make use of e-learning resources to design interesting and successful learning opportunities.
- **Scalable Infrastructure:** Provide an e-learning platform that is flexible enough to accommodate varying student demographics and educational levels.
- **Promote Innovation:** Promote the incorporation of state-of-the-art technology into teaching methods.

7.3.3 Resolution of iLearn2.0

To overcome these obstacles, the iLearn2.0 project was started, utilizing cloud computing and e-learning technology.

- **Putting Cloud-Based Platform into Practice:**

  IaaS: Reliable and scalable infrastructure was provided by using cloud services to host the iLearn2.0 platform.

  PaaS: Cloud platforms were used to create customized e-learning systems that facilitate interactive and multimedia-rich content.

  SaaS: Cloud-based software and solutions for education that are easy to access and maintain.

- **Digital Media:** A sizable collection of interactive activities, multimedia tutorials, and digital textbooks was built. Worked in tandem with educators to create curriculum-aligned and interesting digital content.
- **Characteristics of Accessibility:**Implemented tools to assist a variety of learners, including language translation, text-to-speech, and user interface customization; made sure that the desktops, tablets, and cellphones all work with the same platform.
- **Support and Training for Teachers:** Offered thorough training courses to help educators use e-learning resources and incorporate them into their lesson plans; created a support network for ongoing troubleshooting and professional development.
- **Sustainable Projects:**Encouraged the reduction of reliance on printed documents by using digital resources; pushed for the adoption of digital communication platforms and paperless administrative procedures in schools.

7.3.4 Summary of iLearn2.0

The iLearn2.0 study by Fu-Hsuan Chen demonstrates how e-learning and cloud computing can revolutionize the field of sustainable education. An equal, interesting, and ecologically sustainable educational system has resulted from the initiative's effective resolution of Taiwan's major educational issues. For areas looking to improve their educational systems using creative and sustainable methods, the case study is a notableexample.

7.4 UNDERSTANDING DISTANCE EDUCATION WITH CLOUD

Learning through electronic devicesand accessing the learning material online through the Internet is known as virtual learning or distance learning [10]. Some acronyms for the platform that offers e-learning capabilities are learning management systems (LMS), e-learning platforms, electronic learning, virtual learning environments (VLEs), etc.

E-learning offers so many benefits, such asmeasurement, diversity, opening, flexibility, and so forth. Numerous educational establishments lack the infrastructure and resources required to operate an advanced e-learning system. For this reason, the twoleading e-learning software providers, Blackboard and Moodle, now provide cloud-based versions of their core programs. Today, e-learning is widely used for a variety of educational purposes, including academic courses, corporate training, ongoing education, and more. An e-learning system involves trainers and students as one of its minimum number of entities.

In an e-learning environment, students engage in the following activities: completing online courses, taking tests, providing feedback, and sending assignments and projects.

Trainers working on an e-learning system are responsible for managing content, creating tests, grading assignments, assessments, and projects completed by students; providing feedback; and interacting with students through discussion boards. Figure 7.2 illustrates the interplay of various aspects concerned with the E-Learning-Based CloudApproach.

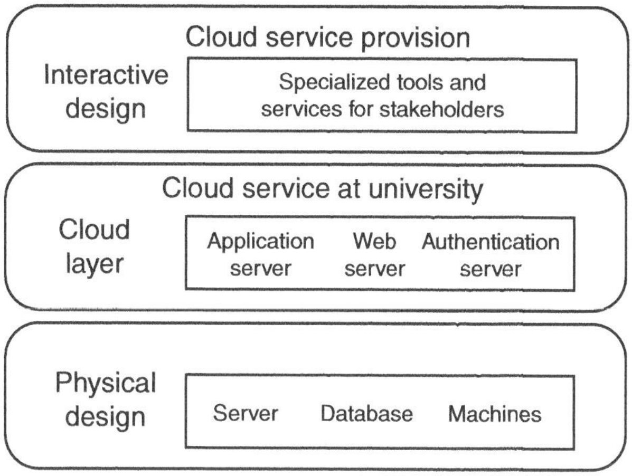

FIGURE 7.2 E-Learning-Based Cloud Approach.

The above architecture depicts the E-Learning-Based Cloud Approach with three layers:

1. Interaction design
2. Cloud layer
3. Physical design

7.4.1 Interaction Design

To enable the development of services, this layer builds upon the virtual resources with a variety of specialized tools, middleware, and services. Thus, it includes the services that the Campus Clouds would be able to support.

The Interaction design layer will provide all the functionalities that can be used by the different stakeholders (including admin, student, teaching faculty, and others).

In this layer, the different learning objects (such as online assignments, lecture notes, test and assessments, video tutorials, lecture notes, etc.) can be used by different users via the Internet.

Service-based learning is expanding quickly with the advent of recently developed cloud service technologies. New concepts such as virtual classrooms, virtual laboratories, and virtual universities are posing a number of new challenges that call for the use of more sophisticated information techniques intended to support e-learning services.

7.4.2 Cloud Layer

Specialized cloud-enabled software on the servers will provide continuous cloud access for the user. Every one of these servers is going to possess specialized collaboration software to facilitate resource sharing. Three servers make up this layer: an application server, a web server, and a server for single sign-on authentication. The primary function of the authentication server is to confirm the validity of the user or the accuracy of the user's name and password that they have provided. Only authorized users are able to access those services and resources. The user must complete the registration form before using the resources. The application server must offer a setting in which stakeholders and end users can effectively run their apps. It doesn't matter whether the user's computer has the particular software installed or not. The web server is responsible for sending the online learning materials to the user's PC.

The layer offers applications (tools and services) for management, hosting, and deployment. The layer can be split into two halves to create an integrated platform for distance education for students and educational institutions. It starts with the technical support framework, which offers the platform service's operational environment. The framework may swiftly create new services and provide a consistent service interface. Second, the layer contains platform service libraries. It can fulfill the need for application services by offering learning and educational institutions an interface for services like teaching, resource, video, identity management, and so on. This environment contains the framework or development language at the layer. The framework can be used by developers to create new applications.

7.4.3 Physical Design

At the base of the cloud framework, it provides virtual hardware resources as a hardware integration, service, and some forms of para-virtualization are used to deliver and consume infrastructure on-demand. The fundamental framework and base services make up this layer. The host computer, hardware, network, and storage—all of which will be visualized—are first provided by the foundation framework.

The network gives users access to a variety of educational tools, such as the Internet, satellite television service, and phone network. Utilize the network construction to your advantage to create a virtual private network on campus.

It requires complete access and control over the infrastructure at the layer to configure additional protocols, such as the active directory. Infrastructure management is elastic, made available on demand, and highly abstracted from the end user. As a result, the educational establishment can expand its infrastructure in response to the demands and requirements of distant learning. Educational institutions do not need to buy servers, network equipment, or storage because virtual hardware resources are offered as a service.

Everything is a cloud computing service. Campus Cloud-based e-learning might have been expanding its learning support services to provide university-level distance learning of the highest caliber. Everything is provided as a service on the local campus cloud system, including teaching tools, educational resources, and even learning. The emergence of cloud service technology, coupled with the swift growth of service-based learning and novel ideas such as virtual labs, virtual classes, and virtual institutes, has given rise to a plethora of new issues that require the development of more advanced information techniques to support e-learning services.

7.5 ADVANTAGES OF CLOUD-BASED E-LEARNING

7.5.1 Virtual Classroom Efficiency

Cloud software creates a powerful virtual classroom environment and helps educational institutions set up virtual classrooms for students while cutting down on infrastructure expenditures [11]. This approach also minimizes material expenses for teachers and students while facilitating collaboration with qualified remote coaches, serving as cost-effective resources. Instructors may design and deliver online courses from any place, giving students the freedom to save money and time by taking virtual tests from any location.

7.5.2 Ease of Access

Cloud technology ensures unparalleled accessibility, allowing users to effortlessly access topic details, different applications, and information anytime, from any place. Users can enroll in interesting topics with their group classes without the limitations of space and time, ensuring uninterrupted content delivery. Furthermore, access via mobile devices enhances learning flexibility for students on the go.

7.5.3 CostEfficiency

Cloud computing offers extensive cost savings, benefiting both students and providers. Students no longer need to buy the costly infrastructure as well as books, as these learning resources are readily available on cloud-based platforms.

7.5.4 Safe Information Management

In addition to ease of use and financial savings, cloud computing ensures secure data storage. Organizations leveraging cloud-based teaching methods can implement Virtual Private Network (VPN) protocols to safeguard data. These protocols automatically encrypt outgoing data and traffic, ensuring the integrity of learning content transmission. Furthermore, students can safeguard their private data by utilizing VPNs for cloud-based learning applications.

7.5.5 Scalability and Accessibility

Cloud computing extends its reach across educational institutions, allowing for increased scalability and accessibility. Schools, colleges, and universities can rapidly expand their training programs and accommodate more students, thereby effectively managing server loads and interruptions caused by a high volume of users simultaneously accessing resources.

7.5.6 Agility and Innovation

Cloud-based learning enables students to experiment more often and innovate faster. With improved Internet speeds, students can engage in innovative learning experiences and create new tools and features that surpass traditional methods, fostering continuous improvement and experimentation.

7.5.7 Enhanced Student Support

Cloud computing in education opens up opportunities for students to broaden their horizons, offering an alternative to traditional education systems. Students seeking remote learning options or studying abroad can benefit immensely from cloud technology. Additionally, working professionals can enhance their skills through virtual classes, accommodating their schedules and career aspirations.

7.6 SUMMARY

The global educational landscape has undergone a significant transformation, with technology rapidly integrating into traditional learning environments. To improve the distance learning experience, educational institutions have quickly made investments in digital tools and learning management systems. Ascloud computing offers unmatched scalability, accessibility, and cost-effectiveness, it has become a key enabler of remote education. Through the use of cloud-based platforms, educators and students may collaborate and access learning materials from any location, resulting in inclusive and personalized learning environments. Additionally, cloud computing guarantees safe data storage and promotes innovation in methods of delivering education. Even though cloud-based e-learning has the ability to change education, issues such aspoor Internet access still need to be resolved to guarantee fair access. All things considered, the advent of cloud computing has brought about a revolution in distance education by creating immersive and adaptable learning environments that are not limited by physical location.

REFERENCES

1 Kaynak, Baran, Osman Tuna, UgurOzbek, AliAksoy, Ahmet Ozmen, M. Baris Horzum, and BurakGol. 2023. "Uzep: A Cloud-Based Distance Education Platform for Higher Education Institutions."*Turkish Online Journal of Distance Education* 24 (4): 220–237. https://doi.org/10.17718/tojde.1188032.

2 Afanasiev, Ilya Vladimirovich, Nataliya VladimirovnaVysotskaya, Valery NikolaevichAlferov, and Natalia AnatolyevnaGrigorieva. 2021. "The Use of Cloud Resources and Services in Distance Learning of Students in the Context of Restrictions Caused by the Pandemic."*Revista Tempos e EspaçosEm Educação* 14 (33): e16103. https://doi.org/10.20952/revtee.v14i33.16103.

3 Al-Malah, Duha Khalid Abdul-Rahman, Ibtisam AAljazaery, Haider Th SalimAlrikabi, and Hussain Ali Mutar. 2021. "Cloud Computing and Its Impact on Online Education."*IOP Conference Series: Materials Science and Engineering* 1094(1): 012024. https://doi.org/10.1088/1757-899x/1094/1/012024.

4 Thavi, Riddhi, Rujuta Jhaveri, VaibhavNarwane, BhaskarGardas, and Nima JafariNavimipour. 2024. "Role of Cloud Computing Technology in the Education Sector."*Journal of Engineering, Design and Technology* 22 (1): 182–213. https://doi.org/10.1108/JEDT-08-2021-0417.

5 GevkoV, VivcharO, SharkoV, RadchenkoO, BudiaievM, TarasenkoO.2021."CloudTechnologies in Business Management."*Udc 378.14* 4 (39): 294–301.
6 Deb, Moumita, and AbantikaChoudhury. 2021. "Hybrid Cloud: A New Paradigm in Cloud Computing."*Machine Learning Techniques and Analytics for Cloud Security*, no. December 2021, 3–23. https://doi.org/10.1002/9781119764113.ch1.
7 Pažun, Brankica, and ZlatkoLangović. 2020. "Cloud Computing Concept in Education Systems."*Serbian Journal of Engineering Management* 5 (2): 25–32. https://doi.org/10.5937/sjem2002025p.
8 He, Wu, DanCernusca, and M'hammedAbdous. 2010. "Exploring Cloud Computing for Distance Learning."*Online Journal of Distance Learning Administration* 14:1–5. www.westga.edu/~distance/ojdla/fall143/he_cernusca_abdous.pdf.
9 Chen, Fu Hsuan. 2021. "Sustainable Education through E-Learning: The Case Study of Ilearn2.0."*Sustainability (Switzerland)* 13 (18). https://doi.org/10.3390/su131810186.
10 Xu, Wenyi. 2023. "An Improved Computational Solution for Cloud-Enabled E-Learning Platforms Using a Deep Learning Technique."*International Journal of E-Collaboration* 19 (1): 1–19. https://doi.org/10.4018/IJeC.316664.
11 Bazarbaevna, Bekchonova S.2020. "Use of "Cloud Technologies" That Store and Transmit."*European Journal of Research and Reflection in Educational Sciences* 8 (9): 19–23.

Section II

Pedagogical Changes and Multi-faceted Aspects of Clouds in E-Learning

8 Transformative Pedagogy

Collaborative Learning with Cloud Architecture and Virtual Programming Labs

Zulfiya Usmonova and Mohamed Uvaze Ahamed Ayoobkhan

8.1 INTRODUCTION

Education is learning new things to get a deep understanding of the subjects that can be applied to daily life. Many reasons stand beyond the need for quality education, such as providing stability that considers better career opportunities, ensuring financial security with money-saving tactics, achieving self-dependency, and gaining self-confidence. In a world where education plays an important role in becoming successful, the learning environment that gives this education directly affects the quality of the resultant knowledge. The purpose of this chapter is to explain the concepts of collaborative learning, the importance of cloud architecture in collaborative learning, the implementation techniques, and an overview of Virtual Programming Labs (VPLs), as well as security measures, optimizing options, and future trends. The chapter begins by introducing the differences between physical and online classrooms and reviewing the transition to digital and cloud-based learning. The next section discusses collaborative learning in detail, its role in modern education, and its benefits over traditional methods. Moving onwards, cloud architecture is discussed by touching on its significance in education and the role of Service-Oriented Applications in e-learning. In the next section, the VPLs, their benefits, design principles, and practical deployment tips are covered. Finally, the last two sections provide an overview of the security measurements, strategies for optimizing performance within virtual programming environments, and future directions and trends in this area. The chapter offers insights into the practices of collaborative learning enhancement with the help of digital technologies.

From the beginning, the most common and optimal environment for learning is considered to be physical classrooms – offline/on-site learning, but the situation with the COVID-19 pandemic introduced a new direction in education systems –online learning, which changed the old perspective to fresh innovations. Additionally, the emergence of digital technologies has transformed the education sector, reshaping the traditional model of teaching and learning. They have revolutionized pedagogy by offering innovative teaching methods that lead to different learning styles. The study process for students has been enriched with different media components such

DOI: 10.1201/9781003472537-10

as animations, images, graphics, and videos, while online assessments and data analytics have enabled teachers to identify students' strengths and weaknesses and provide personalized learning experiences that enhance their academic performance (Singh et al., 2023). The transition that the world has experienced from offline learning to online brought many changes to our usual lifestyle, and this movement began in the late 2000s when it can be observed how the newly offered online courses by institutions started to become more popular among student bodies.

The movement toward online education started years before and reached its peak during the pandemic in 2020 when the increase of online educational platforms stepped up dramatically. The education system was one of the most severely affected areas touched by lockdowns, along with the financial and healthcare systems, and the closure of most educational institutions caused the sudden shift from offline education to online, which was considered a method of protecting teachers and students from spreading COVID-19 at that time. Consequently, nowadays, there is a new teaching model – online education, e-learning.

8.2 RISE OF COLLABORATIVE LEARNING IN CLOUD-BASED LEARNING ENVIRONMENTS

Using groups to improve learning through cooperation is known as *collaborative learning*. To resolve issues, finish tasks, or pick up new knowledge, groups of two or more students collaborate with each other. Unlike rote memorization of facts and figures, this approach actively involves learners in processing and analyzing information and concepts (Valamis Group Ltd., 2023). When working on projects together, students are engaged to cooperate as a team to understand the ideas being covered. The students in a group get more understanding of concepts by clarifying such one, thinking from different viewpoints, and trying to defend their own compared to learning as individuals. They also get a chance to learn from others' skills, experience, and resources.

Collaborative and cooperative learning are two different research methods, they are similar in many ways, and have unique characteristics because of their divergent beginnings and entwined developmental trajectories. These distinctions are generalizations of the two strategies about the degree of concessions each strategy makes in terms of assured accountability. Both strategies can be used in a variety of ways, and after years of development, many of the differences appear to be vague (Yang, 2023). This section will solely focus on collaborative learning and its different aspects, such as benefits and types. It is important to know why this way of education is currently considered to be one of the most effective ones, in what forms it shows up, and the advantages vs. disadvantages of collaborative learning being applied to virtual and physical classroom education.

The reason collaborative learning is preferred in the modern study era is because of its benefits that are divided into organizational and individual (Valamis Group Ltd., 2023).

1. *Organizational benefits*:
    - developing leadership skills by applying their knowledge in organizing, assigning, and teaching situations so that they can learn how to support both themselves and others while leading in such scenarios;

- increasing skills and knowledge needed to be a qualified employee as each employee will have something to teach to others and learn something from others by observing and supervising their groupmates;
- improving relationships across teams and departments is ensured as collaborative learning engages individuals to improve their network within the company.

2. *Individual benefits*:
   - making learning an engaged process by organizing thoughts and presenting them in real time to other peers, as well as being able to defend your ideas, which leads to continuous learning and getting more knowledge;
   - promoting learning from others' points of view – students can find out about different viewpoints and, as a result, learn more;
   - improving critical thinking in scenarios where the learner should be able to support their arguments with new information gathered if the arguments are lacking or vice versa;
   - promoting listening to criticism and being able to construct your constructive criticism points.

Before diving straight into the approaches of collaborative learning, it is important to make sure that the groups have been announced before the start of studies so that students/learners can slightly adapt. Also, the rules of how the groups will operate and be graded should be thoroughly explained. Lastly, before each activity, everything should be planned beforehand by the instructor and ready for implementation; collaborative learning is a very powerful approach if it is correctly constructed in the realms of the classroom.

Several types of collaborative learning can be applied in a class within the online learning environment (University of Maryland, 2024):

1. *Problem-based learning* – each group of students is given a specific problem where they need to understand the requirements to solve it and begin proposing different possible solutions, which leads to constructive discussion.
2. *Jigsaw classroom* – each member of the group takes different parts of the topics and individually investigates them; afterward, the students teach each other the things they have learned.
3. *Small group discussion* – the group has proper guidance taken from instructors, and the group starts a discussion by following the given instructions, where they are usually asked to share some product.
4. *Peer teaching* – a peer of students works together by taking turns in teaching different concepts to each other, thereby enhancing overall understanding through teaching.

Comparison of traditional and cloud-based learning environments: In this section, the implementation of collaborative learning in different environments, particularly in physical and online classrooms, is discussed by focusing on the advantages and disadvantages of each approach.

A physical classroom (or traditional classroom) is a place where teachers and students have a face-to-face learning environment and can interact with each other during class hours or office hours. Inside such classrooms, different equipment and furniture, starting from desks and chairs and ending with projectors and portable computers, help students dive into the academic environment. At the same time, the physical presence of the teachers can make them less distracted.

An online classroom is a digital space where educators and learners can interact, teach, and learn remotely, in most cases via the Internet. They provide all opportunities given by the physical classrooms, including but not limited to virtual office hours, live lectures, discussions with students, online whiteboards, screen sharing, and many more; the advantages can be found in Table 8.1 (Jain, 2024). Online classrooms are customizable and can be accessed through different devices such as PCs, laptops, and smartphones.

Although they were thought to be very effective, the lockdown (due to COVID-19 in 2020) has shown some of the disadvantages they tend to have, which are shown in Table 8.2 (Streamlyn Academy, 2023).

Both approaches have their benefits and proper limitations, so while making a decision on which environment suits the needs, Tables 8.1 and 8.2 can be used as

TABLE 8.1
Comparison of Advantages

Physical Classroom	Online Classroom
Personal interaction with teachers and classmates: • opportunities to have a face-to-face conversation with classmates and teachers; • leads to the improvement of teamwork and real-life communication skills; • better socialization and networking.	Individual approach: • emphasizes the individual approach to each student because online classrooms tend to give statistics about the academic performance of each individual and the whole class.
Less distraction: • the presence of the teacher encourages students to less procrastinate; • the academic environment motivates them to focus on lessons; • no distractions such as phone calls, kids, television, or social media.	Flexibility: • students can attend lessons from any location and at a convenient time that can be changed easily; • the assignments can be completed at any part of the day and don't affect their other work; • the recorded lectures can be watched at any time from any device.
Access to resources: • students can use libraries. Laboratories, and computers that not every student has at home.	Cost-effective: • require fewer materials, minimum expenditures include e-books and Internet connection; • no need for expensive textbooks, lab tools, or transportation fees;

TABLE 8.1 (Continued)
Comparison of Advantages

Physical Classroom	Online Classroom
Development of discipline: • In face-to-face environments, students are more engaged in learning how to appreciate each other, have good manners, and have positive and open-minded behavior. • setting up a routine – waking up early and preparing for the lessons can result in better self-discipline.	Management of study materials: • all materials will be available to students from any location with a stable Internet connection, they also can get materials before the start of the class; • materials can be accessed from different multimedia options; • having continuous access to the study materials facilitates candidates' independent learning; • email system can be used between teachers and students.
Structured learning environment: • strict schedules and detailed curriculum; • helps to stay on track and focused; • practices that have been applied before ensure that all important material is being covered.	E-learning courses: • help to improve the understanding of class materials; • can be useful for self-development; • students who did not have access to physical lectures can indeed attend courses of such lectures; • achievement of extra certificates and knowledge from different tutorials.
	Different testing methods: • the use of more diverse and visually attractive testing methods and platforms can be used; • online quizzes give results faster and provide better analytics that can be used by teachers later.

a reference by considering the curriculum, requirements, time limits, and financial conditions as well as transportation possibilities.

8.3 CLOUD ARCHITECTURE

Cloud computing is the on-demand access of computing resources – physical servers or virtual servers, data storage, networking capabilities, application development tools, software, AI-powered analytic tools, and more – over the internet with pay-per-use pricing (Stephanie & Ian, 2024). It has a significant impact on the daily lives of millions of Internet users who rely on different applications such as Google Gmail, Netflix, and even online video games. Cloud computing is also irreplaceable in various business settings, starting from small startups to global enterprises, as it

TABLE 8.2
Comparison of Disadvantages

Physical Classroom	Online Classroom
Number of students in a class: • for example, teachers cannot handle the number of questions asked by a lot of students at the same time; • there may not be enough resources for all students in the class; • the pace of instruction – some students require more time to learn, while some tend to learn more quickly.	No scope for socializing: • due to a lack of communication and fewer face-to-face talks with peers or other students, it becomes difficult to socialize.
Traveling: • for students who live far away from the education building, it is costly to travel every day both financially and in the means of time; • more finance is spent on meals, tolls; • difficult for students with disabilities.	Technical issues: • in some areas, there may not be a stable Internet connection and students are unable to attend online classes; • the devices may be out of date and getting new ones requires extra expenditures.
Less flexibility: • students have to follow strict schedules and attend at specific locations; • the schedules and locations are not changed in any case except the ones that are accepted by the administrative office; • with fixed schedules, it is difficult to have part-time jobs, or internships that are crucial for university students.	Distractions: • students may attend the classes from home where the environment is not primarily intended for educational purposes; • presence of real-life distractions such as sudden phone calls, kids playing around, or delivery service bringing the package which leads to loss of focus.
The subject–object approach to teacher–student relationships predominates (Sharofat & Ruxsora, 2021).	Motivational problems: • for some students, procrastination arises when there is no one to help them physically or to study together; • the excess of social media leads to motivation to become weaker.
Expenses: • all equipment in the classroom has a reasonable cost, so the charge from students is also noticeable; • teacher's salary and administrative work expenses also are included in the tuition fee; • the expenses can create a financial division between students from different schools/education centers resulting in unequal attitudes toward each other.	

allows applications and data to be accessible from anywhere, which can result in remote work availability. It provides the framework for seamless customer engagement, computing power, and other resources that can be used for generative AI or quantum computing. A cloud services provider at a remote data center manages the pay-as-you-go or monthly subscription fees that are usually required to access cloud-based technology services (Yasar et al., 2023).

The rapid advancement of cloud computing technology has resulted in significant and swift changes to the services offered by the cloud. In addition to the industry, the education system, which was able to enhance its learning patterns and vision with the aid of this technology, has also adopted these changes. A new direction in the education sphere was raised, which is now stated as e-learning systems.

8.3.1 The Benefits of Cloud-Based Learning

The popularity of e-learning systems and tools is rising day by day and becoming widely acknowledged as a qualified learning method. The number of courses in English offered by the LinkedIn platform (one of the most popular and prestigious platforms for job hunting and recruitment) has already exceeded 10,000 (Online Courses, Training, and Tutorials on LinkedIn Learning), which is evidence of e-learning popularity. All these e-learning tools are a combination of resources provided by cloud computing.

The role of cloud in learning is important, as it allows educators and learners to make use of all the listed advantages of online classrooms that were discussed above. Here are the advantages of cloud-based applications that can benefit both teachers and students:

1. Students' reach – the learners can pursue their diploma by enrolling in online courses. This mode of learning is particularly beneficial for those who may not thrive in or have access to traditional classroom settings, providing them with an alternative way to continue their education.
2. Less expensive or subscription-based textbooks – high-quality printed books are expensive, and libraries always have a limited number of such books, cloud-based textbooks are less expensive as they are not printed and delivered to different locations.
3. No outdated learning materials – previously highly costly books, after several years, become outdated and not relevant anymore, and the replacement of all such books is very costly, while cloud-based materials can be easily updated on a real-time basis.
4. Environment – with the help of the cloud, an academically positive environment can be set up where all learners have access to high-quality materials that create different mindful collaborations between learners and academia.

Given that the Internet is a public media with minimal regulation, the cloud not only offers many benefits, but it also presents certain challenges:

1. Security – where the data stored is mostly not known.
2. Privacy – cloud computing makes use of virtual computing technology, which allows user data to be distributed across multiple virtual data centers that may

be situated geographically apart. There may be disagreements about local legal systems' protection of data privacy.
3. Long-term viability – the methods that allow the system to operate even if the cloud provider fails or gets owned by another company.

The solution suggested by Salunkhe and Sandeep Kelkar (Salunkhe & Sandeep, 2024) encourages the use of data encryption to ensure security, minimizing the storage of personal information in the cloud for privacy purposes. As extra measurements, it is suggested to use different access levels for security and have several back-ups for cloud providers fails/shuts.

By exploiting the suggested solutions to the emerging issues, cloud can be used in educational environments without fear, and by this, the understanding of the capabilities and the role of cloud-based learning in modern education systems can be reached.

8.3.2 Service-Oriented Architecture

In a service-oriented architecture (SOA), services function independently and provide functionality or data exchanges to their consumers. The client sends a request for the needed information with input data to the service, and the service then executes the task with the received data and sends the output as a response. For example, if the system wants to perform the registration service, it sends all required information to the service where the service processes the input data and sends back the response stating if the registration was successful or not. In general, SOA (Sanchhaya Education Private Limited, 2023):

1. enables users to create applications by combining numerous features from already-existing services;
2. includes a set of design guidelines that serve to organize the creation of systems and offer ways to combine different parts to create a cohesive, decentralized system;
3. SOA-based computing transforms functionalities into a collection of interoperable services that can seamlessly integrate into diverse software systems across various business domains.

The adoption of SOA in education helps address issues with adaptability by boosting agility, reusing services, and simplifying the integration of new systems. The integration and collaboration of multiple educational tools and systems are made easier in educational settings by cloud computing's SOA. It makes it possible for organizations to effectively put together, employ, and reuse teaching and learning resources. This methodology facilitates tailored educational experiences, easy access to learning materials, and the scalability required to adjust to evolving demands in education. The process involves defining a set of services that can include instructional features like content delivery, student information systems, and assessment tools. These services are then implemented to be interoperable, which means that data exchange for communication is established seamlessly.

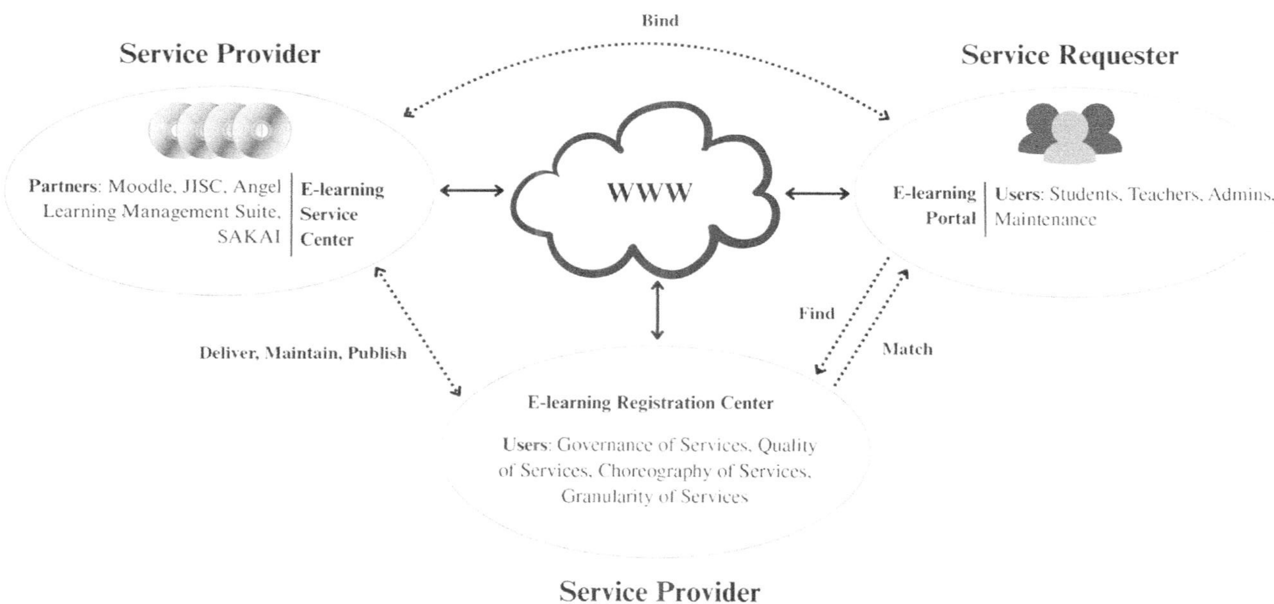

FIGURE 8.1 An Image Representing a Service-oriented Architecture (SOA) for an E-earning System.

The basic parts of a general e-learning system are:

1. audio and video conferencing;
2. virtual classroom/labs;
3. shared whiteboard;
4. application sharing;
5. chat/instant messaging;
6. web-based teaching materials.

SOA divides these parts into individual services, and the developers make them available over a network so that the users' ability to combine and reuse functions in the creation of applications is promoted. These services – and the users who use them – communicate with one another by exchanging data in a standard format or by arranging for an activity to be coordinated between two or more services. The policies and procedures that govern the provision and consumption of services are also included in the SOA. As personal information is private, and security and privacy are considered as important aspects of the education system, only authorized and verified users should have access to such private data.

Figure 8.1 is a diagram that represents an SOA for an e-learning system, and there are three main parts involved:

1. Service Provider: an organization or system that offers e-learning services; responsible for maintaining, delivering, and publishing these services on the web.
2. Service Registry: central directory where services are listed and can be found by potential users or other systems; a place where the characteristics of services such as governance, choreography, quality, and granularity are managed ("E-learning Registration Center"). It acts as a broker to ease the matching and binding of services between providers and requesters.
3. Service Requester: the end-users of the e-learning services, such as students, teachers, administrators, and maintenance personnel. They access the services through an "E-learning portal," which usually provides a user interface for interacting with the different e-learning services offered by the partners.

The service requester uses a web interface to search for and find appropriate e-learning services, and when a service is selected, the system "binds" the requester to the service provider and establishes a connection that allows the requester to use the service. This binding is made easier because of the information stored in the Service Registry. There is also an interaction directly between the service provider and requester, which is probably the use of the e-learning services after they have been discovered and agreed upon through the registry.

8.4 VIRTUAL PROGRAMMING LABS AS LEARNING TOOLS

According to creator Juan Carlos Rodríguez-del-Pino, the creator of VPL for Moodle Learning Management System, "VPL is an activity module that manages programming assignments and whose features are:

1. Enable to edit the program source code in the browser
2. Students can run interactive programs in the browser
3. You can run tests to review the programs.
4. Allows searching for similarity between files.
5. Allows setting editing restrictions and avoiding external text pasting." (Juan, 2021).

In the early studies of coding, students often need constant monitoring of their code from the instructors' side, as they are not aware of the correctness of their work. VPLs are one of the methods that help to contribute to the solution of this problem.

VPL is an open-source (plug-in) software product that allows the management of programming assignments on Moodle and is designed to enhance learning and practice, as well as assess the programming skills of students/learners. Students can write their code in different (available) languages, compile it, see the output, and, in most cases, see the grading for their output, the requirements that instructors set. Usually, the student does not need to install the whole software to implement the actions above. The key features of a VPL consist of the following:

1. *accessibility* – they are accessible from any device that has a connection to the Internet;
2. *support for multiple languages* – general VPL should support several programming languages;
3. *assignment submission* – instructors can use VPL to give students programming tasks, and the VPL collects their work and grades it with the predefined test cases and specific criteria;
4. *immediate feedback* – VPLs usually provide immediate feedback on the code submitted, which includes syntax or logical error messages, so that students can learn from their mistakes and improve their skills;
5. *security and isolation* – VPL should be able to run code in isolation so that no malicious code (or incorrect code) affects the other systems or users.

VPLs are mostly used in educational systems that tend to teach programming to their learners or in tech-related companies for training or upskilling employees, and also by groups of self-motivated learners – individuals who want to sharpen their programming skills with their friends. VPLs are very useful in distance learning environments, online classrooms, and online courses where traditional PC labs are not available or accessible. The ability for students to share resources and files with others is another advantage of VPL. VPL encourages collaborative learning by giving users a way to communicate with one another.

This section discusses the general VPL platforms, their benefits and educational value, cloud infrastructure in VPLs, and their implementation strategies and design principles.

8.4.1 Educational Value of Virtual Programming Labs

At the upper levels of education (universities), programming is typically a solitary task. This can be highly upsetting for struggling students, who often feel alone and ashamed to seek clarification on assignments or tasks. Having numerous mistakes in their code can be discouraging and annoying for inexperienced programmers, as traditional compilers' feedback is often complicated. Due to the size of programming classes, lecturers and instructors face the challenge of having to spend more time compared to the optimal time suggested for grading student work. In such cases, VPLs provide an interactive learning environment where each student can practice programming for real-life problems and improve their understanding of different computer science concepts. They give practical experience with instant feedback and offer accessibility so that each student can complete lab tasks from anywhere and at any time – VPLs support numerous flexible learning opportunities.

Both students and teachers experience the paradigm shift due to the usage of VPLs. The reason for this is that now the teacher needs to pay more attention to the curriculum and lesson preparation (as well as preparing assignments and setting up testing for solutions) before students start their course. Even if this process takes a lot of time, after lessons and assignments, the effort needed for student grading will be much less.

By considering all above aspects, it can be derived that the educational value of VPLs can be seen in the following ways:

1. VPLs can enable students to practice programming in real-world scenarios by improving their understanding of concepts;
2. VPLs can give learners immediate and personalized feedback (e.g., error messages, hints, or solutions);
3. VPLs also give the students a chance to focus and experiment on several parts of the code without adverse consequences;
4. VPLs can help to avoid the technical problems that may arise while setting up the programming software (installing integrated development environment (IDE), configuration issues, etc.).

8.4.2 VPLs Enhancing Collaborative Learning

The students can gain skills that are important in tech industries, which tend to have the collaborative nature of product development, such as communication, problem-solving, and teamwork, with the help of VPLs that simulate the real-world programming environment. Here are the several methods by which VPLs can improve the collaborative learning environment:

1. *Shared Coding Environment* – students can work on the same piece of code at the same time to complete the given assignments, which leads to real-time interaction and problem-solving among team members.
2. *Version Control (VC) Integration* – students can learn the basics of Git/VC, which counts as an essential skill to optimize collaboration within software development.
3. *Peer Review and Feedback* – students can share their codes with their peers and get feedback on their work, which helps them to learn how to accept

critique and how to make constructive criticism as well as how to analyze and understand others' code that is going to be an essential skill in the programming career.

4. *Instructor Intervention* – as groups of students work through coding tasks, instructors can join the VPL and offer advice or suggestions for improvement.
5. *Interactive Learning* – some VPLs can help students stay more engaged and interested by providing gamification elements and interactive activities that make students work in a group and solve different real-life problems.

8.4.3 Design Principles and Implementation Strategies

Integrating virtual labs into e-learning software (as a Learning Management System) involves considering several factors. For example, embed the virtual lab in the e-learning software using the appropriate method, such as an iframe, link, or launch button. Additionally, provide learners with clear and consistent instructions and expectations on how to access and use the virtual lab. Furthermore, incorporate the virtual lab as part of the learning path, such as a pre-requisite or an assessment. Additionally, monitor and support learners' progress and performance in the virtual lab with feedback, scaffolding, or troubleshooting. Lastly, collect and analyze data from the virtual lab to measure completion rates, scores, time spent, or code quality (Hoffman & Eric, 2024).

One of the most exciting and difficult tasks that schools and education systems are currently engaged in is designing activities that integrate inquiry and collaborative learning into virtual labs. The correct design and implementation of the VPL into the education system ensure that the full potential of the VPLs can be employed and that there will not be any technical issues or logical controversies. The strategies considered important are shown in Table 8.3.

8.4.4 Moodle

Moodle is a software application used for e-learning activities. It is a basic IDE that does not require any installation or configuration. It helps with (Komar, 2023):

1. setting up simple management of submissions and evaluations;
2. integration with Moodle Gradebook;
3. the control of the assignment environment;
4. running and evaluating the code without downloading the required software or IDEs for this;
5. building the test cases and customizing the evaluation;
6. identifying the code similarity and plagiarism.

Moodle supports languages such as ADA, Assembler-x86, Lisp, Mips, Groovy, Pascal, Scheme, Shell, Perl, Prolog, Verilog, SQL, Python, Java, JavaScript, C, C++, C#, Go, R, and many more (Rodríguez-del-Pino, 2021). It is crucial to choose the required range of accepted languages that your curriculum and assignment consider while creating the assignment.

TABLE 8.3
Suggested Strategies for VPL Implementation

Strategy	Explanation
Needs Assessment	Find and test the curriculum needs, and state the programming languages and tools that have to be included.
Cloud Platform Selection	Search for available cloud service providers and choose the one that fits your needs by considering scalability, reliability, support, and cost.
Lab Design and Development	Create the lab activities that follow your learning outcomes by using tools that align with real-world programming scenarios.
Infrastructure Setup	Set up development environments, cloud servers, and required software on the cloud platform.
Integration with LMS	For a smooth user experience, connect the VPLs with an already-existing learning management system.
Access Management	To keep the integrity of the labs and the students' work, make sure that secure access control measures are in place.
Testing and Piloting	Initiate pilot tests that help to find technical and usability issues with a small group of students.
Training	Conduct training sessions with instructors and students to make sure that they are familiar with VPL and provide guides.
Support and Maintenance	Set regular updates and maintenance for the lab environments, and also a support system for technical problems.
Monitoring and Analytics	Use monitoring tools to analyze the student participation, performance, and usage, and then utilize the information to enhance and improve the labs.
Feedback Loop	Set up a feedback collection environment that helps to constantly improve VPLs.

Basic steps to consider while creating new VPL activity (Komar, 2023):

1. Create a new VPL activity.
2. Set the name, the description, and the deadline of the activity.
3. Set the limits for the number of files that can be uploaded by students.
4. Set the grade of the activity.
5. Save the activity.

The benefits of using Moodle VPL has not only all the benefits of general VPLs but also the following: it is a simple, non-threatening IDE and provides an opportunity for repetition. However, it also has challenges, such as having different compilers that result in different error messages and results and not supporting binary files. Generally, the VPL environment requires some technical issues like plug-in installs for specific tasks, a Linux web server, and finally, a jail server or firewall access. It is also necessary to configure Moodle, register students, create groups, and, of course, prepare assignments and test cases. It is important to carefully evaluate and consider all the advantages and disadvantages of VPL before implementing it in your system.

8.5 ENSURING SECURITY AND OPTIMIZING PERFORMANCE

As was previously mentioned, using cloud computing for collaborative learning is generally thought to be among the best choices available. It allows users to access and store learning materials and other data remotely on servers. Transferring data to cloud environments, however, may result in privacy concerns or the loss of crucial documents. So, when deploying VPLs, it is important to consider security issues, especially the ones related to the personal information of the users.

Fortunately, newer technologies provide a variety of methods for successfully reducing these difficulties, which benefits the system as well as users. The integrity and confidentiality of data during transmission can be ensured by the usage of encryption mechanisms and algorithms. Modern encryption techniques protect private data traveling through collaborative learning environments from being accessed by unauthorized parties or intercepted by hostile entities. In a similar vein, user authentication is an essential way to confirm the identities of people who want to access VPLs. Stricter user login requirements, such as passwords and entrance codes for particular courses or subjects inside VPLs, can be used to establish a secure infrastructure. Strong authentication prevents unwanted attempts to misuse educational resources by guaranteeing that resources are only accessible to the intended recipients. This protects sensitive information from being misused (Farokhi, 2020).

In collaborative learning environments facilitated by cloud systems, optimizing work processes is important to ensure efficiency and deliver high-quality educational experiences. Two techniques used for this purpose are data caching and workflow parallelism. Data caching stores frequently accessed data in temporary storage closer to users, so the need for repeated data retrieval from remote servers will be less. Caching allows the users to experience significant performance improvements and reduced latency. Data caching techniques also offer several additional advantages, including enhanced performance, bandwidth optimization, and cost reduction, all of which contribute to improving system responsiveness. Workflow parallelism, on the other hand, involves decomposing complex tasks into smaller, independent subtasks that can be executed concurrently. This approach maximizes computational resources and improves processing times. In collaborative learning environments, workflow parallelism optimizes resource utilization and enhances system responsiveness. By using this technique, the system can experience faster execution, scalability, and resource efficiency. This is achieved by distributing complex tasks into subtasks across multiple processing units and cloud instances, which leads to enabling quicker responses and reducing overall execution time. These strategies not only upgrade the efficiency of collaborative learning platforms but also contribute to a more seamless and enriching educational experience for users. By exploiting data caching and workflow parallelism, educators and administrators can unlock the full potential of cloud-based learning environments, collaboration, and knowledge acquisition among learners (Wang et al., 2024).

8.6 LOOKING AHEAD: TRENDS AND FUTURE DIRECTIONS

Technological advancements and the demand for more adaptable and easily accessible learning solutions are driving a significant transformation in the education sector (Prathiksha, 2023). With its revolutionary approach to education, cloud-based learning has transformed traditional learning models and encouraged collaboration between educators and students. The upcoming era of e-learning systems is tightly connected with the rising trend of EdTech – Education Technologies. Educational technology, or Edtech as it's often called, encompasses using technology and tools to enhance the learning experience (Jiek, 2024). EdTech provides a lot of benefits for learners who can show their full potential, for educators who are not bound by different limitations, and for institutions that can provide opportunities to more students than they used to. Here are some of such benefits that can be listed and also considered as current trends of revolutionizing e-learning environments:

1. *Personalized Learning* – with the help of EdTech (a combination of data analytics and machine learning algorithms), teachers can analyze the student's strengths and weaknesses, and by using this information, the adaptive learning systems can create customized learning paths that guarantee each student receives individualized instruction and support.
2. *Cost-effectiveness* – through cost savings and increased efficiency, EdTech optimizes the delivery of education and saves up resources for other important issues; it is done by eliminating the need for expensive physical servers or data centers. Instead, the institutions are encouraged to use the scalable resources from cloud server providers where they can, based on their demand, control the amount of EdTech they need during different periods.
3. *Accessibility and Equity* – by enhancing accessibility and equity in education for students with different needs and learning styles, EdTech helps close the gap; the reason is that access to learning materials is available from any geographic location and any smart device that results in inclusion and the rise of learners from diverse backgrounds.
4. *Collaborative Learning* – students and teachers can interact, exchange knowledge, and grow with one another in a collaborative learning environment that is fostered by EdTech: virtual classrooms, real-time collaboration tools, and discussion forums help learners interact with others without considering the physical distances or limitations.

The way that people interact with educational content, collaborate, and learn is being completely transformed by cloud-based education. For teachers and students around the world, cloud-based education offers new opportunities due to its affordability, scalability, and accessibility. Through personalized instruction and collaborative learning environments, cloud-based education gives students the tools they need to succeed in the digital age.

Here are the top 10 digital trends in education and educational technology:

1. Cloud computing.
2. Mobile/online learning.

3. Artificial intelligence.
4. On-demand video learning.
5. Augmented and virtual reality.
6. Data and analytics.
7. Gamification.
8. Social media/collaborative learning.
9. Interactivity in the classroom.
10. Personalized learning, adaptive learning, and automated assignments.

Almost half of the trends already were discussed in this chapter, which is proof that education also flows to the side of digitalization. EdTech is becoming increasingly important in changing conventional learning paradigms and offering dynamic, inclusive learning experiences to all students as technology advances. Educational institutions and organizations can set the standard for accessible, collaborative, and genuinely transformative learning in the future by adopting cloud-based solutions.

8.7 CONCLUSION

The chapter discusses the important roles of cloud architecture and VPLs within collaborative learning environments. It explains how e-learning has evolved and reshaped educational systems, leading to a new era of digital education. Collaborative learning is analyzed, focusing on its definition, benefits, and various implementable types within online settings. Furthermore, the chapter outlines the disparities between collaborative learning in traditional and virtual environments. Moreover, it underscores the significance of cloud architecture in bolstering e-learning systems' functionality and the utility of VPLs. The educational merit of VPLs in facilitating real-world problem-solving, fostering collaborative coding sessions, and seamless integration with platforms like Moodle is thoroughly explored. The integration of cloud architecture and VPLs into collaborative learning frameworks signifies a noticeable advancement in educational technology, accelerating efficiency, inclusivity, and engagement. As we embark on this new era of virtual education, there remains a wealth of exploration and experimentation ahead. Looking ahead to future trends outlined in the concluding section, it becomes evident that educational systems will continue to undergo digital transformation, leveraging cloud technologies and embracing the latest EdTech trends to deliver optimal education to all learners.

REFERENCES

Farokhi, Farhad. *Privacy in Dynamical Systems.* Springer Nature, 2020. http://books.google.ie/books?id=x8C_DwAAQBAJ&pg=PR7&dq=978-981-15-0492-1&hl=&cd=1&source=gbs_api.

Hoffman, Reid, and Eric Ly. "Online Courses, Training and Tutorials on LinkedIn Learning." *LinkedIn.* Accessed March 20, 2024. www.linkedin.com/learning/search?entityType=COURSE.

Jain, Isha. "Physical vs Virtual Classroom: Which Is Better." *Careers360*, January 19, 2024. Accessed March 15, 2024. https://engineering.careers360.com/articles/physical-vs-virtual-classroom-which-better.

Jiek, Chern. "Top 10 Digital Trends in Education & Educational Technology: Transforming the Future of Learning." *Senpai Corner*, March 14, 2024. www.senpaicorner.com/post/digital-trends-in-educational-technology.

Juan Carlos Rodríguez-del-Pino. "Languages Supported – Virtual Programming Lab for Moodle (VPL) 3.4.3+ Documentation." 2021. Accessed March 22, 2024. https://vpl.dis.ulpgc.es/documentation/vpl-3.4.3+/languagesupported.html.

Komar, Meir. "Integrating Virtual Programming Labs in Higher Education: Benefits, Challenges, and Best Practices." *ResearchGate*, August 14, 2023. https://doi.org/10.13140/RG.2.2.23442.02243.

Prathiksha, S.S. "Cloud-Based Education: Revolutionizing Learning and Collaboration." *LinkedIn*, July 27, 2023. Accessed March 12, 2024. www.linkedin.com/pulse/cloud-based-education-revolutionizing-learning-prathiksha-s-s/.

Rodríguez-del-Pino, J. C. Languages supported - Virtual Programming Lab for Moodle (VPL) 3.4.3+ documentation, 2021. https://vpl.dis.ulpgc.es/documentation/vpl-3.4.3+/languagesupported.html

Salunkhe, Uday, and Sandeep Kelkar. "A Study on the Scope of Cloud Computing in Management Education." *AIMA Journal of Management & Research* 10, no. 2/4 (2016). Accessed March 19, 2024. https://apps.aima.in/ejournal_new/articlesPDF/Uday-Salunkhe.pdf.

Sanchhaya Education Private Limited. "Service-Oriented Architecture." *GeeksforGeeks*, January 10, 2023. Accessed March 26, 2024. www.geeksforgeeks.org/service-oriented-architecture/.

Sharofat, Sobirova, and Ruxsora Karimova. "Advantages and Disadvantages of Traditional and Non-Traditional Lessons, Goals, Objectives and Types." *European Journal of Innovation in Nonformal Education* 1, no. 2 (2021): 233–236. https://inovatus.es/index.php/ejine/article/download/110/92.

Singh, Bharat, Varun Gupta, Animesh Jain, Tarun Vashishth, and Shashank Sharma. "Transforming Education in the Digital Age: A Comprehensive Study on the Effectiveness of Online Learning." International Journal of Scientific Research in Engineering and Management 7, no. 7 (July 2023): 1–11.

Streamlyn Academy. *Classroom vs. Online Learning: 4 Advantages and Disadvantages – 2023*. Streamlyn Academy, September 28, 2023. Accessed March 27, 2024. https://streamlynacademy.com/blog/classroom-vs-online-learning/.

Susnjara, Stephanie, and Ian Smalley. "What Is Cloud Computing?." *IBM*, February 14, 2024. Accessed March 02, 2024. www.ibm.com/topics/cloud-computing.

University of Maryland. *Teaching and Learning Transformation Center*. tltc.umd.edu. Accessed March 21, 2024. https://tltc.umd.edu/instructors/resources/collaborative-learning.

Valamis Group Ltd. *Collaborative Learning*. June 22, 2023. Accessed March 27, 2024. www.valamis.com/hub/collaborative-learning.

Wang, Xiaoda, Yuan Tang, Tengda Guo, Bo Sang, Jingji Wu, Jian Sha, Ke Zhang, Jiang Qian, and Mingjie Tang. "Couler: Unified Machine Learning Workflow Optimization in Cloud." *2024 IEEE 40th International Conference on Data Engineering (ICDE)*, pp. 5224–5237. IEEE, March 12, 2024.

Yang, Xigui. "A Historical Review of Collaborative Learning and Cooperative Learning." *TechTrends*, January 21, 2023. https://doi.org/10.1007/s11528-022-00823-9.

Yasar, Kinza, Wesley Chai, and Stephen J. Bigelow. "Cloud computing." *Cloud Computing*, December 27, 2023. Accessed March 20, 2024. www.techtarget.com/searchcloudcomputing/definition/cloud-computing.

9 Challenges and Solutions in Industrial IoT Education after Navigating the Cloud

Satyajeet Shinge and Urmila Shrawankar

9.1 INTRODUCTION

The Industrial Internet of Things (IIoT), which has been impacting industrial operations with incredible interconnectivity and intelligence since the digital revolution, has emerged as a revolutionary force. Industry adoption of IIoT holds the potential to boost production, efficiency, and innovation, but it also raises a new need: a qualified workforce that can navigate this complex environment. The adoption of IIoT solutions has been greatly aided by the integration of cloud technologies, which make it possible to gather, analyze, and manage data effectively across remote industrial environments. However, while educational institutions work to give students the knowledge and skills they need to succeed in the connected businesses of the modern world, this integration also brings with it a host of new obstacles (Lu, 2022). Education for IIoT involves acquiring knowledge and skills in key areas such as IoT fundamentals, industrial communication protocols, data analytics, machine learning (ML), cloud and edge computing, cyber security, and system integration. Formal education programs, including degree programs and certifications, provide foundational knowledge, while professional development opportunities like workshops, online courses, and hands-on projects offer practical experience. Collaborative learning through research programs and professional networks also plays a crucial role in staying updated with the most recent developments and advised processes in IIoT. This comprehensive educational approach ensures that individuals are well-equipped to design, implement, and manage IIoT systems effectively.

This chapter delves into the multifaceted challenges and pragmatic solutions in IIoT education post-cloud integration. It explores the intricacies of preparing the next generation of professionals to harness the full potential of IIoT within industrial settings. Drawing upon insights from academia, industry, and technological experts, this chapter sheds light on the evolving educational landscape shaped by the

DOI: 10.1201/9781003472537-11

convergence of IIoT and cloud technologies. It examines the nuances of curriculum development, the dynamic nature of technological advancements, and the diverse skill set requirements, resource constraints, security considerations, awareness gaps, and the integration of IIoT education into existing academic frameworks. Moreover, this chapter underscores the critical importance of collaborative efforts between academia and industry in addressing these challenges. By fostering partnerships, knowledge exchange, and joint initiatives, stakeholders can work toward standardizing curricula, ensuring relevance through continuous updates, offering interdisciplinary programs, securing resources for practical learning experiences, and raising awareness about the significance of IIoT education (Lu, 2022).

As we navigate through the complexities of IIoT education post-cloud integration, this chapter serves as a roadmap for educators, policymakers, industry leaders, and students alike. By embracing the challenges and implementing innovative solutions, we can cultivate a workforce poised to drive sustainable growth, innovation, and competitiveness in the digital era of connected industries (Shinge & Urmila, 2022).

9.2 INDUSTRIAL INTERNET OF THINGS

IIoT represents a critical advancement in the integration of internet-connected technologies within industrial environments, aimed at revolutionizing the way industries operate. Unlike the broader consumer-focused IoT, IIoT is specifically tailored to sectors such as manufacturing, energy, logistics, and healthcare. It involves the deployment of interconnected sensors, actuators, and devices on machinery and equipment to gather and exchange real-time data. This data is then utilized to monitor and manage industrial operations with a level of precision and efficiency previously unattainable. By continuously collecting data from various processes, IIoT enables companies to gain actionable insights that drive improvements in operational efficiency, reduce costs, and enhance productivity.

A significant benefit of IIoT lies in its ability to facilitate predictive maintenance. Traditional maintenance schedules often lead to either over-maintenance or unexpected equipment failures, both of which can be costly. IIoT solves this by predicting when an equipment component is likely to break down using real-time data and sophisticated analytics, enabling maintenance to be carried out only when required. This not only minimizes downtime but also extends the lifespan of machinery and reduces maintenance costs. Additionally, IIoT systems can streamline supply chain operations by providing visibility into every stage of the production and distribution process. Improved supply chain agility, lead time reduction, and inventory optimization are all aided by this increased visibility (Akram & Kumar, 2020).

Moreover, IIoT plays a pivotal role in the development of smart factories. These factories leverage IIoT technologies to create highly automated and adaptive production environments. In a smart factory, machines and systems communicate with each other and make autonomous decisions to optimize production processes. This level of automation reduces the need for human intervention, minimizes errors, and enhances the ability to respond quickly to changes in demand or production conditions (Bellavista et al., 2019). For example, if a machine detects a defect in a product, it can automatically adjust its parameters to correct the issue, ensuring consistent product quality and reducing waste.

The transformative impact of IIoT extends beyond operational efficiencies to include the creation of new business models and revenue streams. By leveraging the vast amounts of data generated by IIoT devices, companies can develop innovative services such as predictive analytics, remote monitoring, and performance optimization solutions. These services not only provide additional value to customers but also open up new markets and opportunities for businesses. Moreover, IIoT's capabilities are improved by integration with emerging technologies like artificial intelligence (AI) and ML, enabling more complex data analysis and decision-making procedures. As industries continue to embrace IIoT, it is poised to drive significant advancements in industrial productivity, sustainability, and competitiveness (Akram & Kumar, 2020).

9.3 CLOUD TECHNOLOGY

Cloud technology is one that provides the distribution of computing services—such as storage, servers, databases, networking, analytics, and software over the internet to provide flexible resources, faster innovation, and economies of scale. A cloud service provider can give individuals or companies with on-demand access to technology resources in place of owning and managing physical data centers and servers. IIoT applications benefit greatly from cloud computing's scalable storage, real-time data processing, and sophisticated analytics features. It enables industries to manage vast amounts of data generated by IoT devices efficiently, integrating this data into centralized repositories for comprehensive analysis. Cloud platforms facilitate real-time monitoring and control, allowing for immediate responses to operational changes and issues. Additionally, the integration of ML and AI through cloud services enables predictive maintenance and process optimization, reducing downtime and maintenance costs while improving overall efficiency (Bellavista et al., 2019).

Moreover, cloud technology ensures robust security and compliance, protecting sensitive industrial data with advanced encryption and identity management features. Its scalability and cost-efficiency, through elastic resource allocation and pay-as-you-go models, make it an ideal solution for varying industrial demands. By connecting various enterprise applications and IoT ecosystems, cloud platforms foster collaboration and streamline the development and deployment of IIoT solutions, driving operational efficiency and competitive advantage.

9.4 THE CLOUD-BASED LEARNING ENVIRONMENT FRAMEWORK FOR IIOT EDUCATION

Personalized learning, reflection, and feedback are all supported by cloud technologies that must be integrated into a cloud-based learning environment framework for IIoT education, which is shown in Figure 9.1.

The central component is the learning management system (LMS), which serves as the core platform for hosting course materials, facilitating interactions, and supporting

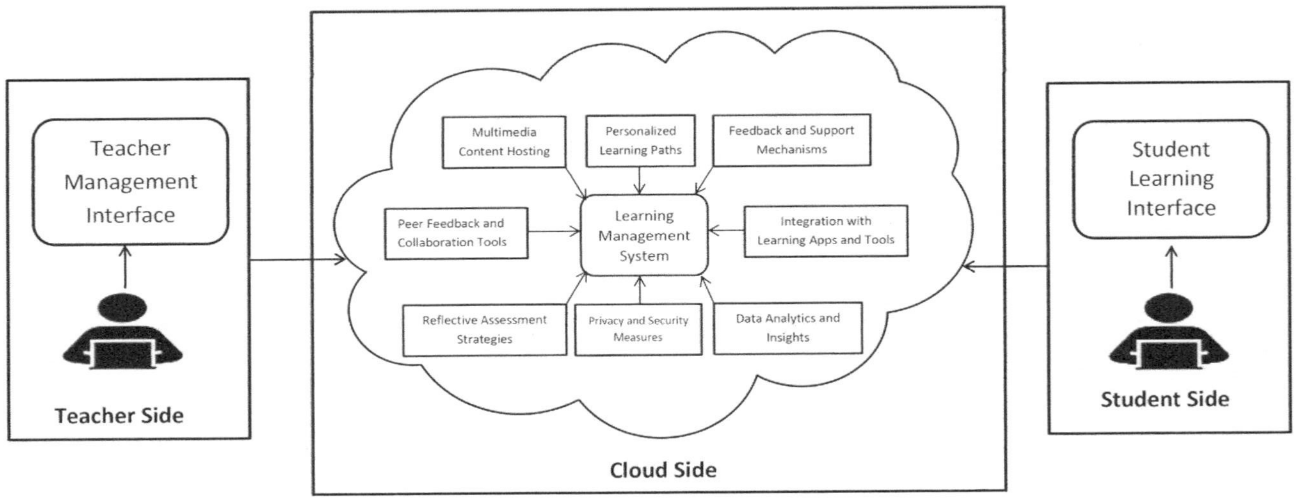

FIGURE 9.1 Cloud-Based Reflective Learning Environment's Framework for IIoT Education.

reflective practices. The LMS is surrounded by a number of cloud-based reflective learning environment components and functionalities which are explained below.

1. *LMS*: Utilize a cloud-based LMS to host course materials, assignments, and discussions. Incorporate features for students to document their reflections within the LMS, such as blogs, journals, or discussion forums dedicated to reflective practices
2. *Multimedia Content Hosting*: Use cloud storage and streaming services to host multimedia content, including videos, podcasts, and interactive simulations, which can stimulate reflection and deeper engagement with course materials.
3. *Peer Feedback and Collaboration Tools*: Integrate cloud-based collaboration tools like discussion forums, chat rooms, and collaborative document editing platforms to facilitate peer feedback and collaborative reflection among students.
4. *Personalized Learning Paths*: Utilize cloud-based adaptive learning tools to provide individualized instruction based on the needs, preferences, and learning styles of each student. Learning analytics, content recommendations, and adaptive tests may all be part of this.
5. *Reflective Assessment Strategies*: Design assessment tasks that encourage reflection, critical thinking, and metacognitive skills. Use cloud-based assessment tools to administer and evaluate reflective assignments, such as reflective essays, self-assessments, or portfolio assessments (Machii & Kyalo, 2016).
6. *Data Analytics and Insights*: Employ cloud-based learning analytics tools to gather data on student engagement, progress, and reflective practices. Analyze this data to gain insights into students' learning processes, identify areas for improvement, and provide timely feedback.
7. *Integration with Learning Apps and Tools*: Integrate cloud-based learning apps and tools that support reflective practices, such as digital annotation tools, mind mapping software, and reflective journaling apps. This allows students to incorporate various technologies into their reflective learning process.
8. *Feedback and Support Mechanisms*: Offer cloud-based communication channels, such as email, instant messaging, and video conferencing, for students to seek feedback and support from instructors, mentors, or peers during their reflective learning journey.
9. *Privacy and Security Measures:* Protect student data and make sure data protection laws are followed by putting strong privacy and security safeguards in place. Secure sensitive data kept in the cloud-based reflective learning environment using encryption, access controls, and frequent security assessments.

9.5 CHALLENGES IN INDUSTRIAL IOT EDUCATION AFTER NAVIGATING THE CLOUD

Following are the challenges for educating IIoT after integration with cloud.

1. *Complexity of Technology Integration*: The integration of technology in IIoT systems poses a significant challenge due to the diverse components involved, such as sensors, actuators, cloud platforms, and networking protocols.

Educators face the task of teaching students how to effectively integrate these components to build functional IIoT solutions. This requires covering topics like sensor and actuator functionalities, secure device-to-cloud connectivity, cloud-based data storage and analysis, and communication protocols. Hands-on experience is essential for reinforcing theoretical knowledge and developing practical skills in designing, developing, and deploying IIoT systems. Through comprehensive instruction and practical projects, educators can prepare students to navigate through the complexities of technology integration in IIoT and excel in modern industrial environments (Naveed et al., 2019).

2. *Skill Gap*: The widening gap between industry demands for IIoT roles and the skills possessed by graduates highlights the pressing need for comprehensive training programs. IIoT education should prioritize equipping students with a diverse skill set, including proficiency in data analytics, cyber security, cloud computing, and hardware integration. Students must develop competencies in analyzing large data volumes, implementing robust cyber security measures, leveraging cloud platforms for efficient data processing, and integrating hardware into IIoT systems. By addressing this skill gap through rigorous training, educators can ensure graduates are prepared to meet IIoT industry demands and foster innovation in industrial settings.
3. *Rapid Technological Advancement*: The rapid evolution of the IIoT presents a significant challenge for educators, requiring them to continuously update the curriculum to keep pace with emerging technologies and standards. Educational programs must be regularly updated to ensure students acquire the latest knowledge and skills demanded by the industry. However, staying current in the dynamic IIoT sector requires educators to identify and integrate new technologies and standards, adapt teaching methodologies, and engage in ongoing professional development. Despite these challenges, educators can enhance curriculum relevance by fostering agility, leveraging industry partnerships, and embracing interdisciplinary collaboration to prepare students for the evolving industrial landscape (Urmila & Dhule, 2021).
4. *Resource Constraints*: Resource constraints present a significant challenge for educational institutions seeking to establish and maintain IIoT laboratories with necessary hardware, software, and cloud infrastructure. Limited budgets often hinder students' access to hands-on experience crucial for mastering IIoT technologies and real-world applications. To address this, educators can explore solutions like partnering with industry for shared resources, utilizing cost-effective alternatives such as virtual laboratories, and advocating for increased funding from academic institutions and government initiatives. By overcoming resource constraints, educators can ensure students receive practical training essential for success in the dynamic IIoT field and contribute to industrial innovation (Naveed et al., 2019).
5. *Security and Privacy Concerns*: For the deployment of IIoT systems, security and privacy concerns are paramount, particularly in critical infrastructure sectors. Educators must educate students on the specific cyber threats targeting IIoT environments and equip them with knowledge of security

protocols, encryption techniques, and access control mechanisms tailored to IIoT systems. Emphasizing the importance of robust security measures throughout IIoT deployment, educators empower students to protect against potential attacks and safeguard critical infrastructure assets from security breaches and privacy violations.

6. *Lack of Standardization*: The lack of standardization in IIoT education poses a significant challenge, resulting in varied teaching approaches and skills imparted to students across institutions. This lack of consistency complicates both employer assessment of job applicants and student credit transfer between programs. Additionally, the absence of standardized curricula hampers the evaluation of graduates' proficiency levels in IIoT-related disciplines. To address this, collaboration between educators and industry stakeholders is crucial to establish common frameworks and guidelines for IIoT education. Standardization efforts can improve the recognition of educational credentials, enhance transparency in learning outcomes, and instill confidence among employers in graduates' skills, ultimately strengthening the IIoT workforce (Mukherjee et al., 2018).
7. *Limited Awareness*: Limited awareness about the potential of the IIoT and its career opportunities presents a challenge for students, educators, and industry professionals. To address this, educational institutions promote IIoT through workshops, outreach initiatives, and partnerships with businesses. These efforts aim to educate individuals about IIoT's transformative impact on industries, showcase career paths, and emphasize the importance of acquiring relevant skills. By engaging with students and professionals through informative sessions and hands-on workshops, institutions can bridge the awareness gap and empower individuals to explore opportunities in the field, fostering a more informed and prepared workforce for the digital age (Odeh et al., 2017).

Addressing these challenges will require a concerted effort from educators, industry leaders, and policymakers to ensure that IIoT education programs remain relevant and effective in preparing students for the future of work in a connected world.

9.6 SOLUTIONS FOR INDUSTRIAL IOT EDUCATION AFTER NAVIGATING THE CLOUD

After navigating the cloud in IIoT education, several solutions can be implemented to enhance learning and prepare students for careers in this field:

1. *Hands-on Lab Environments*: Hands-on lab environments play a crucial role in providing students with practical experience in deploying and managing IIoT systems. These labs should offer cloud-based virtual environments that simulate real-world industrial scenarios, allowing students to interact with various components like sensors, actuators, and cloud-based analytics platforms. Through hands-on experimentation, students can learn to configure, monitor, and troubleshoot IIoT systems, enhancing their problem-solving skills and understanding of IIoT complexities. These immersive learning experiences

foster deeper proficiency in IIoT technologies by offering a safe environment for exploration and experimentation with different configurations and scenarios.

2. *Project-Based Learning*: It is an effective approach to engaging students in the IIoT field, encouraging them to undertake hands-on projects that address real-world industrial challenges. These projects involve designing, building, and implementing IIoT solutions in areas like process optimization, predictive maintenance, energy efficiency, or supply chain management. By applying theoretical concepts to practical scenarios, students gain the skills of critical thinking, problem-solving, teamwork, and communication, necessary for careers in the IIoT. Furthermore, project-based learning fosters creativity and innovation as students explore various solutions and technologies, preparing them for the dynamic landscape of the IIoT industry.
3. *Collaborative Learning Platforms*: Implementing cloud-based collaborative learning platforms is beneficial for enhancing collaborative learning in the IIoT domain. These platforms provide virtual spaces where students can interact with peers, exchange ideas, and collaborate on IIoT projects effectively (Odeh et al., 2017). Features such as discussion forums facilitate meaningful conversations and knowledge sharing, while group chat functionalities promote real-time communication and teamwork. Document-sharing capabilities enable seamless collaboration on project documentation and resource-sharing, while version control features ensure the integrity of project files. By leveraging these platforms, students can develop essential teamwork skills, deepen their understanding of IIoT concepts, and collectively address complex challenges in the field.
4. *Online Courses and Tutorials*: Providing cloud-based online courses, tutorials, and training modules is essential for enriching the learning experience in the IIoT domain. These resources should cover diverse aspects of IIoT technology, offering flexibility and accessibility for students to learn at their own pace. Interactive elements, practical demonstrations, and real-world examples enhance understanding, while assessments and quizzes allow students to evaluate their progress. By leveraging cloud-based platforms for online learning, educational institutions empower students to acquire essential IIoT skills, stay updated with industry trends, and pursue continuous professional development in this rapidly evolving field (Zhou Youhua, 2022).
5. *Industry Partnerships*: Establishing partnerships with industry stakeholders considerably enhances the educational experience for students in the IIoT field. Through collaboration with industry partners, educational institutions provide students access to real-world IIoT applications, case studies, and insights from experts (Qing & Miao, 2022). These partnerships facilitate opportunities like internships, co-op programs, and guest lectures, enabling students to gain hands-on experience, exposure to industry practices, and insights into emerging technologies. Internships and co-op programs allow using theoretical knowledge in practical and building professional networks, while guest lectures offer unique perspectives and trends shaping the IIoT landscape. Strong industry partnerships ensure that IIoT curriculum remains

aligned with industry needs, preparing students for successful careers in this dynamic field.

6. *Continuous Learning and Professional Development*: In the rapidly developing sector of IIoT, professional growth and continuous education are essential (IIoT). Educational institutions can support students by providing access to cloud-based resources for ongoing learning and skill enhancement, such as webinars, online workshops, conferences, and community forums focused on IIoT topics. Participation in these events allows students to stay abreast of industry trends and best practices, ensuring their skills remain marketable and competitive. Encouraging continuous learning reinforces the importance of staying updated in the dynamic IIoT field. Moreover, facilitating connections with IIoT professionals and experts creates valuable networking opportunities for students to collaborate, exchange ideas, and explore career paths.
7. *Evaluation and Feedback Mechanisms*: Cloud-based evaluation and feedback mechanisms are essential for effective IIoT education outcomes. These tools enable continuous assessment of student progress and performance. Instructors utilize online quizzes, assignments, and peer evaluations to gauge comprehension of IIoT principles and practical application. Automated feedback tools provide timely guidance for improvement, enhancing instructional strategies. Leveraging cloud platforms streamlines assessment, promotes transparency, and fosters student engagement and success in IIoT education.

By implementing these solutions into practice, educational institutions may provide a thorough and efficient learning environment for IIoT education, giving students the information, abilities, and real-world experience they need to thrive in the quickly developing IIoT sector.

9.7 CONCLUSION

Addressing the educational challenges posed by the IIoT requires bridging the knowledge gap between academia and industry needs. This chapter highlights challenges such as curriculum standardization, rapid technological evolution, diverse skill requirements, resource limitations, security considerations, and integration into existing educational frameworks. Proposed solutions include collaborative curriculum development, continuous updates, interdisciplinary programs, resource allocation for practical experience, and targeted awareness initiatives. By fostering collaboration between academia and industry, we can equip a skilled workforce to navigate smart and connected industries. These efforts will drive innovation and efficiency, leading to a seamless transition toward a future powered by IIoT technologies.

REFERENCES

Akram, F., & Kumar, R. (2020). Analysis of Collaborative and Convenient E-Learning on Cloud Computing. *International Conference on Smart Electronics and Communication (ICOSEC).*

Bellavista, P., Berrocal, J., Corradi, A., Das, S. K., Foschini, L., & Zanni, A. (2019). A survey on fog computing for the Internet of Things. *Pervasive and Mobile Computing*, 52, 71–99. https://doi.org/10.1016/j.pmcj.2018.12.007

Lu, Q. (2022). Research on flipped classroom teaching mode of computer basic courses based on education cloud platform. *China Management Informatization*, 25(8), 233–235.

Machii, J. K., & Kyalo, J. K. (2016). Assessment of cloud computing adoption for e-learning by institutions of higher learning in Nairobi county Kenya. *International Journal of Scientific Research and Innovative Technology*, 3(2), 9–20.

Mukherjee, M., Shu, L., & Wang, D. (2018). Survey of fog computing: fundamental, network applications, and research challenges. *IEEE Communications Surveys & Tutorials*, 20(3), 1826–1857. doi: 10.1109/COMST.2018.2814571.

Naveed, Q.N., Qureshi, M.R.N.M., Shaikh, A., Alsayed, A.O., Sanober, S., & Mohiuddin, K. (2019). Evaluating and ranking cloud-based e-learning critical success factors (CSFs) using combinatorial approach. *IEEE Access,* 7(10), 157145–157157.

Odeh, M., Garcia-Perez, A., & Warwick, K. (2017). Cloud computing adoption at higher education institutions in developing countries: a qualitative investigation of main enablers and barriers. *International Journal of Information and Education Technology*, 7(12), 921–927.

Qing, Q.L., & Miao, X.(2022). Hybrid teaching practice based on education cloud platform. *IC Application* 39 (3), 224–225.

Shinge, S.R., & Urmila, S. (2022). Cloud-based cost effective IIoT model towards Industry 5.0. *Research Reports on Computer Science*. https://doi.org/10.37256/rrcs.2320232632

Urmila, S., & Dhule, C. (2021). Cloud Computing Technologies for Smart Agriculture and Healthcare: Virtualization Technology for Cloud-Based Services. *Chapman and Hall/ CRC.*

Zhou Youhua, Y.H. (2022). Information technology hybrid teaching based on smart education cloud platform. *Office Automation*, 27(11), 21–23.

10 Cloud-Powered Distance Learning

Breaking Geographical Barriers in Education

Vinay Kumar Yandrapalli and Shubham Sharma

10.1 INTRODUCTION

In the ever-evolving landscape of education, distance learning has emerged as a pivotal solution to bridging the educational divide, enabling learners from all corners of the globe to access quality education. As we progress through the digital age, integrating cloud computing into distance learning platforms has revolutionized education delivery, rendering it more accessible, flexible, and inclusive than ever before (Alam 2022) This chapter explores the significant role that cloud technology plays in enhancing distance learning and breaking down the geographical barriers that have historically restricted educational opportunities.

Cloud computing, a technology that enables internet-based access to data and applications, is currently leading the way in educational innovation (Li et al. 2021). Its ability to provide scalable resources on demand has proven to be a game-changer for academic institutions worldwide. With cloud-based solutions, educators and students can interact in real time, regardless of physical location, and access vast learning resources without heavy infrastructure investments (Khan et al. 2021). This shift toward cloud-powered education systems offers numerous advantages, including reduced costs, enhanced collaborative opportunities, and a level of customization that traditional learning environments struggle to match. Particularly in distance learning, cloud technology facilitates a more dynamic, interactive, and personalized educational experience that can adapt to the unique needs of each learner.

While distance learning has made significant strides in making education accessible, it often struggles with issues such as lack of real-time interaction, limited access to resources, and difficulty personalizing learning experiences (Ali and Alourani 2021). Traditional online learning environments sometimes offer a one-size-fits-all approach, which can hinder the learning process for those who need more tailored educational support (Alam 2022). Furthermore, the dependency on physical infrastructure and the high costs associated with scaling educational resources pose substantial challenges for expanding access in underserved regions.

DOI: 10.1201/9781003472537-12

This chapter explores how cloud computing can address these fundamental gaps in traditional distance learning systems. By leveraging cloud technology, educational institutions can offer scalable, flexible, and more interactive learning environments. This exploration is crucial for understanding how technological advancements can help overcome longstanding educational barriers, making learning more accessible, personalized, and efficient.

In this chapter, we delve into how cloud computing technologies can significantly enhance distance education delivery. Here are the critical areas for our exploration:

1. We explore how the integration of AI and cloud computing can customize learning experiences to meet individual needs. This personalized approach allows educational content and pacing to adjust dynamically based on a learner's progress and understanding, which can lead to improved educational outcomes.
2. We discuss the implementation of virtual labs on cloud platforms, which provide students with practical, hands-on experience in subjects such as science and engineering without the need for physical lab equipment. Students worldwide can access these virtual labs from any location, enhancing their access to practical learning.
3. We explore developing and using cloud-based collaborative platforms that enable students and teachers to interact in real time. These platforms facilitate live discussions, feedback, and group projects, replicating the interactive aspects of traditional classrooms in a digital environment.
4. We detail strategies for the effective deployment of cloud services in educational settings. This includes choosing the right type of cloud service (e.g., IaaS, PaaS, or SaaS) based on institutional needs, planning for scalability to accommodate varying numbers of users, and ensuring cost-effectiveness without compromising quality.
5. We address the crucial data security and privacy aspects of cloud-based educational systems. Given the sensitive nature of personal and academic data, this section outlines best practices for securing data and protecting privacy, ensuring that institutions can maintain trust and comply with regulatory requirements.

Through these detailed points, the chapter aims to provide a comprehensive look at the transformative potential of cloud computing for reshaping distance learning. Each area highlights the advancements and addresses practical considerations and challenges, offering a balanced view of the current and future state of cloud-powered education. This structured approach ensures the information is clear and actionable for educational stakeholders looking to adopt and optimize cloud technologies.

This chapter contributes to the broader discourse on enhancing distance learning through technology by offering a comprehensive overview and actionable insights. It provides educators, administrators, and policymakers with valuable information on harnessing cloud computing to extend educational opportunities and elevate the quality of education, fostering a more inclusive and informed global society.

10.2 RELATED WORKS

Exploring the potential of cloud computing in education reveals diverse approaches and methodologies that highlight the technology's capacity to enhance distance learning. One study focused on asynchronous learning platforms, utilizing a mixed-methods approach that combined quantitative user engagement data with qualitative feedback from participants. This analysis revealed improved engagement and retention among learners, although it identified a notable gap in the capacity for real-time interaction (Wu and Plakhtii 2021). Research has developed an AI-powered model that adapts the learning materials and pace to each student's performance, as determined by machine learning algorithms on large interaction datasets. This model markedly enhanced learning outcomes, yet it underscored the necessity for robust data collection methods to ensure its effectiveness (Lakshmi et al. 2022).

Additionally, the implementation of virtual labs, specifically in the context of chemistry education, demonstrated significant potential. Through a controlled experiment comparing groups of students, those using cloud-based virtual labs showed superior conceptual understanding, validating the practical utility of virtual environments in science education (Luna-Encalada et al. 2021). These studies collectively emphasize the transformative capabilities of cloud technology in education while also pointing to areas that require further refinement, such as data handling and the provision of real-time educational interactions.

In the quest to enhance educational delivery through cloud computing, various research initiatives have explored different facets of its application. Notable research examines the use of cloud-based collaborative tools in rural schools to improve student interaction. A longitudinal study documented improvements in collaboration but also highlighted significant challenges with internet connectivity, highlighting the inherent dependencies on robust infrastructure (Wu et al. 2020). Concurrently, another research effort focused on the strategic deployment of cloud services within higher education. This study employed a strategic framework, analyzed through case studies across multiple universities, demonstrating that cloud adoption could significantly reduce costs and enhance institutional flexibility. However, it also raised concerns about potential issues such as vendor lock-in and data sovereignty, which could impede the autonomy of educational institutions (Aljawarneh 2020).

Another study scrutinized the integrity and security of data within cloud-based educational systems and proposed a new security model. This model, tested through simulations, effectively reduced the incidence of data breaches. Nevertheless, it underscored the necessity for continuous monitoring to safeguard against evolving cybersecurity threats (Maiia 2020). These studies collectively underscore the multifaceted impact of cloud computing on education, highlighting its transformative potential and the challenges that need addressing to maximize its benefits.

The continued expansion of cloud computing in education has prompted diverse investigations into its scalability, technological integration, data management, and infrastructure requirements. A pivotal study on the scalability of cloud platforms examined their ability to handle surges of online learners, particularly during peak times. The study affirmed the platforms' robust scalability through simulations of user load variations, but it also emphasized the need for more sophisticated load forecasting techniques to better manage future demands (Kovalevskaia 2021). Simultaneously, research into integrating augmented and virtual reality (AR/VR) technologies within cloud-based educational settings highlighted their potential to significantly enhance student engagement and comprehension. This study, which focused on engineering education, identified the high costs associated with setting up such technologies as a significant barrier, despite notable improvements in learning outcomes when using AR/VR tools (Khan et al. 2021).

Furthermore, a detailed analysis of data management practices within cloud-based educational systems sheds light on the intricacies of data lifecycle management. The study looked at system architectures and data flows to give useful tips for managing data and to bring attention to the ongoing problems with data interoperability that might make it harder for educational processes to run smoothly (Ivanova 2021). Finally, we examined the critical issue of internet dependency, specifically its impact on remote learners. The research utilized surveys and interviews to illustrate how the digital divide hinders effective learning through cloud-based systems, advocating for significant policy interventions to enhance broadband access in underserved areas. This study emphasized that reliable high-speed internet remains a cornerstone for implementing cloud education, particularly in remote and rural settings (Cheng 2020).

The comprehensive review of recent literature on cloud computing in education highlights the significant advancements and persistent challenges in this field. These studies collectively demonstrate cloud technology's potential to revolutionize educational delivery by enhancing accessibility, interaction, and personalization. However, they also highlight crucial gaps that require attention to fully utilize this technology in various learning environments.

10.3 PROPOSED APPROACH

10.3.1 Enhancing Real-Time Interaction in Distance Learning

This subsection aims to enhance real-time interaction capabilities in cloud-based distance learning platforms. Improved real-time interaction facilitates better engagement, immediacy in feedback, and a stronger sense of community among students and teachers.

Strategies

1. Integration of Real-Time Communication Tools:
   - Incorporate video conferencing tools that support high-definition video and audio to provide a classroom-like experience. To enhance interactivity, key features should include screen sharing, breakout rooms, and real-time polling.
   - Implement chat functionalities that allow students to ask questions and interact during lectures, which promotes a more inclusive learning environment.

2. Latency Reduction Techniques:
   - Utilize edge computing to process data closer to the user's location. This significantly reduces latency, enhancing the synchronicity of real-time interactions.
   - Adopt real-time protocols, such as WebRTC (Web Real-Time Communication), which supports browser-based real-time communication. WebRTC facilitates direct, peer-to-peer communication, bypassing server relays and reducing delay.
3. Load Balancing and Scalability:
   - Implement algorithms for dynamic resource allocation that can adjust the computational and bandwidth resources in real time based on the current demand.
   - Use a predictive scaling algorithm that forecasts the resources required at different times based on historical data.

Let $\left(N(t)\right)$ represent the number of users at time (t),and $\left(R(t)\right)$ represent the resources allocated. The goal is to minimize resource wastage while avoiding under-provisioning:

$$R(t) = \alpha \cdot \max_{\tau \in [t-'' t, t]} N(\tau) \tag{10.1}$$

where (α) is a scaling factor to ensure there is always a buffer of resources, and (Δt) is the look-back period for maximum usage estimation

Figure 10.1 illustrates the process flow for managing and facilitating real-time interaction within a cloud-based educational system. The flow begins with user login and progresses through connection to the nearest data center, which utilizes edge computing to reduce latency. If sufficient resources are not available, a load balancing check ensures their availability and dynamically allocates additional resources. The system then launches the real-time communication tools, such as WebRTC, enabling various interactive features like video, chat, and other real-time interactions. The session concludes once the interaction ends, showcasing an efficient system that supports seamless communication and learning.

10.3.2 Cost-Effective Implementation of AR/VR Technologies

This subsection aims to detail strategies for implementing AR and VR technologies in educational settings cost-effectively. These technologies can significantly enhance the learning experience by providing immersive and interactive environments, but they often come with high costs.

Strategies

1. Utilization of Open-Source Tools:
   - Many open-source tools can reduce the overall cost of softwarc in AR and VR setups.

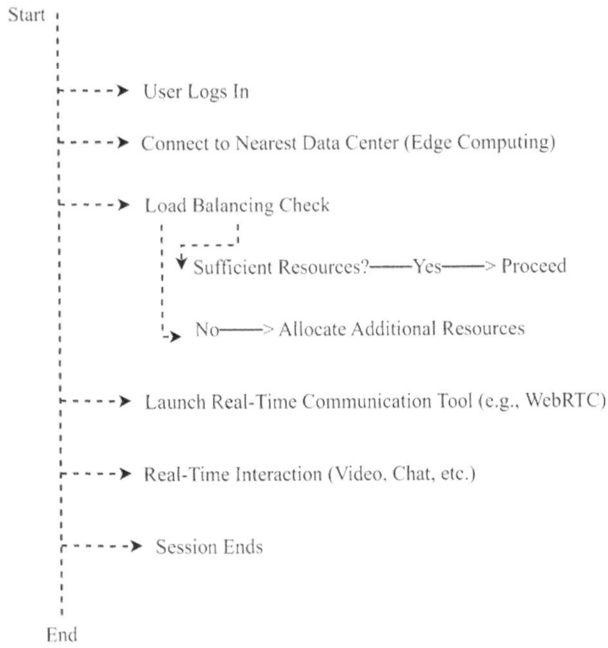

FIGURE 10.1 Flow Chart of Real-Time Interaction System in Cloud-Based Education.

- Educators and IT departments can customize open-source AR/VR platforms such as A-Frame (for VR) and AR.js (for AR) to their specific educational needs without the licensing costs associated with proprietary software.

2. Shared Cloud Services for AR/VR:
   - Complex AR and VR graphics are rendered using cloud computing. This approach offloads the graphical computation from local devices to the cloud, allowing institutions to use less expensive hardware.
   - Develop a cost–benefit analysis model that compares the upfront and ongoing costs of local versus cloud-rendering solutions for AR and VR. Let C_L be the cost of local rendering setups per user, and C_C be the cost of cloud-based rendering per user. The total cost for N users can be calculated as:

$$\text{Total Cost} = N \times \left(\gamma \cdot C_L + (1-\gamma) \cdot C_C\right) \tag{10.2}$$

where γ is the proportion of the workload handled locally.

3. Partnerships with Technology Providers:
   - Form strategic partnerships with tech companies that specialize in AR and VR technologies. These partnerships can provide access to cutting-edge technology at reduced costs, or even on a shared-cost model.

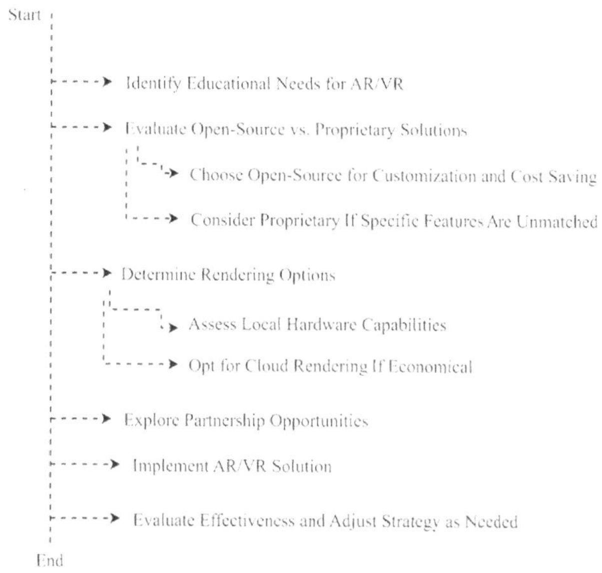

FIGURE 10.2 Decision-Making Flowchart for Implementing Cost-Effective AR/VR Technologies in Education.

- Such collaborations can also foster technological enhancements tailored to educational needs and potentially offer students opportunities for internships and hands-on experience with AR and VR.

Figure 10.2 presents a detailed decision-making flowchart for strategically implementing AR/VR technologies in educational settings, focusing on cost-effectiveness. The flowchart identifies the educational needs for AR/VR technologies and evaluates the trade-offs between open-source and proprietary solutions. It guides decision-makers through assessing local hardware capabilities versus the potential benefits of cloud rendering. The chart also emphasizes the importance of exploring partnership opportunities with technology providers to reduce costs and enhance technological capabilities. The process concludes with the implementation of the chosen AR/VR solution, followed by an evaluation phase to measure effectiveness and make necessary adjustments.

10.3.3 Strengthening Data Security and Advocating for Improved Internet Access

This subsection aims to concurrently address the crucial aspects of enhancing data security in cloud-based educational systems and advocating for policies that ensure improved internet access. This dual focus acknowledges the interdependence of robust security measures and reliable internet connectivity in optimizing the efficacy and reach of cloud-powered education.

Strategies

1. Data Security Enhancements:
   - Ensure the protection of sensitive information from unauthorized access by implementing state-of-the-art encryption protocols for all data transmitted and stored in the cloud.
   - Conduct regular security audits and vulnerability assessments to identify and mitigate potential security threats. Adopting continuous monitoring systems should complement these audits to detect and respond to security breaches in real time.
   - Strengthen user authentication mechanisms by implementing multi-factor authentication (MFA) across all access points. Employ robust access control policies that ensure users can only access data pertinent to their roles and responsibilities.
2. Internet Accessibility Initiatives:
   - Work with government bodies and Internet Service Providers (ISPs) to advocate for and implement policies to extend broadband infrastructure, particularly to underserved areas.
   - Encourage the creation and expansion of subsidy programs that make internet access more affordable for educational institutions and economically disadvantaged students.
   - We support the establishment of community internet access points, such as WiFi-enabled public libraries and community centers, that provide reliable internet access in remote areas.
3. Integrated Policy Development:
   - To ensure alignment and mutual reinforcement of initiatives for improving internet access and data security, establish joint task forces comprising educators, technologists, policymakers, and community leaders.
   - Initiate public awareness campaigns to educate stakeholders about the importance of data security and reliable internet access, highlighting how these elements are critical to the success of digital education.
4. Technological and Policy Synergy:
   - Develop adaptive policy frameworks that can dynamically adjust to technological advancements in data security and evolving needs for internet infrastructure.
   - Implement mechanisms to regularly assess the effectiveness of security measures and internet access initiatives, allowing for timely adjustments based on feedback from educational institutions and users.

This approach ensures a secure educational environment by merging the strategies for strengthening data security with those aimed at enhancing internet access. It broadens its reach to include a more extensive and diverse student population. The integrated approach acknowledges the importance of secure, continuous access to educational resources, as well as the critical role of reliable internet connectivity in achieving this. Such comprehensive measures are essential to foster a safe and inclusive digital learning landscape where all students, regardless of geographical or economic circumstances, can benefit from advanced educational technologies.

10.4 OUTCOMES AND IMPLICATIONS

10.4.1 Enhanced Learning Experiences

We expect integrating enhanced real-time interactions, AR, and VR technologies into cloud-based educational platforms to significantly enhance student engagement by creating immersive learning experiences that mimic physical interaction. Features such as live discussions and instant feedback promote active participation. At the same time, AR and VR tools help visualize complex concepts, making learning more accessible and engaging, particularly for experiential subjects like science and engineering. Additionally, students from remote or underserved areas will find quality educational resources more accessible because of advancements in cloud infrastructure and improved internet access initiatives. Secure and scalable cloud solutions ensure that more students can simultaneously access these resources without performance lapses, promoting inclusivity. These technologies not only make education more accessible but also more equitable, especially for students requiring specific accommodations, fundamentally transforming the educational landscape into a more dynamic, inclusive, and effective environment.

10.4.2 Technological Advancements

Cloud-based educational technologies, AR/VR, and enhanced data security measures can propel technological advancements significantly. These technologies catalyze innovation by facilitating immersive and interactive learning experiences previously unfeasible with traditional methods. AR and VR, for instance, allow students to engage deeply with material that benefits from visual and experiential learning, revolutionizing fields such as medical education, engineering, and science. Moreover, the continuous enhancement of cybersecurity within educational platforms ensures these innovations remain sustainable and secure. This protects users and builds trust in digital educational systems, encouraging wider adoption. We anticipate that these evolving technologies will drive further innovations in educational practice and technology deployment, thereby expanding applications and improving technology. This cycle of innovation and improvement will likely yield significant advancements in the educational technology landscape, enhancing both the effectiveness and reach of digital learning globally.

10.4.3 Policy and Societal Changes

We expect implementing cloud-based educational technologies to trigger significant policy and societal changes, primarily due to the influence of broadband infrastructure and digital equity. Advocacy for improved internet access will likely prompt policy changes that could increase investment in digital infrastructure, making high-speed internet more accessible, especially in underserved areas. This, in turn, supports the broader goal of digital equity, ensuring that all students, regardless of geographic or economic barriers, have access to quality education. We anticipate that these policy shifts will impact society by promoting economic development. Enhanced access to education broadens the skilled workforce, potentially reducing economic disparities and fostering economic growth. Moreover, as digital education becomes more embedded in societal norms, it encourages a shift toward lifelong learning and continuous professional development, aligning instruction more closely with evolving industry demands. This policy-driven transformation will likely lead to a more informed, educated, and equitable society, underpinning communities' sustainable growth and resilience worldwide.

10.4.4 Challenges and Considerations

Implementing cloud-based educational technologies presents several challenges and considerations that require attention to ensure successful adoption and sustained impact. One primary challenge is resistance to change, particularly from educational institutions accustomed to traditional teaching methods. Overcoming this often requires substantial change management efforts, including training educators and administrators to adapt to new technologies. Another significant concern is technological literacy among users, which varies widely and can hinder the effective use of advanced digital tools. Planning and budgeting for initial setup costs and ongoing maintenance is a logistical and financial challenge in ensuring equitable access to these technologies.

Additionally, there are considerations around the scalability of digital solutions to handle increased user loads without degradation in performance or service quality. Addressing these challenges necessitates a thoughtful approach to implementation, including robust support systems, clear communication strategies, and continuous feedback mechanisms to adapt and refine technological deployments. This will guarantee the complete realization and long-term sustainability of the benefits of digital education.

10.5 CONCLUSION AND FUTURE WORK

This chapter has explored integrating cloud computing technologies into distance education, highlighting their potential to revolutionize learning environments by enhancing real-time interactions, implementing cost-effective AR/VR technologies, and ensuring robust data security. We also discussed the critical role of improved internet access in expanding educational opportunities. Our proposed approach uses cloud computing to create dynamic, inclusive, and secure educational settings. By enhancing real-time interaction capabilities, deploying AR/VR technologies cost-effectively, strengthening data security, and advocating for policies that ensure universal internet access, we aim to address the gaps identified in traditional and digital education systems. We designed these strategies to be scalable and adaptable, meeting the diverse needs of the global student population. We expect implementing these strategies to result in more engaging and interactive learning experiences, higher levels of student retention, and broader access to educational resources. Integrating AR/VR technologies, in particular, should make complex subjects more accessible and enjoyable, thus enhancing the quality of education. Meanwhile, projections suggest that improved data security measures and reliable internet access will foster trust in digital learning platforms, expanding their reach to underserved communities.

There is substantial scope for further research into the long-term impacts of these technological interventions on student outcomes and educational equity. Future studies could explore more advanced, cost-effective cloud solutions and evaluate their scalability and effectiveness across educational contexts. Additionally, ongoing policy adjustments and technological advancements will likely provide new opportunities and challenges, necessitating continuous adaptation and evaluation of digital education strategies.

REFERENCES

Alam, Ashraf. "Cloud-based e-learning: Scaffolding the environment for adaptive e-learning ecosystem based on cloud computing infrastructure." In *Computer Communication, Networking and IoT: Proceedings of 5th ICICC 2021*, Volume 2, pp. 1–9. Springer Nature Singapore, 2022.

Aljawarneh, Shadi A. "Reviewing and exploring innovative ubiquitous learning tools in higher education." *Journal of Computing in Higher Education* 32, no. 1 (2020): 57–73.

Ali, Ashraf, and Abdullah Alourani. "An investigation of cloud computing and E-learning for educational advancement." *International Journal of Computer Science Network Security* 21, no. 11 (2021): 216–222.

Cheng, Yung-Ming. "Students' satisfaction and continuance intention of the cloud-based e-learning system: roles of interactivity and course quality factors." *Education + Training* 62, no. 9 (2020): 1037–1059.

Khan, Shahnawaz, Ayman Al-Dmour, Vikram Bali, Mustafa Raza Rabbani, and K. Thirunavukkarasu. "Cloud computing based futuristic educational model for virtual learning." *Journal of Statistics and Management Systems* 24, no. 2 (2021): 357–385.

Kovalevskaia, Natalia, Emma Nikolaevna Gilyazeva, Olga Fedorovna Lobazova, Irina Albertovna Duborkina, and Antonina Pavlovna Sokolova. "Impact of digital services of hybrid cloud-based learning environment on efficiency of education." *Revista Tempos E Espaços Em Educação* 14, no. 33 (2021): e15297–e15297.

Lakshmi, G., S. Brindha, J. Divya, and N. Shobhanali. "AI-powered digital classroom." In *2022 International Conference on Communication, Computing and Internet of Things (IC3IoT)*, pp. 1–6. IEEE, 2022.

Li, Feng, Hui Lu, Meiqian Hou, Kangle Cui, and Mehdi Darbandi. "Customer satisfaction with bank services: The role of cloud services, security, e-learning and service quality." *Technology in Society* 64 (2021): 101487.

Luna-Encalada, Washington, Jonny Guaiña-Yungan, and Fernando Molina-Granja. "E-learning ecosystem's to implement virtual computer labs." In *Learning Technology for Education Challenges: Proceedings of the 9th International Workshop, LTEC 2021*, Kaohsiung, Taiwan, July 20–22, 2021, pp. 77–89. Springer International Publishing, 2021.

Marienko, Maiia V. "The current state of using the cloud-based systems of open science by teachers of general secondary education." In *Proceedings of the 1st Symposium on*

Advances in Educational Technology (AET 2020), Volume 2, pp. 466–472. Science and Technology Publications.

vanova, Tatyana, Valentina Terzieva, and Malinka Ivanova. "Intelligent technologies in E-learning: Personalization and interoperability." In *Proceedings of the 22nd International Conference on Computer Systems and Technologies*, pp. 176–181. 2021. Association for Computing Machinery.

Wu, Huaming, Ziru Zhang, Chang Guan, Katinka Wolter, and Minxian Xu. "Collaborate edge and cloud computing with distributed deep learning for smart city internet of things." *IEEE Internet of Things Journal* 7, no. 9 (2020): 8099–8110.

Wu, Wei, and Anastasiia Plakhtii. "E-learning on cloud computing." *International Journal of Emerging Technologies in Learning (iJET)* 16, no. 10 (2021): 4–17.

11 The Comprehensive Study for Enhancing Security in Cloud-Based Learning Environments through Blockchain

Jagdish Pimple, Arti Burghate, Shraddha Raut, and Anil Band

11.1 INTRODUCTION

Cloud computing has changed the face of education in recent years by offering adaptable and scalable solutions to satisfy the various demands of teachers and students. The confidentiality, integrity, and availability of sensitive educational data are under risk due to the major security concerns brought about using cloud technology in educational contexts. According to recent studies, insider threats, cyberattacks, and data breaches are some of the main issues (Bin Sarhan and Altwaijry, 2022; Sarkar et al., 2022).

Moreover, the potential of blockchain technology to tackle security concerns in cloud environments has attracted interest. The application of blockchain in protecting federated learning frameworks and integrating it with cloud computing has been covered in studies by Qammar et al. (2022), Gai et al. (2020), and Zou et al. (2021), showing both the advantages and difficulties in improving security and privacy.

Additionally, encryption methods are essential for protecting data in cloud-based learning settings. While Ogala et al. (2023) underlined the significance of sophisticated cryptographic techniques for preserving data integrity and secrecy, Goel et al. (2024) suggested using homomorphic encryption.

Additionally, to react quickly to new threats, adaptive security frameworks designed specifically for cloud-based learning platforms have been put forth (Kaur and Aggarwal, 2021); Alenezi (2023) emphasizes how crucial it is for digital learning environments to continuously adapt to emerging security threats.

Educating users about cybersecurity remains paramount for the effectiveness of technical measures. Sahid and Maleh (2023) suggested integrating virtual cloud-based labs into educational curricula to enhance cybersecurity awareness and competence among users of cloud-based learning systems.

DOI: 10.1201/9781003472537-13

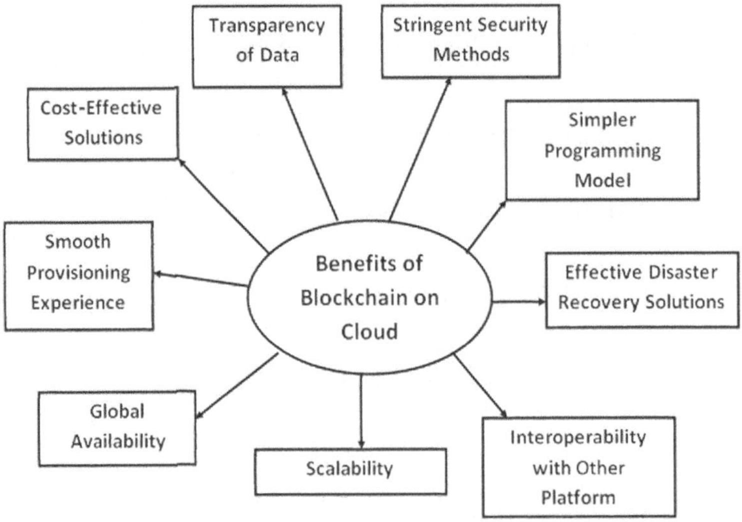

FIGURE 11.1 Benefits of Blockchain on Cloud.

Considering the multifaceted nature of security challenges in cloud-based learning environments, this comprehensive study aims to explore the role of blockchain technology in enhancing security. By synthesizing existing literature and analyzing key findings, this study seeks to provide insights into effective strategies for mitigating security risks and fostering a secure learning environment in the cloud.

Blockchain technology holds significant promise for enhancing e-learning in cloud computing environments due to several key reasons:

1. **Security and Trust:** Blockchain technology provides a decentralized, unchangeable ledger that records all interactions and transactions inside the e-learning ecosystem. By guaranteeing data integrity, authenticity, and transparency, this reduces the likelihood of fraud, tampering, and unauthorized access. In cloud-based e-learning systems that store and communicate sensitive student data and instructional materials, blockchain technology can strengthen security protocols, promote user confidence, and thwart cyberattacks.
2. **Credentialing and Certification:** Academic credentials, certifications, and accomplishments can be safely and verifiably stored and managed via blockchain-based credentialing systems. Employers, educational institutions, and other stakeholders can share tamper-proof digital badges and certifications that e-learning systems are able to produce by utilizing blockchain technology. This reduces the possibility of credential fraud in the cloud environment, expedites the verification process, and strengthens the legitimacy and mobility of credentials.
3. **Decentralization and Accessibility:** Blockchain technology removes the need for centralized servers and middlemen by enabling decentralized

e-learning material distribution and storage. In remote or underserved locations where access to traditional educational infrastructure may be limited, this decentralized method improves accessibility, scalability, and availability of educational materials. Blockchain technology can be used by cloud-based e-learning platforms to build peer-to-peer networks for content sharing, teamwork, and decentralized learning communities.

4. **Data Privacy and Ownership:** Users that use cloud-based e-learning environments give their personal information and learning data to third-party cloud providers, making data privacy and ownership critical concerns. Blockchain provides ways to protect user privacy and give people more control over their data. By using cryptographic methods like private key management and zero-knowledge proofs, blockchain helps users to keep control over their learning data while allowing only those who are allowed access. In cloud-based e-learning systems, this improves data sovereignty, user autonomy, and privacy protection.
5. **Smart Contracts and Micropayments:** Smart contracts built on blockchain technology allow parties to automatically and self-execute agreements within predetermined parameters. Smart contracts can be used in e-learning to support a variety of interactions and transactions, including content licensing, course enrollment, assessment grading, and royalties paid to content authors. Furthermore, blockchain facilitates microtransactions with cryptocurrency tokens, opening up easy and affordable monetization options for cloud-based e-learning services and content.

11.2 LITERATURE SURVEY

Cloud computing has revolutionized educational environments by offering scalable and flexible solutions, yet it also introduces significant security challenges. Insider threats, cyberattacks, and data breaches are among the primary concerns highlighted in recent studies (Bin Sarhan and Altwaijry, 2022; Sarkar et al., 2022). The integration of ML and AI has emerged as a critical approach to enhancing security in these environments.

Blockchain technology is increasingly recognized for its potential to address security issues in cloud environments. Qammar et al. (2022) discussed the application of blockchain to secure federated learning frameworks, and Gai et al. (2020) along with Zou et al. (2021) reviewed the integration of blockchain with cloud computing, highlighting its benefits and challenges in enhancing security and privacy.

Encryption techniques are essential for protecting data in cloud-based learning environments. Goel et al. (2022) proposed the use of homomorphic encryption to secure data without compromising system performance. Ogala et al. (2023) emphasized the importance of advanced cryptographic methods for maintaining the integrity and confidentiality of data in knowledge management systems. Adaptive security frameworks that respond dynamically to emerging threats are crucial. Kaur and Aggarwal (2021) proposed an adaptive security framework tailored for cloud-based learning platforms, focusing on real-time threat detection and response mechanisms. Alenezi (2023) underscored the importance of continuously adapting digital learning environments to new security challenges through innovative solutions.

Educating users about cybersecurity remains vital for the effectiveness of technical measures. Sahid and Maleh (2023) suggested integrating virtual cloud-based labs into educational curricula to enhance cybersecurity awareness and competence among users of cloud-based learning systems. Overall, the literature indicates that enhancing security in cloud-based learning environments requires a multifaceted approach involving advanced technologies such as AI, ML, blockchain, and encryption. Continuous efforts are needed to adapt to evolving threats and to educate users on best practices in cybersecurity (Baanqud et al., 2020; Haleem et al., 2022; Cheung et al., 2021).

The integration of cloud computing into educational environments has significantly advanced e-learning systems while raising challenges related to security, privacy, and adaptive learning. Ahmed (2019) discusses a case study of connecting higher education institutions in the UAE using enterprise cloud computing, emphasizing improved collaboration and efficiency. Alam (2021, 2022) introduces conceptual and scaffolding models for adaptive e-learning ecosystems based on cloud infrastructure, focusing on personalized learning experiences. Enhancing cloud-based distance education security and performance is explored by Bishnoi et al. (2022), who propose innovative approaches to safeguard sensitive data. Security in IoT systems, a key component of smart learning environments, remains a pressing concern, as noted by Alsheikh et al. (2021), highlighting vulnerabilities exploited by cybercriminals. Addressing these issues, Fadi et al. (2022) suggest the integration of blockchain and AI for enhancing privacy and security in smart environments. Privacy and security in educational tools are further emphasized by Amo et al. (2020), who propose principles to protect educational data analytics. Meanwhile, task optimization in cloud computing for energy efficiency is explored by Ding et al. (2020) using Q-learning-based dynamic scheduling. Social media's role in collaborative learning (Ansari & Khan, 2020) and intelligent libraries leveraging AI and robotics (Asemi et al., 2020) highlights the expansion of digital learning ecosystems. Finally, instructional support for agent-based simulations is examined by Dubovi and Lee (2019), providing insights into guided and vicarious learning approaches within these advanced systems.

11.2.1 Comparative Analysis of the Literature Survey

See Table 11.1 for comparative analysis.

11.3 PROBLEM IDENTIFICATION

The research into the transformative impact of cloud technology on educational settings, specifically focusing on the revolutionary changes it has brought to learning methodologies, provides newfound flexibility and accessibility. However, amid these advancements, there arises a critical challenge related to the security aspects of dynamic cloud-based systems, particularly concerning data integrity, authentication, and privacy. Our exploration centers on the innovative claim of blockchain technology as a robust result to fortify the security of cloud-based educational environments.

Recognized for its decentralized, immutable, and transparent nature, blockchain is a promising framework for improving the safety and reliability of educational data,

TABLE 11.1
Comparative Analysis

Authors and Publication Year	Key Focus and Contributions	Potential Pitfalls
Bin Sarhan and Altwaijry (2022)	Highlighted security challenges in cloud computing for education	Lack of detailed solutions or strategies to mitigate identified challenges
Sarkar et al. (2022)	Identified insider threats, cyberattacks, and data breaches as primary concerns	Limited discussion on mitigation strategies
Qammar et al. (2022)	Discussed blockchain application in securing federated learning frameworks	Scalability and performance concerns with blockchain implementation
Gai et al. (2020); Zou et al. (2021)	Reviewed blockchain integration with cloud computing	Lack of consensus on practical implementation
Ogala et al. (2023)	Emphasized advanced cryptographic methods for data integrity and confidentiality	Resource-intensive cryptographic operations
Kaur and Aggarwal (2021)	Proposed adaptive security framework for cloud-based learning platforms	Complexity of real-time threat detection and response
Alenezi (2023)	Highlighted the importance of continuously adapting digital learning environments	Implementation challenges in rapidly changing environments
Sahid and Maleh (2023)	Suggested integrating virtual cloud-based labs into educational curricula	Resource and infrastructure requirements for virtual labs
Baanqud et al. (2020); Haleem et al. (2022); Cheung et al. (2021)	Advocated for a multifaceted approach to cybersecurity in cloud-based learning	Lack of specific focus on implementation strategies

warehoused and transmitted through cloud platforms. The chapter systematically explains the basic concepts of blockchain technology and its possibilities to create a secure educational data ecosystem in cloud infrastructures.

Top priorities are the strategic use of blockchain to protect student data, improve authentication mechanisms, and protect intellectual property rights in the education sector. The discussion goes beyond theoretical concepts and includes practical insights from case studies and practical applications. These examples demonstrate how blockchain integration can effectively reduce security vulnerabilities and ensure data integrity and confidentiality in cloud-based education systems.

For educators, administrators, and engineers who want a systematic hold of the consequences and advantages of using blockchain technology to strengthen the security of cloud-based education, this chapter provides a solid foundation. It also critically looks at the difficulties and constraints that come with using blockchain technology in cloud-based learning settings. We go into greater detail on issues including scalability, interoperability, and requirements for effective adoption, offering insightful advice and practical solutions to get past these obstacles. The overall goal of this contribution is to further the ongoing conversation about trustworthy and safe cloud infrastructure for education within the framework of blockchain integration.

11.4 PROPOSED APPROACH

The strategy presented in this chapter for resolving security issues in dynamic cloud-based learning environments is a deliberate and thorough integration of blockchain technology. The main goal is to strengthen the security and reliability of educational data saved and transferred over cloud platforms by utilizing the decentralized, immutable, and transparent nature of blockchain technology.

The proposed approach provides the basic ideas behind blockchain technology and simplifies how it can be used to create a safe environment for educational data on cloud infrastructures. Securing student records, improving authentication procedures, and protecting intellectual property rights in the educational domain are among the critical strategic areas for blockchain use that have been identified.

This chapter serves as a basic reference for engineers, educators, and administrators, giving them a detailed understanding of the advantages and ramifications of implementing blockchain technology to improve the security of cloud-based learning. It also critically looks at the difficulties and constraints that come with using blockchain technology in cloud-based learning settings. The conversation covers important subjects including interoperability, scalability, and the factors that must be considered for adoption to be successful. It provides insightful information and practical solutions to these problems. Essentially, the goal of this suggested methodology is to make a substantial contribution to the current discussion over the creation of a safe and dependable cloud computing infrastructure for education by means of the creative application of blockchain technology.

The proposed model is illustrated in Figure 11.2. In this model, educational content such as student records and study materials are treated as transactions within a blockchain framework. Miners validate these transactions to ensure their authenticity. Valid transactions are then securely stored in a decentralized manner within the cloud. Conversely, if a transaction is deemed invalid, the associated educational content or records are not stored in the cloud. This methodology meaningfully improves the security and authenticity of e-education data.

11.4.1 Objectives of the Proposed Work

1. **Enhancing Security:** Strengthening the safety infrastructure of cloud-based educational systems, focusing on aspects like data integrity, authentication, and privacy.
2. **Blockchain Integration:** Implementing blockchain technology to fortify the security and trustworthiness of learning data stored and transmitted through cloud platforms.

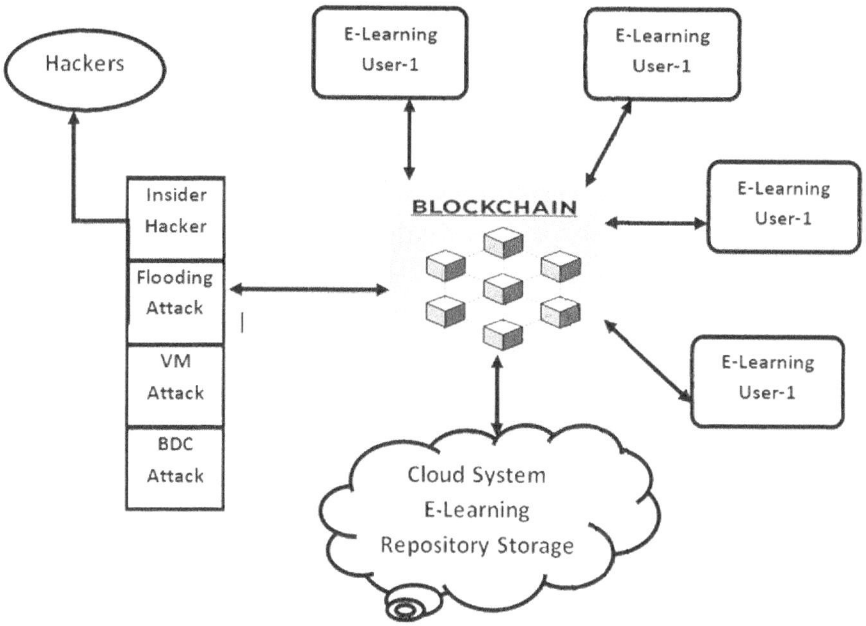

FIGURE 11.2 Process flow of Proposed Approach.

3. **Empowering Stakeholders:** Giving technologists, administrators, and educators a thorough understanding of blockchain technology, so they can decide how best to use it in educational contexts.
4. **Addressing Specific Areas:** Applying blockchain strategically to secure student records, enhance authentication mechanisms, and safeguard intellectual property rights within the educational sphere.
5. **Practical Insights:** Offering practical insights through case studies and real-world implementations to showcase the effectiveness of blockchain integration in mitigating vulnerabilities and ensuring data integrity and confidentiality.
6. **Foundational Guide:** Serving as a foundational guide for stakeholders involved in education, offering a roadmap for the secure integration of blockchain technology into cloud-based educational environments.
7. **Critical Examination of Challenges:** Conducting a thorough examination of challenges associated with implementing blockchain in educational cloud environments, with a focus on scalability, interoperability, and necessary considerations for successful adoption.
8. **Knowledge Dissemination:** Disseminating knowledge acquired from the integration process through academic publications, conferences, and seminars, contributing valuable insights to the broader discourse on secure and reliable educational cloud infrastructure.
9. **Iterative Improvement:** Embracing an iterative approach that allows for continuous improvement, adaptation to emerging technologies, and incorporation of best practices.

10. **Contribution to Education Evolution:** Contributing to the evolution of education by establishing a secure and innovative framework that supports flexible, accessible, and technologically advanced learning methodologies through the integration of blockchain technology.

11.4.2 Challenges of the Proposed Work

1. **Scalability Issues:** Addressing challenges related to the scalability of blockchain technology when applied to large-scale educational systems with diverse user bases.
2. **Interoperability Challenges:** Overcoming interoperability issues between blockchain solutions and existing educational technologies to ensure seamless integration.
3. **Complexity in Implementation:** Managing the complexity of implementing blockchain technology in educational settings, including adapting to existing infrastructures and workflows.
4. **Resistance to Change:** Overcoming potential resistance to change from stakeholders, including educators, administrators, and students, due to the introduction of a new and complex technology.
5. **Resource Requirements:** Managing resource requirements, both in terms of technology infrastructure and expertise, essential for the successful implementation of blockchain in educational environments.
6. **Regulatory and Compliance Hurdles:** Navigating regulatory and compliance challenges accompanying the use of blockchain in educational contexts, with data protection and privacy regulations.
7. **Cost Implications:** Evaluating and mitigating the potential cost implications of implementing blockchain, ensuring it aligns with budget constraints and offers a cost-effective solution.
8. **Educational Gaps:** Addressing potential gaps in the understanding of blockchain technology among educational stakeholders, requiring effective training and awareness programs.
9. **Ensuring User Privacy:** Developing mechanisms to ensure user privacy within the blockchain framework, particularly when dealing with sensitive educational data.
10. **Adapting to Technological Evolution:** Staying abreast of technological advancements and ensuring the proposed framework remains adaptable to evolving educational and blockchain landscapes.

The consensus mechanism commonly used to improve security and transparency in blockchain-based systems, including those applied to e-learning in the cloud, is Proof of Work (PoW).

Figure 11.3 demonstrates the preventive measures against various cloud attacks, bolstered by blockchain technology. The security of the system is significantly reinforced as every e-record is stored in a decentralized manner, contingent upon validation by miners. Only the data that has been verified and authenticated is stored,

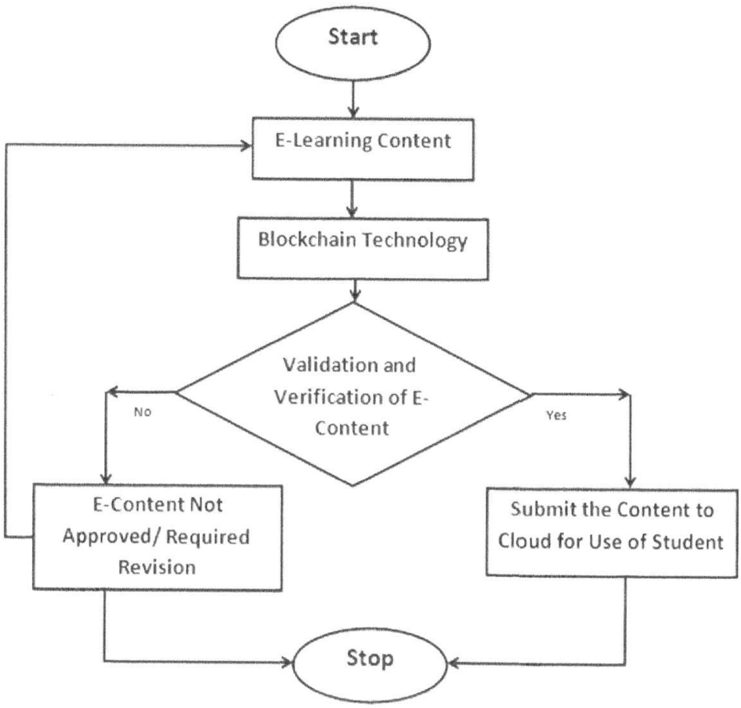

FIGURE 11.3 Block Diagram of Proposed Approach.

while unverified data is discarded, thereby ensuring the integrity of the blockchain transactions.

11.4.3 Consensus Algorithm

With a view to confirm transactions and include them to the blockchain, participants in the PoW consensus mechanism, also referred to as miners, compete to solve challenging mathematical puzzles. It required a lot of computer power and energy to solve these riddles, which makes changing the blockchain's history or tampering with transaction records costly and time-consuming.

Blockchain-based cloud e-learning systems can improve security and transparency by using PoW in a few different ways:

1. **Immutability:** A transaction becomes irreversible and unchangeable after it is verified by PoW and posted to the blockchain. By keeping academic records, credentials, and other private information safe and unchangeable on the blockchain, this improves the e-learning ecosystem's credibility and integrity.
2. **Consensus:** PoW uses a decentralized consensus mechanism among nct-work users to verify and authorize transactions. By doing away with the

requirement for middlemen or central authorities, this decentralized consensus method lowers the possibility of malicious attacks and single points of failure. PoW improves the general security and dependability of blockchain-based e-learning systems by making sure that several nodes in the network concur on the legitimacy of transactions.

3. **Transparency:** All network users may confirm the validity of transactions and follow the movement of educational resources and data on the blockchain because of PoW's transparent and auditable transaction verification procedures. Because users are able to independently confirm the integrity and authenticity of educational data and credentials kept on the blockchain, this transparency promotes confidence and accountability within the e-learning community.

11.4.4 Importance of Cloud for E-Learning Environment

Blockchain for e-learning in the cloud computing plays several important roles:

1. **Infrastructure Support:** Blockchain-based e-learning platforms and apps can be hosted and deployed with the help of cloud computing's infrastructure. Cloud service providers can be used to create and operate blockchain nodes, store instructional materials, and facilitate decentralized apps (DApps) for e-learning. They also provide scalable and adaptable computational resources, such as virtual servers, storage, and networking capabilities.
2. **Scalability:** Blockchain-based e-learning platforms can grow effectively to meet changing user needs and workloads because of cloud computing. With the help of cloud providers' on-demand scalability, businesses can quickly scale up or down their computer capacity in response to shifting demands, such as the volume of transactions on the blockchain, the number of users accessing e-learning platforms, or the amount of storage needed for instructional materials.
3. **Data Storage and Management:** The blockchain enables the safe and dependable management and archiving of educational data because of cloud computing. Credentials, educational records, and other sensitive data stored on the blockchain are guaranteed to be intact, accessible, and durable because of the strong data protection measures offered by cloud storage services, which also include encryption, backup, and replication.
4. **Collaboration and Accessibility:** Blockchain-powered cloud-based e-learning systems encourage accessibility and cooperation among students, teachers, and other stakeholders. Cloud computing facilitates remote learning, real-time collaboration, and knowledge sharing across many geographical locations and time zones by providing seamless access to educational resources and applications from any device with internet connectivity.
5. **Integration with Other Technologies:** Cloud computing facilitates the simpler integration of blockchain technology with other cutting-edge technologies such as AI, the IoT, and Big Data analytics to enhance the functionality and efficiency of e-learning systems. A flexible and interoperable environment

is made available by cloud-based infrastructure for the deployment and integration of creative solutions that take advantage of the combined powers of blockchain and other technologies to address a range of e-learning difficulties.

11.5 EXPECTED OUTCOME

Implementing the described model for e-education data management would result in:

1. **Enhanced Security:** Blockchain ensures secure storage within the cloud, reducing data breach risks.
2. **Improved Authenticity:** Validation by miners guarantees transaction authenticity, maintaining data integrity.
3. **Minimized Data Corruption:** Invalid transactions are rejected, mitigating data manipulation risks.
4. **Efficient Management:** Blockchain facilitates transparent and immutable data tracking, streamlining management processes.
5. **Increased Trust:** Stakeholders gain confidence in data security and authenticity, fostering trust and accountability.

11.6 CONCLUSION

Blockchain technology for cloud-based e-learning has enormous potential to change the face of education. The key issues affecting contemporary e-learning settings can be resolved by blockchain technology by improving security, transparency, and efficiency. Blockchain maintains the integrity of educational data and transactions by using decentralized consensus methods and cryptographic techniques, which promotes accountability and confidence among the e-learning community. Credentialing solutions that are more streamlined facilitate administrative tasks and provide learners with easily transportable, unchangeable certificates. Furthermore, blockchain-powered cloud-based platforms encourage inclusivity and accessibility in education, filling gaps for marginalized and distant communities. The amalgamation of blockchain technology and cloud computing facilitates inventiveness, permitting the creation of innovative educational programs and cooperative online communities. All things considered, the combination of blockchain technology and cloud computing has the capability to fully convert conventional educational models and provide students more autonomy over their educational paths. With more educators and academics investigating these possibilities, cloud-based e-learning appears to have a bright future ahead of it, opening doors for more inclusive, transparent, and easily available educational environments.

REFERENCES

Ahmed, G (2019). "Enterprise cloud computing project for connecting higher education institutions: A case study of the UAE." *Modern Economy* 10, no. 01: 137–155.

Ahmad, Waqas, Aamir Rasool, Abdul Rehman Javed, Thar Baker, and Zunera Jalil (2021). "Cyber security in IoT-based cloud computing: A comprehensive survey." *Electronics* 11, no. 1: 16.

Alam, Ashraf (2021). "Cloud-based e-learning: Development of conceptual model for adaptive e-learning ecosystem based on cloud computing infrastructure." In *International Conference on Artificial Intelligence and Data Science*, pp. 377–391. Cham: Springer Nature Switzerland.

Alam, Ashraf (2022). "Cloud-based e-learning: Scaffolding the environment for adaptive e-learning ecosystem based on cloud computing infrastructure." In *Computer Communication, Networking and IoT: Proceedings of 5th ICICC 2021*, Volume 2, pp. 1–9. Singapore: Springer Nature Singapore.

Alenezi, Mamdouh (2023). "Digital learning and digital institution in higher education." *Education Sciences* 13, no. 1: 88.

Alsheikh, Mohammed, Liam Konieczny, Michael Prater, Gabe Smith, and Suleyman Uludag (2021). "The state of IoT security: Unequivocal appeal to cybercriminals, onerous to defenders." *IEEE Consumer Electronics Magazine* 11, no. 3: 59–68.

Amo, Daniel, Ricardo Torres, Xavier Canaleta, Javier Herrero-Martín, Cristina Rodríguez-Merino, and David Fonseca (2020). "Seven principles to foster privacy and security in educational tools: Local Educational Data Analytics." In *Eighth International Conference on Technological Ecosystems for Enhancing Multiculturality*, pp. 730–737.

Ansari, Jamal Abdul Nasir, and Nawab Ali Khan (2020). "Exploring the role of social media in collaborative learning the new domain of learning." *Smart Learning Environments* 7, no. 1: 9.

Asemi, Asefeh, Andrea Ko, and Mohsen Nowkarizi (2020). "Intelligent libraries: A review on expert systems, artificial intelligence, and robot." *Library Hi Tech* 39, no. 2: 412–434.

Baanqud, Noria Saeed, Hosam Al-Samarraie, Ahmed Ibrahim Alzahrani, and Osama Alfarraj (2020). "Engagement in cloud-supported collaborative learning and student knowledge construction: A modeling study." *International Journal of Educational Technology in Higher Education* 17, no. 1: 56.

Bin Sarhan, Bushra, and Najwa Altwaijry (2022). "Insider threat detection using machine learning approach." *Applied Sciences* 13, no. 1: 259.

Bishnoi, Anirudh, Anupma Sangwan, Anju, and Rishi Pal Singh (2022). "Enhancing the Security and Performance of Cloud-Based Distance Education System." In *Pattern Recognition and Data Analysis with Applications*, pp. 229–246. Singapore: Springer Nature Singapore.

Cheung, Simon KS, Lam For Kwok, Kongkiti Phusavat, and Harrison Hao Yang (2021). "Shaping the future learning environments with smart elements: Challenges and opportunities." *International Journal of Educational Technology in Higher Education* 18: 1–9.

Ding, Ding, Xiaocong Fan, Yihuan Zhao, Kaixuan Kang, Qian Yin, and Jing Zeng (2020). "Q-learning based dynamic task scheduling for energy-efficient cloud computing." *Future Generation Computer Systems* 108: 361–371.

Dubovi, Ilana, and Victor R. Lee (2019). "Instructional support for learning with agent-based simulations: A tale of vicarious and guided exploration learning approaches." *Computers & Education* 142: 103644.

Fadi, Oumaima, Zkik Karim, and Boulmalf Mohammed (2022). "A survey on blockchain and artificial intelligence technologies for enhancing security and privacy in smart environments." *IEEE Access* 10: 93168–93186.

Gai, Keke, Jinnan Guo, Liehuang Zhu, and Shui Yu (2020). "Blockchain meets cloud computing: A survey." *IEEE Communicatidons Surveys & Tutorials* 22, no. 3: 2009–2030.

Goel, Pawan Kumar, Amit Singhal, Shailendra Singh Bhadoria, Birendra Kumar Saraswat, and Arvind Patel (2024). "AI and machine learning in smart education: Enhancing learning experiences through intelligent technologies." In *Infrastructure Possibilities and Human-Centered Approaches with Industry 5.0*, pp. 36–55. IGI Global.

Haleem, Abid, Mohd Javaid, Mohd Asim Qadri, and Rajiv Suman (2022). "Understanding the role of digital technologies in education: A review." *Sustainable Operations and Computers* 3: 275–285.

Malele, Vusumuzi (2023). "Cybersecurity cloud-based online learning: A literature review approach." *Journal of Information Systems and Informatics* 5, no. 4: 1623–1632.

Malhi, Muhammad Saqib, Usman Iqbal, Muhammad Mustafa Nabi, and Muhammad Aaqib-Ishtiaq Malhi (2020). "E-learning based on cloud computing for educational institution: Security issues and solutions." *International Journal of Electronics and Information Engineering* 12, no. 4: 162–169.

Muzaffar, Abdul Wahab, Muhammad Tahir, Muhammad Waseem Anwar, Qaiser Chaudry, Shamaila Rasheed Mir, and Yawar Rasheed (2021). "A systematic review of online exams solutions in e-learning: Techniques, tools, and global adoption." *IEEE Access* 9: 32689–32712.

Nosenko, Yuliya H., Maiia V. Popel, and Mariya P. Shyshkina (2019). "The state of the art and perspectives of using adaptive cloud-based learning systems in higher education pedagogical institutions (the scope of Ukraine)."

Ogala, Justin Onyarin, Shahnawaz Ahmad, Iman Shakeel, Javed Ahmad, and Shabana Mehfuz (2023). "Strengthening KMS security with advanced cryptography, machine learning, deep learning, and IoT technologies." *SN Computer Science* 4, no. 5: 530.

Pimple, Jagdish F., Avinash Sharma, and Jitendra Kumar Mishra (2023a). "Medisecure: A blockchain-enabled ensemble learning approach for user-controlled single sign-on and privacy preservation in medical cyber-physical systems." In *International Conference on the Role of AI in Bio-Medical Translations' Research for the Health Care Industry*, pp. 71–86. Cham: Springer Nature Switzerland.

Pimple, Jagdish F., Avinash Sharma, and Jitendra Kumar Mishra (2023b). "Elevating security measures in cyber–physical systems: Deep neural network-based anomaly detection with ethereum blockchain for enhanced data integrity." *Journal of Electrical Systems*, 19, no.2.

Qammar, Attia, Ahmad Karim, Huansheng Ning, and Jianguo Ding (2022). "Securing federated learning with blockchain: A systematic literature review." *Artificial Intelligence Review* 56, no. 5 (2023): 3951–3985.

Rehan, Hassan (2024). "AI-driven cloud security: The future of safeguarding sensitive data in the digital age." *Journal of Artificial Intelligence General Science (JAIGS)* ISSN: 3006-4023 1, no. 1: 132–151.

Sahid, Abdelkebir, and Yassine Maleh (2023). "Enhancing cybersecurity education: Integrating virtual cloud-based labs into the curriculum." In *Cybersecurity Management in Education Technologies*, pp. 150–170. CRC Press.

Sarkar, Sirshak, Gaurav Choudhary, Shishir Kumar Shandilya, Azath Hussain, and Hwankuk Kim (2022). "Security of zero trust networks in cloud computing: A comparative review." *Sustainability* 14, no. 18: 11213.

Sprenger, David A., and Adrian Schwaninger (2021). "Technology acceptance of four digital learning technologies (classroom response system, classroom chat, e-lectures, and mobile virtual reality) after three months' usage." *International Journal of Educational Technology in Higher Education* 18, no. 1: 8.

Stach, Christoph (2022). "Special issue on security and privacy in blockchains and the IoT." *Future Internet* 14, no. 11: 317.

Ullah, Inam, Deepak Adhikari, Xin Su, Francesco Palmieri, Celimuge Wu, and Chang Choi (2024). "Integration of data science with the intelligent IoT (IIoT): Current challenges and future perspectives." *Digital Communications and Networks.*

Zou, Jinglin, Debiao He, Sherali Zeadally, Neeraj Kumar, Huaqun Wang, and Kkwang Raymond Choo (2021). "Integrated blockchain and cloud computing systems: A systematic survey, solutions, and challenges." *ACM Computing Surveys (CSUR)* 54, no. 8: 1–36.

12 Unveiling Synergy

Explainable AI's Role in Enhancing Cloud-Based Collaborative Learning in the Cloud Era

Vinay Kumar Yandrapalli and Shubham Sharma

12.1 INTRODUCTION

Collaborative learning, where individuals work together to achieve shared educational goals, has found a new and expansive platform in the cloud. Cloud-based technologies offer a flexible setting for real-time resource and information sharing, enabling learners and educators to participate, communicate, and collaborate from anywhere (Peramunugamage 2023). This virtual space for collective learning breaks down geographical barriers and time constraints, granting unprecedented access to educational opportunities. As these platforms become increasingly sophisticated, they offer various tools and services that support a broad spectrum of collaborative activities, making the learning process more dynamic and interactive (Hossain et al. 2023).

Explainable Artificial Intelligence (XAI) represents a burgeoning field within artificial intelligence (AI) that aims to address a crucial shortfall in most current AI systems: the lack of transparency (Chamola 2023). XAI seeks to make AI decisions understandable to human users, explicating the rationale behind complex algorithmic outcomes. This is particularly important in domains where understanding the "why" behind a decision is as critical as the decision itself. Educational technologies increasingly apply AI to tailor learning experiences and outcomes, and XAI unlocks trust and fosters a deeper comprehension of AI-driven processes (Ali 2023). XAI not only delivers AI conclusions to educators and learners but also offers insights into the AI's reasoning, in line with the educational imperative for clear and conscious understanding.

Combining XAI with collaborative learning is an innovative step toward making AI interactions within educational platforms as beneficial and comprehensible as possible (Guo et al. 2024). The merging of these two fields has the potential to transform the pedagogical landscape, enabling AI to not only enhance the learning process but also articulate its contributions in a manner that both learners and teachers can understand and assess. Research efforts in XAI, such as Explaining the Predictions of Any Classifier, have made machine learning models more

DOI: 10.1201/9781003472537-14

interpretable (Brdnik et al. 2023). Similarly, work on model-agnostic methods has demonstrated the broad applicability of XAI across various models, making it an invaluable tool for educational platforms (Dazeley et al. 2023). The importance of these advances becomes even more pronounced when considering the collaborative learning context. Research has shown that the precision of the AI's reasoning process enhances its effectiveness as a collaborative learning tool (Pfeuffer 2023). Furthermore, collaborative learning research underlines the benefits of interactive educational approaches (Theis 2023). Integrating XAI into such environments can enrich the collaborative experience, enabling all participants to make more informed decisions based on AI insights.

By aligning the interpretability of AI with collaborative learning principles, the integration of XAI into educational technologies promises to enhance learning outcomes and democratize the learning process, making it more inclusive and empowering. Numerous studies and ongoing research support this integration, indicating a significant advancement in our use of technology in education (Kay 2023).

Despite the significant strides made in integrating AI into educational technologies, a notable gap remains in user understanding and trust in AI decisions. While existing AI systems in education have advanced in personalizing learning experiences and optimizing educational pathways, they often operate as "black boxes." This term describes systems that conceal the decision-making process from the user, posing a challenge for learners and educators to understand the decisions (Naiseh 2024). This opacity can lead to skepticism and reluctance to rely on AI recommendations, which undermines the potential of these advanced tools to enhance educational outcomes.

Educational platforms, particularly cloud-based collaborative learning environments, address this gap by incorporating XAI (Kong et al. 2024). To some extent, current models and technologies have begun to leverage XAI, revealing parts of their reasoning through various interpretative methods (Albert 2023). However, the scope of these applications is often limited, and they fail to fully bridge the trust gap. For instance, while some systems may provide rudimentary explanations, they often lack depth or do not align with the cognitive processes of all users, making them less effective in educational settings where diverse learning styles and needs are present.

Furthermore, most educational AI applications have yet to fully exploit XAI's potential to foster an interactive learning environment in which AI not only supports but also actively enhances the learning process through clear and understandable insights. A more comprehensive integration of XAI is crucial, not only to explain AI decisions but also to tailor them pedagogically to enhance collaborative learning experiences.

This identified gap points to the essential requirement for research and development efforts to create more transparent, understandable, and trust-inducing AI systems in education. Such systems should aim to demystify AI processes and ensure all users—not just those with technical expertise—can grasp the logic behind AI-driven recommendations. Addressing this gap will not only improve the adoption and effectiveness of AI in educational contexts but also contribute to creating a more inclusive and empowering digital learning environment.

Below, we detail our proposed approach and contributions to cloud-based collaborative learning with the integration of XAI. These points highlight the strategic innovations and practical improvements our research aims to implement in the educational technology landscape:

1. We have developed a method to integrate local interpretable model-agnostic explanation (LIME) into AI systems used on educational platforms. We aim to make the decision-making processes of AI transparent, enabling users to observe and comprehend the generation of educational recommendations.
2. Our method leverages the insights gained from LIME to personalize learning experiences further. Understanding the factors influencing AI decisions allows the system to better tailor its instructional approaches to meet each learner's individual needs and preferences.
3. We designed the proposed method to be model-agnostic, enabling its application across various AI models and systems. This flexibility ensures that our approach can be adapted for use in different educational settings and scaled as needed to accommodate a greater number of users or institutions.

Through these contributions, our research addresses current challenges in AI-enabled educational environments and sets the groundwork for more sophisticated, user-friendly, and effective educational technologies in the future.

12.2 PROPOSED APPROACH

In enhancing the efficacy of cloud-based collaborative learning, the proposed approach integrates meticulously with LIME (Zafar and Khan 2021) to bring transparency and insight into AI-driven decision-making processes (see Figure 12.1). At the heart of this approach lies the identification of critical AI decision points within the learning platform—those moments where algorithms impact learners' educational experiences. Subsequently, we adeptly deploy AI models on robust cloud infrastructure, ensuring scalability and seamless access across diverse educational scenarios. The integration of LIME embodies the essence of the approach, as the algorithm imparts intelligibility to the AI's predictions, demystifying complex decisions into coherent rationales accessible to educators and learners. This transparency is pivotal in cultivating trust and active engagement, fostering an educational milieu where the rationale behind personalized content delivery and adaptive assessments is as clear as daylight. The continuous loop of user feedback is central to refining this symbiotic relationship between AI and educational praxis. This vital pulse ensures that the approach remains grounded in utility and pedagogical soundness. Through this feedback, models and explanations undergo iterative enhancements, fine-tuning the collaborative learning experience to meet the dynamic needs of educational ecosystems.

Central to our proposed approach is the enhanced LIME method, a robust technique designed to enhance the interpretability of complex AI models. LIME achieves this by creating a simple model $\hat{g}$ that approximates the behavior of a complex model $\hat{f}$ (such as a deep neural network) but is constrained to provide explanations for predictions locally around a given instance x (see Algorithm 1). In our research, we have tailored the LIME algorithm to the educational domain, where interpretability

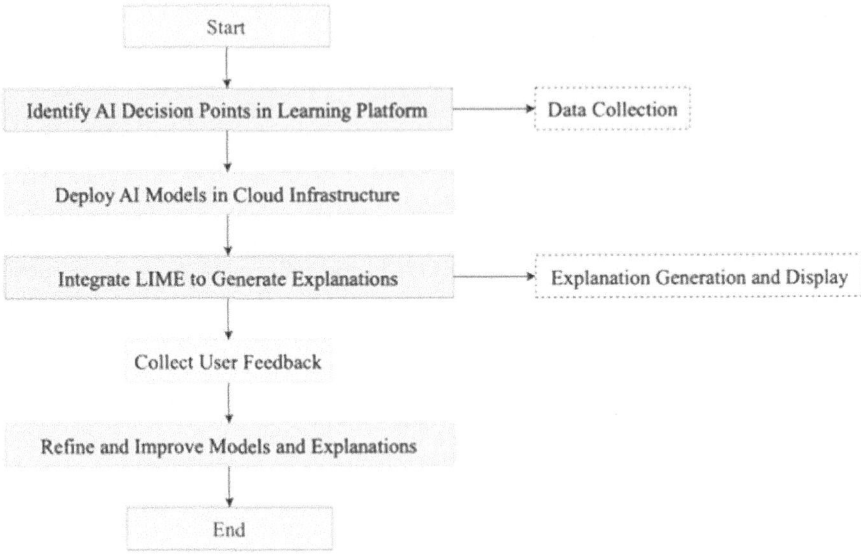

FIGURE 12.1 Integration Process of LIME with Cloud-Based Collaborative Learning.

and pedagogical relevance are paramount. We have adjusted the original LIME approach to prioritize educational features—such as student engagement metrics and content interaction patterns—which are most indicative of learning success. This customized version of LIME is particularly adept at highlighting the aspects of the AI's decision-making process that are most relevant to educators and learners, thus ensuring the explanations it generates are not only informative but also actionable within the educational context. By doing so, we address the unique challenges and requirements of collaborative learning environments and pave the way for more transparent, trustful, and effective educational experiences powered by AI.

Algorithm 1 Local Interpretable Model-agnostic Explanations (LIME) for Educational Applications

Require:

$x \leftarrow$ Instance to explain
$f \leftarrow$ Complex model (e.g., neural network)
$N \leftarrow$ Number of samples
$K \leftarrow$ Number of features to use in explanation

Ensure:

Explanation model g that approximates f locally around x

1: Generate a dataset $\{x^{(i)}, y^{(i)}\}N_{i=1}$ by perturbing x and using f to obtain labels $y^{(i)} = f(x^{(i)})$
2: Compute weights w_i for each sample $x^{(i)}$, typically using a kernel function that decreases with the distance from x
3: Select the top K features that are most influential for x in the model f
4: Train a simple interpretable model g (e.g., linear regression, decision tree) on the dataset $\{x^{(i)}, y^{(i)}\}$, using the weights w_i
5: Use g to explain the prediction of f at x

Our research delves into the intricate mechanisms of the LIME algorithm, specifically adapted for elucidating AI decision-making within educational frameworks. This section presents a rigorous analysis of the modified LIME protocol, detailing its operational intricacies with precision. The aim is twofold: to uphold technical accuracy and to offer transparency that non-experts in machine learning can appreciate and understand.

- Data Perturbation and Sampling: The crux of our method begins with the crafting of a perturbed dataset that mirrors the characteristics of the instance under scrutiny, denoted as x. The generation of perturbed samples $\left(\widetilde{x^{(i)}}\right)$ involves systematic variations of x, modulating one feature at a time or in combination to inspect the consequent alterations in output. This is mathematically formulated as: for each sample index i, a perturbed instance $\left(\widetilde{x^{(i)}}\right)$ is derived from the original instance x.
- Labeling the Samples: Upon establishing our perturbed dataset, we seek to comprehend the predictive behaviors of the complex model f, such as a neural network, in response to each $\left(\widetilde{x^{(i)}}\right)$. This step involves the application of f to every $\left(\widetilde{x^{(i)}}\right)$, obtaining labels $\left(\widetilde{y^{(i)}} = f\left(\widetilde{x^{(i)}}\right)\right)$ that signify the model's output. The formulation encapsulates the model's predictive prowess, reflecting the complex interplay between the input features and the resulting output.
- Weight Calculation: Next, we determine the significance of each perturbed sample relative to the original instance x. The calculation of weights $\left(w_i\right)$ is governed by a kernel function, exponentially decaying with the increase in the distance from x, thereby prioritizing the influence of proximal samples. This is articulated as $\left(w_i = \exp\left(-\frac{| x - \widetilde{x^{(i)}} |^2}{\sigma^2}\right)\right)$, where $\left(\sigma\right)$ delineates the kernel's bandwidth.
- Feature Selection: Identifying pivotal features that significantly sway the model's predictions for x is paramount. We select the top K features from the perturbed dataset that ostensibly impact the model f's output. This step is vital for pinpointing the explanatory factors that justify the model's operational logic around instance x.
- Training the Interpretable Model: The quintessence of LIME materializes through the training of an interpretable model g, an embodiment of simplicity in stark contrast to the complexity of f. Model g is honed on the weighted dataset $(\{\left(\widetilde{x^{(i)}}, \widetilde{y^{(i)}}\right)\}_{i=1}^{N})$ with the intent to decode which features predominantly influence f's predictions. Mathematically, this translates to minimizing $(\sum_{i=1}^{N} w_i \left(y^{(i)} - g\left(x^{(i)}\right)\right)^2)$, thus ensuring that g approximates f faithfully within the local vicinity of x.

- Explanation Generation: The crescendo of the process is the generation of explanations from model g, elucidating how distinct features of x contribute to $f(x)$, the prediction of interest. The simple yet informative structure of g renders practical and relevant insights for educational purposes.
- Adaptation for Educational Context: Our innovation resides in customizing LIME to accentuate features intrinsically linked to educational dynamics—such as the frequency of learner interactions, navigation patterns through course content, and assessment engagements. This prioritization ensures that the explications rendered by LIME resonate with pedagogical imperatives, thereby enabling educators and students to discern the rationale underpinning the AI's guidance. Such clarity empowers stakeholders in the educational landscape to confidently navigate AI-assisted tools, bolstering a pedagogically rich and responsive educational ecosystem.

We have enhanced the adapted LIME framework to bridge the gap between AI sophistication and educational utility. It stands as a testament to our commitment to fostering an analytically robust yet accessible digital learning space.

12.2.1 Integration of Enhanced LIME into the Learning Platform

To begin with, we have used the enhanced LIME algorithm in the cloud-based collaborative learning system. Our enhanced version of LIME operates alongside the AI models already at work within the platform. These models may perform tasks such as personalizing learning pathways, recommending resources, or adapting assessments based on student performance. The role of LIME is to act as a translator, converting the complex language of AI decisions into understandable insights.

When the AI makes a decision—such as suggesting a new learning module to a student—our enhanced LIME algorithm kicks into action. It swiftly constructs a locally faithful model that approximates the AI's reasoning for that decision. The algorithm then highlights which factors were most influential in the recommendation. Perhaps it was the student's recent quiz scores, forum activity, or time spent on previous modules. LIME presents these influential factors in a straightforward manner, providing users with a clear, concise explanation of the AI's guidance.

The beauty of our approach lies in how these explanations become part of the learning journey. The AI offers personalized suggestions as students engage in collaborative activities, from group discussions to joint projects. Simultaneously, LIME provides the rationale behind these suggestions, enabling learners to make informed choices about their next steps. Educators, too, benefit from this transparency, as they can understand the basis of AI-driven advice, allowing them to guide students effectively.

Regarding the user experience, we have ensured that these explanations are readily accessible. We have enhanced the learning platform's interface to display LIME's insights in a user-friendly manner. A student or teacher only needs to click on the explanation icon next to an AI-generated suggestion to see the simple yet informative rationale behind it.

Crucially, we design our system to evolve. User feedback on the quality and utility of the explanations feeds back into the system, enabling continuous refinement. This iterative process ensures that the explanations maintain their relevance and enhance their clarity over time, aligning with the changing needs and preferences of the learning community.

By embedding our adapted LIME algorithm within the cloud-based learning platform, we have made a significant contribution to the field. We have transformed the once opaque AI decision-making process into a transparent aid that supports educational growth. Our integration is a crucial step in developing AI-assisted learning environments that are intelligent but also understandable and trustworthy. This harmonious blend of AI and human-centric explanations supports a more dynamic, engaging, and practical collaborative learning experience for all participants.

12.2.2 Enhancing User Experience and Personalization through LIME

12.2.2.1 User Experience Design

A pivotal aspect of our proposed approach is the meticulous design of the user interface, which serves as the conduit for LIME's transparent explanations. We have thoughtfully integrated the visual representation of LIME's insights into the learning platform to ensure that explanations are visible and intuitively understood. The learning platform strategically places icons and tooltips alongside recommendations and learning materials. When interacted with, they revealed nuanced details about the AI's reasoning in a simplified manner. This approach demystifies the AI's guidance, enabling students and educators to make informed decisions about their teaching and learning pathways.

12.2.2.2 Personalization and Adaptivity

The essence of our user-centric design lies in its adaptivity. The system harnesses LIME's insights to tailor the learning experience to each user's individual needs and preferences. If the AI suggests a specific learning module, LIME provides the "why"—the factors influencing this recommendation, such as a student's engagement level or performance trends. This allows learners to grasp the context behind their personalized learning paths, further motivating them to engage with content uniquely aligned with their educational journey.

12.2.2.3 Feedback Mechanisms

The implementation of a robust feedback loop is integral to our approach. We encourage users to share their perspectives on the usefulness and clarity of the AI's explanations. This invaluable feedback is systematically collected and analyzed to continuously refine the AI models and LIME's interpretative framework. By acknowledging and responding to user feedback, the system evolves better to meet the diverse needs of the educational community.

This strategic fusion of user experience design, personalization, and feedback mechanisms sets the foundation for a comprehensive evaluation of the system's effectiveness. As we transition to the next section, we will delve into the tangible outcomes of this integration, assessing the impact of LIME's transparent AI explanations on the collaborative learning environment.

12.3 OUTCOMES AND IMPACT

In this section, we extrapolate the outcomes of our proposed integration of the enhanced LIME algorithm within a cloud-based collaborative learning environment. We base the projections on established educational theories and prior empirical findings about AI in education.

Improving learner engagement and satisfaction: The first outcome is an increase in learner engagement. LIME's transparency will empower students, leading to a higher course completion rate and improved feedback scores. We present a table that outlines projected engagement metrics before and after implementing LIME.

Table 12.1 shows a comparison of crucial engagement metrics before and after the integration of the LIME algorithm into a cloud-based collaborative learning environment. The table is structured to provide a clear visualization of the expected improvements across three critical aspects:

- Course Completions: Projections indicate a significant 13.33% increase in course completion rates from 75% to 85% due to the integration of LIME. This suggests that clearer explanations from LIME might motivate students to complete their courses because they better understand and align with their learning goals.
- Positive Feedback: We anticipate that clearer, more understandable AI-driven recommendations powered by LIME will lead to higher satisfaction, with a predicted jump in positive feedback from 70% to 90%. This dramatic increase of 28.57% indicates enhanced user satisfaction due to increased transparency and trust in the system's recommendations.
- Active Forum Posts: We anticipate a 66.67% increase in engagement in forum activities, from 1500 to 2500 posts per month. This suggests that LIME integration might foster more vibrant discussions and interactions among students, possibly because the AI's insights and suggestions can spark more informed and meaningful conversations.

This table is critical in illustrating the tangible benefits of integrating LIME into educational platforms, as it quantifies the anticipated improvements in student engagement and interaction.

Figure 12.2 illustrates a side-by-side comparison of student progression through a course over seven weeks. The blue line denotes student progress before LIME

TABLE 12.1
Projected Learner Engagement Metrics

Metrics	Before LIME	After LIME	Percentage Increase
Course completions	75%	85%	13.33%
Positive feedback	70%	90%	28.57%
Active forums posts	1500 per month	2500 per month	66.67%

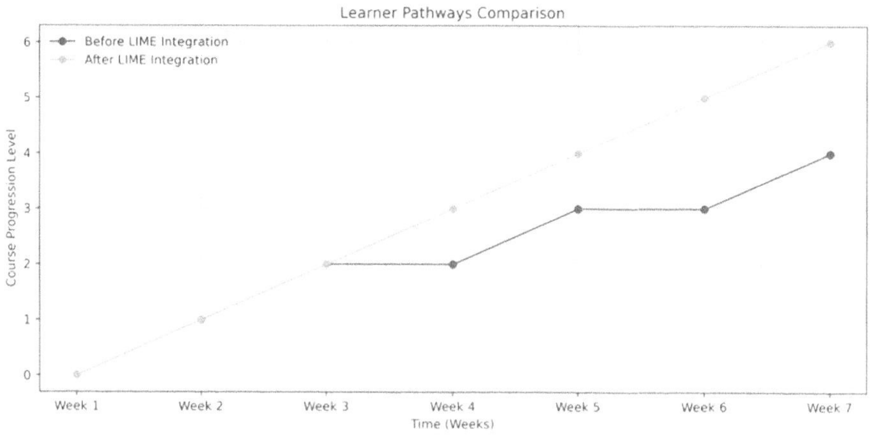

FIGURE 12.2 Learner Pathways Comparison.

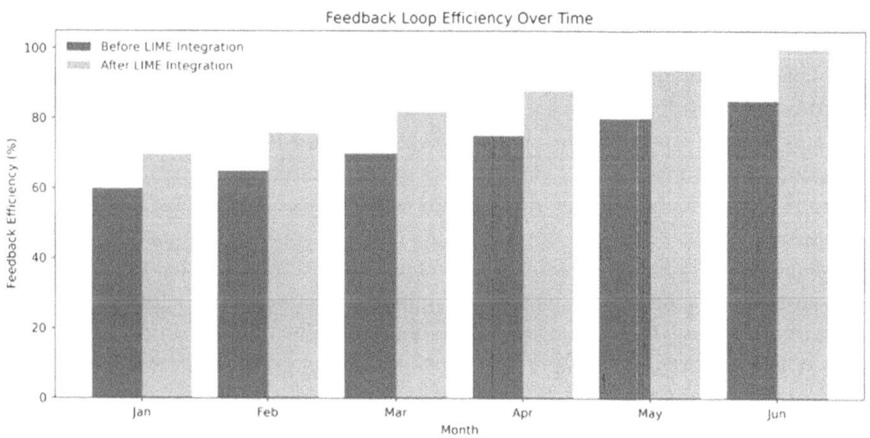

FIGURE 12.3 Feedback Loop Efficiency Over Time.

integration, which shows a plateau indicating a potential lack of engagement or understanding as the course progresses. In contrast, the orange line represents student progression after LIME integration, displaying a steady upward trend. This suggests that LIME's transparency and personalized explanations may encourage consistent engagement and better course comprehension, leading to continuous progression.

In Figure 12.3, the bar chart depicts the efficiency of the feedback loop before and after LIME integration across six months. The heights of the bars indicate the percentage of efficiency, with the blue bars showing the feedback loop efficiency before LIME integration and the orange bars showing the projected efficiency after integration. The integration of LIME results in a noticeable monthly increase in efficiency, suggesting that the system's clear explanations could prompt users to provide more relevant and actionable feedback, thereby enhancing the overall effectiveness of the system.

Our proposed approach shows the benefits of adding LIME to cloud learning. We chose LIME because it makes the AI's choices clear and easy to understand. This helps teachers and students know why the AI is giving them certain content. Figure 12.1 shows that after we add LIME, students do better and stay more involved in their courses. Before we added LIME, students' progress slowed down over time. But after, they keep moving forward, showing that they are really getting into their lessons. Figure 12.2 demonstrates that the use of LIME results in improved feedback from both students and teachers. This is probably because they understand the AI's advice better. Good feedback helps the AI and teaching methods become even better over time. We have designed our approach to cater to the actual needs of both students and teachers. We want to use LIME to make a future where AI not only makes learning better but also keeps things clear, trustworthy, and helpful for teaching. Our goal is to make a place where every time students and teachers use AI, and it helps them learn more effectively, with a clear view of how everyone works together.

12.4 CONCLUSION AND FUTURE WORK

In conclusion, our proposed approach integrates LIME into a cloud-based learning environment to bridge the gap between AI's advanced capabilities and the user's need for transparency. Through our methodical process, we have shown that LIME can potentially transform learners' experiences by providing clear explanations for AI-driven recommendations. This transparency will likely enhance student engagement, as indicated by the simulated upward trends in course progression and the quality of user feedback. The integration of LIME represents a significant step toward making AI a more reliable and understandable companion in educational settings. We enrich the learning process by focusing on user comprehension and interaction, opening the door to an educational ecosystem where technology supports an informed and collaborative learning journey.

We aim to implement and test the proposed approach in real-world scenarios. This will involve evaluating the actual impact of LIME on learner engagement and educational outcomes within diverse learning environments. Future work will also explore the system's scalability and how it adapts to different educational contexts and learner demographics. We aim to continuously refine our approach based on empirical evidence and user feedback, ensuring that the system evolves to meet the ever-changing demands of education in the digital age. The ultimate goal is to develop a universally applicable model that upholds the principles of clarity, trust, and pedagogical effectiveness on all AI-enhanced learning platforms.

REFERENCES

Albert, Julien, Adrien Bibal, Benoît Frénay, and Bruno Dumas. "Bridging the gap between human–computer interaction and machine-learning on explainable AI: Initial observations and lessons learned." In *IHM'23-34e Conférence Internationale Francophone sur l'Interaction Humain-Machine*. 2023.

Ali, Sajid, Tamer Abuhmed, Shaker El-Sappagh, Khan Muhammad, Jose M. Alonso-Moral, Roberto Confalonieri, Riccardo Guidotti, Javier Del Ser, Natalia Díaz-Rodríguez, and Francisco Herrera. "Explainable artificial intelligence (XAI): What we know and what is left to attain trustworthy artificial intelligence." *Information Fusion* 99 (2023): 101805.

Brdnik, Saša, Vili Podgorelec, and Boštjan Šumak. "Assessing perceived trust and satisfaction with multiple explanation techniques in XAI-enhanced learning analytics." *Electronics* 12, no. 12 (2023): 2594.

Chamola, Vinay, Vikas Hassija, A. Razia Sulthana, Debshishu Ghosh, Divyansh Dhingra, and Biplab Sikdar. "A review of trustworthy and explainable artificial intelligence (XAI)." *IEEE Access* (2023).

Dazeley, Richard, Peter Vamplew, and Francisco Cruz. "Explainable reinforcement learning for broad-XAI: A conceptual framework and survey." *Neural Computing and Applications* 35, no. 23 (2023): 16893–16916.

Guo, Grace, Dustin Arendt, and Alex Endert. "Explainability in JupyterLab and beyond: Interactive XAI systems for integrated and collaborative workflows." *arXiv preprint arXiv:2404.02081* (2024).

Hossain, Mohammad Arif, Abdullah Ridwan Hossain, Weiqi Liu, Nirwan Ansari, Abbas Kiani, and Tony Saboorian. "A distributed collaborative learning approach in 5G+ core networks." *IEEE Network* (2023).

Kay, Judy. "Foundations for human–AI teaming for self-regulated learning with explainable AI (XAI)." *Computers in Human Behavior* 147 (2023): 107848.

Kong, Xiangwei, Shujie Liu, and Luhao Zhu. "Toward human-centered XAI in practice: A survey." *Machine Intelligence Research* (2024): 1–31.

Naiseh, Mohammad, Auste Simkute, Baraa Zieni, Nan Jiang, and Raian Ali. "C-XAI: A conceptual framework for designing XAI tools that support trust calibration." *Journal of Responsible Technology* 17 (2024): 100076.

Peramunugamage, Anuradha, Uditha W. Ratnayake, and Shironica P. Karunanayaka. "Systematic review on mobile collaborative learning for engineering education." *Journal of Computers in Education* 10, no. 1 (2023): 83–106.

Pfeuffer, Nicolas, Lorenz Baum, Wolfgang Stammer, Benjamin M. Abdel-Karim, Patrick Schramowski, Andreas M. Bucher, Christian Hügel, Gernot Rohde, Kristian Kersting, and Oliver Hinz. "Explanatory interactive machine learning: Establishing an action design research process for machine learning projects." *Business & Information Systems Engineering* 65, no. 6 (2023): 677–701.

Theis, Sabine, Sophie Jentzsch, Fotini Deligiannaki, Charles Berro, Arne Peter Raulf, and Carmen Bruder. "Requirements for explainability and acceptance of artificial intelligence in collaborative work." In *International Conference on Human–Computer Interaction*, pp. 355–380. Cham: Springer Nature Switzerland, 2023.

Zafar, Muhammad Rehman, and Naimul Khan. "Deterministic local interpretable model-agnostic explanations for stable explainability." *Machine Learning and Knowledge Extraction* 3, no. 3 (2021): 525–541.

Section III

Challenges and Solutions in Educational Clouds

13 Optimizing Learning Environments

A Critical Review of Unified Cloud-Based Platforms for Educational Resource Management

Manoj Bramhe and Jagdish Pimple

13.1 INTRODUCTION

In the rapidly evolving landscape of education, traditional learning methods are facing unprecedented challenges. The digital era has ushered in a new paradigm where learners and educators alike are increasingly reliant on technology to access, create, and disseminate knowledge. However, amid this digital transformation, traditional learning approaches often struggle to keep pace with the dynamic needs and expectations of modern learners.

The emergence of cloud-based learning platforms indicates a paradigm shift in education, offering a revolutionary solution to the limitations of conventional learning methods. These systems offer a scalable, easily accessible, and cooperative learning environment for educators by utilizing cloud computing. From elementary classrooms to higher education institutions and corporate training programs, cloud-based learning platforms are reshaping the way we approach education.

At the heart of this transformation lies the recognition of the challenges inherent in traditional learning approaches. Physical classroom limitations, time constraints, and the need for extensive internet searches are just a few of the obstacles that learners encounter in their educational journey. These challenges not only impede the effectiveness of learning but also undermine the potential for innovation and creativity in the educational process.

The promise of cloud-based learning platforms lies in their ability to overcome these challenges and unlock new possibilities for teaching and learning. By consolidating educational resources onto a unified platform, these platforms provide learners with seamless access to a wealth of materials, including textbooks, multimedia content, interactive simulations, and collaborative tools. Moreover, the scalability and flexibility of cloud technology enable educators to adapt and customize learning experiences to meet the assorted needs and likings of learners.

DOI: 10.1201/9781003472537-16

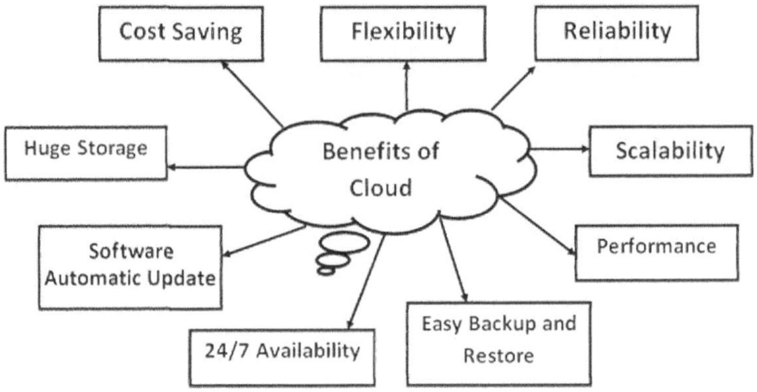

FIGURE 13.1 Benefits of Cloud Computing.

In this chapter, we will discover the transformative potential of cloud-based learning platforms in revolutionizing education. We will examine the key features and benefits of these platforms, as well as the challenges and considerations associated with their implementation. Through case studies, examples, and best practices, we will illustrate how cloud-based learning platforms are reshaping the educational landscape and empowering learners and educators to thrive in the online world.

As we set out on this adventure of exploration and discovery, it is evident that cloud-based learning platforms represent more than just a technological innovation – they are catalysts for change, driving us toward a future where education is accessible, engaging, and transformative for all.

13.1.1 The Role of Cloud Technology in E-Learning

Cloud technology plays a pivotal role in revolutionizing e-learning by addressing inherent challenges and enhancing the overall learning experience. In the context of the proposed framework, leveraging cloud technology is imperative for several reasons. Firstly, cloud-based platforms provide ubiquitous access to educational resources, allowing learners to engage in self-paced learning from anywhere with internet connectivity. This accessibility ensures flexibility and convenience, transcending traditional classroom limitations. Additionally, cloud infrastructure offers scalability, enabling e-learning platforms to dynamically allocate resources to accommodate varying levels of demand and user growth. By centralizing educational resources onto a unified platform, cloud technology mitigates the challenges associated with fragmented content and disparate sources. Learners can seamlessly access a diverse array of materials without navigating through multiple sources, enhancing efficiency and streamlining the learning process. Additionally, cloud computing facilitates communication and cooperation between students, teachers, and administrators with features like discussion boards and real-time collaboration tools. This promotes interaction, knowledge sharing, and collaborative learning experiences. Moreover, cloud-based solutions offer cost efficiency by eliminating the need for educational organizations to invest in on-premises infrastructure and enabling pay-as-you-go resource consumption models. Furthermore, cloud providers enhance data security and privacy for e-learning platforms by putting strong security measures in place to safeguard confidential data and guarantee compliance with data privacy laws. In essence, cloud technology serves as a foundational enabler for e-learning, providing accessibility, scalability, centralized resource management, collaboration tools, cost efficiency, and security, all of which are crucial for optimizing the learning process and fostering a seamless and effective educational journey.

13.1.2 Overview of Unified Cloud-Based Platforms

Unified cloud-based platforms for educational resource management offer a comprehensive solution for organizing and accessing a wide range of educational materials. These platforms typically provide features such as centralized storage, search functionality, collaboration tools, and user authentication mechanisms. By leveraging cloud technology, they enable users to access educational resources from any location with an internet connection, facilitating flexible and convenient learning experiences. Additionally, these platforms often incorporate features for content curation, personalization, and analytics, enabling teachers to efficiently monitor students' progress and customize learning experiences to meet their needs.

13.1.3 Effectiveness of Unified Cloud-Based Platforms

Several studies have investigated the effectiveness of unified cloud-based platforms for educational resource management in enhancing learning outcomes and facilitating collaboration among users. Research suggests that these platforms can improve access to educational materials, streamline content delivery, and foster communication and association among learners and educators. Additionally, unified cloud-based platforms have been found to support personalized learning approaches, enabling educators to customize content and activities to meet the diverse needs of learners. However, challenges such as data privacy concerns, technical issues, and digital divide issues need to be addressed to maximize the effectiveness of these platforms.

13.2 CLOUD ENVIRONMENT FOR E-LEARNING

The introduction of cloud computing has changed how we approach many areas of our lives, including education, in recent years. Cloud computing offers a flexible, scalable, and cost-effective solution for delivering e-learning content and services. This introduction will explore the benefits and features of utilizing cloud environments for e-learning purposes.

13.2.1 Scalability

One of the primary benefits of cloud computing for e-learning is scalability. Educational institutions often experience fluctuations in demand for online resources, especially during peak times such as enrollment periods or exam seasons. Cloud environments can effortlessly scale up or down to accommodate these fluctuations, ensuring consistent performance and uninterrupted access to learning materials.

13.2.2 Accessibility

Cloud-based e-learning platforms enable learners to access educational content anytime, anywhere, and through any internet-connected device. This accessibility fosters a more inclusive learning environment, allowing students to engage in learning activities at their own pace and convenience.

13.2.3 Cost-Effectiveness

Educational institutions can stop spending money on pricey software licensing and hardware infrastructure because of cloud computing. Alternatively, customers can pay for the services they use as needed, utilizing cloud services to minimize upfront expenditures and lower the total cost of ownership. Furthermore, when compared to traditional IT solutions, cloud environments offer economies of scale, which enables institutions to enjoy cheaper per-unit expenses.

13.2.4 Collaboration and Communication

Cloud-based e-learning systems make it easier for teachers, administrators, and students to collaborate and communicate with each other. Collaborative document editing, live chat, discussion boards, and other features allow for participatory learning and build a sense of community among students.

13.2.5 Security and Data Privacy

Cloud service companies make significant investments in security protocols to safeguard private student information kept on cloud servers. They put strong encryption, access control, and compliance frameworks into place to guarantee the privacy, availability, and integrity of data. Furthermore, cloud environments lower the risk of data loss from hardware malfunctions or natural catastrophes by enabling automatic backups and disaster recovery procedures.

13.2.6 Customization and Personalization

Cloud-based e-learning platforms provide educational institutions with the ability to tailor the learning process to the unique needs and preferences of each student. To improve learner engagement and satisfaction, machine learning algorithms can evaluate user data and offer tailored recommendations for courses, resources, and learning routes (see Figure 13.2).

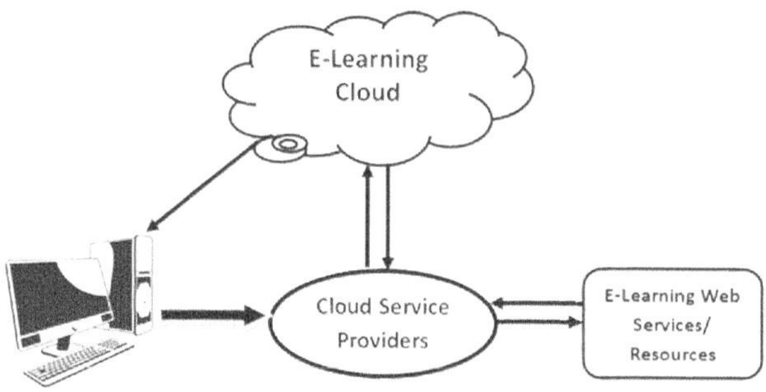

FIGURE 13.2 Model for Cloud-Based E-Learning.

13.2.7 Cloud vs. Traditional Approach

See Table 13.1 for comparison of cloud vs. traditional approach.

13.3 LITERATURE SURVEY

With regard to the scalable and adaptable solutions for resource management and learning optimization, cloud-based platforms have become essential elements of contemporary educational environments. This review of the literature critically looks at the most recent advancements in unified cloud-based platform research and development with the goal of improving learning environments and educational resource management. This survey, which draws from a wide range of studies, examines several facets of recommender systems, adaptive e-learning environments, content recommendation systems, and personalized learning strategies in e-learning, with an emphasis on their uses, difficulties, and prospective solutions.

The effectiveness of individualized learning tactics in raising academic achievement and student motivation was covered by Makhambetova et al. (2021). To shed light on the functions and classifications of content recommenders in e-learning environments, Joy and Pillai (2022) reviewed and categorized the available options. Murtaza et al. (2022) examined the problems, difficulties, and solutions associated with AI-based personalized e-learning systems, highlighting the significance of utilizing artificial intelligence for customized learning experiences.

El-Sabagh (2021) highlighted the impact of an adaptive e-learning environment on students' engagement and learning outcomes and advocated an environment based on learning styles. Dahdouh et al. (2019) explored large-scale e-learning recommender systems built on Spark and Hadoop, offering scalable solutions for individualized learning experiences.

Dumont and Ready (2023) promoted inclusive and equitable learning settings while examining the potential of individualized learning for educational equity. A personalized learning path recommendation system using multi-algorithm approaches was presented by Ma et al. (2023) with the goal of offering customized learning trajectories for each learner.

TABLE 13.1
Comparison of Cloud vs Traditional Approach

Aspect	Traditional Methods Comparison	Cloud-Based Learning Comparison
Accessibility	Limited access to resources, often tied to physical classrooms.	Learners can access resources anytime, anywhere, on any device with internet connectivity.
Scalability	Limited scalability, often requiring significant upfront investments in infrastructure.	Scalable resource allocation based on demand.
Resource Management	Fragmented content across various sources, leading to inefficiencies.	Centralized platform for easy access to diverse educational materials.
Collaboration	Collaboration may be limited, hindering interaction and knowledge sharing.	Facilitates seamless collaboration and communication among learners, educators, and administrators.
Cost Efficiency	Upfront capital expenditures for infrastructure may be required.	Cost-efficient pay-as-you-go model, eliminating the need for significant upfront investments in infrastructure.
Security	Security vulnerabilities associated with physical storage of data.	Robust security measures implemented by cloud providers.
Adaptability	Slower to adapt to advancements in technology and pedagogy.	Rapid innovation and adaptation to changing needs and technologies.
Customization	Limited customization options in traditional settings.	Ability to customize learning experiences based on individual learner preferences and needs.
Real-Time Updates	Updates and changes may require time and resources to implement.	Real-time updates and improvements can be implemented seamlessly.
Data Analytics	Limited or no data analytics capabilities.	Utilization of data analytics for insights into learner behavior, preferences, and performance.
Disaster Recovery	May lack robust disaster recovery mechanisms.	Built-in disaster recovery measures for data protection and continuity of learning.

According to Lee et al. (2020), learning analytics provide information on cutting-edge techniques and emerging trends in the analysis of educational data, enabling well-informed choices for learning optimization. Zhang et al. (2021) examined recommender systems in e-learning, their features, and their applications, highlighting the significance of tailored recommendations in improving learning outcomes.

Shemshack and Spector (2020) conducted a thorough literature study on terms related to individualized learning, offering a thorough synopsis of terms used in the field. In 2022, Roy and Dutta (2022) provided a comprehensive analysis and research viewpoint on recommender systems, emphasizing their potential uses and future developments in e-learning settings. The technology adoption of digital learning technologies was examined by Sprenger and Schwaninger (2021), with an emphasis on mobile virtual reality, e-lectures, classroom response systems, and classroom chat. Cheung et al. (2021) promoted the integration of intelligent technology for improved learning experiences by examining the opportunities and challenges of designing future learning environments with smart elements.

In conclusion, this literature survey provides a comprehensive overview of research efforts aimed at optimizing learning environments through unified cloud-based platforms for educational resource management. By synthesizing findings from diverse studies, this survey contributes to the understanding of current trends, challenges, and opportunities in leveraging cloud-based technologies for personalized and efficient learning experiences.

13.3.1 Comparative Analysis of Literature Survey

See Table 13.2 for comparative analysis of literature survey.

13.4 PROBLEM FORMULATION

The problem statement extracted from the literature survey focuses on the inefficiencies and challenges present in traditional learning approaches, particularly regarding the accessibility of relevant educational content. It highlights the cumbersome process learners face when navigating through multiple sources, including textual documents, audio files, and video files, to find desired materials. This process not only consumes time but also leads to frustration and inefficiency. Moreover, traditional learning methods are constrained by physical classroom limitations and time constraints, exacerbating the difficulty of accessing educational resources seamlessly. Additionally, the complexity of internet-based learning further complicates the process, requiring learners to sift through numerous sources, resulting in inefficiencies. Managing multiple credentials across different websites adds another layer of complexity to the learning process, often leading to replication and creation of various credentials, detracting from the learning experience. Thus, there is a clear need for a transformative solution that centralizes educational resources, optimizes search functionality, and simplifies user access through a single sign-in system. With the help of this solution, students will be able to concentrate on learning material instead of overcoming technological obstacles in the digital age.

13.5 PROPOSED APPROACH

The comprehensive framework aimed at revolutionizing the learning process through cloud-based technology. The framework is designed to address the inherent challenges

TABLE 13.2
Comparative Analysis of Literature Survey

Author Name and Year of Publication	Main Focus	Key Findings and Methodologies/ Approaches
Makhambetova et al., 2021	Personalized learning strategies	Examined personalized learning strategies to improve academic performance and student motivation.
Joy and Pillai, 2022	Content recommenders in E-learning	Provided a review and classification of content recommenders, categorizing their functionalities.
Murtaza et al., 2022	AI-based personalized e-learning	Explored issues, challenges, and solutions related to AI-based personalized e-learning systems.
El-Sabagh, 2021	Adaptive e-learning environment	Proposed an adaptive e-learning environment based on learning styles and measured its impact on students' engagement.
Ma et al., 2023	Personalized learning path	Presented a personalized learning path recommendation method incorporating multi-algorithm approaches.
Lee et al., 2020	Learning analytics	Discussed current trends and innovative practices in learning analytics, providing insights into educational data analysis.
Zhang et al., 2021	Recommender systems in E-learning	Explored recommender systems in e-learning, emphasizing the role of personalized recommendations.
Shemshack and Spector, 2020	Personalized learning terms	Conducted a systematic literature review of personalized learning terms, offering a comprehensive overview of terminology.
Roy and Dutta, 2022	Systematic review of recommender	Provided a systematic review and research perspective on recommender systems, highlighting applications and future directions.
Sprenger and Schwaninger, 2021	Technology acceptance in learning	Investigated the technology acceptance of digital learning technologies, focusing on classroom response systems, chat, e-lectures, and mobile VR.

of traditional learning approaches by streamlining access to educational resources. It mitigates the inefficiencies associated with traditional learning, such as physical classroom limitations, time constraints, and the cumbersome process of internet searches, by consolidating all educational materials onto a unified cloud-based platform. This platform provides learners with easy access to a different collection of materials, including theory and lab study materials, thereby eliminating the need for navigating through numerous links and sources.

A key innovation of the proposed platform lies in its search functionality, which enables learners to efficiently find content by inputting queries. The integrated search engine utilizes previous positive reviews to refine and prioritize results, significantly reducing the time spent on searching through various internet sources. This ensures that learners can promptly access relevant and high-quality educational materials, enhancing the overall learning experience.

Furthermore, the proposed framework simplifies the user experience by introducing a single sign-in system. Instead of managing multiple credentials across different websites, learners can access the entire platform with a single sign-in, eliminating the need for constant replication and creation of various credentials. This streamlined approach not only enhances efficiency but also minimizes the complexities associated with web portal access, thereby facilitating seamless and convenient access to educational resources.

13.5.1 Process Flow of Proposed System

1. **Identification of Challenges:** The process begins with identifying the challenges inherent in traditional learning approaches, including physical classroom limitations, time constraints, and difficulties in accessing relevant educational content.
2. **Introduction of Comprehensive Framework:** A comprehensive framework is introduced to streamline the learning process. This framework leverages cloud technology to create a unified platform for educational resources, addressing the identified challenges.
3. **Consolidation of Educational Resources:** All educational materials, including theory and lab resources, are consolidated onto the cloud-based platform. This consolidation eliminates the need for navigating through numerous links and sources, simplifying access to relevant content.
4. **Enhanced Search Functionality:** A key innovation of the proposed platform is its enhanced search functionality. Learners can efficiently find content by inputting queries, and the integrated search engine utilizes previous positive reviews to refine and prioritize results, ensuring prompt access to high-quality educational materials.
5. **Implementation of Single Sign-In System:** The proposed framework simplifies the user experience by introducing a single sign-in system. Learners can access the entire platform with a single sign-in, eliminating the need for managing multiple credentials across different websites.
6. **Optimization of Learning Experience:** By centralizing educational resources, optimizing search functionality, and implementing a single sign-in system, the proposed framework aims to enhance the overall learning experience. Learners are empowered to focus on educational content rather than grappling with logistical challenges.
7. **Alignment with Evolving Needs:** The innovative approach aligns with the evolving needs of learners in the digital era, fostering a more seamless and

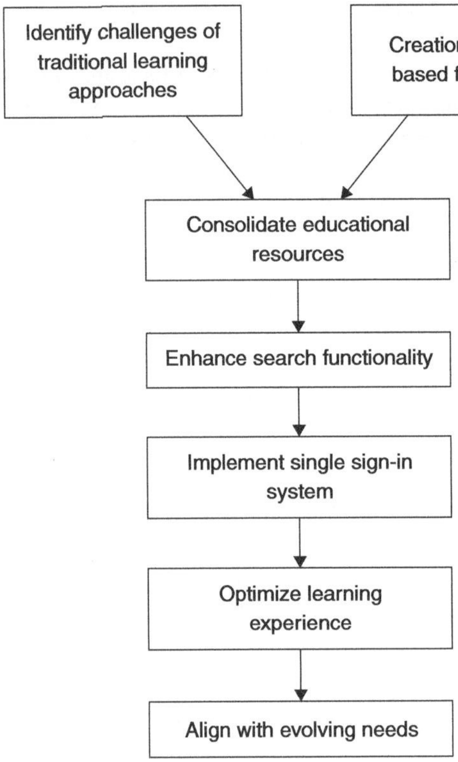

FIGURE 13.3 Block Diagram of Proposed Approach.

effective educational journey. It adapts to changes in technology and learning preferences to continually improve the learning experience (see Figure 13.3).

This block diagram illustrates the sequential flow of the proposed approach, starting from identifying challenges of traditional learning approaches, introducing a comprehensive framework, consolidating educational resources, enhancing search functionality, implementing a single sign-in system, optimizing the learning experience, and finally aligning with evolving needs. Each block represents a distinct step in the process, leading to an improved and more effective educational journey for learners in the contemporary educational landscape.

13.5.2 Identification of Potential Challenges and Limitations

1. **Technical Infrastructure:** Setting up the necessary technical infrastructure to support the cloud-based platform can be complex and resource-intensive. This includes ensuring sufficient storage capacity, network bandwidth, and computing resources to handle the storage and retrieval of large volumes of educational materials.

2. **Data Privacy and Security:** Storing educational materials and user data in the cloud raises concerns about data privacy and security. Protecting sensitive information from unauthorized access, data breaches, and cyberattacks is paramount. Compliance with data protection regulations such as General Data Protection Regulation (GDPR) and ensuring encryption of data in transit and at rest are essential considerations.
3. **User Training and Support:** Educationalists and learners may need training and support to effectively use the platform. Providing comprehensive training materials, tutorials, and user guides can help users navigate the platform's features and functionalities. Ongoing technical support and troubleshooting services are also necessary to address user queries and issues.
4. **Content Migration and Integration**: It can be difficult to transfer current instructional materials from conventional systems to the cloud-based platform. To reduce interruptions to teaching and learning activities, compatibility and smooth integration with current learning management systems (LMS), content repositories, and educational technologies are crucial.
5. **User Adoption and Engagement:** Encouraging widespread adoption and engagement among educators and learners is crucial for the success of the platform. Educators may resist adopting new technologies because of perceived learning curves or concerns about changes to established teaching practices. Strategies for promoting user buy-in, such as conducting pilot programs, soliciting feedback, and highlighting the platform's benefits, are essential for fostering acceptance and usage.
6. **Accessibility and Inclusivity:** Promoting inclusion requires making sure the platform is usable by everyone, including people with different learning needs or impairments. Differentiated learning preferences and abilities can be accommodated by adhering to accessibility standards like Web Content Accessibility Guidelines (WCAG) and offering alternate forms for content.
7. **Scalability and Performance:** As the platform grows in usage and user base, scalability and performance become critical considerations. The platform must be able to handle increased demand without degradation in performance or downtime. Regular monitoring, capacity planning, and optimization of resources are necessary to maintain responsiveness and reliability.
8. **Cost Management:** Managing the costs associated with hosting, maintaining, and upgrading the cloud-based platform can be challenging. Balancing the need for robust features and functionalities with budget constraints requires careful planning and resource allocation. Implementing cost-saving measures such as resource optimization, usage-based pricing models, and negotiating contracts with cloud service providers can help control expenses.

Addressing these challenges requires collaboration among stakeholders, including educators, administrators, IT professionals, and cloud service providers. By proactively addressing technical, organizational, and user-related issues, organizations can successfully implement and leverage unified cloud-based learning platforms to enhance teaching and learning experiences.

13.5.3 Application of the Proposed Framework

The application of the proposed framework for cloud-based learning has extensive implications across various educational settings and contexts. Some key applications include the following:

1. **Higher Education Institutions:** Universities and colleges can leverage the framework to enhance their e-learning platforms, providing students with centralized access to educational resources, facilitating collaboration among faculty and students, and optimizing the learning process. The framework can support diverse disciplines and courses, ranging from humanities to science, technology, engineering, and mathematics (STEM) fields, offering a comprehensive learning experience.
2. **K-12 Education:** The framework can be applied in K-12 schools to modernize traditional teaching methods and engage students in interactive and personalized learning experiences. Teachers can use the platform to deliver multimedia-rich content, track student progress, and provide targeted interventions to support individual learning needs.
3. **Corporate Training:** Organizations can adopt the framework to develop cloud-based training platforms for employee learning and development. By centralizing training materials, providing on-demand access to resources, and integrating collaboration tools, companies can streamline employee training processes and ensure continuous skill development.
4. **Professional Development:** The framework can also be utilized for professional development purposes, enabling professionals to access educational resources, participate in online courses, and collaborate with peers in their field. This application supports lifelong learning initiatives and fosters continuous professional growth.
5. **Distance Learning and Remote Education:** Particularly relevant in situations such as the COVID-19 pandemic, the framework can facilitate distance learning and remote education initiatives. Educational institutions and organizations can use the platform to deliver remote instruction, engage learners in virtual classrooms, and maintain continuity of learning during periods of disruption.
6. **Specialized Training Programs:** The framework can cater to specialized training programs and certifications across various industries, such as healthcare, IT, finance, and engineering. By offering tailored learning pathways, interactive simulations, and real-world case studies, the platform can prepare learners for specific roles and skill requirements.
7. **Global Learning Communities:** With its accessibility and scalability, the framework can support global learning communities, enabling collaboration and knowledge sharing among learners from diverse backgrounds and geographical locations. This fosters cross-cultural understanding, promotes global citizenship, and facilitates the exchange of ideas on a global scale.

13.6 EXPECTED OUTCOME

The expected outcome of the proposed approach is to revolutionize the learning process by leveraging cloud-based technology to overcome the challenges inherent in traditional learning approaches. By implementing a comprehensive framework, the aim is to streamline access to educational resources, thereby mitigating inefficiencies associated with traditional methods. Through consolidation onto a unified cloud-based platform, all educational materials, including theory and lab resources, will be readily accessible to learners, eliminating the need for navigating through multiple sources.

A key innovation of the proposed platform is its search functionality, which enables learners to efficiently find content by inputting queries. By utilizing previous positive reviews to refine and prioritize results, the integrated search engine significantly reduces the time spent on searching through various internet sources. This ensures prompt access to relevant and high-quality educational materials, ultimately enhancing the overall learning experience.

Moreover, the proposed framework simplifies the user experience by introducing a single sign-in system. This eliminates the need for learners to manage multiple credentials across different websites, allowing access to the entire platform with a single sign-in. By minimizing complexities associated with web portal access, the streamlined approach facilitates seamless and convenient access to educational resources, ultimately optimizing the learning process for all users.

13.7 FUTURE WORK

There are several areas for future work and enhancements to the proposed system aimed at further improving the learning process and maximizing its effectiveness. One avenue for improvement involves the integration of advanced analytics tools and techniques to gather insights into learner behavior, preferences, and performance. By analyzing data such as user interactions, search patterns, and content usage, the system can provide personalized recommendations, adaptive learning pathways, and real-time feedback to enhance the learning experience. Additionally, there is potential to develop advanced content curation algorithms and methodologies to automatically categorize, tag, and recommend educational materials based on relevance, quality, and learner preferences. This could involve leveraging machine learning algorithms to analyze content metadata, user feedback, and historical usage patterns to improve the accuracy and effectiveness of content recommendations. Furthermore, integrating the platform with existing LMS could provide a seamless and integrated learning experience for educators and learners, enabling single sign-on, data exchange, and course synchronization between the platform and LMS. Additionally, enhancing collaboration features within the platform to facilitate group projects, peer-to-peer learning, and virtual classrooms could foster greater engagement and interaction among learners and educators. Improving mobile accessibility and offline access capabilities would enable learners to access educational resources anytime, anywhere, and on any device, ensuring uninterrupted access to learning materials, even in low-connectivity environments. Furthermore, exploring the integration of gamification elements and interactive learning experiences could enhance learner engagement and motivation, making the learning process more immersive, enjoyable, and effective. Finally, conducting longitudinal studies and rigorous evaluations to assess the long-term impact of the platform on learning outcomes, retention rates, and student satisfaction would provide valuable insights to inform future iterations of the platform. By focusing on these areas for future work and enhancements, the proposed system can continue to evolve and adapt to meet the changing needs and preferences of learners and educators, ultimately leading to a more effective and personalized learning experience.

13.8 CONCLUSION

Unified cloud-based platforms for educational resource management hold significant promise for optimizing learning environments and enhancing the overall learning experience. By centralizing educational resources, streamlining access to content, and facilitating collaboration among users, these platforms offer a scalable and efficient solution for modern educational settings. However, addressing challenges such as data privacy concerns, technical issues, and digital divide issues is crucial to maximizing the effectiveness of these platforms. With careful planning, implementation, and ongoing support, unified cloud-based platforms have the potential to revolutionize learning environments and empower learners and educators in the digital era.

REFERENCES

Alenezi, Mamdouh (2023). "Digital learning and digital institution in higher education." *Education Sciences* 13, no. 1: 88.

Cheung, Simon KS, Lam For Kwok, Kongkiti Phusavat, and Harrison Hao Yang (2021). "Shaping the future learning environments with smart elements: Challenges and opportunities." *International Journal of Educational Technology in Higher Education* 18: 1–9.

Dahdouh, Karim, Ahmed Dakkak, Lahcen Oughdir, and Abdelali Ibriz (2019). "Large-scale e-learning recommender system based on Spark and Hadoop." *Journal of Big Data* 6, no. 1: 1–23.

Dumont, Hanna, and Douglas D. Ready (2023). "On the promise of personalized learning for educational equity." *NPJ Science of Learning* 8, no. 1: 26.

El-Sabagh, Hassan A (2021). "Adaptive e-learning environment based on learning styles and its impact on development students' engagement." *International*

Joy, Jeevamol, and Renumol Vemballiveli Govinda Pillai (2022). "Review and classification of content recommenders in E-learning environment." *Journal of King Saud University – Computer and Information Sciences* 34, no. 9: 7670–7685.

Lee, Lap-Kei, Simon KS Cheung, and Lam-For Kwok (2020). "Learning analytics: Current trends and innovative practices." *Journal of Computers in Education* 7: 1–6.

Ma, Yongjuan, Lei Wang, Jiating Zhang, Fengjuan Liu, and Qiaoyong Jiang (2023). "A personalized learning path recommendation method incorporating multi-algorithm." *Applied Sciences* 13, no. 10: 5946.

Makhambetova, Aliya, Nadezhda Zhiyenbayeva, and Elena Ergesheva (2021). "Personalized learning strategy as a tool to improve academic performance and motivation of students." *International Journal of Web-Based Learning and Teaching Technologies (IJWLTT)* 16, no. 6: 1–17.

Murtaza, Mir, Yamna Ahmed, Jawwad Ahmed Shamsi, Fahad Sherwani, and Mariam Usman (2022). "AI-based personalized e-learning systems: Issues, challenges, and solutions." *IEEE Access* 10: 81323–81342.

Roy, Deepjyoti, and Mala Dutta (2022). "A systematic review and research perspective on recommender systems." *Journal of Big Data* 9, no. 1: 59.

Shemshack, Atikah, and Jonathan Michael Spector (2020). "A systematic literature review of personalized learning terms." *Smart Learning Environments* 7, no. 1: 33.

Sprenger, David A., and Adrian Schwaninger (2021). "Technology acceptance of four digital learning technologies (classroom response system, classroom chat, e-lectures, and mobile virtual reality) after three months' usage." *International Journal of Educational Technology in Higher Education* 18, no. 1: 8.

Zhang, Qian, Jie Lu, and Guangquan Zhang (2021). "Recommender Systems in E-learning." *Journal of Smart Environments and Green Computing* 1, no. 2: 76–89.

14 Navigating the Legal and Ethical Aspects of Cloud-Based Education

Vinay Kumar Yandrapalli and Shubham Sharma

14.1 INTRODUCTION

The integration of cloud-based technologies in education has transformed the landscape of learning, offering unprecedented access to resources and connectivity (Alan 2012). Our research domain explores the legal and ethical dimensions of using these technologies in educational settings. As cloud computing continues to evolve, it not only presents unique opportunities for enhancing educational delivery but also introduces significant challenges that need careful consideration.

Technological advancements in cloud-based education have led to the development of sophisticated platforms that support a wide range of educational activities, from virtual classrooms to data-driven personalized learning experiences (Kovalevskaia et al. 2021). These platforms leverage the scalability and flexibility of cloud computing to meet the diverse needs of educational institutions and learners. However, researchers and practitioners continue to address critical areas of concern related to data privacy, compliance with international laws, and intellectual property rights despite these technological strides (Bennett 2020).

Our literature review identified several gaps in existing research, particularly in addressing comprehensive solutions that encapsulate legal and ethical considerations. Many existing approaches focus on isolated aspects of these challenges, lacking a holistic view that integrates technical solutions and strategic frameworks (Faragardi 2017, Ahmed and Sarkar 2020). This has led to fragmented practices that may not fully protect stakeholders or harness the full potential of cloud-based educational technologies.

In response to these gaps, our proposed approach offers a structured solution to navigate the complex legal and ethical landscapes. We aim to develop a robust framework that addresses these concerns effectively and ensures that the deployment of cloud-based educational technologies is both secure and equitable.

 DOI: 10.1201/9781003472537-17

We can summarize our contributions to this field in the following way:

1. We introduce a comprehensive privacy-by-design framework that enhances data protection from the initial stages of technological implementation.
2. Our proposal includes a unified compliance model that simplifies adherence to international data protection laws such as the General Data Protection Regulation (GDPR) and the California Consumer Privacy Act (CCPA).
3. We outline a digital rights management system tailored for educational content, ensuring intellectual property is respected and adequately managed.
4. We advocate for developing inclusive technologies that address the digital divide, ensuring fair access to educational resources for all learners.
5. Our approach also emphasizes the importance of transparency and accountability through blockchain technology to maintain a secure and verifiable record of data transactions.

The introduction of this book chapter outlines the structure and scope of our discussion on navigating the legal and ethical aspects of cloud-based education. After this introduction, we structure the chapter to first explore the specific legal challenges, then delve into a detailed examination of ethical considerations, and conclude with an exploration of technical solutions and future trends. Through this structure, we aim to provide a detailed and practical guide for educational institutions and e-learning providers to implement effective strategies that uphold legal and ethical standards in cloud-based education.

14.2 RELATED WORKS

Recent research has extensively explored the legal and ethical dimensions of cloud-based education. One research domain focuses on data privacy concerns, highlighting the need for robust mechanisms to protect sensitive student information in the cloud. These studies emphasize the vulnerability of cloud systems to data breaches and potential data misuse, advocating for strict adherence to data protection standards (Chatterjee 2023). Another significant area of research addresses the compliance challenges with international data protection laws. Researchers argue that the global nature of cloud services complicates compliance, especially when educators and service providers must navigate a mosaic of regional and national regulations. This body of work suggests a harmonized approach to facilitate easier management of legal requirements across different jurisdictions (Sultan 2010).

Intellectual property issues also receive considerable attention. The literature discusses the complexities of managing content ownership, particularly when multiple creators and educational institutions are involved. There is a consensus on the need for clear policies that outline the rights and responsibilities of all parties to mitigate disputes and encourage creative collaboration(Bălțătescu 2014). We thoroughly examine ethical considerations, particularly regarding digital equity. Studies in this area highlight the disparities in access to cloud-based resources, underscoring the risk of widening the educational gap between different socio-economic groups. These investigations often propose strategies to increase accessibility and ensure a more equitable distribution of technological benefits(Alam 2022).

The ethical use of educational data is another critical topic. Research in this domain explores the balance between leveraging data for educational advancements and protecting individual privacy rights. While educational data can significantly enhance learning experiences and outcomes, maintaining trust and integrity in educational systems requires responsible and ethical use(Anwar 2021). We also explore in-depth technical solutions to support legal and ethical compliance. Encryption and secure data storage are critical data protection practices. Similar scrutiny scrutinizes user authentication processes for their role in preventing unauthorized access and ensuring legitimate users can benefit from cloud services without undue barriers(Bishnoi 2022).

Future trends in cloud-based education's legal and ethical aspects are the subject of ongoing research. Research predicts that as cloud technologies evolve, so will the legal and ethical frameworks that govern them. They stress the importance of adaptive legal strategies and ethical guidelines to keep pace with technological advancements, ensuring educational practices remain compliant and beneficial for all stakeholders(Kanimozhi 2019). Some studies delve into the transparency and accountability of cloud-based educational platforms. This research underscores the importance of clear communication between service providers and users regarding data usage policies and the mechanisms in place for data protection. The findings suggest that increasing transparency can significantly enhance trust among users, which is critical for the widespread adoption of cloud technologies in education (Malhi 2020). Recent analyses have also prominently featured accessibility issues. These papers advocate for developing inclusive technologies that cater to diverse learning needs and environments. The emphasis is on designing cloud-based solutions that are technically proficient and universally accessible, ensuring that all learners, regardless of their physical or socio-economic conditions, have equal opportunities to benefit from digital education (Vitkar 2012).

We examine the role of ethics in the design and implementation of educational technologies. Researchers in this field advocate for a more comprehensive approach that integrates ethical considerations into the design phase of cloud-based educational tools. This approach ensures that these tools are practical and inherently equipped to handle ethical dilemmas and privacy concerns from the outset (Chatterjee et al. 2023). Together, these studies enrich our understanding of the multifaceted nature of cloud-based education. These studies offer valuable insights into interweaving legal, ethical, and technical concerns into modern educational practices, thereby providing a solid framework for further discussion and development within the field(Sahaya and Christopher 2019)

This literature review sets the stage for a deeper exploration of specific legal and ethical challenges and the development of practical strategies to address them, as detailed in subsequent sections.

14.3 PROPOSED APPROACH

14.3.1 Legal Challenges in Cloud-Based Education

14.3.1.1 Data Privacy: Understanding Student Data Rights and Obligations

To address the legal challenges surrounding data privacy in cloud-based education, our approach begins with the basic principle of "Privacy by Design." This concept entails integrating data protection from the onset of the technology design process rather than as an afterthought. We propose a framework that includes routine audits and the implementation of strict access controls compliant with the least privilege principle, ensuring that only necessary data is accessible to authenticated users.

Moving on to more advanced considerations, we suggest adopting data minimization strategies. This entails collecting only the data that is directly required for completing educational activities, thereby reducing the risk of sensitive data exposure. For instance, to anonymize student data, we could apply a mathematical formula that looks like this:

$$D' = f(D) \tag{14.1}$$

where D represents original data and D' denotes the anonymized dataset, with f being a transformation function that removes identifiable markers while preserving the utility of the data for educational purposes.

14.3.1.2 Compliance with International Data Protection Laws: GDPR, CCPA, and Others

To comply with international data protection laws such as GDPR and CCPA, our proposed approach includes the development of a unified compliance framework. We would structure this framework around the core requirements standard for all pertinent regulations, including data subject rights, consent management, data breach notifications, and transparency requirements.

To advance this framework, we recommend implementing automated tools that help continuously assess and manage compliance. These tools can utilize algorithms to check for deviations from compliance norms and automatically adjust processes to maintain adherence. For example, we could model a compliance verification equation as follows:

$$C = \sum_{i=1}^{n} w_i \cdot c_i \tag{14.2}$$

where C is the compliance score, w_i represents the weight assigned to each compliance parameter based on its importance, and c_i is the compliance status of each parameter, evaluated as either 0 (non-compliant) or 1 (compliant).

14.3.1.3 Intellectual Property Concerns: Content Creation, Ownership, and Usage

Addressing intellectual property concerns in cloud-based education, our approach starts with establishing clear guidelines and agreements on content ownership and usage rights. These agreements should specify who owns the created content (educators, students, or institutions), the conditions for its reuse, and the method of creation of data.

To further refine this approach, we propose developing a digital rights management system specifically tailored for educational content. This system would use encryption to protect intellectual property rights while allowing for controlled sharing under predefined conditions. A set of rules encoded into the platform could govern the system, ensuring that each piece of content adheres to the license terms agreed upon by all parties. An access control formula could represent this:

$$A(x)=1/0$$

$$1 \ \& \ "\{if\, license\, conditions\, are\, met\}$$

$$0 \ \& \ "\{otherwise\}$$

where $(A(x))$ determines access permission for content (x), permitting access only when license conditions are fully met. These proposals are designed to provide a robust framework to tackle the legal challenges in cloud-based education, offering a blend of basic and advanced strategies tailored to the evolving landscape of educational technologies.

14.3.2 Ethical Considerations in Cloud-Based Education

14.3.2.1 Digital Equity and Access: Addressing the Digital Divide

The fundamental aspect of addressing ethical concerns in cloud-based education begins with tackling digital equity and access. Our approach advocates for the development and deployment of universally accessible educational technologies. This involves designing platforms responsive to various devices and supporting low-bandwidth conditions, ensuring that students in underprivileged areas can access educational materials just as effectively as those in more technologically developed regions.

To further this goal, we propose a tiered service model that adapts resource allocation based on the user's technological access. For example, content could be delivered in different formats: high-definition videos for users with robust internet access and text-based materials or lower-resolution videos for users with limited bandwidth. An access function could guide this approach.

$$E(u)=H/L$$

$$\backslash begin\{cases\}$$

$$H \ \& \ "\{if\ bandwidth\} \geq B$$

$$L \ \& \ "\{otherwise\}$$

where $(E(u))$ determines the content format for a user (u), (H) represents high definition, (L) represents low definition, and (B) is the bandwidth threshold.

14.3.2.2 Ethical Use of Educational Data: Balancing Innovation with Privacy

Balancing the innovative use of educational data with privacy concerns requires a structured approach that incorporates ethical principles from the initial design phase of data collection and analysis systems. We suggest implementing differential privacy techniques to ensure that the data used for enhancing educational processes does not compromise individual privacy. For instance, adding random noise to datasets can help mask individual identities while providing valuable insights for educational improvements. We can mathematically represent the application of differential privacy as follows:

$$P(D+\epsilon) \approx P(D) \tag{14.3}$$

where $(P(D))$ represents the probability distribution of the original dataset (D), and (ϵ) denotes the noise added to ensure privacy.

14.3.2.3 Transparency and Accountability in Cloud Platforms

Transparency and accountability are crucial for ethical cloud-based education platforms. Our proposed approach includes the creation of an open governance framework where stakeholders can review and audit processes on a regular basis. This ensures operations remain transparent and accountable to all users—students, educators, and administrators. We recommend establishing a digital ledger system that records all data transactions and changes to institutionalize transparency. This system could utilize blockchain technology to maintain a tamper-proof data access and usage record, enhancing trust and reliability. We could access the ledger using the following equation:

$$L(t) = \sum_{i=1}^{n} \log(i, t_i) \tag{14.4}$$

where $L(t)$ represents the ledger transactions, i indexes each transaction, and (t_i) is the timestamp of transaction i.

These strategies collectively form a robust ethical framework that addresses the digital divide, ensures responsible use of educational data, and fosters transparency and accountability on cloud-based platforms. This multifaceted approach not only aligns with ethical norms but also enhances educational technologies' overall effectiveness and trustworthiness.

14.3.3 Technical Solutions for Legal and Ethical Compliance

14.3.3.1 Encryption and Secure Data Storage: Techniques and Best Practices

A critical element of ensuring legal and ethical compliance in cloud-based education involves robust data protection through encryption and secure storage practices. Our approach recommends the implementation of end-to-end encryption (E2EE) for all data transmitted and stored within the cloud. This ensures that data is only decipherable by the intended recipient, significantly reducing the risk of unauthorized access during transmission or from storage points.

We propose using encrypted databases with multi-factor authentication (MFA) protocols for access to enhance data storage security. To ensure the protection and regular rotation of decryption keys, these databases should implement advanced encryption standards (AES) and key management best practices. A simple representation of the encryption process can be depicted mathematically as follows:

$$C = E_k(D)$$

$$C \;\&:\; "\{the\, ciphertext(encrypted\; data)\},$$

$$D \;\&:\; "\{the\; plaintext\; data\},$$

$$E\_k \;\&:\; "\{the\; encryption\; function\; using\; key\}\; k.$$

14.3.3.2 User Authentication and Access Control: Ensuring Secure and Equitable Access

Our proposed solution emphasizes a multi-layered security approach for user authentication and access control. This starts with implementing strong password policies and extends to more sophisticated biometric authentication methods (e.g., fingerprint or facial recognition) where feasible. Role-based access control (RBAC) systems should strictly govern each user's access to data and resources, ensuring that users can only access information essential for their role within the educational institution.

To swiftly detect and respond to unauthorized access attempts, we propose using an access control matrix in conjunction with continuous monitoring and auditing of access logs. We can formalize the access control with an access control function.

$$A(u,r) = 1/0$$

$$1 \;\&\; "\{if\}u\; "\{\,has\, rights\, to\,\}r$$

$$0 \;\&\; "\{otherwise\}$$

where $A(u, r)$ determines whether user u has access rights to resource r. This model ensures that necessary permissions are granted based on the principle of least privilege, aligning access rights with the specific needs and roles of users.

We also suggest regular training and awareness programs for all stakeholders involved in cloud-based educational systems to support these technical measures. These programs should focus on data security, strong authentication measures, and best data handling and storage practices. This comprehensive approach to encryption, data storage, and user authentication ensures compliance with legal and ethical standards and builds a robust infrastructure capable of protecting sensitive educational data against emerging cyber threats.

14.4 OUTCOMES AND IMPLEMENTATION STRATEGIES

This section details the practical implications and actionable strategies associated with deploying our proposed framework for addressing cloud-based education's legal and ethical challenges. We focus on the concrete benefits these strategies can offer and the steps necessary for effective implementation.

14.4.1 Enhanced Data Protection and Privacy

The implementation of a privacy-by-design framework and data minimization strategies has the potential to significantly enhance the security and privacy of educational data. By embedding data protection features at the initial design stage of educational platforms, institutions can ensure that privacy measures are not just add-ons but integral components of the technological infrastructure. The anticipated outcome is a reduced risk of data breaches and unauthorized access, fostering a safer educational environment. To achieve these outcomes, institutions must revise their system designs to incorporate encryption protocols and secure access mechanisms from the ground up. We should conduct regular training sessions to educate staff on the importance of data privacy and the specific measures implemented on their platforms.

14.4.2 Streamlined Legal Compliance

Our unified compliance model simplifies the adherence to many international data protection laws, such as the GDPR and CCPA, by synthesizing their common elements into a coherent framework. This model facilitates more straightforward management of compliance obligations, thereby reducing administrative burdens and enhancing focus on core educational activities. The practical steps for implementation include integrating compliance software that automatically updates in response to legal changes, ensuring continuous adherence without manual intervention. Educational institutions should also consider establishing a dedicated legal team to monitor compliance and interact with the automated systems to address any discrepancies or updates in real time.

14.4.3 Intellectual Property Management

Introducing a tailored digital rights management system will mitigate issues surrounding intellectual property in educational content creation and distribution. This system will guarantee adherence to predefined agreements, safeguarding the rights of creators and preventing unauthorized use. Educational institutions must develop clear guidelines for content usage and establish secure digital libraries to safely store and access encrypted content, according to user roles and permissions, for effective implementation. We can organize workshops and seminars to acquaint creators and educators with the technological and legal aspects of managing intellectual property in digital environments.

14.4.4 Closing the Digital Divide

By adopting inclusive technology designs and tiered service models, educational institutions can make significant strides in closing the digital divide. This approach ensures that all students have access to quality educational resources, regardless of their socio-economic background or geographical location. Implementing this strategy entails assessing the student body's current technological landscape and adapting educational materials to suit different connectivity scenarios. For instance, providing low-bandwidth alternatives for students in remote areas can ensure continuous access to learning materials. Institutions should also collaborate with technology providers to develop scalable solutions that adjust to varying bandwidth and device capabilities.

14.4.5 Increased Transparency and Accountability

Utilizing blockchain technology for educational data transactions not only improves data exchange security but also increases transparency and accountability in these processes. The immutable ledger of blockchain guarantees the permanent recording of all transactions, which authorized personnel can audit, thereby fostering trust and integrity. To implement this technology, educational platforms must first pilot blockchain integration in smaller, controlled environments to understand its impact and optimize its setup. After successful trials, educational platforms can launch a full-scale implementation and provide extensive training to users on how to interact with and benefit from the new system.

Through these strategies, our proposed approach addresses cloud-based education's pressing legal and ethical challenges. It lays down a roadmap for educational institutions to enhance their technological capabilities securely and competently.

14.5 CONCLUSION

In conclusion, this chapter has extensively explored the multifaceted legal and ethical challenges of integrating cloud technologies in educational settings. We began with a detailed overview of the domain, discussing how cloud-based education has evolved and its significant opportunities for enhancing teaching and learning processes. Despite these advancements, we identified several gaps, particularly in the comprehensive management of data privacy, legal compliance, intellectual property issues, digital equity, and the transparent use of educational platforms. To address these gaps, we proposed a structured approach that offers robust solutions to the identified challenges. Our approach is anchored in the principles of privacy by design and includes a unified compliance framework that simplifies the complexities of adhering to international data protection laws. We also suggested a digital rights management system tailored for educational content, ensuring proper intellectual property rights management. Furthermore, our strategies for closing the digital divide and enhancing transparency and accountability through blockchain technology aim to create a more equitable and trustworthy educational environment. Our proposed solutions are not merely theoretical but come with detailed implementation strategies that educational institutions and e-learning providers can realistically adopt. These include technical enhancements, policy revisions, and continuous education on new systems and compliance requirements. By implementing these strategies, educational stakeholders can better navigate the legal and ethical mazes presented by cloud technologies, thereby enhancing the overall security, efficacy, and accessibility of cloud-based education.

Cloud-based education will continue to evolve, bringing new challenges and opportunities. Future research should focus on continuously updating and refining the legal and ethical frameworks as new technologies and regulations emerge. There is a particular need for further development in artificial intelligence and machine learning in education, which pose new challenges for data privacy and ethical use. Additionally, as global connectivity improves and more educational institutions adopt cloud-based solutions, researchers should explore the impacts of these technologies on global educational disparities. Studies could investigate how cloud-based education can be leveraged to close the digital divide and enhance cross-cultural learning and collaboration. Finally, with the increasing use of blockchain and other secure transaction technologies in education, future work could explore more advanced applications. This includes their ability to secure and verify transactions, as well as create new forms of educational credentials and certifications that are universally recognized and verifiable.

REFERENCES

Ahmed, Monjur, and Nurul I. Sarkar. "Privacy in cloud-based computing." In *Social, Legal, and Ethical Implications of IoT, Cloud, and Edge Computing Technologies*, pp. 239–252. Pennsylvania: IGI Global, 2020.

Alam, Ashraf. "Cloud-based e-learning: Scaffolding the environment for adaptive e-learning ecosystem based on cloud computing infrastructure." In *Computer Communication, Networking and IoT: Proceedings of 5th ICICC 2021*, Volume 2, pp. 1–9. Singapore: Springer Nature, 2022.

Anwar, Mohd. "Supporting privacy, trust, and personalization in online learning." *International Journal of Artificial Intelligence in Education* 31, no. 4 (2021): 769–783.

Bălțătescu, Ionela. "Cloud computing services: Benefits, risks and intellectual property issues." *Global Economic Observer* 230 (2014): 230–242.

Bennett, Erik Carl. *Jumping into the Cloud: Privacy, Security and Trust of Cloud-based Computing within K-12 American Public Education.* PhD dissertation, City University of New York, 2020.

Bishnoi, Anirudh, Anupma Sangwan, Anju, and Rishi Pal Singh. "Enhancing the security and performance of cloud-based distance education system." In *Pattern Recognition and Data Analysis with Applications*, pp. 229–246. Singapore: Springer Nature, 2022.

Chatterjee, Paramita, Rajesh Bose, Subhasish Banerjee, and Sandip Roy. "Enhancing data security of cloud-based LMS." *Wireless Personal Communications* 130, no. 2 (2023): 1123–1139.

Faragardi, Hamid Reza. "Ethical considerations in cloud computing systems." *Proceedings* 1, no. 3 (2017): 166. MDPI.

Kanimozhi, S., A. Kannan, K. Suganya Devi, and K. Selvamani. "Secure cloud-based e-learning system with access control and group key mechanism." *Concurrency and Computation: Practice and Experience* 31, no. 12 (2019): e4841.

Kovalevskaia, Natalia, Emma Nikolaevna Gilyazeva, Olga Fedorovna Lobazova, Irina Albertovna Duborkina, and Antonina Pavlovna Sokolova. "Impact of digital services of hybrid cloud-based learning environment on efficiency of education." *Revista Tempos E Espaços Em Educação* 14, no. 33 (2021): e15297–e15297.

Malhi, Muhammad Saqib, Usman Iqbal, Muhammad Mustafa Nabi, and Muhammad Aaqib-Ishtiaq Malhi. "E-learning based on cloud computing for educational institution: Security issues and solutions." *International Journal of Electronics and Information Engineering* 12, no. 4 (2020): 162–169.

Sahaya Stalin Jose, G., and C. Seldev Christopher. "Secure cloud data storage approach in e-learning systems." *Cluster Computing* 22, no. 5 (2019): 12857–12862.

Sultan, Nabil. "Cloud computing for education: A new dawn?" *International Journal of Information Management* 30, no. 2 (2010): 109–116.

Vitkar, Swati. "Cloud-based model for e-learning in higher education." *International Journal of Advanced Engineering Technology* 3, no. 4 (2012): 38–42.

Weber, Alan S. "Cloud computing in education." In *Ubiquitous and Mobile Learning in the Digital Age*, pp. 19–36. New York, NY: Springer New York, 2012.

15 Navigating Remote Learning

Cloud-Powered Tools Transforming Education

Uma Yadav and Shweta Bondre

15.1 INTRODUCTION

A paradigm shift in the distribution and acquisition of information has been sparked by the combination of cloud computing and education. With the help of several cloud-based applications, remote learning has become a disruptive force in education in this digital age. Both instructors and students are enjoying the flexibility and accessibility provided by remote learning platforms as they are no longer constrained by geographical restrictions. This chapter begins a thorough investigation of the revolutionary effects of remote learning technologies on contemporary education (May & Denton, 2022). It explores the origins of remote learning throughout history, following its development from the earliest mail courses to the most advanced digital platforms available today. Students and teachers may now communicate and collaborate in real time using video conferencing services like Zoom, Microsoft Teams, and Google Meet (Haugsbakk, 2020). A unified center for course delivery, content administration, and evaluation is provided by learning management systems (LMS) like Moodle, Canvas, and Blackboard, giving instructors the freedom to create individualized learning experiences. Slack and Microsoft 365 are two examples of collaborative technologies that promote productivity and cooperation. They also make project management and communication in virtual settings easy.

Additionally, cutting-edge approaches to project management and document collaboration such as Trello, Microsoft Office 365, and Google Workspace further improve the efficacy and efficiency of remote learning. Teachers may design dynamic and captivating learning experiences that go beyond the confines of conventional classrooms by utilizing the power of these technologies. The goal is to give educators and administrators useful insights for improving their remote teaching and learning strategies by showcasing best practices and lessons learned (Balbín et al., 2023). To enable students to succeed in the digital era and beyond, instructors should embrace the transformational potential of remote learning technologies (de Menezes, de Almeida, de Andrade Lima, & Sousa, 2023).

DOI: 10.1201/9781003472537-18

15.2 HISTORICAL ROOTS OF REMOTE LEARNING

The origins of distant learning may be found in antiquity, when academics used instructional books and written communication to share information. However, with the introduction of correspondence courses in the 18th century, the formalization of remote learning became increasingly apparent (Edula, Shengcheng, Sasaki, Viladiro, & Roy, 2023). Remote learning developed in tandem with technical breakthroughs over time, moving from postal letters to radio and television transmissions and ultimately to the digital age made possible by the internet and cloud computing. This section examines the early developments in distance learning, emphasizing their critical role in democratizing educational access and laying the groundwork for the revolutionary effects of contemporary instruments for remote learning.

15.2.1 Early Forms of Distance Education and Correspondence Courses

15.2.1.1 18th Century Beginnings

The origins of distant learning may be found in antiquity, when academics used instructional books and written communication to share information. However, with the introduction of correspondence courses in the 18th century, early correspondence courses and remote learning programs were creative responses to the problems of providing education for those who could not attend regular colleges or universities because of financial limits, schedule conflicts, or other reasons. These pioneering efforts established the foundation for distance education and provided a paradigm for the creation of educational models that were not limited by geographical locations.

15.2.1.2 Expansion in the 19th Century

The development of postal systems and printing technology in the 19th century contributed to a significant shift in the field of remote education. Organizations and institutions in North America and Europe took advantage of these changes to provide a growing range of correspondence courses covering everything from practical skills and humanities to languages and sciences. These courses democratized access to education in ways never seen before, reaching people in both urban and rural areas, because of effective communication channels and extensive distribution networks (Sahoo et al., 2023).

15.2.1.3 Role in Accessible Education

Throughout history, correspondence courses have been a shining example of accessible education, helping underprivileged and disadvantaged groups overcome obstacles to education. The opportunities they offered were especially significant for those living in rural and isolated regions, where access to traditional educational institutions was either nonexistent or severely restricted. These people found that correspondence courses provided a lifeline to career and academic growth, enabling them to further their education without having to move or disrupt their lives. Furthermore, correspondence education has proven to be an invaluable tool for people with impairments who sometimes have a difficult time enrolling in traditional educational settings (Chatterjee, Bose, Banerjee, & Roy, 2023). Correspondence courses helped learners with disabilities get over physical obstacles and achieve their academic goals by sending course materials straight to their homes and allowing them to study whenever and wherever it was most convenient for them (Angelova, Kiryakova, & Yordanova, 2015).

15.2.1.4 Innovations in Instructional Materials

The success and efficacy of correspondence courses were largely due to innovations in instructional materials, which enabled teachers to provide students with interesting and educational information even when they were located far away. These carefully crafted resources offer thorough coverage of the course subject while supporting independent study (Chatterjee, Bose, Banerjee, & Roy, 2022a). The creation of teaching guidelines and standardized texts, especially for correspondence courses, was one noteworthy breakthrough. Teachers and publishers worked together to provide excellent resources that were well-organized, comprehensible, and supportive of individual study. Furthermore, improvements in printing technology made it possible to produce educational materials in large quantities at a reasonable price, which opened up access to a wider range of people (Choudhary, Shrimali, Choudhary, & Goswami, 2023). In addition, the use of internet platforms and digital formats in modern remote learning has made it easier to create dynamic and interactive learning materials like simulations, virtual laboratories, and films (Ekuase-Anwansedo & Smith, 2019).

15.2.1.5 Challenges and Limitations

Even with its advantages, early distance learning had a number of drawbacks and restrictions that affected its usefulness and accessibility. The sluggish communication rate that comes with correspondence-based learning was one major obstacle. Due to the reliance on postal mail for the transmission of assignments, homework, and feedback, student–teacher interactions were frequently delayed, and there were few possibilities for in-the-moment cooperation. All things considered, early correspondence courses and distance learning programs set the foundation for the creation of remote learning models that are still being developed today. These programs demonstrated the creative spirit of educators and organizations working to remove social and geographic obstacles from education.

15.2.2 Evolution of Remote Learning with Advancements in Technology

The evolution of remote learning has been closely intertwined with advancements in technology, spanning several centuries and marked by significant milestones that have revolutionized the way education is delivered and accessed. Figure 15.1 illustrates the evolution of remote learning with advancements in technology. The figure showcases key stages in this evolution, from traditional classroom settings to the integration of multimedia tools and advancements in communication technologies (Utami, Arif, & Satrio, 2021). It visually depicts the progression toward online learning platforms and highlights future trends, such as the integration of artificial intelligence (AI) and

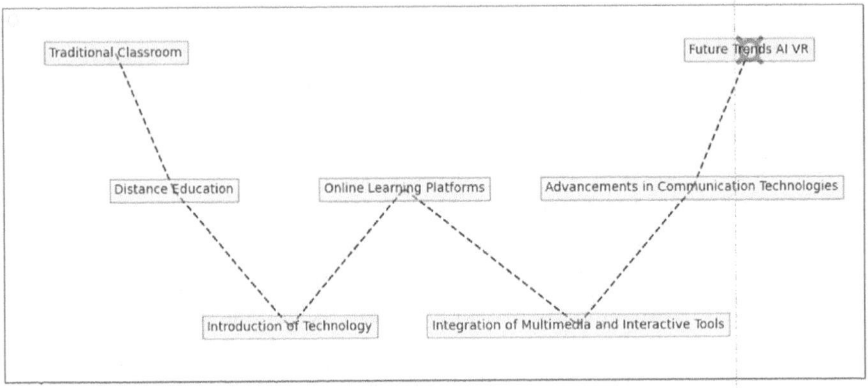

FIGURE 15.1 Evolution of Remote Learning with Advancements in Technology.

virtual reality (VR), which hold the potential to further transform the landscape of remote education.

15.2.2.1 Early Technological Innovations

In the early to mid-20th century, radio and television broadcasts were used as mediums for distance education, allowing educators to reach a broader audience through audio and visual content. Educational programs and lectures were broadcast over the airwaves, enabling learners to engage with course materials from the comfort of their homes.

15.2.2.2 Emergence of Audiovisual Technologies

The development of videotape recorders and multimedia presentations in the mid-20th century further enhanced remote learning capabilities. These technologies allowed for the creation of pre-recorded lectures, instructional videos, and multimedia resources that could be distributed and accessed remotely.

15.2.2.3 Advent of the Internet and Digital Learning

1. **Widespread Adoption of the Internet:** The advent of the internet in the late 20th century marked a transformative moment in the evolution of remote learning. The internet provided a global network for communication, collaboration, and information sharing, laying the foundation for the development of digital learning platforms and online educational resources.
2. **Digital Learning Platforms and Online Courses:** The proliferation of digital learning platforms and online courses in the late 20th and early 21st centuries revolutionized the landscape of remote learning. LMS, such as Moodle, Canvas, and Blackboard, emerged as central hubs for course delivery, content management, assessment, and communication. These platforms provided educators with the tools and infrastructure needed to design and deliver online courses, facilitating asynchronous learning and enabling students to engage with course materials at their own pace and convenience.

3. **Interactive Multimedia and Virtual Learning Environments:** With the rise of digital technologies, interactive multimedia and virtual learning environments became increasingly prevalent in remote education. Educators began to incorporate multimedia elements, such as videos, animations, simulations, and VR experiences, into online courses to enhance engagement and interactivity.

15.2.2.4 Mobile Learning and Personalized Education

1. **Mobile Devices and Apps:** Mobile learning apps and platforms enable learners to engage with course materials on the go, providing flexibility and convenience for busy lifestyles.
2. **Personalized Learning Experiences:** Adaptive learning algorithms and data analytics tools enable educators to tailor instruction to individual student needs, providing targeted support and feedback based on learner progress and performance (Chen & Almunawar, 2021).

15.2.2.5 Emerging Technologies and Future Directions

1. **Artificial Intelligence and Machine Learning:** The integration of AI and machine learning technologies holds immense promise for the future of remote learning. AI-powered chatbots, virtual tutors, and intelligent tutoring systems can provide personalized support and guidance to students, augmenting the role of educators and enhancing the learning experience.
2. **Augmented Reality and Virtual Reality:** Augmented reality (AR) and VR technologies are poised to revolutionize remote education by creating immersive and interactive learning environments. AR and VR experiences enable students to visualize abstract concepts, explore virtual simulations, and participate in hands-on activities, enhancing engagement and comprehension (Chatterjee, Bose, Banerjee, & Roy, 2022b).
3. **Blockchain and Credentialing:** Blockchain technology has the potential to transform credentialing and accreditation in remote education. Blockchain-based credentials provide a secure and tamper-proof way to verify academic achievements and qualifications, enabling learners to showcase their skills and credentials to employers and educational institutions with confidence.

From early experiments with radio broadcasts to the rise of digital learning platforms and immersive virtual environments, technology has played a central role in shaping the future of remote learning, unlocking new possibilities for learners and educators alike.

15.2.3 Significance of Cloud Computing in Revolutionizing Remote Education

It is impossible to overestimate how much cloud computing has revolutionized distant learning; it has completely changed how educational information is handled, saved, and distributed, bringing in a new era of flexibility, accessibility, and teamwork.

15.2.3.1 Flexibility and Scalability

Scalable and adaptable options for organizing and storing instructional materials are offered by cloud computing. Cloud-based systems, in contrast to conventional on-premises infrastructure, are easily able to adapt to variations in demand, thus enabling educational institutions to scale resources up or down as needed. Regardless of how many users or how much content is downloaded, this scalability guarantees that students always have access to the course contents and resources.

15.2.3.2 Accessibility and Anytime, Anywhere Learning

Online learning environments and cloud-based LMS provide anytime, anywhere access to educational materials. Students may participate in learning activities from any internet-connected device, at home or at work, by storing course materials, lectures, assignments, and collaboration tools in the cloud. Because of this accessibility, learners may engage in remote education programs from anywhere in the world, eliminating geographical constraints.

15.2.3.3 Collaboration and Communication

Students, teachers, and administrators can work together and communicate easily because of cloud computing. Real-time collaboration, document sharing, and video-conferencing platforms are examples of cloud-based applications that allow students to work together on group projects, have conversations, and get immediate feedback from teachers. Furthermore, cloud-based communication solutions improve efficiency and productivity for teachers and administrators by streamlining administrative duties like scheduling, grading, and course announcements.

15.2.3.4 Cost-Effectiveness and Resource Optimization

By removing the requirement for sizable upfront expenditures in hardware, software, and infrastructure, cloud computing provides educational institutions with cost-effective alternatives. Pay-as-you-go cloud services let organizations pay only for the resources they use, saving them money on the overhead of operating physical servers and data centers. Because of its affordability, educational institutions are able to invest in creative teaching and learning projects, distribute resources more effectively, and provide education to a wider audience.

15.2.3.5 Compliance and Data Security

Sensitive educational data is protected by strong security measures and compliance processes offered by cloud computing. To protect data from unwanted access and guarantee the confidentiality and integrity of student and institutional information, cloud service providers use encryption, access controls, and multi-factor authentication. Furthermore, cloud-based solutions satisfy legal and commercial standards for privacy and data security, giving both educational institutions and students peace of mind.

15.2.3.6 Data Protection and Adherence

The utilization of cloud computing in remote education facilitates innovation and experimentation by offering a dynamic and adaptable platform for evaluating novel teaching approaches, educational materials, and technological advancements. Teachers may increase student engagement and improve learning outcomes using cloud-based tools to create gamified learning experiences, tailored learning paths, and interactive multimedia material. Additionally, instructors may make data-driven decisions and continuously enhance remote education methods by using cloud-based analytics and machine learning algorithms to obtain insights into student behavior and performance.

Cloud computing has completely changed distance learning by offering scalable, easily available, and cooperative solutions that enable teachers and students to participate in learning activities at anytime, anywhere. Educational institutions may overcome geographical obstacles, improve cooperation and communication, maximize resources, guarantee data security and compliance, and encourage creativity and experimentation in teaching and learning by utilizing the power of the cloud (Carr, 2022).

15.3 PIVOTAL TOOLS SHAPING REMOTE LEARNING

Numerous technologies have emerged as key facilitators in the fast-changing field of remote education, changing the way that learning is facilitated, managed, and experienced. Among these LMS, video-conferencing platforms, collaborative tools, and creative approaches to project management and document collaboration stand out as essential components of contemporary remote learning settings (Keshavarz & Mirmoghtadaie, 2023). This will lead to increased effectiveness, efficiency, and participation in virtual learning settings.

15.3.1 Video-Conferencing Platforms

15.3.1.1 Overview of Zoom, Microsoft Teams, and Google Meet

Zoom has rapidly become one of the most popular video-conferencing platforms worldwide, renowned for its user-friendly interface and robust features. Zoom offers cross-platform compatibility, allowing users to join meetings from desktop computers, laptops, tablets, and smartphones. Its popularity surged during the COVID-19 pandemic, as it became a go-to solution for remote work, education, and social interactions. Microsoft Teams is an integrated communication and collaboration platform that offers video-conferencing capabilities alongside chat, file sharing, and project management tools. It is part of the Microsoft 365 suite, seamlessly integrating with other Office applications such as Outlook, Word, Excel, and PowerPoint. Google Meet, formerly known as Google Hangouts Meet, is part of the Google Workspace suite and is designed for secure video conferencing and collaboration. It offers features such as live captioning, screen sharing, and integration with Google Calendar and Gmail.

15.3.1.2 Features and Functionalities Facilitating Real-time Communication and Collaboration

All three platforms—Zoom, Microsoft Teams, and Google Meet—offer high-quality video and audio, ensuring a seamless communication experience for participants through advanced codecs and adaptive streaming algorithms that optimize performance even under challenging network conditions. Screen sharing allows presenters to showcase presentations, documents, websites, or software applications in real time, which is invaluable for lectures, demonstrations, and project collaboration. Virtual backgrounds enable users to replace their real-life backgrounds with custom images, adding privacy and professionalism to video conferences. Breakout rooms allow hosts to divide participants into smaller groups for focused discussions and activities, fostering engagement and collaboration. Chat and messaging features facilitate text communication during video calls, enabling participants to ask questions, share links, and provide feedback without interrupting the meeting flow. Integration with productivity tools is a key strength of these platforms, allowing seamless access to calendars, email clients, and document collaboration services, thus enhancing workflow and productivity. Security and privacy controls, including encryption, password protection, waiting rooms, and participant controls, address growing concerns and ensure the integrity of virtual meetings.

15.3.2 Learning Management Systems

LMS has revolutionized the way educational content is delivered, managed, and assessed in remote learning environments (Bates, 2019). Among the most widely used LMS platforms are Moodle, Canvas, and Blackboard, each offering a comprehensive suite of tools and features designed to facilitate course delivery, content management, and assessment.

15.3.2.1 Introduction to Moodle, Canvas, and Blackboard

Moodle, Canvas, and Blackboard are three prominent LMS that cater to a diverse range of educational needs. Moodle is an open-source LMS renowned for its flexibility and customization options, designed by educators for educators. It features a user-friendly interface and a wide array of tools for course creation, content sharing, assessments, and communication forums. Canvas, a cloud-based LMS developed by Instructure, is known for its intuitive interface and modern design. It offers comprehensive tools for course creation, content management, assessment, and communication, making it a favored choice among educational institutions of all sizes. Blackboard is a leading LMS platform widely used by educational institutions to deliver online courses and support hybrid learning environments. It boasts a robust set of features for course management, content creation, assessment, and communication.

15.3.2.2 Role of Learning Management Systems in Course Delivery, Content Management, and Assessment

LMS platforms such as Moodle, Canvas, and Blackboard play a central role in course delivery by providing educators with a centralized platform for organizing and delivering course materials, lectures, assignments, and assessments. Educators can create and customize online courses, upload multimedia content, and schedule activities and assessments to align with course objectives and learning outcomes. These platforms support various delivery formats, including synchronous and asynchronous learning, accommodating different learning preferences and schedules. Content management is another critical feature of LMS platforms, offering robust tools for creating, organizing, and sharing educational resources like documents, videos, presentations, and interactive multimedia content. Educators can develop structured learning modules, organize content into folders or categories, and customize the layout and design of course pages to enhance usability and accessibility for students.

15.3.3 Collaborative Tools

Collaborative tools play a pivotal role in virtual learning environments, facilitating communication, cooperation, and knowledge sharing among students and educators. Among the leading collaborative tools are Slack and Microsoft 365, each offering a suite of features designed to streamline collaboration and enhance productivity in remote education settings.

15.3.3.1 Examination of Slack and Microsoft 365

Slack and Microsoft 365 are powerful tools that enhance communication and collaboration in educational settings. Slack is a popular messaging and collaboration platform used by educational institutions to facilitate real-time interaction among students, educators, and administrators. It offers channels for group discussions, direct messaging for one-on-one communication, file sharing, and integration with other productivity tools and services. Features like threaded conversations, mentions, and reactions help users stay organized and engaged in virtual learning environments. Microsoft 365, formerly known as Office 365, provides a comprehensive suite of productivity tools for remote collaboration. It includes Microsoft Teams, OneDrive, SharePoint, and Office Online applications such as Word, Excel, and PowerPoint. Microsoft 365 enables real-time document collaboration, co-authoring, version control, and integration with other Microsoft and third-party applications.

15.3.3.2 Importance of Collaboration in Virtual Learning Environments

Collaboration in virtual learning environments fosters engagement and interaction among students, creating opportunities for discussion, brainstorming, and peer learning. Tools like Slack and Microsoft 365 enable students to communicate, share ideas, and collaborate on projects in real time, regardless of geographical location or time zone. Collaborative activities promote active learning by encouraging students to participate in discussions, problem-solving, and group projects, helping them develop critical thinking, communication, and teamwork skills essential for today's interconnected world. Moreover, collaborative tools enhance accessibility and inclusivity by providing alternative channels for communication and participation. Students who might hesitate to speak up in traditional classroom settings can engage more comfortably in online discussions and activities, contributing to a more inclusive learning environment. Collaborative tools facilitate connections, networking, and relationship-building, creating a supportive learning community where students can seek assistance, share resources, and work together on shared goals and interests.

15.3.4 Innovative Solutions for Document Collaboration and Project Management

In the realm of remote education, efficient document collaboration and project management are essential for ensuring seamless workflow and productivity among students and educators. Google Workspace, Microsoft Office 365, and Trello stand out as innovative solutions that offer robust features for document collaboration and project management, empowering users to collaborate effectively and manage tasks efficiently in virtual learning environments.

15.3.4.1 Overview of Google Workspace, Microsoft Office 365, and Trello

Google Workspace, Microsoft Office 365, and Trello are essential tools for enhancing productivity and collaboration in virtual learning environments. Google Workspace, formerly known as G Suite, includes applications such as Google Docs, Sheets, Slides, Drive, and Gmail. It enables real-time document collaboration, version control, and file sharing, allowing students and educators to work together seamlessly on assignments, projects, and presentations. Features such as comments, suggestions, and revision history foster collaboration and creativity. Microsoft Office 365 offers a comprehensive suite of productivity tools, including Word, Excel, PowerPoint, OneDrive, and Outlook. Trello is a web-based project management tool that uses boards, lists, and cards to organize tasks and workflows. Educators can create project boards, assign tasks to students, set deadlines, track progress, and collaborate on projects in real time. With customizable boards, task cards, checklists, and due dates, Trello provides a flexible and intuitive platform for managing projects and assignments, enhancing productivity in virtual learning environments.

15.3.4.2 Enhancing Productivity and Workflow Management in Remote Education

Google Workspace, Microsoft Office 365, and Trello are instrumental in streamlining collaboration, document management, and task organization in virtual learning environments. Google Workspace and Microsoft Office 365 enable real-time document editing, file sharing, and centralized document management, allowing students and educators to work seamlessly on assignments, projects, and group activities, regardless of geographical location or time zone. With features such as version control, file-sharing permissions, and offline access, these platforms ensure users have access to the latest versions of documents and can collaborate effectively on shared files. Trello enhances task organization and tracking by providing visual boards, lists, and cards to manage projects and assignments. Users can create tasks, assign due dates, add labels and attachments, and monitor progress through customizable workflows. Features such as task assignments, comments, and notifications help users stay organized and focused on their goals. All three platforms support time management and prioritization by allowing users to set deadlines, create reminders, and organize tasks by priority.

15.4 CHALLENGES AND SOLUTIONS

In the dynamic landscape of remote education, educators and institutions face various challenges spanning technology, pedagogy, and security. Addressing these challenges is crucial to ensuring the effectiveness and success of remote learning initiatives. This section explores key challenges in remote education and proposes strategic solutions to overcome them, fostering a conducive environment for learning and collaboration.

15.4.1 Technology Challenges

In the digital realm of remote education, technology acts as both an enabler and a barrier. Connectivity issues and hardware/software compatibility challenges significantly hinder the seamless flow of learning in virtual environments. Students and educators often face variations in internet connectivity, device capabilities, and software compatibility, which can impede access to online resources and participation in virtual classrooms. Addressing these challenges requires a concerted effort to bridge the digital divide. Institutions must invest in infrastructure upgrades, such as broadband expansion and Wi-Fi hotspot distribution, to ensure widespread internet access.

15.4.2 Pedagogical Challenges

Navigating the transition from traditional face-to-face instruction to online delivery presents educators with a myriad of pedagogical challenges. Adapting teaching strategies for the virtual realm demands a paradigm shift in instructional design, content delivery, and student engagement. Educators must shift from traditional methods to engaging virtual experiences, which involves designing interactive content and fostering student-centered learning—tasks that can be daunting for those new to remote teaching. To address this, comprehensive educator training programs in online pedagogy are essential, equipping teachers with the necessary skills and knowledge to design and deliver effective online courses. These programs should emphasize instructional design principles, technology integration strategies, and best practices for engaging online learners. Maintaining student engagement in virtual classrooms poses another significant challenge. Utilizing tools such as videos, quizzes, group discussions, and collaborative projects can enhance student engagement by promoting interaction and peer-to-peer learning, fostering a dynamic and engaging online learning environment.

15.4.3 Security Challenges

In the digital age, safeguarding sensitive data and protecting against cybersecurity threats are paramount concerns for educational institutions engaged in remote education. Data privacy concerns and cybersecurity threats pose significant risks to student privacy and institutional security, threatening the integrity and confidentiality of educational data. Unauthorized access, data breaches, and cyber attacks can compromise the confidentiality and integrity of educational data, undermining student privacy and institutional security. Mitigating these risks requires the implementation of robust security measures such as encryption, access controls, and multi-factor authentication. By prioritizing security and adopting a proactive approach to risk management, educational institutions can create a safe and secure remote learning environment conducive to student success and academic excellence.

15.5 BEST PRACTICES

In the rapidly evolving landscape of remote education, implementing best practices is crucial for ensuring the effectiveness and success of online learning initiatives. This section explores key best practices and success stories in three critical areas: training, communication protocols, and inclusive learning spaces (Halder & Saha, 2023). By prioritizing these practices, educational institutions can create engaging, supportive, and inclusive environments conducive to student success and academic excellence in remote education.

15.5.1 Training: Importance of Comprehensive Training Programs for Educators and Students

In the realm of remote education, comprehensive training programs for both educators and students are essential pillars of success. These programs serve as the bedrock upon which effective online teaching and learning can thrive. Educators require training not only in the technical aspects of online platforms but also in pedagogical strategies tailored to the virtual classroom environment. Similarly, students benefit from training sessions that familiarize them with the tools, resources, and expectations of remote learning.

15.5.2 Establishment of Clear Communication Protocols and Expectations

Educational institutions should outline expectations regarding communication frequency, channels, response times, and etiquette to ensure effective collaboration and coordination in virtual environments. By setting clear communication protocols, institutions can enhance efficiency, streamline workflows, and cultivate a culture of open communication conducive to academic success.

15.5.3 Creation of Inclusive Environments Accommodating Diverse Learning Needs

Educational institutions must prioritize accessibility and diversity in their online learning environments, ensuring that every student has equitable access to educational resources and opportunities. This includes providing accommodations for students with disabilities, offering multilingual support, and fostering a culture of inclusivity and respect for diversity.

15.6 FUTURE TRENDS AND INNOVATIONS

As remote education continues to evolve, future trends and innovations hold the promise of transforming the learning experience and shaping the future of education. This section delves into emerging trends in remote learning, focusing on the integration of AI, AR, and VR, as well as gamification and microlearning, and their potential impact on the future of education.

15.6.1 Integration of Artificial Intelligence in Education

AI is poised to revolutionize the field of education, offering personalized learning experiences, intelligent tutoring systems, and data-driven insights into student performance. By harnessing the power of AI algorithms and machine learning techniques, educators can tailor instruction to individual learning styles and preferences, identify areas of improvement, and provide targeted interventions to support student learning and success. AI-powered educational platforms can analyze vast amounts of data to generate personalized recommendations, adaptive learning pathways, and real-time feedback, empowering students to learn at their own pace and maximize their potential.

15.6.2 Augmented Reality and Virtual Reality in Remote Learning

AR and VR technologies offer immersive and interactive learning experiences that transcend the limitations of traditional classroom settings. By incorporating AR and VR simulations, virtual field trips, and immersive storytelling into remote learning environments, educators can transport students to virtual worlds and engage them in experiential learning activities that promote exploration, discovery, and critical thinking. These technologies enable students to visualize abstract concepts, manipulate virtual objects, and collaborate with peers in virtual environments, enhancing their understanding and retention of course material and fostering a deeper connection to the subject matter.

15.6.3 Gamification and Microlearning for Enhanced Engagement

Gamification and microlearning strategies are revolutionizing the way students engage with course content and interact with learning materials in remote education settings. By incorporating game elements such as points, badges, leaderboards, and rewards into online courses, educators can motivate students, promote active participation, and increase learning retention. Microlearning, on the other hand, involves delivering bite-sized, focused learning activities that are easy to digest and can be accessed anytime, anywhere.

The integration of AI, AR, and VR, as well as gamification and microlearning, represents exciting opportunities to reimagine the future of education and enhance the quality and effectiveness of remote learning. By embracing these emerging trends and innovations, educators and institutions can create engaging, immersive, and personalized learning experiences that empower students to succeed in the digital age and prepare them for the challenges and opportunities of tomorrow's world.

15.7 CONCLUSION

As we conclude this chapter, it is evident that remote education has emerged as a powerful force shaping the future of learning. Throughout this exploration, we have uncovered key insights and takeaways that underscore the transformative potential of remote learning tools in revolutionizing education. From the integration of AI to the utilization of AR and VR, as well as the implementation of gamification and microlearning strategies, educators and institutions have at their disposal a wealth of innovative technologies and approaches to enhance the quality and effectiveness of remote education. Throughout this chapter, we have examined the historical roots of remote learning, the evolution of remote learning with advancements in technology, and the pivotal tools shaping remote learning today. We have delved into the challenges and solutions facing remote education, explored best practices and success stories, and discussed future trends and innovations that hold the promise of transforming the learning experience. Remote learning tools have the transformative potential to democratize access to education, personalize learning experiences, and foster collaboration and creativity in virtual learning environments. From videoconferencing platforms and LMS to collaborative tools and innovative solutions for document collaboration and project management, these tools empower educators and students to connect, communicate, and collaborate regardless of geographical location or time zone. Similarly, educational institutions must prioritize investment in infrastructure, resources, and training to support the effective implementation of remote learning initiatives.

REFERENCES

Angelova, N., Kiryakova, G., & Yordanova, L. (2015). Cloud-based LMS for E-learning. *Trakia Journal of Science*, 13(Suppl. 1), pp. 386–391. Retrieved from https://doi.org/10.15547/tjs.2015.s.01.066

Balbín, A. M., Caetano, N. S., Conde, M., Costa, P., Felgueiras, C., Fidalgo-Blanco, Á., … Sein-Echaluce, M. L. (2023). Trends on Communication, Educational Assessment, Sustainable Development, Educational Innovation, Mechatronics and Learning Analytics at TEEM 2022. In *Lecture Notes in Educational Technology,* pages 699-716. Retrieved from https://doi.org/10.1007/978-981-99-0942-1_73

Bates, A. W. T. (2019). *Teaching in a Digital Age*. Second Edition. teachonline.ca. Tony Bates Associates Ltd.

Carr, J. E. (2022). Teaching in a Digital Age – Second Edition. *Open Learning: The Journal of Open, Distance and e-Learning*, 37(3). Retrieved from https://doi.org/10.1080/02680513.2022.2056008

Chatterjee, P., Bose, R., Banerjee, S., & Roy, S. (2022a). Cloud Based LMS Security & Exam Proctoring Solution. *Journal of Positive School Psychology*, 6(3), pp 3929–3941.

Chatterjee, P., Bose, R., Banerjee, S., & Roy, S. (2022b). Enhancing Security of Cloud Based LMS by Deploying Secure Loopback Protocol. *International Journal of Mechanical Engineering*, 7(1).

Chatterjee, P., Bose, R., Banerjee, S., & Roy, S. (2023). Enhancing Data Security of Cloud Based LMS. *Wireless Personal Communications*, pp. 1123–1139. Retrieved from https://doi.org/10.1007/s11277-023-10323-5

Chen, C. K., & Almunawar, M. N. (2021). Cloud Learning Management System in Higher Education. In *Research Anthology on Architectures, Frameworks, and Integration Strategies for Distributed and Cloud Computing*, pp. 1564–1586. Retrieved from https://doi.org/10.4018/978-1-7998-5339-8.ch076

Choudhary, R. K., Shrimali, D., Choudhary, D., & Goswami, S. (2023). Study on adoption of mobile cloud based learning management system for Indian Universities. In *AIP Conference Proceedings* (Vol. 2521). Retrieved from https://doi.org/10.1063/5.0112823

de Menezes, J. B. F., de Almeida, A. C. A., de Andrade Lima, M. V., & Sousa, T. M. (2023). Ethics and Learning Analytics: A Necessary Combination for Scientific Rigor. *Praxis Educativa*, 18. Retrieved from https://doi.org/10.5212/praxeduc.v.18.21370.016

Edula, R., Shengcheng, L., Sasaki, H., Viladiro, R., & Roy, D. (2023). Personalized Learning Systems in Smart Education: A Review of the Literature & Pilot Feasibility Discussion. In *AIP Conference Proceedings* (Vol. 2909). Retrieved from https://doi.org/10.1063/5.0182560

Ekuase-Anwansedo, A., & Smith, A. (2019). Effect of Cloud Based Learning Management System on the Learning Management System Implementation Process: Faculty and Student Perspectives. In *Proceedings ACM SIGUCCS User Services Conference*. Retrieved from https://doi.org/10.1145/3347709.3347835

Halder, S., & Saha, S. (2023). *The Routledge Handbook of Education Technology*. Retrieved from https://doi.org/10.4324/9781003293545

Haugsbakk, G. (2020). Special Issue: 30 Years of ICT and Learning in Education – Major Changes and Challenges. *Seminar.Net*, 16(2). Retrieved from https://doi.org/10.7577/seminar.4043

Keshavarz, M., & Mirmoghtadaie, Z. (2023). Book Review: Teaching in a Digital Age: Guidelines for Designing Teaching and Learning–Third Edition, authored by Anthony William (Tony) Bates (Tony Bates Associates Ltd., 2022). *The International Review of Research in Open and Distributed Learning*, 24(2),pp. 192–195. Retrieved from https://doi.org/10.19173/irrodl.v24i2.7063

May, L., & Denton, J. (2022). Emergency Designs: Lessons for the Rapid Implementation of Online Teaching. In *Professional and Practice-based Learning* (Vol. 29), pp. 85–96. Retrieved from https://doi.org/10.1007/978-981-19-5587-7_7

Sahoo, M. K., Gouda, B. S., Pratihari, P., Satapathy, A. K., Pradhan, S. S., & Nayak, S. (2023). Intelligent Big Data Analytics: A Perspective for Online Education System. In *Intelligent Technologies for Sensors: Applications, Design, and Optimization for a Smart World, pages 17*. Retrieved from https://doi.org/10.1201/9781003314851-17

Utami, A. D. W., Arif, S., & Satrio, P. U. D. (2021). Understanding Usability and User Experience Cloud-Based Learning Management System from Teacher Review. In *7th International Conference on Electrical, Electronics and Information Engineering: Technological Breakthrough for Greater New Life, ICEEIE 2021*. Retrieved from https://doi.org/10.1109/ICEEIE52663.2021.9616959

16 Leveraging Multicloud Technology for Seamless Education in Rural Areas

Shweta Barhate, Snehal Narale, and M. P. Dhore

16.1 INTRODUCTION

The implementation of cloud computing technology for the education field has already proven to be successful in many aspects. Rural education stands with many challenges such as delay, availability of educational resources, online seminars, classes for the students. The rift was a very big challenge as the rural area students have many issues like low bandwidth, no availability of online educational resources, and the biggest problem was the cost needed to model a repository of educational resources. This problem can be resolved by multicloud technology.

India's rural education system faces several obstacles, a few of which can be insufficient infrastructure, low enrolment, high dropout rates, and lack of seamless education. The multicloud technology helps the user to deal with the critical areas by shifting remote entirely or partially from the university. The multicloud strategy forms the most flexible and cost-effective solution to the students from the rural areas. Most of the data is to be shared and stored among the servers, which enables the students to access it from anywhere and anytime with location independence.

16.1.1 Multicloud Architecture

Multicloud architecture has a number of advantages like flexibility, reliability, low response time, and low cost. This architecture allows the user to have a cost-effective solution as compared to other technologies. The organization has to choose a specific cloud vendor whose policies align with the goals of the institution as each cloud vendor has a different approach. The security needs to be taken care of as a very high number of students are involved. Multicloud proposes the idea that organizations/institutions use multiple cloud providers' public clouds. Using numerous vendors for cloud hosting, storage, and application maintenance, as opposed to relying on a single cloud provider, is the primary distinction between multicloud and other types of clouds. Flexibility, dependability, low cost, and low response time are just a few benefits of multicloud architecture. Compared to competing technologies, this architecture gives the user a more affordable alternative. Each cloud vendor has a different

DOI: 10.1201/9781003472537-19

strategy; thus, the company needs to select a particular cloud vendor whose policies match the institution's objectives. Due to the large number of learners involved, security needs to be considered seriously.

16.1.2 Benefits of Multicloud for Education

An educational institution may have multiple branches, based on the courses it offers and the number of students who use its services throughout time. This ensures that even if cloud's functioning is impacted for the time being, other deployed cloud systems can still be utilized.

Selecting the right cloud provider is crucial as multicloud computing can benefit the business. You can learn how the system can become cloud-native, upload software to the cloud, and use the right tool sets by speaking with different cloud providers and developing strategies with them. Consequently, multicloud technology has several advantages for education, including improved learning outcomes, safe data storage, and enhanced accessibility, better learning experiences, lower costs, less hardware needed, scalability across many geographies, etc.

16.1.3 Shift to Multicloud Architecture from Hybrid Cloud

Prior research has demonstrated that hybrid cloud architecture yielded positive outcomes in terms of reduced response times, improved availability, expedited processing times, and lower deployment costs. Multicloud and hybrid cloud are two architectures that are useful for cloud deployment in rural education, but each has its own set of uses and guidelines for how it should be used. Organizations using a multicloud architecture may combine various public or private suppliers or utilize a number of private or public clouds. This guarantees both scalability and steady service delivery. When an enterprise uses a hybrid cloud, it combines the use of public and private clouds.

Regardless of the infrastructure used, in this scenario the establishment of a virtual desktop infrastructure is necessary. Students use this action to create a virtual desktop environment that can be accessed and used on a distant server. Students can study at their own pace and there is no difference in this way.

16.1.4 Content Delivery Network as a Service

Content delivery network (CDN) as a service study examines the distribution of educational materials via cloud to students in rural areas. Rural education faces several obstacles, chief among them being latency resulting from inadequate bandwidth, as well as scalability, expense, and high response times mostly from cloud locations. Approaching the resolution of the aforementioned issues, CDNs and their points of presence (PoPs) are a suitable solution. PoPs, a network of geographically dispersed servers, make up a CDN. To reduce the distance between the user and the content they are attempting to view, these servers are positioned strategically throughout the globe. In response to user requests, the CDN caches instructional materials on servers that are closest to it.

16.2 LITERATURE REVIEW

P. K. Paul, Ritam Chaterjee, and Sreeramanna Aithal (Paul et al. 2023) in their book discussed the importance of ubiquitous nature of cloud computing. The authors stressed on the fact that cloud-based learning allowed face-to-face education with the advantages of traditional environment along with the help of modern techniques and tools. The authors specify that the work is theoretical in nature but deals with intricacies regarding development and implementation of cloud environment for education.

Abderahim El Mhouti, Mohammad Erradi, and Azeddine Nasseh (El Mhouti et al. 2018) in their paper focused on the research area of applications of cloud computing in e-learning. The paper in its initial phase analyzes the challenges while implementing e-learning followed by cloud-based solutions for e-learning issues. The paper first evaluates the types of e-learning materials available and different forms of e-learning. The authors systematically move toward solution to e-learning problems through the discussion of different cloud deployment models. The paper thoroughly discusses the architecture of cloud-based learning management system.

The architecture suggests a Design Security Multi-Tenancy Access Control using role-based access control and identity management. Identity management is used in the architecture to ascertain the user's identity and the roles that correspond with the services. The processing performance of cloud multi-tenant services can be enhanced while hardening the security and privacy of cloud applications by achieving application independence and data isolation through the use of role-based assignments, which can be used to quickly and effectively manage a user's access rights (Gupta 2016).

Wei Li and Ling Guo (Li and Guo 2022) in their paper have worked mainly on the use of cloud resources for building better English education repositories. The paper mainly focused on the current state of English education repositories. It proposes to build a private cloud to provide open English education platform as a step toward better access and provisioning of English resource repository. The paper provides a private architecture as a base toward educational management subsystem consisting of four modules with different functionalities.

A. K. Gupta, R. K. Dwivedi, and K. Mukherjee (Gupta et al. 2020) in their paper have focused on the point that the majority of Indians live in provinces that have the potential to become financial powerhouses and nations. However, most of these people are completely ignorant of the potential of information innovation to advance business opportunities and tasks. This paper analyzed how cloud computing industry globally can help people in the provinces overcome the challenges, which will ultimately result in country zone advancement and the nation's overall financial advancement with respect to education sector.

Mohammad Rezah Meshbahi, Amir Massoud Rehmani, and Mehdi Hosseinzadeh (Meshbahi et al. 2018) explained the significance of improving cloud computing's high availability and dependability to increase customer satisfaction and stop revenue losses in cloud environments. This document offers a high availability and reliability reference roadmap for cloud computing. The paper breaks down the availability and reliability problem into four basic issues, the solutions to which lead to increased availability and dependability.

Ware Sayali and Jadhav Varsha (Sayali and Varsha 2016) examined data storage practices that are kept on a single cloud. The largest issue facing modern data storage is data security and privacy because of single data storage. The researcher suggests a multicloud feature-based solution in this work. The split format of the data is what is kept on many clouds. To provide the suggested system more functionality, homomorphic encryption and decryption techniques are employed. Segments of the data are split. The suggested solution, which is similar to a Redundant Array of Independent Disks (RAID) system, stores the backup of that data across several clouds.

Kamalpreet Kaur and Kanwalvir Singh Dhindsa (Kaur and Dhindsa 2015) suggested a technique for cost-optimized resource scheduling based on clustering. By allocating weights to the various quality attributes, the k-means clustering algorithm classifies these workloads for clustering-based resource scheduling. Comparing the suggested technique to the current resource scheduling technique, the experimental results obtained in the cloud environment unmistakably show that the latter offers lower cost performance.

Hamza Ali Imran, Usama Latif et al. (Imran et al. 2020) gave a comprehensive analysis of multicloud technology and the prototypes created to reduce the difference between the services offered by cross-vendor unique clouds. Researchers covered a variety of factors in this work, including time, cost, performance, security, and others, that cloud users need to consider while alternating between various multicloud services. The upcoming generation of multicloud cloud is predicted to have lower operation costs, greater coordination between many single-cloud interfaces, and better latency.

Jiangshui Hong, Thomas Dreibholz et al. (Hong et al. 2019) provided a summary of cloud computing technologies, focusing on multicloud networks in particular. The issues associated with cloud computing were examined in this research. It also covered how some of these problems might be resolved by using multicloud architectures like hybrid clouds or multiclouds. The purpose of this study was to evaluate open topics in the field of multicloud computing and to present a contemporary perspective on the state of the art in this area. In addition to illuminating the difficulties that cloud computing faces and outlining how multicloud computing resolves some of these problems, this paper also focuses on the potential future integration of multicloud platforms with other cutting-edge technology.

S. M. Barhate and M. P. Dhore (Barhate and Dhore 2023) in their paper evaluated the resource consumption and power efficiency during interoperability in hybrid cloud. Hybrid cloud is a potent blend of private and public clouds that has become the most popular cloud model in recent years. The data must be moved between the private and public clouds as needed when using a hybrid cloud strategy. This study examines how well a hybrid cloud performs when data is moved between clouds. To facilitate efficient data migration in hybrid clouds, this article addresses solutions for data distribution and consolidation. The CloudSim simulator has been utilized to investigate the performance concerns associated with various data migration strategies, while ensuring compatibility.

A. B. Singh (Singh 2017) discussed the concept of load balancing in a distributed environment like cloud computing. The paper discusses that load balancing helps to use resources efficiently and with less complexity. It also discusses that there are various problems while dealing with load balancing like security, fault tolerance, etc. This paper surveys various problems as well as the solutions, which were suggested with respect to cloud computing. Furthermore, the paper also discusses various algorithms like Round Robin Algorithm, Throttled Algorithm, Modified Throttled, Min-Min Scheduling Algorithm, Priority algorithm, etc.

16.3 PROPOSED METHODOLOGY

16.3.1 Modeling an Architecture for Efficient Multi EduCloud

The experimental work is done in the Cloud Analyst toolkit. The kind of architecture (Figure 16.1) to be designed for multicloud should be working on low bandwidth, highly scalability, with relatively low response time and processing time, and most importantly very low cost as this cloud would be used by rural students.

16.3.2 Modeling of Clustered Multi EduCloud

Modeling Clustered Multicloud considering lower bandwidth has the following key stages involved:

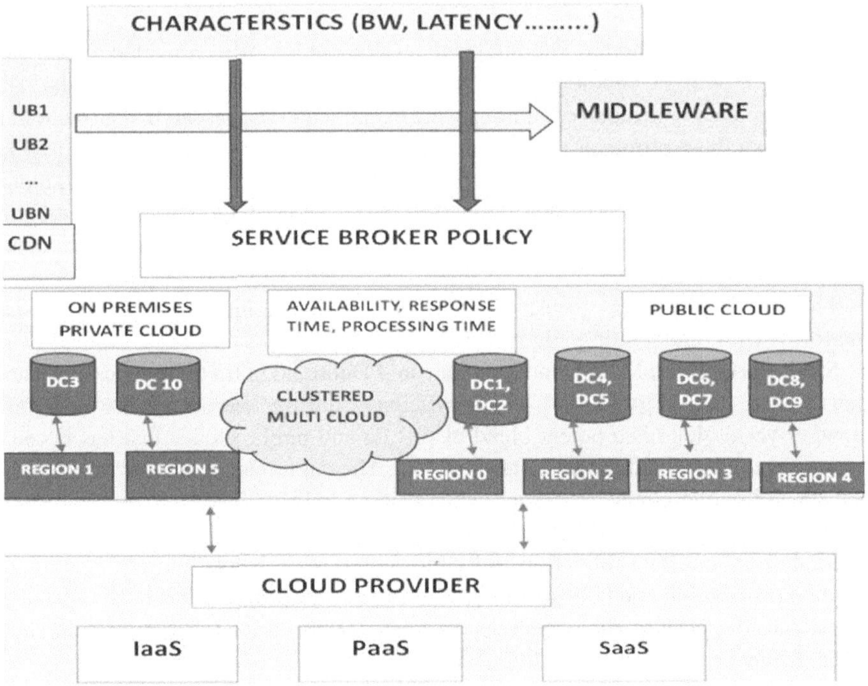

FIGURE 16.1 Proposed Multi EduCloud Architecture for Rural Education.

1. Modeling a multicloud makes a combination of different types of cloud data centers.
2. The concept behind using a specific cloud deployment model is that a cloud with more virtual machines within it would be larger and classified as public, while a cloud with more hosts within it would be smaller and have a higher configuration classified as private.
3. Bandwidth is set as per public and private cloud. It will affect the performance of the system.
4. Users in that particular location would only be able to access private clouds, but users in any region could access public clouds.
5. The request made by the user or client is initially routed by default to the private cloud and, if necessary, is dynamically routed to the public cloud upon exceeding a certain threshold.
6. The basic multicloud architecture involves a combination of multiple clouds with a number of hosts and virtual machines with respect to the requirement of the cloud per region.
7. The most important part of multicloud is the service broker policy, which is the key role player that enhances the performance of the system (like response time, processing time, and cost)
8. As the region-wise time slot varies, multicloud architecture is modeled region-wise across the world accordingly.
9. Based on user's location, server load, and network conditions, the CDN's domain name system (DNS) server's forward content requests to the closest edge server. This results in lowering response times.
10. To further reduce the response time, clustering of data centers with same peak working hours is done.

16.4 RESULTS AND DISCUSSION

The experimental work involves modeling of a clustered CDN multicloud, which helps in better scalability, availability, and low-cost multicloud, which is very feasible for providing educational resources to rural education. The methodology is implemented so as to maintain low bandwidth to simulate the working of EduCloud. The clustered multicloud is then tested for various parameters so as to check the response time, processing cost, and grand total cost of the EduCloud.

The experimental work considered the following important metrics:

- Response time
- Bandwidth
- Data center processing times
- Grand total cost

The multicloud is modeled to have 10 data centers and 13 user bases. The service broker policy is set to optimized response time, and load balancing algorithm is considered as throttled load balancing algorithm. Then region-wise clustering of

	Average (ms)	Minimum (ms)	Maximum (ms)
Overall Response Time:	50.62	36.88	65.01
Data Center Processing Time:	0.98	0.05	2.03

Export Results

Response Time By Region

Userbase	Avg (ms)	Min (ms)	Max (ms)
UB10	51 171	40 889	61 26
UB11	50 586	41 838	61 447
UB12	50 471	38 501	63 509
UB13	50 42	37 484	64 482
UB1	50 574	40 38	61 881
UB2	51 347	41 653	61 65
UB3	51 202	40 651	65 013
UB4	51 146	39 172	62 525
UB5	50 78	36 879	60 879
UB6	50 787	40 255	60 381
UB7	50 725	38 129	62 009
UB8	50 951	41 331	61 884
UB9	50 998	41 825	62 635

FIGURE 16.2 Snapshot of Average Response Time of Multicloud Architecture from Cloud Analyst Toolkit.

Cost

Total Virtual Machine Cost :	$37.50
Total Data Transfer Cost :	$1.40
Grand Total :	$38.90

Data Center	VM Cost	Data Transfer Cost	Total
DC10	5	0.690	5.69
DC2	2.5	0.034	2.53
DC1	2.5	0.03	2.5
DC4	5	0.092	5.09
DC3	5	0.191	5.19
DC6	2.5	0.103	2.60
DC5	2.5	0.103	2.60
DC8	5	0.032	5.03
DC7	5	0.00	5.0
DC9	2.5	0.031	2.53

FIGURE 16.3 Snapshot of Simulation Results for Grand Total Cost of Proposed Multicloud Architecture from Cloud Analyst Toolkit.

user bases is done depending upon the peak hours' start and peak hours' end. The following results have been observed as follows:

The bandwidth of each data center was reduced from 1000 to 500 mbps for a few data centers, and for private data centers it was kept at 1000 mbps. This being a simulation study, the idea was to study the response time, data center processing time, and grand total cost when the multicloud was deployed using less bandwidth.

The results (Figures 16.2 and 16.3) showed that even on lower bandwidth, the multicloud showed the average response time as 50.68 ms and the average data center processing time to be 1.05 ms, whereas the grand total cost was 38.90 $. These metrics were showing high response times for other service broker policy, and load balancing algorithm combinations are not desirable for this research problem.

16.5 CONCLUSIONS

It can very well be concluded that multicloud architecture empowered with clustering as well as CDN is highly suitable for rural education, as in rural education the quality, time, and cost of accessing the education all are compromised. The architecture which works on lower band width is indeed matching the real environment of rural education and is still showing promising results.

The experimental work involves modeling of a clustered CDN multicloud that helps in better scalability, availability, and low-cost multicloud, which is very feasible for providing educational resources to rural education.

Thus, it can be very well concluded that multicloud architecture that is both scalable and available as well as of low cost demonstrates good quality of service (QOS) results.

REFERENCES

Barhate, S., M. Dhore. 2023. "Evaluating Data Migrations with Respect to Interoperability in Hybrid Cloud." In *Lecture Notes in Electrical Engineering*, LNEE 946. Springer, 795–804.

El Mhouti, Abderrahim, Mohamed Erradi, Azeddine Nasseh. 2018. "Using Cloud Computing Services in E-Learning Process: Benefits and Challenges." *Education and Information Technologies* 23: 893–909.

Gupta, A. K., R. K. Dwivedi, K. Mukharjee. 2020. "Cloud Computing Towards Rural Development in India." *International Journal of Computer Sciences and Engineering* 8 (1): 159–165.

Gupta, Sonia. 2016. "Multi Tenancy Access Control Using Cloud Service in MVC." *International Journal of Scientific & Engineering Research* 7 (1): 1170–1174.

Hong, Jiangshui, Thomas Dreibholz, Joseph Adam Schenkel, Jiaxi Alessia Hu. 2019. "*An Overview of Multi-Cloud Computing.*" In *Primate Life Histories, Sex Roles, and Adaptability*. Springer, 1055–1068.

Imran, Hamza Ali, Usama Latif, Ataul Aziz Ikram, Maryam Ehsan, Ahmed Jamal Ikram, Waleed Ahmad Khan, Saad Wazir. 2020. "Multi-Cloud: A Comprehensive Review." *IEEE 23rd International Multitopic Conference (INMIC)*. IEEE, 2–6.

Kaur, Kamalpreet, Kanwalvir Singh Dhindsa. 2015. "Clustering Based Cost Optimized Resource Scheduling Technique in Cloud Computing." *i-Manager's Journal on Cloud Computing* 2 (3): 8–18.

Li, Wei, Ying Guo. 2022. "A Secure Private Cloud Storage Platform for English Education Resources Based on IoT Technology." *Computational Math Methods* 2022 (1): 1–12.

Meshbahi, Mohammad Rezah, Amir Massoud Rehmani, Mehdi Hosseinzadeh. 2018. "Reliability and High Availability in Cloud Computing Environment: A Reference Road Map." *Human Centric Computing and Information Sciences* 8 (1): 2–31.

Paul, P. K., Ritam Chaterjee, P. S. Aithal, Ricardo Saavedra. 2023. "Cloud Computing and Its Impact in Education, Teaching and Research – A Scientific Review." In *Emergence and Research in Interdisciplinary Management and Information Technology*. Routledge, 1–26.

Singh, A. B. 2017. "A Survey of Load Balancing Techniques in Cloud Computing." *Advances in Computing* 7 (2): 2–34.

Ware Sayali, Jadhav. 2016. "Multi Cloud Architecture to Enhance Security and Privacy." *Imperial Journal of Interdisciplinary Research (IJIR)* 2 (3): 29–301.

17 Framework for Bridging the Skill Gap between Higher Education Institutions and Industry

A Machine Learning Approach

Saleema J. S., Lakshmi Shankar Iyer, and Lakshmi Sankaran

17.1 INTRODUCTION

The rapid pace of technological change has created a growing demand for skilled professionals in various industries worldwide. However, a significant challenge has emerged: while industries seek candidates with specific skill sets, recent university graduates are searching for job opportunities that align with their qualifications. Adding to the complexity, the International Labour Organization (ILO) predicts that the global unemployment rate will reach 5.7% by 2022, largely due to the ongoing pandemic. Moreover, the skill gap (SG), resulting from a disparity between labor market demand and supply, contributes to diminished employability. The concept of the SG highlights this mismatch between skill demand (SD) and skill supply (SS), and forward-thinking nations view it as an opportunity rather than a mere challenge. Within organizations, human resource professionals actively identify SGs among employees to optimize workforce planning by harnessing the existing skill sets of their staff. Access to a skilled workforce stands as a pivotal factor that distinguishes successful organizations from others. In addition to embracing more inclusive hiring practices, organizations must strategize methods to equip their employees with the necessary skill sets. Approaches such as apprenticeships, which provide practical on-the-job training programs for entry-level employees, and partnerships with external workforce development agencies, all contribute to the cultivation of a more diverse and capable workforce.

DOI: 10.1201/9781003472537-20

17.1.1 Motivation

The advent of the Fourth Industrial Revolution has set the stage for a growing SG, characterized by evolving job roles, widespread technology adoption, and increased data availability. This imbalance between SS and the shifting demands of the job market has disrupted industries across the board. Minimizing this SG stands as a top priority for all stakeholders striving to match the right talent with the right roles. A NASSCOM (2020) study revealed that 55% of organizations, including IT giant Capgemini, recognize the increasing need for science, technology, engineering, and mathematics (STEM) skills. The World Economic Forum (Milano, 2019) has also noted that the SG widens when academia fails to emphasize the new-age skills sought after by organizations. The future prosperity of nations hinges on the young workforce entering the job market from higher education institutions (HEIs). To thrive in this era of 21st-century disruptive technological development, the workforce must acquire new knowledge, skills, and work habits. Studying STEAM education through the TAM algorithm model to enhance the learning outcomes of higher vocational engineering students were presented (Huang and Liu, 2022). To meet the evolving demands of the job market, HEIs must periodically update their curricula. This necessitates proactive reforms in education and training to cultivate skills aligned with potential employment opportunities. However, a noticeable gap persists between the SDs of the industry and the skills supplied by higher education. Consequently, it becomes imperative to equip and prepare higher education students for the constantly changing workplace landscape. Identifying the SG and instigating proactive changes at the HEI level can help prevent talent shortages and mass unemployment among students (Steyn & Eybers, 2024).

HEIs design courses tailored to the specific skill sets required for each program. However, given the dynamic nature of industry SDs, HEIs may encounter challenges in keeping pace with these changes. Organizations cannot solely address the SG; they require support from HEIs to cultivate talent pools equipped with skills relevant to current business needs. While some organizations collaborate with educational partners to nurture talent pipelines, many rely on HEIs to independently identify and develop future skills. Prominent organizations embracing this approach, often referred to as Education 4.0, include FICCI, Deloitte, KPMG, PWC, Goldman Sachs, among others (Nayar, 2020). This study aims to assess and reduce the gap between academia and industry through dynamic, inbuilt course adjustments

17.1.2 Objectives/Hypothesis

The envisioned HEISG framework endeavors to quantify this disparity through the application of machine learning (ML) methods. Central to this assessment are the skill scores associated with both supply and demand: exit skill scores originating from HEIs and entry skill scores required by industries, respectively. The skill index (SI) is then constructed by combining the exit scores from HEIs with the entry scores from the industry.

17.1.3 Contribution to Literature/Paper Originality

1. In this initial phase, the project yields an SI by mapping exit scores from student profiles (SPs) to entry scores from job descriptions (JDs). The resulting cosine similarity score serves as an indicator of the gap between the supply skill vector and the demand skill vector. For instance, if the threshold is set at 0.3, only candidates B_2 and B_1 meet the criteria for job A_1, while only candidate B_2 aligns with job A_2. The percentage of candidates falling below this threshold is calculated within each HEI hierarchy. Typically, a threshold similarity score of 70% is deemed acceptable for students to qualify for job applications. If fewer than 50% of total students fail to meet this threshold, it signals the existence of an SG for the current job demand. HEIs identified with such gaps are encouraged to implement curriculum adjustments and provide appropriate training to both faculty and students.
2. To ensure alignment with future job profiles, periodic assessments by the industry are conducted to verify the established eligibility criteria This study's primary emphasis lies in addressing the SG concerning hard skills within diverse domains. Students attain these skills through the myriad courses provided by their respective educational institutions. The course structures are carefully tailored to align with industry demands for an array of skill sets. The central objective of this study is to bridge the gap between the skills acquired in academia and the ever-evolving industry requirements, thereby identifying areas of misalignment.
3. Furthermore, this study endeavors to formulate a framework for addressing SGs utilizing ML techniques. The insights generated by this research lead to recommendations aimed at reducing this gap, ultimately enhancing the employability prospects of students who graduate from HEIs.

17.1.4 Future Work

In forthcoming research, the authors plan to assess the effectiveness of this framework by utilizing sample datasets drawn from both the intended demographic groups within their institutions and those external to them.

17.1.5 Structure of this Work

This work is structured into three parts as given below, with the corresponding sections, subsections, and paragraph texts.

Input for this study starts with Abstract section, then an Introduction, which will give an overview of the Problem, Motivation for this study, A crisp Hypothesis, with a solution proposed.

Process part of this study covers a detailed Literature Survey consisting of the following four subsections, skill assessment from HEI, SD from industry, strategies to fill the gap and leveraging ML approach. Here the Methodology of the study is presented with the innovative framework named HEISG and the work implemented with the ML-based analysis.

Output of the work consists of Conclusion, which also covers Future research.

17.2 LITERATURE REVIEW

In its 2017–18 report, the National Skill Development Corporation (NSDC) pinpointed that the IT and ITeS industries, along with related research and development, collectively contribute approximately 8% to the overall gross domestic product (GDP) of the Indian subcontinent (Deloitte, 2019). These industries were projected to generate direct employment opportunities for roughly three million individuals. Key drivers behind this substantial talent pool included the automation of public distribution systems, e-Governance initiatives, the Digital India program, the National Knowledge Network, and the integration of education through Information and Communication Technology (ICT). India has emerged as one of the world's fastest-growing start-up ecosystems, resulting in a high demand for employees possessing contemporary skill sets. A significant number of these start-ups consistently seek out skilled talent, with nearly 50% of employers reporting difficulties in filling positions in certain specialized domains. These circumstances prompted this research to delve into the disparity between the available skills and those in demand. The research employs an ML approach to identify and quantify the gap between the SS from HEIs and the SD from the industry.

17.2.1 Skill Assessment from Higher Education Institution

In the realm of higher education, students who graduate from HEIs equipped with specific skills eagerly enter the job market, seeking positions that align with their acquired expertise. From an academic research perspective, HEIs recognize the importance of catering to future talent needs. Several global studies, selected for discussion here, shed light on how HEIs address the training of their students.

One noteworthy observation is that while dedicated analytics tools in the market have garnered attention, top-tier universities have been somewhat hesitant to experiment with them for an extended period. In a UK study, it was suggested that substantial potential could be unlocked by applying analytics to the extensive static data available within HEIs. Predictive techniques, employing student admission test scores, have been employed to enhance university entry probabilities (Iqbal et al., 2017). In some private universities in India, collaborative efforts among students have led to improvements in their overall skill levels. This extensive data analysis aims to empower students to adapt effectively to the ever-evolving external environment (Paul et al., 2018). By 2018, the United States recognized the need for factual and procedural knowledge to develop new market-based programs. Motivational factors were crucial for academic staff to contribute to these innovative initiatives. One program revealed that a shift in organizational culture within the education sector was necessary to support and align with changes in teaching methods to meet external stakeholder goals. In the Middle East, a gap analysis of students' skills at Qatar University identified the need for 21st-century business skills (Ashley, Schaap, and Bruijn, 2019). Singapore, in anticipation of an automation-driven economy during the Fourth Industrial Revolution, introduced three initiatives: Smart Nation Singapore, Skills Future, and the creation of new universities. After departing formal education via HEIs, students' primary motivation is to enter the job market.

They aim to share the skills acquired from HEIs with industry sectors, thus validating their acquired knowledge globally (Sukackė et al., 2022). Recognizing sharing as a fundamental need, education institutions worldwide must proactively ensure that students' skill development remains relevant to their employers, whether locally or globally. HEIs achieve this through periodic curriculum updates, traditionally operating on a five-year update cycle. However, the trend suggests a shorter, three-year update cycle may be on the horizon, reflecting the rapid pace of technological advancements. Incorporating these changes into the curriculum fosters continuous learning for both faculty and students. The pace of learning has become a critical factor in modern education systems (Gleason, 2018). In Vietnam, a survey conducted in 2018 assessed final-year university graduates' skills across various parameters, revealing an intriguing model among Vietnamese students. Principal component analyses, statistics, T-tests, and ANOVA tests were employed to analyze this model. The results indicated that graduates often lacked essential skills required for their roles, with factors like socioeconomic background and culture playing a significant role (Nghia, 2018). In India, NASSCOM initiated a five-year plan in 2019 aimed at reskilling one million professionals. This ambitious plan aligns the number of (re)skilled individuals with potential employees and fresh students, focusing on emerging new technologies. Industry leaders emphasized the motto "Re-skill or else perish" (NASSCOM, 2020). Latin American policy decisions have demonstrated the predictability of education outcomes through statistical analysis of students' course completion rates. Predictive models help identify a student's probability of completing a degree and can even forecast potential dropouts early in their academic journey (Musso et al., 2020). Process innovation plays a vital role in initiating, designing, implementing, and embedding technological transformations within HEIs. A study conducted in the Netherlands explored a bottom-up approach to projects within higher education, while top-down management processes ensure broader changes that incorporate improved educational practices and quality education (Schophuizen and Kalz, 2020). Table 17.1 provides a consolidated list of the studies discussed in this chapter, categorized by the research country. While these studies offer valuable insights, it is important to note that this chapter covers a selection of essential research to establish the proposed framework, and there may be numerous other insightful reports and statistics in this field.

17.2.2 Skill Demand from Industry Sectors

Organizations are achieving remarkable success by implementing policies and initiatives designed to attract and retain highly skilled workers. The initial step in this process involves the industry articulating its skill requirements through job postings on both internal portals and external platforms. The Executive Summary of the "Human Resource and Skill Requirements in the IT-ITeS" report by the NSDC (2018) emphasizes that their proposals aim to bridge the gap between job demand and supply through industry–academia collaboration recommendations. One such recommendation could involve instructing the industry to establish entry criteria for each job profile application. These criteria could be embedded within the keywords of a job advertisement, with hyperlinks providing information about required training and certifications. Additionally, promoting cross-sector certifications and degrees can

TABLE 17.1
Analyzed Studies Regarding HEI

Study Based On	Location	Year
The potential of data generated is an opportunity	United Kingdom[a]	2016
AI for curriculum development	India[a]	2017–18
Students' business skills in the 21st century	Qatar, Dubai	2018
Bridging skill gap with industry needs	California, USA[a,b]	2018
The fourth industrial revolution resulting in national initiatives	Singapore[a]	2018
Future of jobs report	Switzerland[a]	2018
Students' completion rate prediction	Latin America, USA[a]	2020
Survey of industry demand	Spain[a]	2020
A yearly conference for HEI practitioners	Washington, USA[a]	2020

Notes:
[a] *India Today* (2020), Gleason (2018), World Economic Forum (2018), Musso et al. (2020), JPMorgan Chase (2023).
[b] Doctoral Thesis.

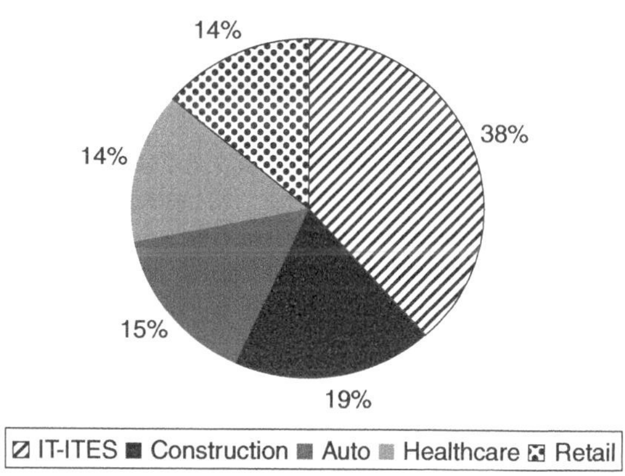

FIGURE 17.1 Training Conducted in Top Sectors.

enhance training infrastructure in regions with lower investment density. NSDC's annual reports classify Indian industries into three categories: priority sectors, large workforce-based sectors, and the informal sector. They also highlight the top five sectors in terms of training and successful job placements. IT-ITeS leads with 38%, while retail ranks fifth with 7%. Government intervention in India completes training programs based on the percentage share depicted in Figure 17.1. In terms of successful placements, the construction sector takes the lead with 34%, as depicted in Figure 17.2.

Transitioning educational institutions to meet the demands of digitalization is imperative, as evidenced by the significant need for disruptive changes. According to the "Quant Crunch" (2017) report by Burning Glass Technologies, the demand for

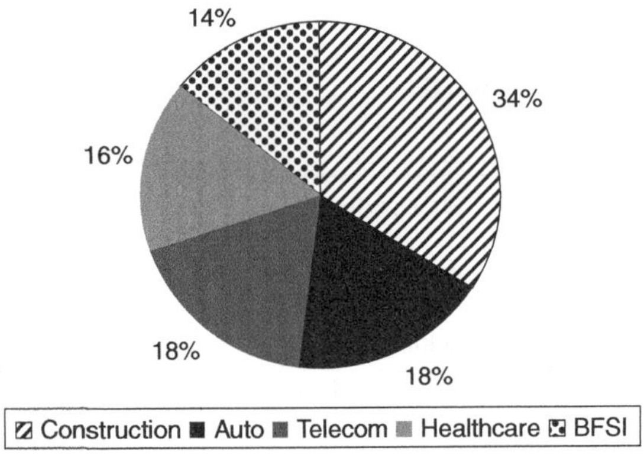

FIGURE 17.2 Successful Placements of Top Sectors.

Data Scientists is projected to surge by 28% by 2020. IBM's prediction in the same report explicitly highlights the challenge in recruiting skilled employees in fields like ML, Big Data, and data science. Recruitment poses challenges due to high hiring costs and the urgent need for new and updated training programs, which can jeopardize an organization's future productivity. IBM, a leader in technology development, conducted this study to analyze the SG between market demands and existing skill sets in businesses. The groundbreaking research aimed to address the shortage of data science and analytics skills through data-driven insights and increased collaboration between HEIs and the industry.

In 2018, a report focused on the distribution of high-skilled roles to bridge the gap between middle-skilled and low-skilled jobs. The report's primary objective was to identify differences between local and global functions across specific regions. It revealed disparities that could be addressed by analyzing surpluses and demand in various occupations, ultimately aiding in projecting employment growth in India over the next ten years. One noteworthy finding from this report is the potential to flip the supply–demand ratio in specific sectors.

The most sought-after job positions typically necessitate some form of post-secondary education or specialized training. It is important to note that the SG is not a singular entity; rather, it accumulates differently across various types of occupations. Establishing stronger connections between industry employers and experts in higher education can expedite the process of obtaining early feedback. Enhanced communication from employers regarding labor market needs is instrumental in preventing mismatches that can affect different segments of the job market in distinct ways. Notably, research within the healthcare sector has unveiled the most pronounced impact, resulting in an expanding SG. Occupations with more advanced training prerequisites tend to exhibit a noticeable gap and consequently endure economic downturns. Conversely, markets focusing on middle-skill jobs often grapple with job losses.

In summary, job position changes have a ripple effect, causing a positive impact on the economy by facilitating the recruitment of individuals into other positions. This phenomenon can result in the displacement of a few skilled workers in high-demand fields (Restuccia and Taska, 2018). Further research, as highlighted in the India Skills Report 2018 (SkillReporter, 2018) by the Confederation of Indian Industries (CII), underscores the collaborative efforts of organizations like PeopleStrong, Wheebox, UNDP, AICTE, AIU, and Pearson, all working toward a common goal: accessing the future global skill capitals. The government is actively committed to skilling the next generation. The report encompasses five key areas: Trends (related to Employability and Hiring), Automation (its Impact on Industry), Future Skills and Future Jobs (for forthcoming work), Apprenticeship (preparing young talent), and Job Preferences (both candidates' and employers' preferences). These five core areas constitute the foundation of the India Skill Gap report for 2018 (CII et al., 2018).

The report integrates two distinct sections based on data derived from the Wheebox Employability Skill Test and the India Intent Survey. Key findings include the attainment of a record-high employability score of 45.60%, along with a positive year-on-year trend in hiring intent. The report also highlights the widespread acceptance of job automation, with Analytics and artificial intelligence (AI) emerging as future job trends, closely followed by robotics. It emphasizes the importance of having requisite skills and participating in apprenticeship programs, both of which are critical steps. The report underscores the strong correlation between economic growth and job creation, as well as the universal requirement for skills and knowledge in the job market. Regardless of whether a country is developed or developing, the focus on skills remains consistent, reflecting a global perspective. Two essential factors in the skill equation are employment seekers and employable candidates. The India Skill Report 2019 elaborates on three noteworthy parameters derived from this equation (AICTE, 2019):

- "New Jobs and New skills – A futuristic perspective"
- "Impact of automation"
- "New-age jobs"

The impact of digitalization on the economy is evident in a comprehensive study encompassing 125 areas of analysis. When applied to the banking sector, this study highlights that bankers require a minimum set of employability skills, including critical, creative, and analytical thinking, to enhance an automated banking environment. Gender also plays a significant role in the availability of these skills (Abbasi, Ali, and Bibi, 2018). Accenture, a leading IT services organization, recognized the need to accelerate skill acquisition in the era of intelligent technologies and published a white paper in 2019 outlining its educational initiatives. The paper underscores the potential cost of a skill crisis for industries and proposes three steps to address it: expediting experiential learning, shifting the focus from institutions to individuals, and empowering vulnerable learners (Accenture, n.d.).The emergence of Industry 4.0 has initiated changes in business processes and work approaches, resulting in the creation of new job profiles within organizations. Job advertisements, rich in information, are available in unstructured or semi-structured formats. Text mining techniques have been employed to delineate the knowledge landscape required in such organizations. The analysis has led to the identification of two distinct groups of job profiles: those solely focused on Industry 4.0 and those related to management and computer science (Pejic-Bach et al., 2020). In 2019, a Higher Education Edition report was jointly released by the New Media Consortium and EDUCAUSE, revealing the misrepresentation of learning initiatives. Overqualification has led to a misalignment of skills, skewing the demand in the job market. Graduates often find themselves inundated with entry-level data jobs that underutilize the skills acquired through formal higher education. Consequently, this analysis calls for an adjustment in demand to rectify the over-skilling pattern observed. The Horizon Report series, which spans over 16 years of research and publication, explores emerging technology-related developments in academia worldwide. It profiles trends, challenges, and advancements in educational technology that are likely to impact teaching, learning, and creative inquiry. The report consists of three sections, serving as a reference and technology planning guide for educators, higher education leaders, administrators, policymakers, and technologists (Figueiredo et al., 2020).

17.2.3 Strategies to Fill the Skill Gap

Several studies have examined the SG from an employment perspective, highlighting the increasing demand for soft skills in contrast to existing hard skills. There are indications that graduates' employability is diminishing, leading to a reduction in their business knowledge. This trend suggests that graduates predominantly acquire hardcore technical skills during their academic education (Feraco et al., 2021). While work experiences and on-the-job learning can help bridge the SG, the expectation is for the workplace to be conducive to continuous learning, evolving beyond a controlled training environment. In this context, having access to various information sources and a supportive employer environment with ample training resources is highly beneficial (Maina et al., 2022). Rhode University conducted an internship program for higher education graduates over a semester, involving a 13-week course with pre- and post-semester macro-level tests administered to both the students and their internship supervisors. The results showed a striking similarity in the feedback provided by both groups, highlighting specific areas in soft skills that required improvement. This feedback proves invaluable for students as they near the completion of their university degrees, enhancing their prospects in the job market. In academic education and industry, technical and social competencies often align. However, there is a noticeable gap in methodological competence, leading industries to extend the training periods for graduate engineers until this gap is adequately addressed. The proposed solution involves implementing a learning factory within one of India's premier institutions as part of its curriculum, serving as a roadmap for other institutions to follow similar learning factory implementations (Kusumo et al., 2022). Another approach to gap analysis is Student Performance Index Classification Enumeration (SPICE), which aims to improve students' performance indices by evaluating the existing parameters within educational institutions. SPICE predicts quality, efficiency, and latency, highlighting individual strengths and weaknesses across various disciplines. It identifies patterns related to motivation, satisfaction, and growth prospects for job seekers. In 2019 the India Skill Report, accessible on the AICTE website, provides insights into the employable talents possessed by students

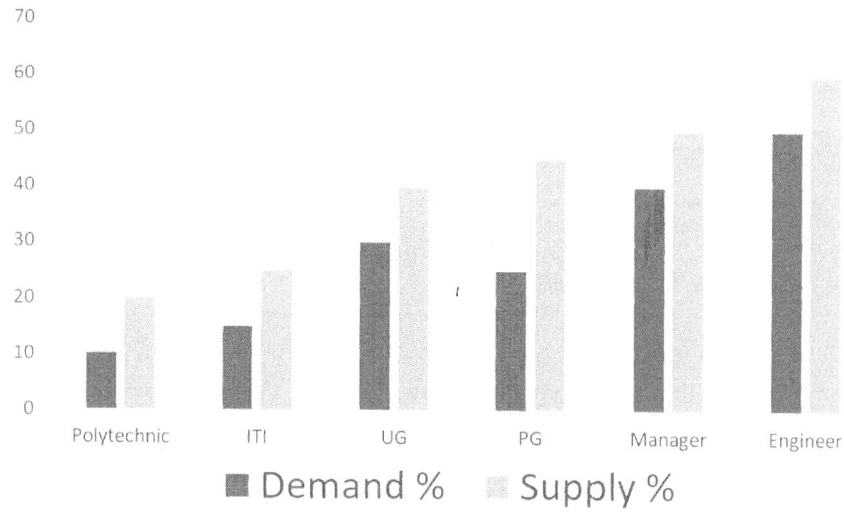

FIGURE 17.3 Consolidated View of Supply and Demand of Skills.

based on their degree or college leaving certificates. The authors of this report deem these findings a significant resource for identifying the SG analysis on the supply side—the composition of an organization's workforce based on the same set of degrees used as recruitment criteria. The report includes a chart depicting the percentage of contributions to each field (CII et al., 2019). As depicted in Figures 17.1 and 17.3, opportunities in the top sectors underscore training as the foremost solution advocated by the industry (Nayar, 2020). Bridging the gap between the classroom and the boardroom results in a narrowing of the SG and an increased awareness of digital skills, fostering corporate connections, industry meetings, and interviews at all levels within organizations (Deloitte, 2020). In the pursuit of mitigating SG accelerators, the World Economic Forum in 2020 addressed both national and global SGs while preparing countries for the future of work. The forum identified four key focus areas to expedite the resolution of global SGs:

- Lifelong learning and upskilling
- Future readiness and employability
- Innovative skills funding models
- Skills anticipation and job market insight

The envisioned commitment and a bold challenge were set to encourage each citizen to undertake 101 days of additional learning by the year 2022. The devised plan aims to swiftly address the evolving skill requirements in key sectors, as outlined in the Future of Jobs report. This approach entails a comprehensive strategy designed to implement actions simultaneously in four crucial directions, aligning with the four SGs. These directions encompass national-level initiatives, global learning networks, the availability of SG playbooks, and the enhancement of country-specific portfolios based on the multifaceted recommendations presented

TABLE 17.2
Year-wise Analysis of Training

Year	Training Expenditure	Hours of Training
2017	$1075	46.7
2018	$986	42.1
2019	$1286	–

Source: Bohne (2019).

in the report by the World Economic Forum in 2020 (World Economic Forum, 2020). In the New York City Skill Gap report from JPMorgan Chase & Co in 2020, solutions for addressing critical, in-demand jobs in the city are primarily focused on healthcare professionals, followed by technology jobs. The firm has committed to investing $250 million over a span of five years in a global initiative aimed at preparing markets to meet the needs of emerging high-growth, high-demand, middle-skill jobs. This initiative involves establishing a demand-driven workforce development system and providing training to both youth and adults for middle-skill occupations in high demand. The analysis presented in this report is derived from job postings data in NYC spanning from July 2013 to June 2014. Notably, the report highlights the challenges contributing to SGs in New York City while also identifying numerous opportunities to transition individuals into more lucrative employment prospects (JPMorgan Chase, 2020).

According to Table 17.2, organizations invest significant time and resources in the quest for top talent, but they recognize the importance of providing comprehensive training to new employees during the onboarding process (Statista, 2022). This investment is crucial to ensure that new hires fully understand their job responsibilities. Inadequate training can result in subpar work quality and may ultimately lead to employee turnover (Bohne, 2019). A survey conducted by Training mag.com magazine between May and July 2019, involving responses from 100 employees drawn from the Dun & Bradstreet database, shed light on the training practices of various industries, corporations, and educational institutions. However, it is important to note that the survey results are somewhat skewed, primarily representing the perspective of the industry. Notable findings include a substantial allocation of resources to training staff on the payroll and expenditures on external agencies for content acquisition. Additionally, 44% of respondents expressed plans to invest in online learning and development tools and systems. Alternatively, one can consider any of the three datasets to analyze the cost per learner in talent development. In a survey conducted in Europe, involving nearly 400 students, the aim was to gain a better understanding of students' computational thinking skills. The findings revealed that motivation to learn was significantly enhanced through peer learning. This highlights the importance of instructors innovating their teaching approaches, particularly by implementing flipped classroom instructions. Such instructional strategies are already in use in HEIs (Gong et al., 2020).

17.2.4 Leveraging Machine Learning Approach to Fill the Gap

Higher education institutions are staying up to date with curriculum updates by leveraging the straightforward analytical techniques available in the field of data science and ML. These courses present a significant opportunity as future job skills, enabling individuals to master the tools associated with data analysis across various sectors of society and industry. By implementing a few simple text mining steps to validate curriculum development, HEIs can streamline the interactions required between different academic disciplines. This approach underscores the importance of integrating data science and ML techniques into various fields to ensure the relevance of the courses. Furthermore, the study proposes data mining steps to guide the development of university-level curricula in disciplines that are embracing this emerging trend, spanning various research domains. When compared to manual analysis conducted by staff across different departments in the traditional manner, machine-driven analysis yields more comprehensive insights. This is primarily because ML techniques excel at recognizing complex patterns across textual data, a task that can be challenging for human analysts. The accuracy of results obtained through machine-driven analysis demonstrates the clear advantages of utilizing these techniques (West, 2017). ML has the capability to enhance research by building applications with a focus on econometrics, enabling the prediction of new research questions. The quality of data input into hypotheses, and subsequently the accuracy of predictions, plays a pivotal role in this process. It is noteworthy that there exists heterogeneity in the treatment of ML models across various fields, which has led to the development of new theories

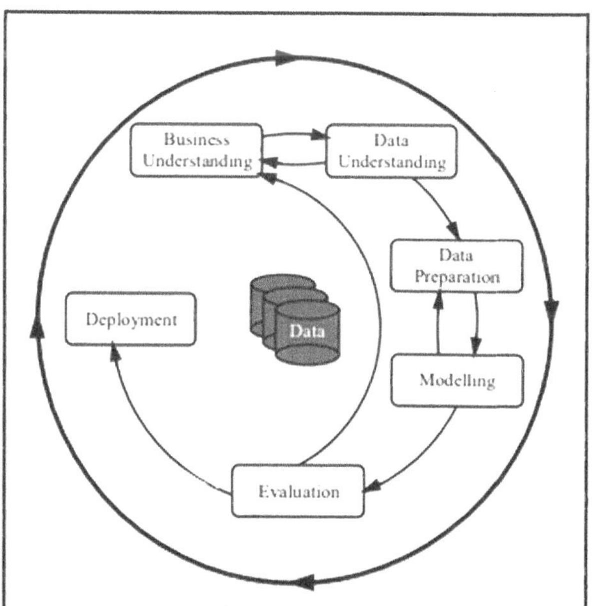

FIGURE 17.4 The CRISP Model.

TABLE 17.3
Consolidated Challenges in MOOC

No	Issues	Pros	Cons	Suggestions
1	A fully automated learning environment	Scaling is a boon	Self-driven self-learning	Full automation suggests the necessary skills
2	Pre-tests checking for basic mathematics and programming skills	Pre-test score-based prediction for course completion status	Strained learning despite a low score in the pre-test	Need one to one collaboration with academic experts for engaged learning
3	Time between tests	Learning curve increases with time lags	Problem and solution space increases with laps in the time	Resulting in a range of skill set to explore
4	Trail on exercise	Mass roll-out	Case-by-case coaching	Measures cases
5	Actual programming to workout exercise	Acquire practical knowledge with sample datasets	The real dataset will be far from the sample	Skill not developed is offset with rigorous workouts

Source: Seya et al. (2019).

(Mullainathan and Spiess, 2017). ML, as a branch of AI, cannot be simply viewed as a tool or process; it represents a field of study and a problem-solving approach. The current methods employed to address the widening SG worldwide have resulted in a generation of graduates lacking employable skills, exacerbating unemployment issues and hindering the development of tools that enhance machine intelligence. However, the synergy between human talent, intelligence, and machine capabilities holds promise for skill development in product creation. Therefore, unemployment should be viewed as a destabilizing factor, underscoring the importance of fostering learning skills through AI and Big Data-driven curriculum design, creating a comprehensive learning cycle (*India Today*, 2018; Alonso-García, de-Cózar-Macías, and Blazquez-Parra, 2020).

The future of employment calls for a symbiotic relationship between humans and machines, necessitating an amalgamation of learning from both entities (Xing and Marwala, 2017). Massive open online courses (MOOCs), particularly in areas like ML, deep learning, and AI, face specific challenges related to learner completion rates (Seya et al., 2019). A consolidated list of pros and cons sheds light on potential strategies to mitigate these challenges, transforming issues into learning opportunities (Table 17.3). This approach leads to improved teaching methods, emphasizing that one-size-fits-all solutions are not suitable for all learners and that customization based on individual needs is crucial. Ultimately, the effectiveness of machine-led teaching depends on the learner's commitment to becoming an efficient self-learner (Xing and Marwala, 2017). In the field of software programming, a structured approach with processes and tools is essential. While AI and ML algorithms are increasingly taught through automation, concerns have arisen among software developers about code quality. The study suggests that a focus on strengthening existing tools and reducing diversification in tool development can enhance the quality of code written by developers. This approach encourages software researchers to actively participate in improving coding environments, thereby fostering a culture of experimentation and skill development among developers (Marijan et al., 2019).

The literature review underscores the existence of a SG among graduates in terms of employability. Industries are reducing training for fresh college graduates due to cost optimization, and the digital disruption underscores the need for HEIs to prepare graduates with digital and ICT skills. To address this, we propose a framework, higher education institution skills gap (HEISG), which aims to identify dynamic industry demands and provide comprehensive training within HEI campuses to bridge the SG. This framework employs ML techniques to understand skill factors from both HEIs and industry sectors, facilitating a holistic view of supply and demand and enabling strategic decisions to reduce the SGs.

17.3 METHODOLOGY

This article follows a two-phase methodology. The first phase involves designing and presenting a comprehensive framework for assessing the SGs between HEI and the industry. In parallel, the second phase entails the practical exploration of this proposed framework, leveraging an ML approach. This step aims to gain insights into the framework's opportunities and challenges, serving as a preliminary assessment before expanding the research to encompass various cities and states across India. The primary metric utilized for evaluating the existing SG is the SI, which is computed by comparing the supply skill scores originating from HEIs with the demand skill scores derived from the industry. Throughout the implementation of the ML component, the Cross-Industry Standard Process for Data Mining (CRISP-DM) methodology was employed as a structured approach to guide the research process. Refer Figure 17.4.

17.3.1 Framework for Skill Gap Identification

The primary objective of this research is to establish a connection between the SS originating from HEI and the SD within the industry. The framework presented in Figure 17.5 illustrates the essential components of this research effort. Below, we provide a breakdown of the key features integrated into the HEISG framework and an overview of the associated process details.

17.3.2 HEI Skill Acquisition Track

Conducting a SG analysis necessitates the acquisition of data from both HEI and industries. Therefore, the collection of data from these two distinct segments is of

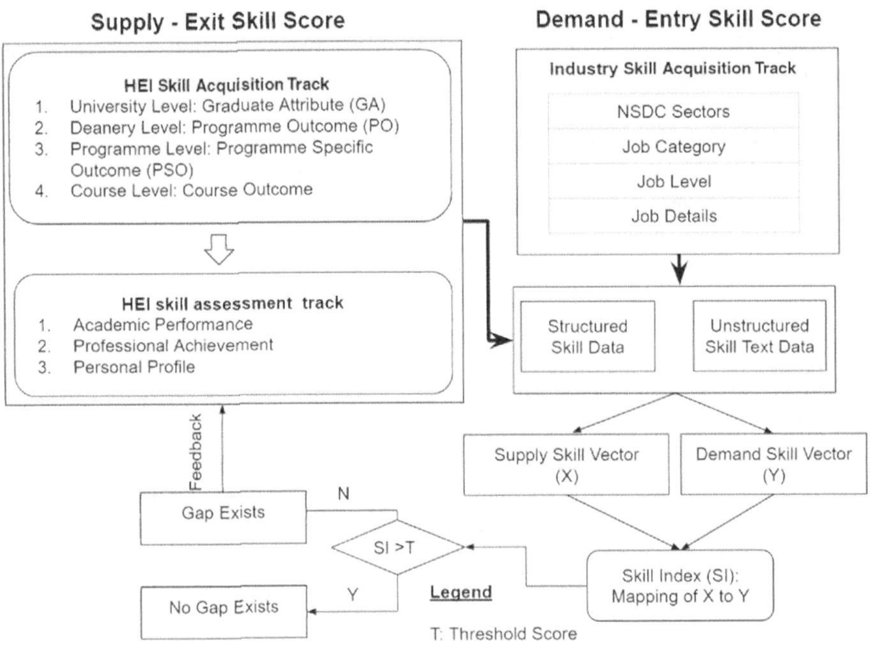

FIGURE 17.5 HEISG Framework.

paramount importance in accurately assessing the gap between them. However, in the Indian context, accessing open data from these sectors is often challenging. Consequently, this research suggests an approach that involves extracting the maximum available data from HEI websites, considering the four levels of knowledge and skill-providing sources.

University Level. The graduate attributes of any HEI encompass the essential skills and qualities that a student possesses upon completing their education. These attributes serve as a foundation for various disciplines or departments to ensure that their program outcomes are aligned with these skills and help in the design of a curriculum that meets these objectives.

Deanery/School Level. The program outcome of any deanery/school is a directive for the departments to prepare their students to accomplish upon completion of the degree—standard taxonomies used for designing these outcomes.

Program Level. A subtle and expected outcome standards are set by each HEI program that they focus on as a skilled provider.

Course Level. Outcomes of students depend on the type and duration of the course. Mainly the core and elective courses focus on the hard skill that any student anticipated to acquire by the end of the term.

Constructing a skill hierarchy for HEI will help in designing ontology or work corpus for skill vector generation. The first three are planning levels for skill, whereas the course level is the implementation level designed during the curriculum development stage.

HEI Skill Assessment Track. The graduating students' tracked skills from three different dimensions: academic performance, professional achievement, and personal profile. The assessment tracks support consolidating the structured and unstructured data forms of an individual, and the aggregated scores of all skill acquisition levels discussed earlier.

Academic Performance: Course-wise assessment record with skills and competency scores provides adequate information of an individual student. A critical stage that helps in deriving the supply skill score of HEI is academic performance.

Professional Achievement: In HEI, apart from academic performance assessment, each student will get the opportunity to participate in non-academic programs. The generated scores for the courses and the capture of relevant skills happen at this level.

Personal Profile: This level gathers skills both from individual and placement offices of the HEI that include all external sources and the track record of the student/department/deanery available in the placement office.

17.3.3 Industry Skill Acquisition Track

There are various sources from which market demand created by industry sectors can be obtained. The primary source of information is the Indian government's NSDC portal, which categorizes jobs relevant to the outgoing students of HEIs. Additionally, public and private job portals can be utilized for web scraping to extract information on industry skills demand. Academic partnership surveys conducted by different industry sectors can also provide insights into job trends and job listings. Each industry typically categorizes jobs based on job levels and provides detailed JDs, which can be valuable sources of information for understanding market demand.

Skill Vector Generation: To process the data retrieved from both HEI and industry sources, skill scores need to be derived based on their respective levels. Exploratory data analysis will be conducted at all three tiers of skill gathering, addressing the mutual needs of both HEI and Industry. The structured and unstructured data require intensive preprocessing before generating feature vectors for both HEI and industry sectors.

Empirical models utilizing various ML algorithms from the existing literature will support this stage of the framework. The selection and tuning of the model will be highly dependent on the input data.

The similarity between vectors is defined by equation as in Figure 17.6. Similarity scores between A_i and B_j vectors will be determined to identify the gap between the existing skills of a student and the available demand. The results will be presented later in the same section.

Skill Index: Mapping skills at supply to demand defines a metric and threshold for identifying a gap between HEI and industry. The choice of threshold (T)

$$similarity(A,B) = \frac{A \cdot B}{\|A\| \times \|B\|} = \frac{\sum_{i=1}^{n} A_i \times B_i}{\sqrt{\sum_{i=1}^{n} A_i^2} \times \sqrt{\sum_{i=1}^{n} B_i^2}}$$

FIGURE 17.6 Similarity Calculation Formula.

TABLE 17.4
Stages in the Empirical Study

Stage	Process Adopted
Data Collection	Data scraping and synthetic data imputation
Data Processing	Data pre-processing; feature extraction
Modeling	Similarity score
Feedback	Recommendation based on threshold limits

determines the level of the organization. A hierarchical level representation depicts the flow that can be aggregated or separated based on *T*'s value at each stage. The default metric is the distance measure to understand the similarity or dissimilarity scores across the skill vectors of supply and demand. Alternate SI metrics is on the nature of feature vectors.

Feedback: It is applicable only if there is a gap in supply and demand skill between HEI and industries, so this component is optional for HEISG. Recommendations suggested for HEI if the SI score is less than that of the relevant industry's standard T. The guidance can be mapped to any HEI layer for incorporation in their strategies or procedures. As the skill sets are dynamic due to the rapid disruptions in information technology and unpredictable environmental and social changes, there is a high necessity of a healthy handshake among the HEI and industries to boost education and the nation's economy.

17.3.4 Skill Gap Analysis Using Machine Learning Approach

This article's authors piloted the proposed HEISG framework. The current work has used the natural language processing (NLP) approach of ML algorithms. The sequence of processes detailed in Table 17.4 is the empirical stage of adoption. As outlined in the HEISG framework, the primary objective is to identify SGs between HEI disciplines and industry sectors. The pilot phase of this work has adopted the methodology illustrated in Figure 17.7.

To obtain the necessary data, open data from HEIs has been collected through their respective web portals for SPs, and JDs have been sourced from public job portals using open-source code-based scrapers. The document preprocessing steps have been carried out with the assistance of NLP (Shaikh, 2017) toolkits, which include: tokenization of words, removal of stop words, stemming/lemmatization, and building skill-based word corpus. The SC depicted in Figure 17.7 serves as a storage

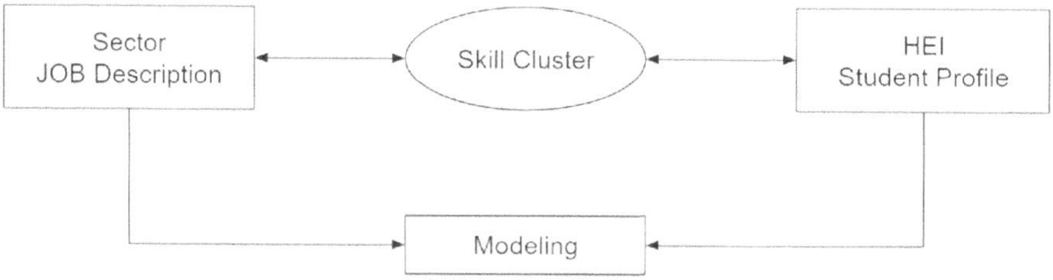

FIGURE 17.7 Block Diagram of the Empirical Model for the Pilot Study.

repository that encompasses all pertinent words required for generating the SI across both HEI and industry domains. It is structured based on a word hierarchy, which establishes a domain ontology for sectors, levels, and qualifications from an industry perspective, as well as for the deanery, program, and course levels from HEI. This framework has been developed with the aim of achieving standardization in skill data representation and management. In the pilot implementation, a set of sample words stored in the SC is relevant to both the supply skill vectors from the SP and the demand vectors from the JD. As illustrated in Figure 17.7, during the modeling phase, the skill mapping from supply to demand is conducted using the cosine similarity index, which helps determine the gap between a student's existing skills and the industry's skill requirements (Qin et al., 2020). The data extracted for this study is original, and the standard NLP processes have been applied. Therefore, there is no immediate need to test this model's behavior against false data. However, testing with synthetic or simulated data may be considered as part of future work by the authors.

17.4 RESULTS AND DISCUSSION

The results obtained during the pilot process are discussed in this section. The structure of the preprocessed data generated through scraping from the public domain for SP and JD is as follows:

JD: *M* Documents: $D_1, D_2, \ldots, D_M$;
SP: *N* Documents: $S_1, S_2, \ldots, S_N$;
JD Skill Vector: $A_i \Rightarrow (a_1, a_2, \ldots, a_p)$ $for\ i = \{1, 2, 3, \ldots, M\}$; $a_p \in SC$
SP Skill Vector: $B_j \Rightarrow (b_1, b_2, \ldots, b_q)$ $for\ j = \{1, 2, 3, \ldots, N\}$; $b_q \in SC$

Using the equation shown in Figure 17.5, similarity scores of A_i and B_j vectors have been determined to find the gap between the existing skill of a student and available demand. The expected dataset of SC inputs includes terms from HEI and job sectors without their hierarchy relationship, which is given below:

HEI Qualifications. Professional (BE, MBA, MCA, BCA, BBA), science, humanities, arts, etc.
Job Sectors. Telecommunication, IT, manufacturing, pharmaceutical, healthcare, etc.

TABLE 17.5
Sample Similarity Scores of JDs and SPs

$S(A_i, B_j)$	B_1	B_2	B_3
A_1	0.314138	0.38998192	0.21761683
A_2	0.2982207	0.48541511	0.07286329

Job Roles. Software engineer, HR manager, software developer, graphics designer, web designer, technical writer, chemist, pharmacist, business analyst, data analyst, etc.

Skills. Digital marketing, data analysis, UI/UX design, Big Data, AI, business intelligence, Python, JAVA, NoSQL, problem-solving, project management, etc.

Two sample JDs (A_1, A_2) and three sample SPs (B_1, B_2, B_3) from the above dataset illustrate the pilot model's results and probable recommendations.

- A_1: (BE, MCA, telecommunication, software engineer, JAVA, SQL, data analysis, problem-solving)
- A_2: (MBA, MCA, healthcare, data analyst, Python, NoSQL, data analysis, problem-solving)
- B_1: (BE, JAVA, NoSQL, data analysis, problem-solving, Big Data)
- B_2: (MCA, JAVA, Python, NoSQL, data analysis, problem-solving, UI, UX design)
- B_3: (MBA, Python, SQL, data analysis, project management, business intelligence)

The similarity scores between the JDs and SPs have been ranked for each SP to identify the probable jobs relevant to the candidate. For each JD, suitable candidates may be rated from the industry perspective. As shown in Table 17.5 for both JDs, candidates B_2, B_1, and B_3 have been ranked in that order. Experts from both HEI and the industry define and decide on the threshold score for identifying the eligibility index to assess qualified professionals with the right skill sets. For example, if the threshold is set at 0.3, then only B_2 and B_1 are eligible for A_1, and only B_2 is suitable for A_2. The percentage of candidates below the threshold index is available from each HEI hierarchy.

Approximately a threshold similarity score of 70% is acceptable for a student to apply for a job. If less than 50% of total students are not eligible, then the SG for the available demand is proven to exist. HEIs with such gaps are recommended to make relevant curriculum changes and provide adequate training to staff and students. Industry assessment is conducted periodically to confirm the eligibility criteria set for future job profiles (Venkatraman et al. 2018), and apprenticeships are one way to improve employment in the digital economy while HEIs explore new ways of implementing new curriculums

17.5 CONCLUSION AND FURTHER RESEARCH

The rapid advancements in technology and the era of Industry 4.0 have led to a continuous need for curriculum updates by HEIs. Digital disruptions have raised expectations within organizations, resulting in a significant shift toward the demand for future-focused skills. This study's primary objective is to assess the gap between the skills supplied by HEIs and the skills required by the industry, utilizing the HEISG framework. It appears that the responsibility for closing this gap lies more with HEIs than with the industry. Thus, the proposed framework aims to identify and address this gap by providing the right candidates with the necessary skills as per industry demand. Applying recommendations generated through AI and ML techniques to curriculum development helps reduce the demand–supply gap (*India Today*, 2018).

The HEISG framework, as proposed, seeks to measure this gap using ML techniques. It relies on skill scores related to supply and demand to determine the existing gap. Exit skill scores are derived from HEIs, while entry skill scores are determined by industry needs. By comparing SPs from HEIs and JD from industry, this pilot work calculates the SI, which serves as a decision parameter for recommendations based on dynamically set industry thresholds. The resulting cosine similarity score (SI) indicates the gap between the supply and demand skill vectors. Based on these findings, HEIs can use the SI as a score to design and adapt their curricula. This cyclical process aims to minimize the gap between the skills demanded by the industry and those supplied by HEIs.

As this is an ongoing process, JDs from various sectors are subject to dynamic changes based on industry needs. HEIs share equal responsibility for keeping their curricula up to date, as mandated by education authorities, and being responsive to industry demands. In cases where curriculum changes within a year may not be practical, HEIs can establish additional training programs and internship projects to keep pace with the ever-changing job market requirements. By aligning students' needs with organizational needs, these need-based jobs can help minimize the gap between the two, ultimately reducing the amount of additional training required for students upon joining the workforce. This, in turn, leads to improved economic prosperity for a country by harnessing the raw talent provided by HEIs, who are well-prepared for the job market.

A recent trend among students completing their higher secondary education is taking a break of a year or more before pursuing full-time higher education. This break allows them to contemplate their career options more thoroughly before making decisions about their academic path. Given the myriad opportunities, especially those arising from the 2020 pandemic, online learning is expected to evolve into a blended learning approach, becoming the new norm. This approach will provide students with greater personalization and more frequent opportunities for beneficial changes in their education journey.

ACKNOWLEDGEMENTS

The authors would like to thank the immense support rendered to this work, and in general to allocation of the major research project to us by the Center of Research Projects. The authors are indebted to their university for allowing the research hours to be put in for this work.

REFERENCES

Abbasi, Farhad Khurshid, Amjad Ali, and Naila Bibi. 2018. "Analysis of Skill Gap for Business Graduates: Managerial Perspective from Banking Industry." *Education + Training* 60(4): 354–67. https://doi.org/10.1108/et-08-2017-0120.

Accenture. n.d. "Talent & Organization/Human Potential Services I Accenture." n.d. www.accenture.com. Accessed 11 June 2024. www.accenture.com/gb-en/insights/future-workforce/transforming-learning.

AICTE. 2019. "United Nations Development Programme." Available at: www.aicte-india.org/sites/default/files/Annual%20Report%2018-19.pdf. Accessed: 11 June 2024.

Alonso-García, María, Óscar D. de-Cózar-Macías, and Elidia Beatriz Blazquez-Parra. 2020. "Viability of Competencies, Skills and Knowledge Acquired by Industrial Design Students." *International Journal of Technology and Design Education* 31(3): 545–63. https://doi.org/10.1007/s10798-020-09561-6.

Ashley, Sue, Harmen Schaap, and Elly de Bruijn. 2019. "Exploring Differences between International Business Undergraduates' Conceptual Understanding." *Studies in Higher Education*, October, 1–14. https://doi.org/10.1080/03075079.2019.1672642.

Bohne, Raphael. 2019. Factors driving digital learning over the next two to three years.

CII, PeopleStrong, Wheebox, UNDP, AICTE, AIU, & Pearson. 2018. "India Skills Report 2018." *UNDP*. Available at: www.undp.org/india/publications/india-skills-report-2018. Accessed: 11 June 2024.

CII et al. 2019. www.aicte-india.org/sites/default/files/India Skill Report-2019.pdf

Deloitte. 2019. "Ten years on: The G20 Employement Process." Available at: https://www2.deloitte.com/content/dam/Deloitte/global/Documents/About-Deloitte/gx-ioeg20-implementation-report.pdf. Accessed: 11 June 2024.

Deloitte. 2020. Deloitte's Voice of the Workforce Report. Available at: www.deloitte.com/uk/en/services/consulting/research/deloittes-voice-of-the-workforce-report.html. Accessed: 11 June 2024.

Feraco, Tommaso, Dario Resnati, Davide Fregonese, Andrea Spoto, and Chiara Meneghetti. 2021. "Soft Skills and Extracurricular Activities Sustain Motivation and Self-Regulated Learning at School." *The Journal of Experimental Education* 90(3): 1–20. https://doi.org/10.1080/00220973.2021.1873090.

Figueiredo, H., Biscaia, R., Rocha, V., & Teixeira, P. 2015. "Should We Start Worrying? Mass Higher Education, Skill Demand and the Increasingly Complex Landscape of Young Graduates' Employment. *Studies in Higher Education*, 42(8): 1401–1420. https://doi.org/10.1080/03075079.2015.1101754

Gleason, N. W. 2018. *Higher education in the era of the fourth industrial revolution*. Springer Nature.

Gong, D., Yang, H. H., and Cai, J. 2020. "Exploring the key influencing factors on college students' computational thinking skills through flipped-classroom instruction." *International Journal of Educational Technology in Higher Education*, 17(1). doi:10.1186/s41239-020-00196-0.

Huang, Y., Liu, X. 2022. "The Analysis and Research of STEAM Education Based on the TAM Algorithm Model to Improve the Learning Effectiveness of Higher Vocational Engineering Students." *Evolutionary Intelligence* 15: 2597–2607. https://doi.org/10.1007/s12065-021-00619-5.

"How Artificial Intelligence Is Helping Universities Design a Curriculum for Future Jobs That Don't Exist Now." 2018. *India Today*. Available at: www.indiatoday.in/education-today/featurephilia/story/artificial-intelligence-can-design-curriculum-to-prepare-for-future-jobs-html-1404544-2018-12-07. Accessed 11 June 2024.

IBM. "The Quant Crunch." 2017. *Web.archive.org*. 27 June 2017. Available at: http://web.archive.org/web/20170627143049/www.ibm.com/analytics/us/en/technology/data-science/quant-crunch.html.

Iqbal, Muhammad Munwar, Muhammad Usman, Zeshan Iqbal, Muhammad Umar Chaudhry, Muhammad Farhan, and Muhammad Ashraf. 2017. "E-Assessment and Computer-Aided Prediction Methodology for Student Admission Test Score." *EURASIA Journal of Mathematics, Science and Technology Education* 13(8). https://doi.org/10.12973/eurasia.2017.00939a.

JPMorgan Chase. 2020. Closing the Skills Gap. Preparing New Yorkers For High-Growth, High-Demand, Middle-Skill Jobs.

JPMorgan Chase. 2023. *Closing the skills gap*. Available at: www.jpmorganchase.com/content/dam/jpmc/jpmorgan-chase-and-co/documents/54841-JPMC-GAP-REP-AW6.pdf. Accessed: 11 June 2024.

Kusumo, H. et al. 2022. "Kampus Merdeka: College Educational Breakthrough to Address the Wide Gap between Industry and Academia." *KnE Social Sciences*: 499–508. [Preprint]. doi:10.18502/kss.v7i19.12470.

Maina, M. F., Guàrdia Ortiz, L., Mancini, F. *et al.* 2022. "A Micro-Credentialing Methodology for Improved Recognition of HE Employability Skills." *International Journal of Educational Technology in Higher Education* 19, 10. https://doi.org/10.1186/s41239-021-00315-5.

Marijan, Dusica, Weiyi Shang, and Rakesh Shukla. 2019. "Implications of Resurgence in Artificial Intelligence for Research Collaborations in Software Engineering." *ACM SIGSOFT Software Engineering Notes* 44(3): 68–70. https://doi.org/10.1145/3356773.3356813.

Milano, Miguel. 2019. "The Digital Skills Gap Is Widening Fast. Here's How to Bridge It." *World Economic Forum*. 12 March 2019. Available at: www.weforum.org/agenda/2019/03/the-digital-skills-gap-is-widening-fast-heres-how-to-bridge-it/.

Mullainathan, S., and Spiess, J. 2017. "Machine Learning: An Applied Econometric Approach." *Journal of Economic Perspectives* 31(2): 87–106. doi:10.1257/jep.31.2.87.

Musso, M. F., Hernández, C. F., and Cascallar, E. C. 2020. "Predicting Key Educational Outcomes in Academic Trajectories: A Machine-Learning Approach." *Higher Education* 80(5): 875–94. doi:10.1007/s10734-020-00520-7.

NASSCOM. 2020. "NASSCOM VISION and PRIORITIES." www.nasscom.in/sites/default/files/FutureSkills_An_Industry_Response.pdf. Accessed: 11 June 2024.

Nayar, Lola. 2020. www.skillreporter.com/2018/05/news/skilldevelopment/we-are-making-higher-education-more-skill-centric-ugc-chairman/

Nghia, T. L. 2018. "The Skills Gap of Vietnamese Graduates and Final-Year University Students." *Journal of Education and Work*, 31(7–8): 579–94. doi:10.1080/13639080.2018.1559280.

NSDC. 2018. "Annual Report 2017–18 – NSDC." 2018. *NSDC*. Available at: www.nsdcindia.org/sites/default/files/files/Annual-Report-NSDC-2017-18.pdf. Accessed 11 June 2024.

Paul, Prantosh, P. S. Aithal, A. Bhuimali, and K. Kumar. 2018. "Emerging Degrees and Collaboration: The Context of Engineering Sciences in Computing & IT—An Analysis for Enhanced Policy Formulation in India." *International Journal on Recent REsearches in Science Engineering and Technology (IJRRSET)*, 5 (12): 13–27.

Pejic-Bach, Mirjana, Tine Bertoncel, Maja Meško, and Živko Krstić. 2020. "Text Mining of Industry 4.0 Job Advertisements." *International Journal of Information Management* 50 (February): 416–31. https://doi.org/10.1016/j.ijinfomgt.2019.07.014.

"Publications." 2024. *World Economic Forum*. 10 January 2024. Available at: https://www.weforum.org/publications/the-future-of-jobs-report-2018/

Qin, Chuan, Hengshu Zhu, Tong Xu, Chen Zhu, Chao Ma, Enhong Chen, and Hui Xiong. 2020. "An Enhanced Neural Network Approach to Person–Job Fit in Talent Recruitment." *ACM Transactions on Information Systems* 38(2): 1–33. https://doi.org/10.1145/3376927.

Restuccia, Dan, and Bledi Taska. 2018. "Different Skills, Different Gaps: Measuring and Closing the Skills Gap," January, 207–26. https://doi.org/10.5771/9783957103154-207.

Schophuizen, Martine, and Marco Kalz. 2020. "Educational Innovation Projects in Dutch Higher Education: Bottom-Up Contextual Coping to Deal with Organizational Challenges." *International Journal of Educational Technology in Higher Education* 17(1). https://doi.org/10.1186/s41239-020-00197-z.

Seya, Keisuke, Nobuyuki Kobayashi, and Seiko Shirasaka. 2019. "Method of Creating Story-Based Lectures from a Past-To-Present Perspective That Helps Non-Technical Adult Learners Understand AI." Available at: www.weforum.org/publications/the-future-of-jobs-report-2020/digest. Accessed 11 June 2024.

Shaikh, Javed. 2017. "Machine Learning, NLP: Text Classification Using Scikit-Learn, Python and NLTK." *Medium*. Towards Data Science. 23 July 2017. Available at: https://towardsdatascience.com/machine-learning-nlp-text-classification-using-scikit-learn-python-and-nltk-c52b92a7c73a.

SkillReporter. 2018. "We are making higher education more skill-centric': UGC chairman, Skill Reporter." Available at: www.skillreporter.com/2018/05/news/skilldevelopment/we-are-making-higher-education-more-skill-centric-ugc-chairman. Accessed 11 June 2024.

Statista. 2022. "Workplace Training: Spending per Employee 2022." n.d. *Statista*. Available at: www.statista.com/statistics/738519/workplace-training-spending-per-employee. Accessed 11 June 2024.

Steyn, Adriana, and Sunet Eybers. 2024. "Unlocking the Power of Micro-Credentials in Commerce Degrees: A Practical Example," January, 225–36. https://doi.org/10.4102/aosis.2024.bk454.15.

Sukackė, V. et al. (2022) "Towards Active Evidence-Based Learning in Engineering Education: A Systematic Literature Review of PBL, PJBL, and CBL." *Sustainability* 14(21): 13955. doi:10.3390/su142113955.

Venkatraman, Sitalakshmi, Tony de Souza-Daw, and Samuel Kaspi. 2018. "Improving Employment Outcomes of Career and Technical Education Students." *Higher Education, Skills and Work-Based Learning* 8(4): 469–83. https://doi.org/10.1108/heswbl-01-2018-0003.

West, Jason. 2017. "Validating Curriculum Development Using Text Mining." *The Curriculum Journal* 28(3): 389–402. https://doi.org/10.1080/09585176.2016.1261719.

World Economic Forum. 2020. *Closing the Skills Gap Accelerators*. Available at: www3.weforum.org/docs/WEF_Closing_the_Skills_Gap_Accelerator_1pager.pdf. Accessed 11 June 2024.

Xing, Bo and Marwala, Tshilidzi. 2017. Implications of the Fourth Industrial Age for Higher Education. https://ssrn.com/abstract=3225331

Section IV

Panoramic Applications of Educational Clouds

18 E-Learning Recommender System for Deaf and Hard of Hearing Learners

Anisha Poly and P. K. Nizar Banu

18.1 INTRODUCTION

Hearing impairment, including both deafness and hard of hearing conditions, collectively referred to as DHH, is an invisible sensory disability categorized under physical disabilities. As per the Rights of Persons with Disabilities Act (2016), deaf individuals experience hearing loss in speech frequencies above 70 decibels (dB) in both ears, while hard of hearing refers to those who experience hearing loss ranging from 60 to 70 dB in speech frequencies in both ears, with both measurements being in decibels. Apart from the above definitions, individuals whose hearing threshold is above 20 dB are said to have hearing loss, which may range from mild to moderate, severe, and profound (World Health Organization, 2023).

Educational upbringing is essential for this group, as quality education provides better employability, eventually leading to improved living standards (Mandke & Chandekar, 2019). Compared to their hearing peers, DHH individuals have lower employable rates, which might arise from the limited access to formal education and learning resources. Technology can play an important role to mitigate the challenges faced by DHH learners in accessing education. e-Learning is a most promising solution through which global access to education is facilitated during the time of COVID-19 (Aljedaani et al., 2021). The flexibility of e-Learning, allowing access at anytime, anywhere, and at our own pace, makes it the most adaptable way to deliver instruction for DHH learners (Poly & Banu, 2023). Generally, DHH learners are often considered a homogeneous group, overlooking the diversity, including the range of variations in their hearing impairment, preferences in communication and learning style, learning modalities, and technological use (Poly & Banu, 2024; Singh, 2019). This is an arduous task for educators to recognize this diversity and deliver the instructions in line with their vivid range of learning needs and preferences. The adaptability of e-Learning can be further extended by untapping the potential of machine learning algorithms to tailor the instructions according to the unique needs and preferences of DHH learners, thus addressing their diversity.

DOI: 10.1201/9781003472537-22

e-Learning assists the DHH learners in their learning using a variety of digital instructional forms such as sign language video, animations, text adaptations, images, or text documents, referred to as learning objects (LOs) (Mohd Hashim & Tasir, 2020). It allows students to spend more time to revise and refer to the contents at their own space and time, thereby enhancing their autonomous learning skills (Elliot et al., 2020). Systematically adapting LOs to individual learners based on the relevant learner characteristics will personalize the e-Learning environment and enhance the learning process. However, personalization will be effective only if the e-Learning environment is able to capture dynamic changes in learner characteristics, thus constituting the adaptation (Tetzlaff et al., 2020).

Recommendation systems that intelligently adapt learning content to learner characteristics are a key component of an adaptive e-Learning system, tailoring learning content to individual learner needs and thus providing personalization. This inherent feature of recommender systems can be adopted to effectively tailor learning contents to DHH learners, who exhibit diversity in terms of their degree of hearing loss, educational background, preferences in communication, learning style, learning modalities, and technological use (Raji et al., 2023). This may help increase the level of learning engagement for DHH learners and, in turn, optimize academic performance, thereby reducing the academic gap between DHH learners and their hearing peers.

Tag-based recommendation is an approach in recommendation systems to automatically analyze the user preferences and provide recommendations based on the keywords, so-called tags (Wan & Niu, 2020). Tagging is an implicit way to rate or give an opinion about the learning content. Tag-clustering is an efficient way to gather similar tags together from the implicit feedback of DHH learners about their e-Learning activities, such as watching a video, doing exercises, or taking a test. While there are numerous research studies on such automatic e-Learning recommendation systems for hearing learners, there is a noticeable gap in the studies carried out concerning DHH learners. So, the main objectives of this study are as follows:

1. To analyze the existing challenges faced by DHH learners in e-Learning.
2. To analyze and summarize the research happening in the field of personalized e-Learning recommender systems.
3. To investigate the possibility of tag-clustering to enhance the recommendation results for DHH.
4. To propose a personalized model of tag-based recommender systems that use tag clusters for DHH learners.

This chapter is organized as follows. Section 18.1 introduced the benefits of adaptive e-Learning to DHH learners over classroom learning. Section 18.2 details the challenges faced by the DHH learners in the e-Learning environment, while Section 18.3 offers an overview of e-Learning recommender systems. In Section 18.4, we examine the need for a DHH-friendly recommender system, followed by a discussion on the components of such a system in the subsequent section. Section 18.6, seeking the possibility of tag-clustering to enhance the recommendation results for DHH learners, and a hybrid model of recommender system is proposed in Section

18.7. Finally, the chapter concludes with a comprehensive discussion of the findings and implications outlined throughout the study.

18.2 CHALLENGES IN E-LEARNING FOR DHH

18.2.1 e-Learning

e-Learning is an interactive learning facilitated by electronic technologies, wherein learning content is available online and provides automatic feedback to the users to create a learning experience (Muniasamy & Alasiry, 2020). There are two aspects of e-Learning, such as technological and pedagogical (Aljedaani et al., 2022). The technological aspect encompasses hardware components such as multimedia stations, network servers, or a personal computer and network connections. It also includes software components such as authoring software, web server software, browsers, and media players.

Pedagogical perspective focuses on e-Learning content, how people learn, their progress in learning, adapting content delivery based on preferred learner characteristics such as learning style. Learning content, referred to as LOs, is distributed to learners over the internet through a software application called Learning Management Systems (LMS) that organizes, documents, and records e-Learning courses. This can take place in two forms such as synchronous and asynchronous where the former supports the real-time interaction between the learner and instructor while the latter focuses on the self-paced learning. This makes the educational system adopt the LMS and other e-Learning possibilities to enhance the academic performance of DHH learners (Elliot et al., 2020).

18.2.2 Adaptive e-Learning

While e-Learning provides the learning experience anytime, anywhere, and anyhow, adaptive e-Learning makes it more personalized by dynamically delivering the right content to the right person with the help of intelligent technologies such as machine learning and artificial intelligence (Zayet et al., 2022). As this is a learner-centered approach, learner characteristics such as learning style, interests, knowledge level, and parameters related to deafness in the case of DHH learners are used to build the learner profile. Personalized recommender systems in e-Learning then analyze the learner profile to determine the current cognitive level and deliver the right learning materials to offer adaptivity and personalization, respectively (Murtaza et al., 2022). As adaptive learning offers more personalized and dynamic learning experiences, it is a better choice for DHH learners (Poly & Banu, 2023), as they have more preferences in learning and communication as compared to their hearing peers (Luangrungruang & Kokaew, 2022a; Raji et al., 2023).

18.2.3 Challenges in e-Learning

18.2.3.1 Technological Challenges

Technological challenges encompass the hardware and software challenges, including limited and unstable internet accessibility, unavailability of hearing aids or digital devices such as personal computers and smartphones, disruptions during online sessions, and concerns regarding the quality of multimedia contents, as well as lower digital literacy in using online learning platforms. Mohammed (2021) details that poor video quality and low level of digital literacy in setting up and navigating online platforms pose major technical challenges for DHH learners. Limited access to good internet connectivity, smart gadgets, and specialized DHH-friendly applications is hampered by online learning for DHH (Kotwal et al., 2022). Lack of technical knowledge for in-service training for teachers to prepare quality e-Learning contents also serves another barrier for DHH learners (Yazçayır, 2023).

18.2.3.2 Pedagogical Challenges

Pedagogical challenges cover issues related to LMS and its contents, as well as challenges related to personalization. According to McKeown and McKeown (2019), accessibility challenges with LMS and its contents may span across three levels for DHH learners: LMS accessibility challenges, course accessibility challenges, and communication and language challenges.

An LMS or other learning websites serve as the entry point for accessing information, thus constituting the first level of challenge for deaf learners. *Accessibility challenges* with LMS for DHH learners may arise when LMS lacks text alternatives for any non-text content, such as controls that accept user input, fail to provide captions or sign language interpretation for audio content, present modules without meaningful sequence, or include audio without background sounds (Madhesh, 2021). *Course accessibility challenges*, the second level, regards the course content and materials. This includes the unavailability of short online modules and a variety of contents such as sign language videos, images, videos with subtitles, and short keywords for text documents (Aljedaani et al., 2023). The third level of challenges is with *communication and language* as DHH learners have a lower reading level compared to their hearing peers (McKeown & McKeown, 2019). *Personalization challenges* pay attention to make e-Learning more adaptable to the specific needs of the DHH learners by recommending appropriate learning content. DHH learners often receive similar content that overlooks their individual preference and needs in learning and communication (Poly & Banu, 2024).

The pedagogical challenges can be reduced if the e-Learning system is adaptable to the personal needs and preferences of DHH learners in accessibility, communication and learning, and knowledge level. The recommender systems are the tools that offer adaptability, thus avoiding the one-size-fits-all challenge of e-Learning systems. So, it is therefore important to overview how the recommender systems work and what are the different techniques employed to offer personalization.

18.3 OVERVIEW OF CURRENT E-LEARNING RECOMMENDER SYSTEMS

Recommender systems are the software tools and techniques that deliver suggestions to the user for the items to be of use (Zayet et al., 2022). This will help them to avoid the information overload in online learning, thus boosting the learning gain of the learners. The main approaches in the recommender systems are as follows:

1. Collaborative filtering (CF)-based methods
   CF methods find the similarity between items or users and cluster them based on the similarities (Jena et al., 2023). The key concepts used are item-based and user-based CF, where the former finds the similar items that the user interacted with in the past while the latter identifies the users with similar preferences to the target user (Aggarwal, 2016). The essence of the CF method is to find the similarity either between the users or items. CF-based methods can be broadly classified into memory-based and model-based methods. Memory-based methods are also called neighborhood CF methods, as they predict the user-item ratings based on the similar neighbors. Although memory-based methods are simple to implement, they need large inline memory space to store the huge rating matrix when a massive number of users are involved in the problem. Model-based methods are here to solve this problem with the help of data mining and machine learning models (Khanal et al., 2019). CF-based methods suffer from the new user cold start problem and the rating sparsity problem (George & Lal, 2019).
2. Content-based (CB) methods
   Another common approach for recommendation is CB filtering, in which the user profile depicts the item description based on the user's own choice (Aggarwal, 2016). In CB methods, similarity is calculated between the attributes of items that the user has liked in the past rather than between the users with similar interest. These systems rely on two sources of data: the item description table, where the content-specific attributes of items are in textual format, and the user profile, generated from the user feedback such as the explicit ratings for the items or implicit actions like clicking or browsing an item (Aggarwal, 2016). This is helpful in the case of a new item problem where a smaller number of ratings are available for the respective item.
3. Knowledge-based methods
   Knowledge-based methods are a better choice for highly customized applications like e-Learning, which require a more sophisticated set of content recommendations. These systems are based on the direct specifications of the user needs rather than historical data, which helps them to overcome the cold start problem. Recommendations are generated based on the cumulative sum of user-specified data, item-specific attributes (such as details regarding course, lectures, exercise, quizzes, or forums), and domain knowledge on how the item meets user demands (George & Lal, 2019). Ontology-based recommender systems are a subset of knowledge-based methods. Ontologies are the formal explicit description of concepts in a domain consisting of objects, classes, properties, relationships, rules, and constraints (Rahayu et al., 2022). It can be used to store the information of learners and learning resources. Ontologies, which do not rely on historical data, can effectively tackle the cold start problem (Jeevamol & Renumol, 2021), but the creation of ontologies is expensive.
4. Tag-based methods
   Tags are the keywords attached to digital LOs, providing easy access and retrieval of learning content. There are two types of tags: one is the standard

metadata that describes the digital objects using implicit keywords, and the other is free text assigned by learners that defines their own understanding of a learning item (Shoja & Tabrizi, 2019). As the user-defined tags reveal more on their understanding or preferences about a learning item, it can efficiently improve the recommendations. Tag-based methods can work from two perspectives. One is tag recommendation for users, which will ease the process of tagging an item by recommending the most appropriate tags. The second perspective is to make the learning content recommendation based on previously used tags. The former uses the collaborative tagging approach, while the latter uses the CB filtering approach. The main challenges associated with tag-based recommendation are cold start, redundancy, and lack of semantics (Qassimi & Abdelwahed, 2019). The challenges can be dealt with by forming clusters of similar tags or using hybrid approaches.

5. Hybrid methods

   The aforementioned methods suffer from various issues, such as cold start (two types are there: the new LO problem, when the new LO is added and not used by any of the learners, so no preferences for the LO are stored in the system, and the new user problem arises when the learner has not provided their preference to the system to make efficient recommendations), data sparsity (insufficient entries in the learner–LO matrix as most of the users are not willing to provide the ratings for the LOs that they visited), lack of contextual awareness (contexts regarding time and location) and overspecialization (user receives recommendation only from the items that are similar to their preference) (George & Lal, 2019). Hybrid methods combine two or more methods, exploiting their advantages to provide more effective and personalized recommendation (Qassimi & Abdelwahed, 2019; Jeevamol & Renumol, 2021).

e-Learning system has experienced more extensive growth in developing personalized and adaptive recommender systems for hearing individuals, but there has been comparatively less growth in addressing the learners with disabilities, especially those who are DHH (Chemnad & Othman, 2024). There is very less work focused on the learners with disability in the field of adaptive e-Learning (Poly & Banu, 2023). The adaptivity of e-Learning can be extended to DHH learners through dynamic profiling of them, as their preferences or knowledge level may change over time (Calle-Jimenez et al., 2021). So, this chapter focuses on profiling DHH learners to get the dynamic learning content recommendation in e-Learning, an area that has received less attention in existing studies (Ochukut et al., 2022).

18.4 NEED FOR A DHH-SPECIFIC RECOMMENDER SYSTEM

An adaptive (to the changing preference and progress of the learner) and adaptable (to the personalization based on learner characteristics) recommender systems are the cornerstone of a personalized e-Learning system. For a DHH-specific recommender system, the following attributes constitute a comprehensive learner profile.

1. The nature of hearing impairment: Any level of hearing loss may impact the educational and communication needs of children with hearing impairment. Hearing impairment can vary due to several factors, including the cause of hearing loss, age of onset, types of hearing loss, degree of hearing loss, and whether the hearing loss is by birth or acquired at later ages (Singh, 2019). There are mainly three different types of hearing loss: conductive, sensorineural, and mixed. Conductive hearing loss occurs when the sound waves do not reach the inner ear due to problems in the outer or middle ear. This may be a temporary or permanent situation and can often be treated by medicine or surgery. Individuals with conductive hearing loss may experience challenges in speech clarity and hearing soft sounds. Sensorineural hearing loss occurs when the damage happens to the inner ear, and it often cannot be reversed. These people may have difficulty in understanding speech, and sounds may be unclear or distorted to them. Mixed hearing loss is the combination of conductive and sensorineural (Lieu et al., 2020).
   The severity of hearing loss can be measured in decibels (dB), a unit used to measure the intensity of sound that an individual with hearing impairment can perceive. Each type of hearing loss can be classified from mild to severe, depending upon the severity of hearing loss (Lieu et al., 2020). Table 18.1 refers to these categories. Identifying the type and degree of hearing loss will help to effectively make the first-level recommendations of learning materials in an e-Learning environment.
2. Preferences in communication: There is no single method for DHH learners to communicate; rather, they rely on various combinations of communication methods. This may include natural sign language such as Indian Sign Language (ISL), signed systems, a manual coded sign language that combines the natural sign language, English word order and grammatical markers, sign-supported speech, spoken communication, lip reading, and cued speech that uses hand shapes and placements in addition to mouth movements (Singh, 2019). At times, educators use total communication, which incorporates all of the aforementioned means of communication (Hands & Voices, n.d.).
3. Learning styles: Learning style refers to the preferences of learners when interacting with the learning materials. There are many learning style models in the literature; among them, Visual, Auditory, Read/Write, Kinesthetic

TABLE 18.1
Categories Based on Degree of Hearing Loss

S. No.	Category	Degree of hearing loss (dB)
1	Slight	16–25
2	Mild	26–40
3	Moderate	41–55
4	Moderately severe	56–70
5	Severe	71–90
6	Profound	>90

(VARK) is one of the well-known models (El-Sabagh, 2021). This can be adapted to DHH learners to streamline the learning content according to their learning style (Luangrungruang & Kokaew, 2022b). Learners who prefer a visual learning style can be supplied with the diagrams, charts, presentations, illustrations, and sign language videos. Auditory learners prefer to perceive the information through ears, and this might help those who have slight and mild conductive hearing loss. Read/write learners prefer to use words, and they can be recommended with lecture notes, text/notebook, online forums, peer interactions, and captions, subtitles, or transcripts for video. Kinesthetic learners prefer to learn by practice, and they can be complemented with the exercise or quizzes.

4. Accessibility: DHH learners may have different accessibility preferences while they interact with the digital learning material. This may include captioned video, transcription for audio or video material, sign language videos, visual cues, font size and color, and audio settings. These might help all DHH learners, especially those who have moderate to profound hearing loss.
5. Knowledge, language, and comprehension level: Learner's knowledge level is an important contextual factor in building an adaptive recommendation system. DHH learners may start as a beginner when they register for the first time, progressing to intermediate or advanced levels as they acquire more knowledge over time. Due to differences in language and comprehension levels compared to their hearing peers, it is advisable to recommend short, concise learning materials for them rather than simply translating textbook contents to PDFs or offering captioned video. Additionally, providing a dictionary of the most useful words can be beneficial. The use of user-defined tags may also help DHH learners to effectively mark and organize the learning contents and facilitate recommendations of the most tagged learning resources to similar learners at the same knowledge level.

These factors are important to consider while developing an adaptive e-Learning platform for DHH learners as these exhibit their DHH profile (the nature of the hearing impairment, usage of a hearing aid or having undergone cochlear implantation, reception of speech therapy, and family history of deafness), Personal Needs and Preference (PNP) profile (communication preference, accessibility preference, learning style, and learning modality), and performance profile (their knowledge level, English language literacy, and comprehension level). Acquiring comprehensive data that incorporate these factors, alongside personal information and learning history, is essential for developing DHH-friendly and personalized recommender systems for them.

18.5 COMPONENTS OF DHH-FRIENDLY RECOMMENDER SYSTEM

The traditional model of an adaptive e-Learning system is mainly composed of three modules, including learner model, domain model, and adaptation model (Ochukut et al., 2022). Considering all of the above information, this traditional approach can mold to accommodate the DHH-friendly components.

1. Learner Model: This module is responsible for acquiring the learner data. At the time of new user registration, the learner profile will be built from the scratch and will dynamically update as the learner progresses in the system. It comprises of:
   - Personal information: Learner's demographic data, including age, gender, education level, and proficiency in computer literacy.
   - Deafness profile: This will capture the data regarding the nature of the hearing impairment, usage of a hearing aid or having undergone cochlear implantation, reception of speech therapy, and family history of deafness.
   - PNP profile: Data about the personal needs and preferences of an individual learner. This includes communication preference, accessibility preference, learning style, and learning modality.
   - Performance profile: System gathers and monitors the data about the learners' current knowledge level on the topic, as well as their language proficiency and comprehension level, to assess the appropriate level of complexity of the learning materials delivered. This information is instrumental in designing the course content or web pages tailored to their needs.
   - Learning history: This stores the learner–system interaction data, such as the pages visited, topics learned, and assessment results.
2. Domain Model: This presents the knowledge representation of a particular topic or subject, storing digital LOs such as courses, teaching materials, and tests along with metadata descriptions. The LOs may have the standard metadata tag based on their type, topic, accessibility features, and user-defined tags that describe the content. These annotated LOs are then added to the LO database. This also stores the semantic relationship between the subject components (Ochukut et al., 2022).
3. Adaptation Model: Adaptation model is the bridge between the learner and the domain model. This tells us what to adapt, including the learning path, learning content, user interface, and navigation of links and how to adapt them based on the learner model. The implementation of the adaptation model is the recommendation engine that selects the top-N learning materials based on the learners' requirements to offer personalization. This consists of an adaptive and adaptation module:
   - Recommendation engine: This is tasked with an identification of important learner characteristics, such as learning style or knowledge level, to group the similar learners to present the first level of learning content recommendations (Jeevamol & Renumol, 2021). The recommendation can even be improved by incorporating the learner interaction with the system. The learners' sequential access patterns can be mined to understand the hidden interest in learning content. This is because, even though learners exhibit the same learning style or knowledge level, they might have different capacities to learn certain items. For example, the slow learners may grasp some topics really fast, and vice versa. This can be identified by learner interaction with the learning materials.

18.6 TAG-CLUSTERING AND RECOMMENDER SYSTEM FOR DHH LEARNERS

Tags are the user-assigned keywords with semantic meaning to a digital LO. Tag-clustering is the way to gather similar tags with similar semantic meaning to improve the internet search or provide effective recommendations of learning materials. Tag-clustering involves the following steps: tag similarity computation, which will compute the similarity between the pair of tags using any similarity measure such as cosine or Jaccard index, clustering algorithm, which will cluster the similar tags by employing any of the clustering algorithms, representing the cluster by means of its centroid tag and assign the tags to the most similar cluster with its similarity to the centroid (Shoja & Tabrizi, 2019; Jo et al., 2023).

Tag-clustering helps to identify the underlying pattern between the tags and contents or users, which helps to improve the recommendations. This means that tags in the same cluster are frequently used by the users to tag or group specific types of learning resource. For example, suppose there is a cluster of tags related to "Java," and the possible tags may be Java basics, Java GUI development, Java spring, and Java mobile application used by users. A tag-clustering algorithm will identify the similarity between these tags and assign them to a single cluster called "Java." Whenever the users show any interest in Java-related topics, the recommender system can suggest the contents from the respective "Java" cluster to users. Figure 18.1 shows the recommendation process in CF-based tag-clustering.

Tag-clustering can be adopted to enhance the recommendations for DHH learners for several reasons. It allows them to organize the learning materials in their own way by giving their own words to explain the specific learning resource, which will improve their engagement in learning. It helps to identify the commonalities among the learners in their needs and preferences in communication, learning modality, and accessibility. These factors may change over time as learning progresses and can be

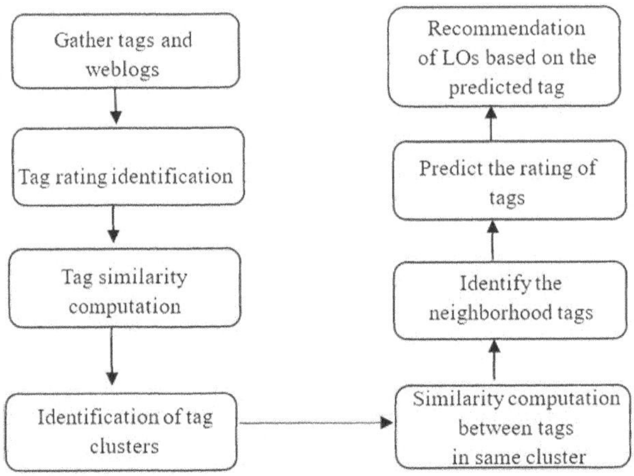

FIGURE 18.1 CF-Based Recommendation of LOs Based on Tag Clusters.

effectively captured by the user-defined tags by identifying the interaction between the specific learning materials tagged in the particular cluster.

DHH learners may experience the information overloading when presented with a huge number of learning resources, and eventually this may make learners' lost. Tag clusters allow users to efficiently discover related contents from a vast array of resources by exploring the automatic recommendations within their area of interest. Furthermore, tag-clustering allows dynamically adjusting the learning path. For example, if a learner is proficient in certain topics but may struggle with others, the system can adjust the sequence of learning activities where the additional support is needed. Overall, tag-clustering offers DHH learners better adaptive learning experiences, effective content recommendations, customized learning paths, and better accessibility and inclusiveness.

18.7 PROPOSED MODEL

The proposed model of an adaptive recommendation engine comprises the following components: learner profile, LO model, data preparation, tag recommendation, and dynamic adaptation engine. Figure 18.2 summarizes the functionality of the proposed model. *The learner profile* component is responsible for storing the information about the learners through explicit and implicit approach. It contains the learners' personal information, deafness-related parameter, PNP profile, performance profile, and the interaction between the LOs. When a user registers for the first time, the system can analyze the tag clusters of similar users to provide the first-level recommendation that matches with the learner profile. As the learner progresses, the dynamic recommendation engine will recommend the contents by adapting new contexts along with the web logs of the learner's sequential access and using tag-based filtering.

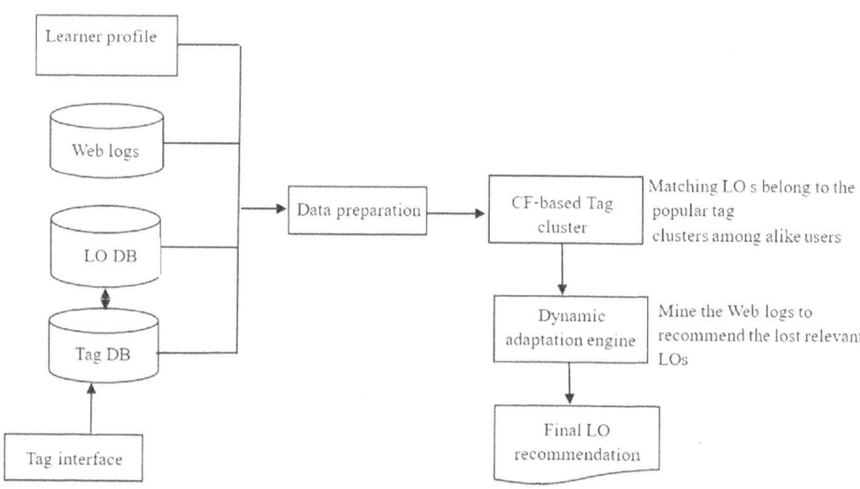

FIGURE 18.2 Proposed Recommendation Model for the DHH-Friendly Recommender System.

The LO model contains information about the learning resources, such as the type, the complexity level, the accessibility level, and the cluster name of tag based on user-defined descriptions for the learning resources. This will be recommended to the target learner based on the preference and accessibility needs, along with co-occurrences of tags among the alike users. *The data preparation* component is responsible for the preprocessing of learners' contextual information, learning resources, and tags into suitable formats for the recommendation engine. The tag recommendation engine predicts the similarity between the co-occurrences of tags and identifies the users who viewed the similar tagged contents. So that it can recommend the contents in the same tag cluster to the neighborhood users. *The dynamic adaptation engine* will filter out the top-N recommended contents given by the tag recommendation engine by incorporating the learners' sequential access patterns. This will ensure the final recommendations received by the learner are incorporating the contextual, accessibility, and learning patterns.

18.8 DISCUSSION AND CONCLUSION

This chapter focused on the need for adaptive e-Learning recommender systems for DHH learners, aiming to enhance learning engagement and facilitate learning progress in web-based learning. As e-Learning is now the most promising and economical way of instruction delivery, prioritizing the adaptation of the environment to meet the specific needs of DHH learners is imperative. Therefore, the first step is to identify the e-Learning challenges experienced by DHH and categorize those as technical and pedagogical. In this chapter, we paid attention to how to mitigate the pedagogical challenges by providing an adaptable e-Learning platform to the needs and preferences of DHH learners by portraying the different aspects of their learning.

The important aspect of an adaptable e-Learning platform is the recommendation engine, by which the environment automatically adjusts the delivery of learning material based on the learners' dynamic needs. So, it was essential to overview the different types of e-Learning recommender systems to identify the most commonly used techniques by the recommendation engines. From the study, it is identified that CF-based and CB methods are most popular, but the latest trend is hybrid recommender systems that use both the methods. The recommendation engines run on any technique, receiving the input from the learner model as the base for the filtration and predicting the process of learning contents. In an e-Learning environment, adaptability is the key, facilitated by a well-profiled learner model that effectively communicates the needs and preferences of the learner. As the learner progresses in learning, the system adapts accordingly, ensuring personalized learning.

This underscores the need for profiling DHH learners, wherein we identified that the component should consist of learners' personal information, their PNP profile, deafness profile, knowledge information, and learning system interaction logs. The LO model is another component, to which the recommendation engine communicates and fetches the learning content by mapping the learner requirements. This retrieval will be more effective if we cluster the LOs based on the user-defined keywords known as tags, assigned to the LO by the learners while interacting with the learning material.

As tags are small keywords with semantic meaning, DHH learners can effectively label the learning contents to which they are interacting with. This will help them to organize the learning materials in their own way by topic name, difficulty level, or accessibility features. Additionally, teachers can monitor their progress level by viewing the tags assigned by them. So, it is identified that tag-clustering is a feasible technique for a DHH-friendly recommender system to filter out the relevant contents.

Finally, a hybrid recommendation approach is proposed by combining the techniques of collaborative-based tag-clustering and sequential pattern mining of access logs to offer the personal-level recommendations for DHH learners based on context, access patterns, accessibility, and personal needs and preferences. The tag-clustering will efficiently reduce the search space by finding out the learning materials from the respective cluster that match the tags, which are the search keywords. As learners progress through the system, the mining of their access patterns will keep the recommendations dynamic and contextual at the individual level. Thus, the proposed model will bridge the gap on adaptive e-Learning recommender systems concerning the DHH learners and will help them to overcome the pedagogical challenges in e-Learning.

REFERENCES

Aggarwal, C. C. (2016). *Recommender systems.* Cham: Springer International Publishing.

Aljedaani, W., Aljedaani, M., AlOmar, E. A., Mkaouer, M. W., Ludi, S., & Khalaf, Y. B. (2021). I cannot see you – the perspectives of deaf students to online learning during COVID-19 pandemic: Saudi Arabia case study. *Education Sciences*, *11*(11), 712. https://doi.org/10.3390/educsci11110712.

Aljedaani, W., Krasniqi, R., Aljedaani, S., Mkaouer, M. W., Ludi, S., & Al-Raddah, K. (2023). If online learning works for you, what about deaf students? Emerging challenges of online learning for deaf and hearing-impaired students during COVID-19: a literature review. *Universal Access in the Information Society,* 22, 1027–1046. https://doi.org/10.1007/s10209-022-00897-5.

Calle-Jimenez, T., Sanchez-Gordon, S., & Arias-Flores, H. (2021). Profiling of e-Learning users with accessibility needs. *Lecture Notes in Networks and Systems*, *275*, 477–485.

Chemnad, K. & Othman, A. (2024). Digital accessibility in the era of artificial intelligence – bibliometric analysis and systematic review. *Frontiers in Artificial Intelligence*, *7*, 1349668. https://doi.org/10.3389/frai.2024.1349668.

El-Sabagh, H. A. (2021). Adaptive e-learning environment based on learning styles and its impact on development students' engagement. *International Journal of Educational Technology in Higher Education*, *18*(1), 1–24. https://educationaltechnologyjournal.springeropen.com/articles/10.1186/s41239-021-00289-4.

Elliot, L., Gehret, A., Valadez, M. S., Carpenter, R., & Bryant, L. (2020). Supporting autonomous learning skills in developmental mathematics courses with asynchronous online resources. *American Behavioral Scientist*, *64*(7), 1012–1030. https://doi.org/10.1177/0002764220919149.

George, G., & Lal, A. M. (2019). Review of ontology-based recommender systems in e-learning. *Computers & Education*, *142*, 103642. https://doi.org/10.1016/j.compedu.2019.103642.

"Hands & Voices." (n.d., March 23). *Handsandvoices.org*. Retrieved March 23, 2024, from www.handsandvoices.org/comcon/index.html.

Jeevamol, J., & Renumol, V. G. (2021). An ontology-based hybrid e-learning content recommender system for alleviating the cold-start problem. *Education and Information Technologies*, 26, 4993–5022. https://doi.org/10.1007/s10639-021-10508-0.

Jena, K. K., Bhoi, S. K., Malik, T. K., Sahoo, K. S., Jhanjhi, N. Z., Bhatia, S., & Amsaad, F. (2023). E-learning course recommender system using collaborative filtering models. *Electronics*, *12*(1), 157. https://doi.org/10.3390/electronics12010157.

Jo, H., Hong, J., & Choeh, J. Y. (2023). Improving collaborative filtering recommendations with tag and time integration in virtual online communities. *Applied Sciences*, *13*(18), 10528. https://doi.org/10.3390/app131810528.

Khanal, S. S., Prasad, P. W. C., Alsadoon, A., & Maag, A. (2019). A systematic review: machine learning based recommendation systems for e-learning. *Education and Information Technologies*, *25*, 2635–2664. https://doi.org/10.1007/s10639-019-10063-9.

Kotwal, R., Chauhan, G. S., & Ghosh, S. (2022). Challenges and opportunities in online learning amid COVID-19: A study on hearing–speech impaired students of Jammu and Kashmir. *Media Watch*, *13*(1), 118–134. https://doi.org/10.1177/09760911221086356.

Lieu, J. E. C., Kenna, M., Anne, S., & Davidson, L. (2020). Hearing loss in children. *JAMA*, *324*(21), 2195. https://doi.org/10.1001/jama.2020.17647.

Luangrungruang, T., & Kokaew, U. (2022a). Adapting Fleming-type learning style classifications to deaf student behavior. *Sustainability*, *14*(8), 4799. https://doi.org/10.3390/su14084799.

Luangrungruang, T., & Kokaew, U. (2022b). E-learning model to identify the learning styles of hearing-impaired students. *Sustainability*, *14*(20), 13280. https://doi.org/10.3390/su142013280.

Madhesh, A. (2021). Full exclusion during COVID-19: Saudi Deaf education is an example. *Heliyon*, *7*(3), e06536. https://doi.org/10.1016/j.heliyon.2021.e06536.

Mandke, K., & Chandekar, P. (2019). Deaf education in India. In H. Knoors, M. Brons, & M. Marschark (Eds.), *Deaf education beyond the western world: Context, challenges, and prospects* (pp. 261–284). Oxford University Press. https://doi.org/10.1093/oso/9780190880514.003.0014.

McKeown, C., & McKeown, J. (2019). Accessibility in online courses: Understanding the Deaf learner. *TechTrends*, *63*, 506–513. https://doi.org/10.1007/s11528-019-00385-3.

Mohammed, N. (2021). Deaf students' linguistic access in online education: The case of Trinidad. *Deafness & Education International*, *23*(3), 217–233. https://doi.org/10.1080/14643154.2021.1950989.

Mohd Hashim, M. H., & Tasir, Z. (2020). An e-learning environment embedded with sign language videos: research into its usability and the academic performance and learning patterns of deaf students. *Educational Technology Research and Development*, *68*(6), 2873–2911. https://doi.org/10.1007/s11423-020-09802-4.

Muniasamy, A., & Alasiry, A. (2020). Deep learning: The impact on future e-Learning. *International Journal of Emerging Technologies in Learning (IJET)*, *15*(01), 188. https://doi.org/10.3991/ijet.v15i01.11435.

Murtaza, M., Ahmed, Y., Shamsi, J. A., Sherwani, F., & Usman, M. (2022). AI-based personalized e-learning systems: Issues, challenges, and solutions. *IEEE Access*, *10*, 81323–81342. https://doi.org/10.1109/ACCESS.2022.3193938.

Ochukut, S. A., Oboko, R. O., Miriti, E., & Maina, E. (2022). Research trends in adaptive online learning: systematic literature review (2011–2020). *Technology, Knowledge and Learning*, *28*, 431–448. https://doi.org/10.1007/s10758-022-09615-9.

Poly, A., & Banu, P. K. N. (2023). A comprehensive study on E-learning environments for deaf or hard of hearing learners. *2023 Advanced Computing and Communication Technologies for High Performance Applications (ACCTHPA)*, 1–7. Ernakulam: IEEE.

Poly, A., & Banu, P. K. N. (2024). Discovering the micro-clusters from a group of DHH learners. In A. S. Munna, H. H. Alharahsheh, A. Ferrazza, & A. Pius (Eds.), *Transforming education for personalized learning* (pp. 159–175). IGI Global. https://doi.org/10.4018/979-8-3693-0868-4.ch010.

Qassimi, S., & Abdelwahed, E. H. (2019). The role of collaborative tagging and ontologies in emerging semantic of web resources. *Computing*, *101*(10), 1489–1511. https://doi.org/10.1007/s00607-019-00704-9.

Rahayu, N. W., Ferdiana, R., & Kusumawardani, S. S. (2022). A systematic review of ontology use in E-Learning recommender system. *Computers and Education: Artificial Intelligence*, *3*, 100047. https://doi.org/10.1016/j.caeai.2022.100047.

Raji, N. R., Kumar, R. M. S., & Biji, C. L. (2023). Closing the gap: Exploring the untapped potential of machine learning in deaf students and hearing students' academic performance. *ProQuest*, *10*, 1449–1475. https://doi.org/10.19101/IJATEE.2023.10101685.

Shoja, B. M., & Tabrizi, N. (2019). Tags-aware recommender systems: a systematic review. In *IEEE International Conference on Big Data, Cloud Computing, Data Science & Engineering (BCD)*, 11–18. IEEE. https://doi.org/10.1109/bcd.2019.8884850.

Singh, S. (2019). Revisiting inclusion of children with hearing impairment: issues and possibilities. In *Disability, Inclusion and Inclusive Education* (pp. 157–174). Springer. https://doi.org/10.1007/978-981-15-0524-9_8.

Tetzlaff, L., Schmiedek, F., & Brod, G. (2020). Developing personalized education: a dynamic framework. *Educational Psychology Review*, *33*(3), 863–882. https://doi.org/10.1007/s10648-020-09570-w.

The Rights of Persons with Disabilities Act. (2016, February 16). *Department of Empowerment of Persons with Disabilities*. Retrieved February 16, 2024, from https://depwd.gov.in/acts/.

Wan, S., & Niu, Z. (2020). A hybrid e-learning recommendation approach based on learners' influence propagation. *IEEE Transactions on Knowledge and Data Engineering*, *32*(5), 827–840. https://doi.org/10.1109/TKDE.2019.2895033.

World Health Organization. (2023, February 27). *Deafness and hearing loss*. www.who.int/news-room/fact-sheets/detail/deafness-and-hearing-loss.

Yazçayır, G. (2023). Teachers' instructional design for e-learning of deaf and hard of hearing students. *International Journal of Modern Education Studies*, *7*(2). https://doi.org/10.51383/ijonmes.2023.342.

Zayet, T. M. A., Ismail, M. A., Almadi, S. H. S., Hussein, M., & Nor, A. M. (2022). What is needed to build a personalized recommender system for K-12 students' E-Learning? Recommendations for future systems and a conceptual framework. *Education and Information Technologies*, *28*(6), 7487–7508. https://doi.org/10.1007/s10639-022-11489-4.

19 Unlocking the Potential of Educational Cloud Platforms for Differently Abled People

Sohini Banerjee, Shweta Barhate, and M. P. Dhore

19.1 INTRODUCTION

The economic growth of any country is greatly influenced by its level of education. As a result of the evolving educational landscape and students' increased interest in technology, it is critical that we consider integrating the latest technologies into our world of education. Cloud computing is one of the trendiest technologies that is widely used today. The use of cloud computing services and technologies in the field of education to improve administrative, teaching, and learning procedures is known as "educational cloud computing."

Differently abled people can range from moderate to severe but most of them require a lot of assistance from the outside community. Educators play a crucial role in assisting them in realising their full potential. It is important to provide them with the resources to function at their best so that they can contribute positively to society and toward the development of the nation. They have a lot of promise, but society and educators in particular must do more to support them in realising that potential. So there is an immense need of implementing all cloud computing resources for differently abled people for taking a giant leap from the traditional educational setup to this latest technological arena.

Here, our fundamental goal is to model educational cloud architecture for differently abled people keeping in mind the academic development of the differently abled learners. The aim of the proposed model for differently abled learners would suggest the components that should be considered in this architecture so that the learner unravels his full potential to become a part of society's success as well as his own.

19.2 CATEGORIES OF DIFFERENTLY ABLED PEOPLE

The Rights of Persons with Disabilities Act (RPwD) was put into effect in 2016 and was officially implemented on April 19, 2017. This act replaced the Persons with

 DOI: 10.1201/9781003472537-23

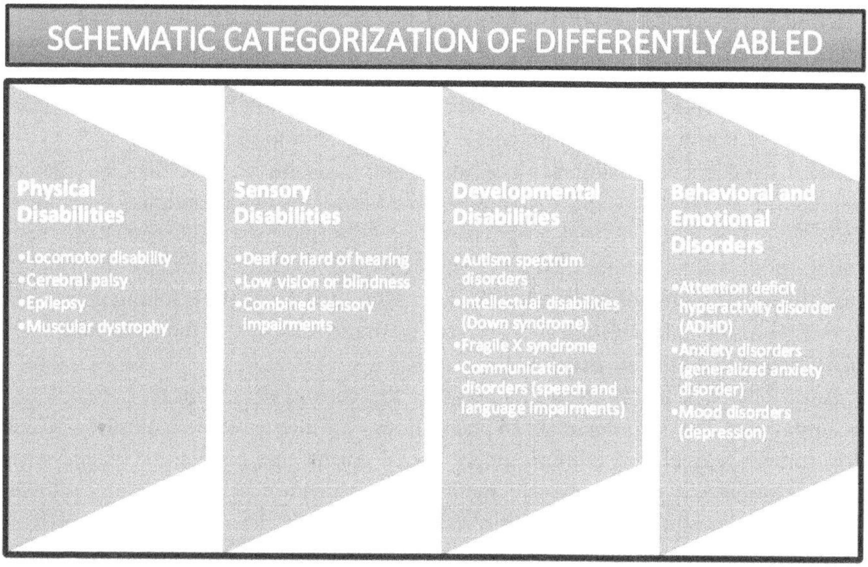

FIGURE 19.1 Categorisation of Differently Abled People.

Disabilities (Equal Opportunities, Protection of Rights, and Full Participation) Act from 1995. Its main goal is to ensure that individuals with disabilities can live their lives with dignity, away from discrimination, and have access to opportunities.

Differently abled people can be classified mainly into four categories: physical, sensory, developmental, and behavioral or emotional. Further people with sensory disabilities can belong to the four primary subcategories as shown in Figure 19.1. They are sensory processing disorder, deafness and loss of hearing, autism spectrum disorder, and blindness and low vision. According to the Census of India 2011 Data on Disability, the proportion of the disabled population with a speech disability is 7.5%, whereas hearing disability scores 18.9%. The epicentre of our study revolves around this 26.4% disabled population of India.

Education for the deaf and mute takes into account the special requirements of people who have hearing and speech impairments. These people have particular difficulties with social contact, communication, and getting access to educational possibilities. The field of deaf and mute education has changed as a result of advances in our understanding of these disabilities and technological improvements. Thus, emphasis is given to inclusive and comprehensive approaches that cater to the specific requirements of deaf and mute people (Olsson 2021).

19.3 TRADITIONAL EDUCATION SYSTEM FOR DIFFERENTLY ABLED

Over the years, differently abled students have had difficulties coping with other students. These issues restricted students' access to high-quality education and prevented them from reaching their full potential. Differently abled people have always been subjected to marginalisation and exclusion from mainstream education. These have hindered their personal growth and their educational achievements. Hence, this problem needs to be actively tackled by catering to their individual needs based on their disability. Hereby we would examine the gradual transition of a conventional system to a new technological landscape with more inclusion.

Traditional school cultures place more emphasis on content than on meeting the individual needs of the differently abled students. Conventional educational institutions frequently restrict progress toward fulfilling the requirements of various student populations. As they are concentrated on delivering curricular information, staff members might not understand the necessity for alternative teaching approaches according to their disabilities. This lack of awareness results in the shortcomings of traditional methods of instruction.

Additionally, it has been discovered that the various sociocultural contexts have an impact on the implementation and efficacy of inclusive education programs. Government regulations, cultural views, social norms, and economic considerations have an impact on how inclusive mainstream education is for students with disabilities. As a result, context-specific strategies that take into account the particular requirements and conditions of every location are required. Therefore, it is crucial that we stress the significance of culturally sensitive approaches to address social inclusion and educational equity.

When a child is first growing and absorbing everything around him, he or she always relies on their ability to hear and attempts to mimic what they hear. The deaf and mute students must learn to discriminate between objects that are presented to them, recognise their many forms, and operate them. It is difficult for them to cope without hearing its voice.

The deaf and hard-of-hearing learners can be categorised into four subcategories based on the intensity of their hearing impairment (see Figure 19.2).

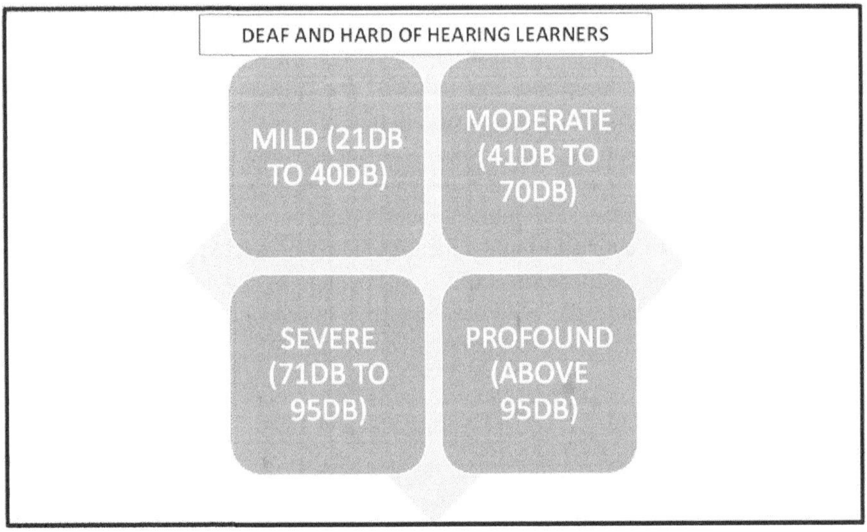

FIGURE 19.2 Categorisation of Deaf and Hard of Hearing Learners.

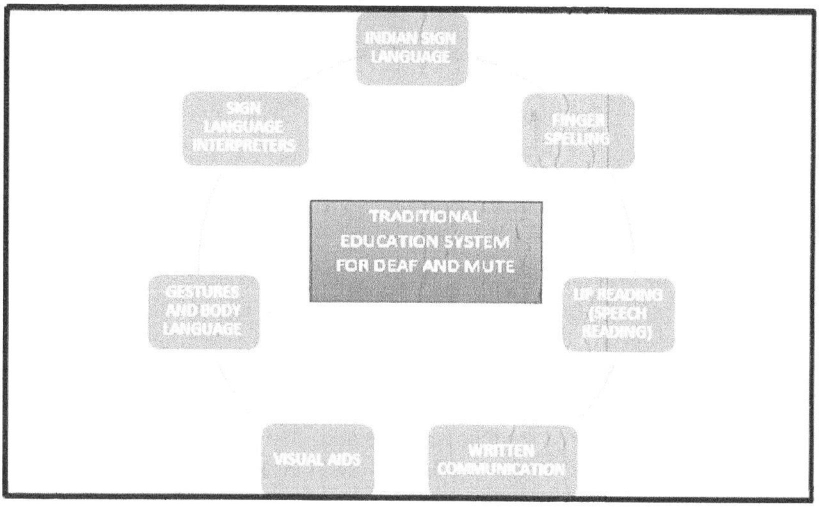

FIGURE 19.3 Traditional Education System for Deaf and Mute.

The total communication method with deaf and mute students makes combined use of aural, oral, and manual modalities. These include the use of lip reading, listening, auditory practice, and speech practice. Manual methods of communication with them are sign language, finger spelling, and cued speech. Figure 19.3 shows the different communication methods used in traditional education system for deaf and mute students.

19.4 ARCHITECTURE OF EDUCATIONAL CLOUDS

A structured approach to teaching and learning created for remote delivery through electronic communication is known as distance learning, or e-learning which can be implemented using cloud computing. Many educational institutions have adopted remote learning because of the increased interaction between students and instructors brought about by the use of technology in the classroom.

Besides the Infrastructure as a Service (IAAS) and Platform as a Service (PAAS), Software as a Service (SAAS) revolves around the service model that provides software allowing users to access it remotely via the Internet. In the world of education use of educational tools, learning management systems (LMS), collaboration platforms, and other software applications operate in the SAAS model (Ahmed and Ahmed 2018).

Each deployment model of cloud private, public, hybrid, and community for education has got its own pros and cons. Hybrid cloud combines the positive aspects of both public and private clouds creating a balance between scalability and security and thus equipping schools and colleges with faster disaster recovery. Collaboration among institutions results in cost-cutting and hence facilitated by the community cloud (Borse and Gokhale 2019).

Many architectural models have been proposed by researchers while exploring the educational cloud. A commercial platform called "Cloud Wisdom Education Architecture" is proposed for cloud computing using the service-oriented architecture (SOA) framework philosophy. The architecture offers solutions for the efficient delivery of educational services and is intended to give a thorough and integrated approach to cloud computing in education. With its three compute nodes, the "Cloud Wisdom Education Architecture" emphasises the use of cloud technologies to improve learning and give students access to virtual labs. This architecture can be implemented for the education of people with special needs. Another architectural model proposed in this domain is V.I.C.E. Vertical Implementation of a Cloud for Education is what the acronym V.I.C.E stands for. The difficulties of scalability, adaptability, and effective resource allocation in educational institutions are the focus of this architecture. The purpose of the V.I.C.E Vertical Architecture is to use cloud computing to improve student learning and give them access to virtual labs. In another model named "VPPL," or "Virtual Practice Programming Lab," a cloud-based platform is created to give students practical experience with software development and programming. To provide students with access to virtual labs and hands-on learning opportunities in the field of computer programming and software development, universities have adopted cloud architecture, which includes the VPPL. The sole objective of eduDS cloud, or educational data analytics and service-oriented cloud architecture, is to provide students with practical experience in distributed big data processing, data storage, and data mining within the data lab. A cloud computing environment constructed within an educational institution using the open-source software platform OpenStack is referred to as a private cloud employing OpenStack in education. This gives the organisation various advantages over using public cloud services, including the ability to manage and control its own cloud infrastructure (Borse and Gokhale 2019).

19.5 RESEARCH PROBLEM

Previous studies suggest that considerate work has been done in the field of cloud computing for the management of educational resources. Several assistive technologies and audio–visual aids have also been designed for differently abled people. Still, there is a substantial gap in the development of a cloud computing model for the education of differently abled people, especially deaf and mute students. This research work proposes modelling of educational cloud architecture for deaf and mute learners.

19.6 RESEARCH METHODOLOGY

Modelling of educational cloud architecture involves the following steps:

1. In the present proposed work, the research gap is identified and the research problem is formulated in the first step of modelling.
2. Then data about deaf and mute students is collected from ten special educators and counsellors using Google Forms.

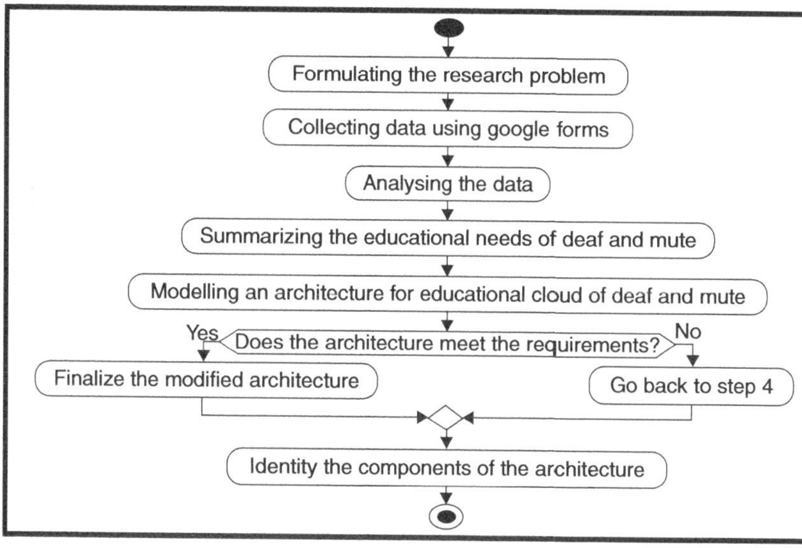

FIGURE 19.4 Flowchart of Research Methodology.

3. The collected data from the linked spreadsheet is then analysed and summarised to understand the educational needs of deaf and mute learners.
4. Accordingly, architecture is modelled for the educational cloud of deaf and mute which caters to the educational requirements of these learners.
5. Then identification of the components of the architecture facilitates modelling with the help of a schematic diagram.

The flowchart for the research methodology is as shown in Figure 19.4.

19.7 NEED OF MODELLING EDUCATIONAL CLOUD ARCHITECTURE FOR DEAF AND MUTE

Analysis of the data collected from the special educators and counsellors through Google Forms shows that deaf and mute learners encounter a lot of difficulties in their educational setup (Mantzikos and Lappa 2020). The typical barriers in their educational environment are as follows:

1. Lack of educational resources and materials for deaf and mute
2. Communication barriers
3. Unavailability of audio–visual content for complex concepts
4. Inability of social interaction with peers
5. Absence of sign language interpreters in regular classrooms
6. Lack of teacher training in visual communication methods.

Hence, there is an urgent need of modelling an educational cloud for the deaf and mute to meet the challenges faced for their educational requirements (Getting Smart

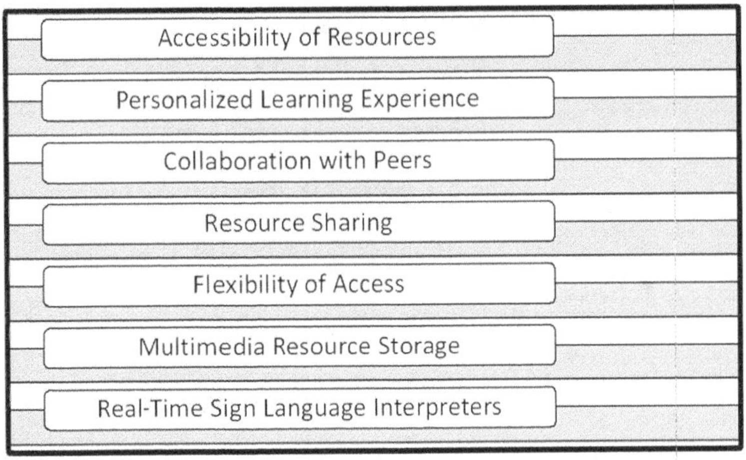

FIGURE 19.5 Need of Educational Cloud Architecture Modelling for Deaf and Mute.

2016). Figure 19.5 summarizes the reasons for modelling the educational cloud environment of deaf and mute.

19.8 PROPOSED ARCHITECTURE FOR EDUCATIONAL CLOUD OF DEAF AND MUTE

Differently abled people have unique requirements and hence they face tremendous difficulties in accessing and interacting with educational content, compelling us to do modifications to the educational cloud architecture. Changes must be made to guarantee inclusion, accessibility, and the best possible learning environment to meet these needs. The modifications are crucial because of the accessibility barriers, limited personalisation, integration challenges, and data and privacy concerns. To study the components of modified educational clouds, we need to broadly bifurcate it into three domains: users, key components, and management tools.

19.8.1 Users

The varied demands and abilities within the differently abled community are reflected in the wide set of users of educational cloud services. A variety of users are connected with the educational cloud architecture for individuals with disabilities, both directly and indirectly helping students and others who assist them in their educational endeavours.

DEAF AND MUTE LEARNERS: The primary user group is basically the core user group, the deaf and mute students. With elements that improve their learning process and remove obstacles to accessibility, the architecture is made to meet their unique demands. They mostly depend on the visual elements of the educational resources.

SPECIAL EDUCATORS, TEACHERS: Educators and lecturers are essential to make the most of the cloud platform. To support students with a variety of requirements, the architecture should give educators the tools and resources they need to track student progress, customise learning routes, and take advantage of the platform's accessible capabilities. They also create individualised digital content for the cloud model to cater to the needs of the differently abled students.

COUNSELORS, THERAPISTS: Educational therapists, speech therapists, occupational therapists, and counsellors also play an important role in this scenario. To provide a comprehensive learning experience for students with special needs, the cloud architecture should include tools that let teachers, support workers, and families communicate and work together more easily.

PARENTS, CAREGIVERS: Involvement of parents and guardians in their children's education is essential. Their requirements should be taken into account in the cloud architecture by offering easily accessible platform information, student progress reports, and tools to help with at-home learning.

EDUCATION ADMINISTRATORS: Head of the institutions, school administrators, policy makers in educational inclusivity also influence the deployment of educational cloud computing. Schools, colleges, and other educational establishments may offer inclusive learning opportunities to a larger spectrum of learners because of the scalability and flexibility of cloud architecture.

RESEARCHERS: Researchers assess the extent to which the current assistive technologies can be implemented in cloud-based learning environments. User experience studies are carried out by researchers with the participation of educators, stakeholders, and students with disabilities along with suggestions for safe data processing and storage aid in the creation of strong security elements in the educational cloud. To determine the long-term impact of educational cloud services on the social and intellectual growth of differently abled people, researchers carry out longitudinal studies which help to guide continuous improvements and modifications to cloud-based educational models.

TECHNOLOGY SUPPORT PERSONNEL: IT specialists overseeing and preserving the cloud infrastructure for education, the developers and specialists in assistive technology ensure adapted tools are operating properly while testing and deploying the educational cloud platform.

19.8.2 Core Components

Core component is the most important tier of the architecture which comprises all the critical tools required for the architecture.

MULTIMODAL COMMUNICATION TOOLS: Multimodal communication tools offer alternate channels for information access, expression, and interaction, so they are essential to the educational cloud architecture for students with disabilities. These resources help students with impairments communicate more effectively and accommodate a variety of learning methods (Wazalwar and Shrawankar 2019). The communication tools beneficial for deaf and mute learners in educational clouds are as follows:

1. Speech-to-text technology
2. Interactive whiteboard
3. Sign language interpretation
4. Real-time captioning
5. Integration of multimedia
6. Video conferencing
7. VR AR tools (Mubin et al. 2024)
8. Chat platforms

ASSISTIVE TECHNOLOGY: For deaf students with residual hearing, assistive technologies provide assistive listening equipment such as cochlear implants, FM systems, high-performance headphones, and hearing aids to improve auditory perception and understanding. Various features of the existing educational cloud platforms like Google Classroom, Canvas, Blackboard Learn, Moodle, Schoology, D2L Brightspace, Edmodo, Nearpod, Kahoot, Turnitin, Microsoft 365, Zoom, ClassDojo, and Apple Classroom provide assistive technologies facilitating the teaching–learning process for people with special needs. Some features of these platforms include accessibility tools (screen reader, keyboard shortcuts, text-to-speech tools, voice typing, captioning), real-time feedback and monitoring (notification to guardians, assignment tracking, feedback to students), differentiated instruction (personalised learning path, assignment customisation, private comments), resource management (calendar integration, multimedia, virtual and augmented reality, centralised information) and collaboration (online discussion, group project, file sharing). Many more assistive technologies can be combined with our educational clouds to enhance their listening skills.

1. Assistive listening devices
2. Alternate input devices
3. Real-time centralised progress tracking
4. Assistive software access
5. Collaborative document editing
6. Intense blinking lights
7. Vibrating notifications
8. Volume and speed control of educational resources
9. Animated sign language websites.

ACCESSIBLE LEARNING MANAGEMENT SYSTEM: For creating an accessible learning environment for the deaf and mute learners' proper instructional strategies and along with the learning environment need to be tailored according to the requirement of the disability to create maximum impact.

EDUCATIONAL CONTENT REPOSITORIES: Multimedia content (visual representation along with closed captioning), application of augmented and virtual reality content, text-based resources, etc., contribute to create a huge repository of educational resources customised for deaf and mute students.

CONTENT DEVELOPMENT NETWORK: Content Development Network (CDN) can be modified for developing an educational cloud for differently abled. This would minimise access time of web content and improve performance by reducing latency.

UNIVERSAL DESIGN FOR LEARNING: The goal of the Universal Design for Learning (UDL) framework is to create learning environments and resources that are efficient and accessible to all students, irrespective of their learning styles, backgrounds, or ability levels. UDL emphasises inclusivity, adaptability, and flexibility in curriculum design, teaching strategies, and assessment procedures. UDL encompasses multiple modes of representation, expression, and engagement for deaf and mute learners (Silvestri and Hartman 2022).

USER FRIENDLY INTERFACE: Navigating through the educational contents for deaf and mute learners becomes easier if the interface is user-friendly. An educational cloud platform with clear menus, navigation buttons, and visual cues like sign language animations would keep these learners engrossed in the cloud platform for longer durations.

WEB CONTENT ACCESSIBILITY GUIDELINES (WCAG) 2.1: A set of guidelines for improving web content accessibility for those with impairments is outlined in the Web Content Accessibility Guidelines (WCAG) 2.1. These standards include a broad spectrum of disabilities, such as neurological, physical, cognitive, auditory, visual, and speech impairments. Information on the web should be perceivable, operable, understandable, readable, and robust (W3C 2023).

19.8.3 Management Tools

Management Tools are necessary for the allocation, controlling, balancing, and implementation of all educational cloud resources.

DATA MANAGEMENT: Data management tools is the umbrella term comprising all the functionalities related to data storage, data integration, data analysis, data security, and data backup. Cloud service providers such as Amazon Web Services (AWS), Microsoft Azure, Google Cloud Platform (GCP), etc. provide cloud-based data storage solutions. Storage of huge amount of teaching–learning resources specially designed for the deaf and mute especially visual content is the primary requisite of this architecture. Educational institutions need to keep the highly sensitive data of differently abled students secure from security breaches. Moreover, data backup and automatic data recovery prevent the loss of essential data about these special learners.

SERVICE MANAGEMENT: The main function of service management tools is the deployment of cloud-based resources. Monitored by Service Level Agreements (SLA) these tools also manage the cloud infrastructure. High-end service management is therefore necessary for the proper functioning of this architecture.

SECURITY MANAGEMENT: Cloud security management envelops a vast area of encryption, user authentication, firewalls, virtual private networks, and data privacy policies. Institutional data of these differently abled learners needs to be secure from any type of breaches.

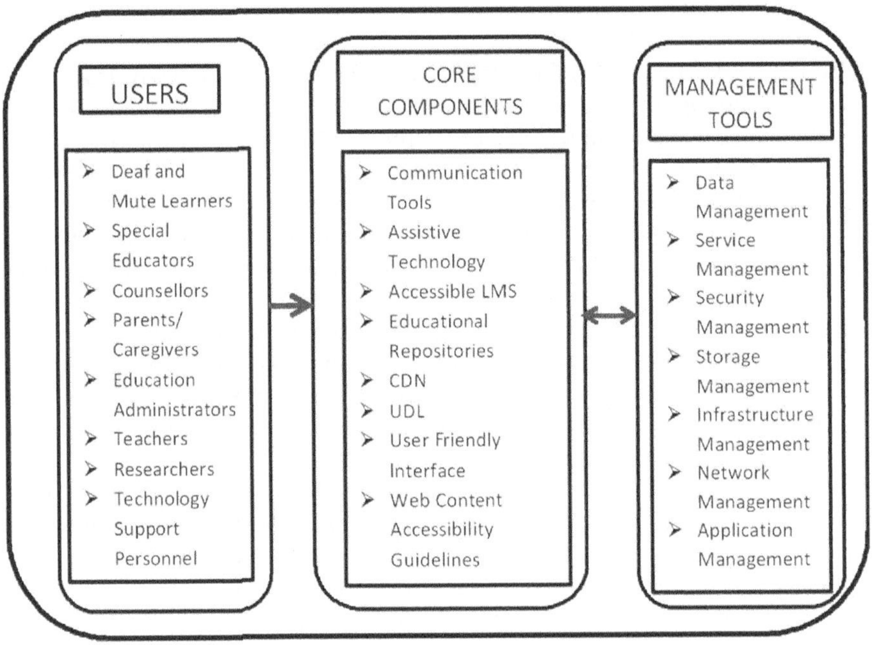

FIGURE 19.6 Architecture for Educational Cloud of Deaf and Mute.

STORAGE MANAGEMENT: Storage virtualisation capabilities of the educational cloud enhance the power of the educational cloud. Maximising storage capabilities and minimising storage costs makes the proposed architecture ideal for storing huge amounts of visual data for these learners.

INFRASTRUCTURE MANAGEMENT: One of the prime factors for the shifting paradigm from traditional cloud computing to a cloud computing model for education is infrastructure management facility provided by cloud providers. Hence, infrastructure management is the backbone for the smooth functioning of cloud operations.

NETWORK MANAGEMENT: For proper accessibility of the educational resources, network management plays a significant role by balancing the network traffic during video conferencing and utilisation of e-learning platforms.

APPLICATION MANAGEMENT: Configuration of software application services along with the user support is taken care of by application management part of educational clouds.

Figure 19.6 shows all the components of the proposed educational cloud.

19.9 WORKING PHILOSOPHY FOR EDUCATIONAL CLOUD OF DEAF AND MUTE

The proposed architecture is designed based on the parameters listed in Figure 19.7.

The average access time for cloud-based resources depends on several factors like relative location of the cloud servers, speed of Internet connection, infrastructure of

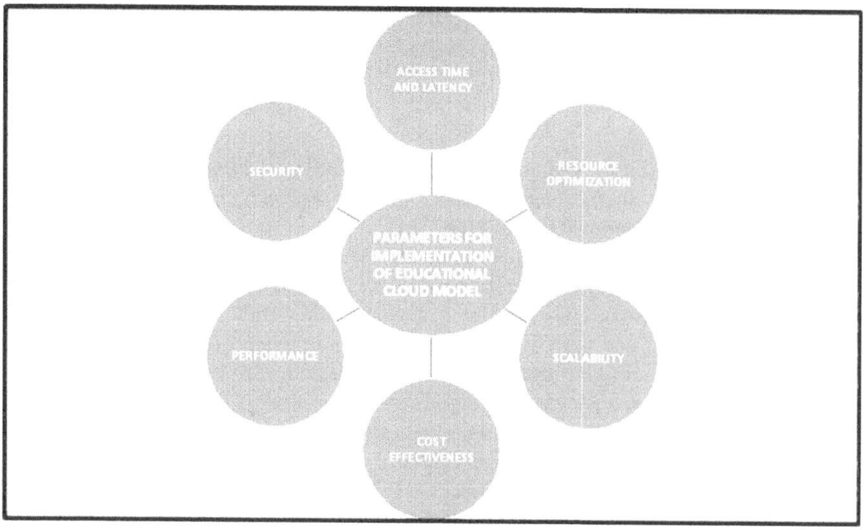

FIGURE 19.7 Parameters for Implementation of Educational Cloud Model.

the cloud service provider, size of the resource file, as well as network congestion. According to the analysed data provided by special educators and counsellors via Google Form, the average access time for searching educational resources for the deaf and mute is more than a minute due to the scarcity of resources for hearing and speech impairment. Accessible LMS in distributed data centres would help in reducing the access time for this architecture. High-end sign language video resources, transcriptions, real-time chat, and many more features of educational clouds lead to resource optimisation for the proposed model. According to the workload requirement, the architecture needs to dynamically allocate the resources and hence provides a scalable solution. Along with assistive technologies, collaboration tools and CDN result in increased performance and thus a cost-effective solution for the differently abled community. Keeping in mind the vulnerability of differently abled people the data security of these educational clouds becomes a major concern.

19.10 CONCLUSION

To conclude, it can be stated that the proposed educational cloud model would cater to the individualised needs of each and every deaf and mute learner by providing an accessible, scalable, and cost-effective solution. In India, approximately 63 million people are deaf among which 2.42 million belong to deaf and mute category. Hence, educational needs of these people need to be immediately addressed and that is only feasible through the implementation of the latest technological tools like cloud computing. Identifying the needs of our focus group and designing the architecture accordingly is the chief objective of this research. Real-world implementation of this educational cloud computing architecture is costly due to the amount of resource usage. Further experimental research work and implementation can be carried out in this arena with proper funding from organisations so that the disabled community gets benefitted.

REFERENCES

Ahmed, Engr Ali, and Ahmed, Huma Ali. 2018. "A proposed model for education system using cloud computing." In *3rd International Conference on Emerging Trends in Engineering, Sciences and Technology (ICEEST)* (pp. 1–4).

Borse, Y., and Gokhale, S. 2019. "Cloud computing platform for education system: A review." *International Journal of Computer Applications* 17(9): 41–45.

Mantzikos, Constantinos N., and Christina S. Lappa. 2020. "Difficulties and barriers in the education of deaf and hard of hearing individuals in the era of COVID-19: The case of Greece – a viewpoint article." Online Submission. *European Journal of Special Education Research* 6(3): 75–95.

Mubin, Siti Azreena, Jacob Sow Tian You, Edwin Pio Rufus Samiraj, and Sharizal Pujahaas Jaafar. 2024. "Supporting and improving deaf and mute learners learning experience." *AIP Conference Proceedings* 2802(1).

Olsson, Sylvia. 2021. "Longing to belong: Deaf and hard of hearing young adults' social interaction, social relationships, and identity." PhD dissertation, Mälardalen University.

Silvestri, Julia A., and Maria C. Hartman. 2022. "Inclusion and deaf and hard of hearing students: Finding asylum in the LRE." *Education Sciences* 12(11): 773.

Wazalwar, Sampada S., and Urmila Shrawankar. 2019. "Multimodal interface for deaf and dumb communication." In *6th International Conference on Computing for Sustainable Global Development (INDIACom)* (pp. 418–422). IEEE.

WEBSITES

Getting Smart. 2016. "10 Challenges deaf students face in the classroom." www.gettingsmart.com/2016/08/21/10- challenges-deaf-students-face-in-the-classroom/

W3C. (2023). "Web Content Accessibility Guidelines (WCAG) 2.1." www.w3.org/TR/WCAG21/

20 E-Interpretation System

Smart Document Learning System Using Educational Clouds

Prerna Mishra and Urmila Shrawankar

20.1 INTRODUCTION

Cloud computing is now a significant part of various sectors of industries, due to its high potential for ameliorating the scalability, accessibility, and reliability of service environments, while reducing operational costs (Alam 2022a, Aceto et al. 2020). Thus, cloud technology is being leveraged by various enterprises for the efficient conduction of business and services. Cloud technology is a new IT service model for providing resources used for accessible computing such as accessible networks, high-end servers, abundant storage, ease-of-access applications, and robust services over the internet (Udhayakumar et al. 2021, Baba et al. 2024). Since the COVID-19 pandemic, cloud technologies are vastly used and deployed for multiple sectors, especially the education sector. With the change in teaching–learning paradigms, educational cloud services have attracted huge attention in smart or e-learning by utilizing recent innovations (Kaur et al. 2022, Al Bashaireh 2023).

E-learning holds various media activities by delivering texts, audio, images, videos and animations, inscribing notes, and lecture delivery from instructors (shown in Figure 20.1). E-learning, being a providential approach, entrusts the purposive use of communication technology and networked data for teaching-training and learning (Baba et al. 2024, Kaur et al. 2022). With the influence of cloud computing, there has been a boom in e-learning modules due to their global availability, especially for academic institutes that have a smaller budget for managing their e-learning systems and services. However, now various universities and educational institutes around the world are adopting cloud computing to enhance the efficiency and convenience of educational services (Jayanthi et al. 2023). A study on recent e-learning systems based on classification, architecture, functions, challenges, and current trends is discussed (Liu and Yu 2023), while also discussing a general architecture for big data-based e-learning systems. The system provides personalized courses and training mechanisms as per the needs and abilities of the student. The impact of immersive digital games in science examining factors influencing their teaching effectiveness and the overall classroom experience was studied (Mutch-Jones et al. 2021). Teachers often adopted a co-teaching approach with the game, enhancing genetics curriculum delivery

DOI: 10.1201/9781003472537-24

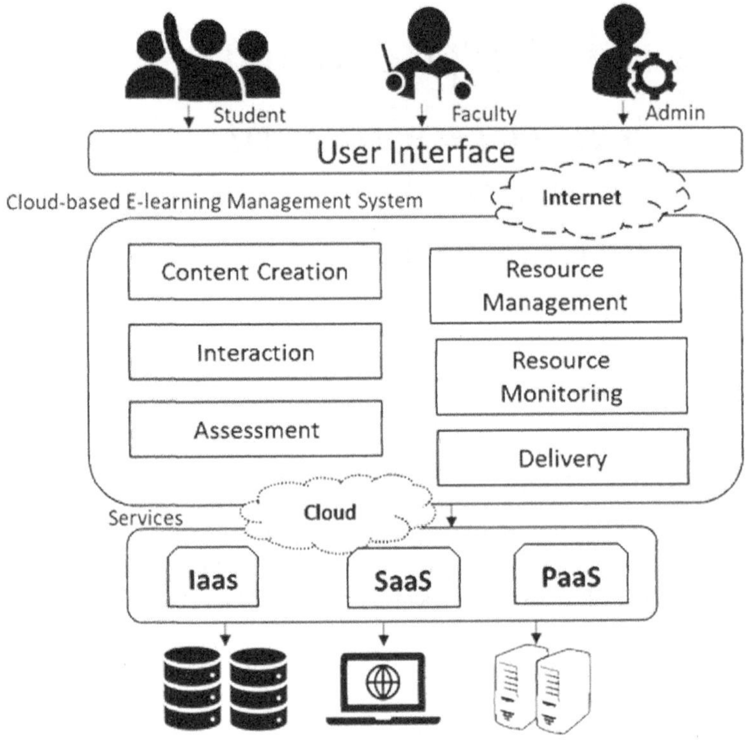

FIGURE 20.1 Cloud-Based e-Learning System.

and instructional methods. Various studies have been performed to investigate the advantages of educational clouds for learning systems (Sweta 2021). However, various cloud-based services are focused only on sharing learning materials, instead of supporting the interpretation of the study materials.

Documents are generally not facilitated for machine understanding (Fu et al. 2020), i.e., it is difficult for the computer to automatically understand and extract the meaning of document components such as paragraphs, equations, images, and tables. Thus, machine learning methods are expected to extract underlying information from different sections of documents and then make intelligent decisions for document interpretation (Binmakhashen and Mahmoud 2019). Moreover, comprehending various types of study materials (or documents) is easier for a sighted user, which at the same time is challenging for visually impaired users (Xiao et al. 2023). The structural variations such as layouts, orientations, and text appearance vary upon the format of the document, i.e., they are never of same. This affects the feature representation and learning capability of the document processing methods, making it challenging for the processing algorithm to adapt to the variedness of the documents (Mishra et al. 2022). As people with special needs are not able to access cloud-based study materials effectively, there is a need for an e-interpretation system that proffers people with special needs a concise real-time interpretation while accessing study materials through educational clouds.

20.1.1 Advantages of Cloud-Based E-Learning

With the advent of educational clouds, e-learning has offered the possibility of an effective teaching–learning process not only in small school premises but also in remote areas (Nasim et al. 2020). A few advantages of cloud-based e-learning are,

- *Easy access*: Students have access to various educational resources and contents without being physically present in the institutions.
- *Group-based or interest-based collaborative learning*: With enhanced learning communication, students can have interactive and collaborative learning from remote locations (Alam and Mohanty 2023).
- *Self-paced learning*: Cloud-based e-learning allows students to integrate studies into their busy schedule, where students can learn at their own pace, learn skills, and develop technological curves as per their availability and ability (Alam 2022b).
- *Resource scalability*: Reaching the teacher becomes accessible and infinite. Enhanced scalability increases the support toward both students and teachers by reducing time, effort, and money for the services.
- *Encourages active learning*: The e-learning environment supports active learning by helping students to be linked with the course, solving assignments, and forming discussion platforms for discussing and reviewing questions, doubts, ideas, and more.
- *Unlimited knowledge*: Students find unlimited resources, materials, information, and all relevant data using cloud communication tools (Xiaomei 2021).

20.1.2 Limitations of Cloud-Based e-Learning

Cloud-based learning has created a favorable environment for a simplified and unified teaching–learning system. However, there are a few factors that affect the growth and usability of the system especially in low-resource countries. A few limitations of cloud-based e-learning are:

- *Access to resources*: Computer and Information and Communications Technology (ICT) resources are the foundations of learning, skills development, and tutoring. However, access to resources depends upon the income and affordability of the family.
- *Poor internet and power facility*: As e-learning systems and ICT depend upon computer and ICT services which require adequate power and internet facilities. Poor power supply and low bandwidth of internet facilities are major reasons for inaccessible educational services.
- *Unsuitable courses*: Few courses require both theory and practical/field work aspects for overall learning, which is not possible in cloud e-learning.

With the swift advancements in technology and the high usage of computers, there lies a perfect opportunity to support a new culture of learning. In this direction, this chapter discusses a smart real-time interpretation system for documents using educational clouds that integrates recent advancements in document processing, and cloud-based services for proving ease-of-access learning mode. The interpretation system enables educational institutes to share various study materials while providing a real-time interpretation of educational content to students with special needs. The cloud-based interpretation system consists of five primary features: a cloud platform, a compatible system for content extraction, an interpretation system, a content displayer, and security systems that are required for deploying learning systems on the educational cloud. However, the real-time interpretation of the document is limited only to a private educational cloud.

20.2 REAL-TIME DOCUMENT INTERPRETATION FOR SMART EDUCATION SYSTEM USING EDUCATIONAL CLOUD

The smart education system proffers document understanding and sharing by integrating various elements required for deploying an educational cloud-based document interpretation system. Figure 20.2 shows the architecture of a cloud-based real-time e-learning system with its five modules required by the interpretation system. The teacher creates and uploads various study materials based on the course content. The materials (documents) are managed in the cloud under the same document file format. The system is accessible over computers, tablets, mobile, tablets, and smart TV. The content displayer displays the interpretation results on different platforms. The content and results are customized as per the need, preference, access capability, and knowledge of the student, especially students with special needs. For structured, systematized, and secured data transmission, the system security provides encrypted and controlled access and usage in the cloud.

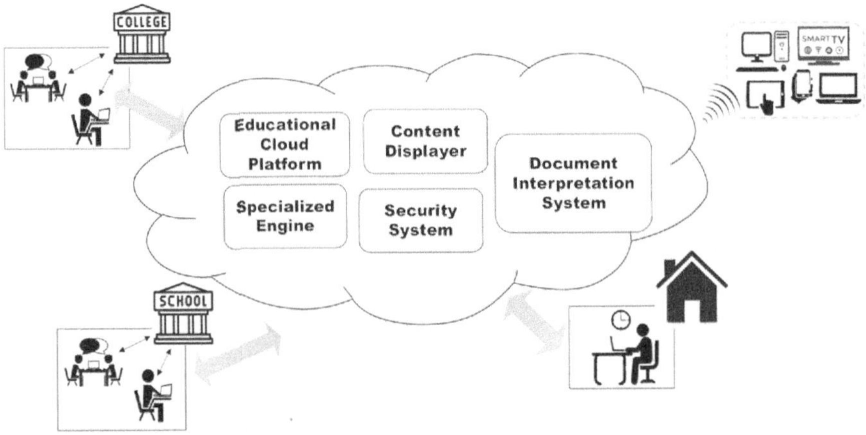

FIGURE 20.2 The Architecture of the Cloud-Based e-Learning System with Real-Time Document Interpretation Service.

20.2.1 Educational Cloud Platform

The proposed interpretation system is employed on a private educational cloud platform for offering a wide infrastructure for deploying a cloud-based educational environment using cloud computing technologies such as synchronization, virtualization, and provision of multiple sharing services. The software and tools required for proposed cloud-based learning services are identified and allotted to respective service models of the cloud (IaaS, PaaS, SaaS). It is observed that many documents available online are either in MS Word (.doc) or PDF (.pdf); thus, these formats are considered as a common file format for unified document processing. Instructors can create and upload a document by inserting contents dynamically or uploading the existing material from the web.

20.2.2 Content Displayer

The role of the content displayer is to display documents and their interpretation on multiple platforms such as smartphones, tablets, laptops, computers, and smart TVs. The displayer displays the documents and their interpretation to the student by converting the document content to HTML, as it is most suitable for various devices and can be loaded in low bandwidth connections too. The interpretation comprises: (1) *image interpretation*, where the intended meaning of the image is portrayed to the student, i.e., "what does an image mean and what message has to be inferred from the image." The images mostly present in any document are categorized as flow diagram which shows the flow of the method, scientific charts, and natural images which show cars, apples, houses, and so on. While scrolling a document, the displayer portrays the interpretation for each image in the panel beside the document; (2) *text interpretation*, where the text from the document page is summarized for each understanding. While active reading, the summarization works page-by-page until the end of the document. For a student with special needs, for example, a student with visual impairment the summarization of text and interpretation of images is provided page-by-page with the help of a screen reader in a way that the document page is comprehended easily by the student.

The system includes a specialized engine which provides personalized learning content or courses to the students as per their needs, preferences, and access ability. The engines use the access patterns, content usage, access ability, difficulty level opted, success rate, and learning genre of a student in the database, analyze; then use machine learning algorithms to infer the learning pattern of a student. The engine is based on a knowledge-based recommendation (Agarwal et al. 2022, Yang et al. 2022) for suggesting learning courses for a student based on his/her learning patterns.

20.2.3 Security System

The security system of the learning environment encrypts data, and data transmission, controls user access and privileges, protects the network, and resolves networking issues within the educational cloud. All the study materials are encrypted usingAdvanced Encryption Standard (AES) and Rivest–Shamir–Adleman (RSA) encryption methods to fulfill file size and latency required for communication amid cloud and learning systems (Alassery 2021), while maintaining secured policies accommodating cloud features such as data preservations, reliability, and durability by reducing any type of attacks on the cloud, or unexpected fault load. The security system also stores a backup of all study material.

20.3 REAL-TIME INTERPRETATION SYSTEM

The chapter proposes a real-time system for document interpretation, which extracts all contents from the document by building relationships between content, irrespective of document structure and orientation (Mishra and Shrawankar 2022). The system comprises three steps: (1) document region detection model, (2) relationship building module, and (3) long short-term memory (LSTM) model.

20.3.1 Document Region Detection Model

Documents possess a possibility for text contents to be placed at different locations within the documents. The text detection models process the object proposals regardless of the size; this reduces the ability of the model to handle a large variety of text/image sizes. Thus, the region proposal network was given feature maps of later (conv4 and conv5) and previous (conv3 and conv2) convolutional operations. Thus, all resultant feature maps are fused and given to the detection model for content localization and classification. The element detection model (shown in Figure 20.3) works in similar ways for document component detection by detecting texts within images of the document.

With the change in text locations, the model tends to misclassify the textual elements and similar graphical elements. Thus, a classifier alignment method (CA) is proposed to overcome element misclassification. The method tries to reduce the alignment distance between element pseudo-labels (classes). Let FM_o be the final output feature map, element classes as $\mathbb{C}$, then pseudo-labels can be given as,

$$P_{\ell e} = \frac{\sum_{e\epsilon R} FM_o\, rel\left(l_e = c\right)}{R_e \mathbb{C}_e} \tag{20.1}$$

where $rel\left(l_e = c\right)$ is a relation function denoting 1 if the label of the element l_e belongs to class c ($c \epsilon \mathbb{C}$), otherwise 0, $P_{\ell e}$ represents the pseudo labels of the element e, R_e is the region of interest. Ground-truth of the training set is employed to extract foreground regions and regions of interest (RoI) with the initial predicted element class $\mathbb{C}_e$. CA was optimized for a model to learn the pseudo-labels and perform the classification tasks accordingly. Google Tesseract 4.0 Engine is used within the bounding box to extract text matter.

20.3.2 Document Content Articulation

This step generates a relationship graph D represented as, $D = (D_V, D_E, D_A)$, where D_V is a set of document regions represented as a vertex, D_E denotes the edges between

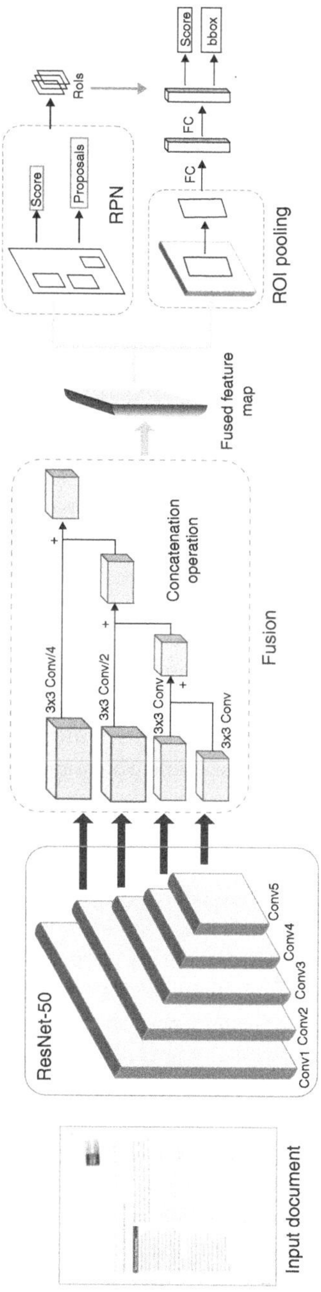

FIGURE 20.3 Element Detection Model.

vertex, and D_A is a set of relationships amid regions. $D_A \subseteq (D_V \times D_E \times D_V)$ is a set of triplets such that, $v = (e_i, r, e_j) \in D_A$, and for any relation, e_i and e_j are interrelated region elements. The aim is to generate a text-image representation ($A_{i,j}$) depending upon the location-based relationship between document regions such that an edge $(i, j) \in E$ denotes the relationships.

20.3.3 Obtaining Content Relationships and Data Extraction

The notion of this step is to adapt relationship triplets to identify superior feature representations between all content of the document (i.e., text–text and text–image relationship). The vector representation of the triplets is, $v = W\ [e_i, r, e_j]$. For extracting confined data from documents, A attention is utilized, which makes final encodings as,

$$\dot{e} = \forall a \in A\left[\sigma\left(\Sigma\, \theta_{i,j} v_{i,j}\right)\right] \tag{20.2}$$

where θ= softmax(v). As now the relations are built, by iteratively learning the edge relationships between different components, the global relationship amid document components is updated. For all region components $D_E = (D_{e1}, D_{e2}, \ldots, D_{eN})$, the LSTM model is used as a decoder to assign adaptive weights to each element's feature representation. The model generates (1) the summary for each detected image stating the meaning of the image or what should be understood from the image and (2) interpretation of the textual matter of the document. Both interpretations are provided page-by-page in a parallel manner. These summaries can be offered to students with special needs using assistive tools (like Braille devices, screen readers, and magnifiers), as per their needs (Wazalwar and Shrawankar 2021, Mishra et al. 2022).

20.4 E-LEARNING IDEOLOGY AND EDUCATIONAL CLOUDS

The numerous benefits of cloud-based education facilitate the teacher-learning process for creating, fostering, and delivering smart learning from any remote location. This creates an effective environment for students by making them aware of the latest technologies and their upgradations while meeting society's needs for continuous rapid learning in suitable forms. The web enables learning systems that have provided active, self, and collaborated learning paradigms with enhanced learning materials and contents. Next-generation e-learning is fused with social acculturation, collaborative, and application-based learning reflected by various utilities and tools like Wikipedia, blogs, online simulators, social networking portals, and so on. The advancements of e-learning have built a strong benchmark in various sectors whose pillars are accessibility, eco-sustainability, employability, online service integration, e-resources services, self/organizational learning, and quality assurance. National Agency for Higher Education (NAHE) report (Ossiannilsson and Landgren 2012) proposes ten quality aspects for analyzing e-learning systems where learning content, virtual environment, communication and cooperation, student assessment, flexibility, adaptability, and support to the uses were considered.

TABLE 20.1
Cloud-Based Learning Platforms

Educational Cloud	Features and Characteristics
Google Educational Cloud	A virtual collaborative learning environment integrating G-Classroom, mail, documents, sheets, calendar, drives, and sites to provide users with an easy personalized environment.
Microsoft Education Cloud	Enables users to improve their skills by collaborative communication using Microsoft email, sites, MS Office, messaging and conferencing applications, plotting graphs, and real-time engagement of users.
Moodle	One of the best e-learning management systems having strong support of documentation and administration with high-security mechanisms.
Blackboard	An e-learning management system that integrates social learning experiences with personalized learning through Blackboard learn, blackboard collaborate, and analytics.
Sakai	An open-source learning management service that provides the same as Moodle.
Cisco Collaborative Knowledge	A centralized e-learning system for business used for handling real-time administration, staff-training, group-planning, and future event organizing, all in the cloud.
DocentEDU	A free tool useful for teachers, which integrates facilities of the google cloud.

Cloud-based educational platforms can be organized as per their support toward cognitive learning, motivation, and social-constructive theories. Although many learning platforms support these learning theories, few might overlook relative vital theories. The pedagogical aspects of cloud-based e-learning platforms deliver a complete advantage to interdisciplinary learning communities at various levels (Kumar and Bhardwaj 2020). The most prominent and significant educational clouds are listed in Table 20.1.

20.5 CONCLUSION

The rate of e-learners is growing rapidly with time and changing technology. The institutes are exploring and utilizing the cloud-based smart learning system for enhancing the learning skills of students and diversifying the teaching-learning mechanisms. Moreover, the institutes are emphasizing and promoting cloud-based e-learning systems for reliable and efficient learning experiences as such systems are cost-effective, faster, and more efficient than traditional e-learning systems. The chapter proposed a smart real-time document interpretation system that summarizes the text and image components of the document. This facilitates the user with special needs who cannot understand documents or depend on assistive tools. Cloud-based interpretation system enables documents and their interpretation accessible on the go for all types of users. The cloud-based multimedia learning system could give the high potential for various techniques to understand documents in ongoing education pedagogical reforms. This shall embody e-learning and ubiquitous learning environments as crucial aspects of an education management system. Additionally, processing and interpretation of various other forms of educational material or content are also essential for extended support toward education, as well as constant upgradation of the e-interpretation system via application-oriented case studies.

REFERENCES

Aceto, Giuseppe, Valerio Persico, and Antonio Pescapé. 2020. "Industry 4.0 and health: Internet of things, big data, and cloud computing for healthcare 4.0." *Journal of Industrial Information Integration* 18: 100129.

Agarwal, Abhinav, Divyansh Shankar Mishra, and Sucheta V. Kolekar. 2022. "Knowledge-based recommendation system using semantic web rules based on learning styles for MOOCs." *Cogent Engineering* 9 (1): 2022568.

Al Bashaireh, Rasha. 2023. "Cloud-Based E-Learning: Concepts, and Its Beneficial Role during the COVID-19 Dilemma." In *Proceedings of Seventh International Congress on Information and Communication Technology*, 491–505. Springer, Singapore.

Alam, Ashraf. 2022a. "Cloud-Based E-Learning: Development of Conceptual Model for Adaptive E-Learning Ecosystem Based on Cloud Computing Infrastructure." In *International Conference on Artificial Intelligence and Data Science*, 377–391. Springer, Cham.

Alam, Ashraf. 2022b. "Cloud-Based e-Learning: Scaffolding the Environment for Adaptive e-Learning Ecosystem Based on Cloud Computing Infrastructure." In *Computer Communication, Networking and IoT: Proceedings of 5th ICICC 2021*, Vol. 2, 1–9. Springer Nature Singapore, Singapore.

Alam, Ashraf, and Atasi Mohanty. 2023. "Design, Development, and Implementation of Software Engineering Virtual Laboratory: A Boon to Computer Science and Engineering (CSE) Education during Covid-19 Pandemic." In *Proceedings of Third International Conference on Sustainable Expert Systems: ICSES 2022*, 1–20. Springer Nature Singapore, Singapore.

Alassery, Hind A. 2021. "Securing fog computing for e-learning system using integration of two encryption algorithms." *Journal of Cybersecurity* 3 (3): 149.

Baba, Khalid, Nour-eddine Elfaddouli, and Nicolas Cheimanoff. 2024. "The role of information and communication technologies in developing a smart campus with its four pillars' architectural sketch." *Education and Information Technologies* 29 (12): 14815–14833.

Binmakhashen, Galal M., and Sabri A. Mahmoud. 2019. "Document layout analysis: A comprehensive survey." *ACM Computing Surveys (CSUR)* 52 (6): 1–36.

Fu, J., B. Zhu, W. Cui, S. Ge, Y. Wang, H. Zhang, H. Huang, Y. Tang, D. Zhang, and X. Ma. 2020. "Chartem: Reviving chart images with data embedding." *IEEE Transactions on Visualization and Computer Graphics* 27 (2): 337–346.

Jayanthi, K., M. Sugantha Priya, S. Saranya, R. Gomathi, and Dahlia Sam. 2023. "E-Learning as a Desirable Form of Education in the Era of Society 5.0." In *Advances in Distance Learning in Times of Pandemic*, 23–51. Chapman and Hall/CRC.

Kaur, Shubhpreet, Tarandeep Kaur, and Ashok Sharma. 2022. "Cloud-enabled education-as-a-service (EaaS)—a review." *ICT Systems and Sustainability* 321: 397–404.

Kumar, V., & A. Bhardwaj. 2020. "Role of Cloud Computing in School Education." In *Handbook of Research on Diverse Teaching Strategies for the Technology-Rich Classroom*, 98–108. IGI Global.

Liu, Mengchi, and Dongmei Yu. 2023. "Towards intelligent E-learning systems." *Education and Information Technologies* 28 (7): 7845–7876.

Mishra, P., S. Kumar, and M. K. Chaube. 2022. "Evaginating scientific charts: Recovering direct and derived information encodings from chart images." *Journal of Visualization* 25: 343–359.

Mishra, Prerna, Santosh Kumar, Mithilesh Kumar Chaube, and Urmila Shrawankar. 2022. "ChartVi: Charts summarizer for visually impaired." *Journal of Computer Languages* 69: 101107.

Mishra, Prerna, and Urmila Shrawankar. 2022. "Human vs. Machine Eye for Chart Interpretation." In *2022 IEEE Region 10 Symposium (TENSYMP)*, 1–6. IEEE.

Mutch-Jones, Karen, Danielle C. Boulden, Santiago Gasca, Trudi Lord, Eric Wiebe, and Frieda Reichsman. 2021. "Co-teaching with an immersive digital game: Supporting teacher-game instructional partnerships." *Educational Technology Research and Development* 69, no. 3, 1453–1475.

Nasim, Raheela, Halim Ullah, Sanam Shahla Rizvi, Almas Abbasi, Sajid Khan, Rabia Riaz, and Anand Paul. 2020. "A cloud-based enterprise resource planning architecture for women's education in remote areas." *Electronics* 9 (11): 1758.

Ossiannilsson, Ebba, and Lena Landgren. 2012. "Quality in e-learning—a conceptual framework based on experiences from three international benchmarking projects." *Journal of Computer Assisted Learning* 28 (1): 42–51.

Sweta, Soni. 2021, "Educational Data Mining in e-Learning System." In *Modern Approach to Educational Data Mining and Its Applications*, 1–12. Springer.

Udhayakumar, S., D. Uma Nandhini, and S. Chandrasekaran. 2021. "Trusted Cooperative E-Learning Service Deployment Model in Multi-Cloud Environment." In *Inventive Communication and Computational Technologies*, 527–535. Springer, Singapore.

Wazalwar, S. S., and U. Shrawankar. 2021. "Distributed Education System for Deaf and Dumb Children and Educator: A Today's Need." In *Proceedings of Integrated Intelligence Enable Networks and Computing. Algorithms for Intelligent Systems*. Springer, Singapore.

Xiao, Shishi, Suizi Huang, Yue Lin, Yilin Ye, and Wei Zeng. 2023. "Let the chart spark: Embedding semantic context into chart with text-to-image generative model." *IEEE Transactions on Visualization and Computer Graphics* 30: 284–294.

Xiaomei, Song. 2021. "Design and implementation of university network education platform based on cloud computing." *Journal of Physics: Conference Series* 1982 (1): 012197.

Yang, Humin, M. Anbarasan, and Thanjai Vadivel. 2022. "Knowledge-based recommender system using artificial intelligence for smart education." *Journal of Interconnection Networks* 22: 2143031.

21 Revolutionizing Education

The Multifaceted Role of Cloud in Modern e-Learning Environment

Josephine A. Anitha

21.1 INTRODUCTION

In the digital age, the evolution of technology has transformed the process of delivery and accessibility of education. Among the numerous innovations, cloud computing has become a force for transformation in the field of e-Learning. The integration of cloud technologies into educational settings has unlocked a plethora of opportunities, reshaping traditional paradigms and redefining the learning experience. The multifaceted aspects of clouds in e-Learning encompass accessibility, scalability, collaboration, personalization, innovation, cost efficiency, and security. Cloud-based platforms provide seamless access to educational resources, scale resources based on demand, enable collaboration among learners and educators, personalize learning experiences, foster innovation in teaching methodologies, offer cost-effective solutions, and implement robust security measures to protect sensitive data. These facets collectively contribute to the transformation of educational practices, enhancing learning outcomes in the digital age.

21.1.1 Background

The background of cloud computing in transforming e-Learning traces back to the early 2000s when advancements in internet technology began to reshape educational practices. Because cloud computing offers internal or external programs that supervise academic achievement in a cloud-based context, it has completely transformed the traditional web-based e-Learning environment. It provides comprehensive software support and ample computing resources that can be accessed at any location and time, as desired by educational institutions (Eljak et al., 2023). Initially, e-Learning relied on standalone computer-based training modules, limiting accessibility and interactivity. Cloud environment provided the infrastructure needed to support dynamic, interactive learning experiences, enabling global participation and

DOI: 10.1201/9781003472537-25

collaboration among learners and educators. Using information and communication technology (ICT) in a novel way, cloud computing allows for the instantaneous provision of flexible and extendable capabilities as a service (Scalera et al., 2020). The COVID-19 pandemic served as a catalyst, expediting the application of cloud-based e-Learning technologies as educational institutions worldwide transitioned to remote learning environments. This rapid shift underscored the significance of cloud computing in ensuring the continuity of education and supporting distance learning initiatives. Looking ahead, the background of cloud computing in transforming e-Learning continues to evolve, driven by ongoing innovations in technology, pedagogy, and learner-centric design. Cloud computing enables the establishment of a dependable, adaptable, cost-effective, self-governing, and Quality of Service assured e-Learning environment (Dong et al., 2009).

21.1.2 Evolution of Cloud-Based e-Learning

Initially, e-Learning primarily relied on standalone computer-based training modules, limiting accessibility and interactivity. With the emergence of the internet, web-based e-Learning platforms began to gain traction, offering greater flexibility and access to a wider audience. The current pick-and-mix model benchmark identifies accessibility, dependability, eco-sustainability, job prospects, integration of digital portfolio services, faculty and students, learning resources, and library services as critical success elements for e-Learning. A number of issues are covered by the e-resources, including organizational learning, pedagogy, personalization, plagiarism, quality control, staff awards and recognition, and raising involvement (Kumar & Sharma, 2021). The advancement of interactive, collaborative learning spaces that surpass geographical limitations, encourages worldwide engagement and cooperation between learners and educators. Looking ahead, the evolution of cloud-based e-Learning is expected to continue, driven by innovations in technology, pedagogy, and learner-centric design. The multifacets of cloud-based e-Learning are given in Figure 21.1.

21.1.3 Role of Cloud Computing in Transforming e-Learning

The two types of e-Learning systems that are now in use are Learning Management Systems (LMSs) and Massive Open Online Course (MOOC) platforms (Liu & Yu, 2023). With cloud-based solutions, learners gain anytime, anywhere access to educational resources, breaking down geographical barriers and fostering inclusivity. In addition, cloud technology allows for customized learning experiences that are specifically designed to meet individual needs, utilizing data analytics and artificial intelligence (AI). The scalability of cloud computing permits institutions of education to adapt quickly to changing demands and deliver innovative teaching methodologies. Additionally, cloud-based e-Learning platforms enhance collaboration among learners and educators, promoting interactive and engaging learning experiences. Overall, the function of cloud computing in e-Learning is transformative, driving efficiency, accessibility, and innovation in education.

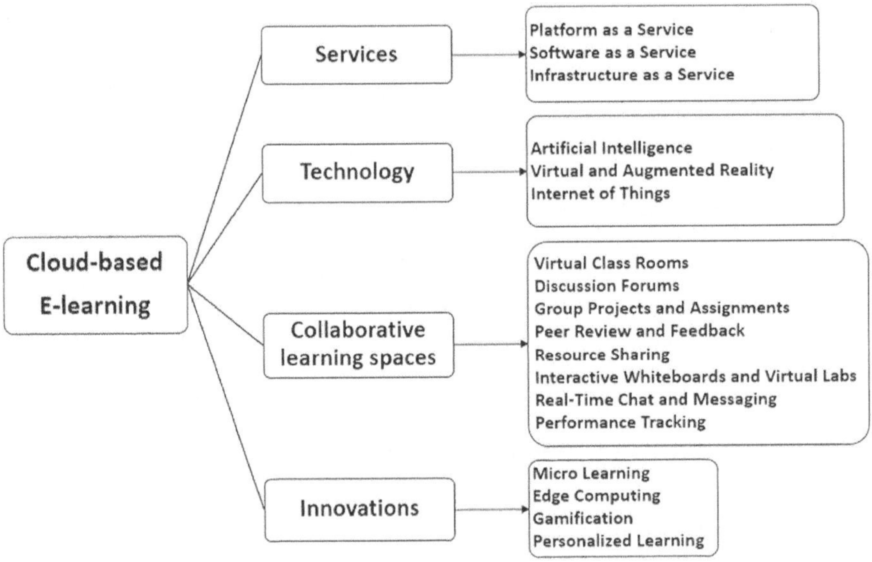

FIGURE 21.1 Multifaceted Aspects of Cloud in e-Learning.

21.2 CLOUD-BASED INFRASTRUCTURE FOR E-LEARNING

Cloud computing technologies have become a powerful and influential factor in the field of e-Learning, providing flexible, effective, and economical ways to deliver educational content and services. Three levels of cloud computing services are distinguished: Platform as a Service (PaaS), Infrastructure as a Service (IaaS), and Software as a Service (SaaS) (Wu & Plakhtii, 2021). SaaS, is a method of licensing and delivering software products to customers upon their request. Cloud computing encompasses a service layer referred to as SaaS. SaaS provides numerous benefits and conveniences, particularly in terms of optimizing resource utilization and accelerating application development. SaaS enables simultaneous usage of an application by multiple tenants while ensuring the protection of each individual tenant (Fithri et al., 2020). PaaS provides a computer platform and solution stack as a service. It often uses cloud infrastructure and supports cloud applications. It eradicates the requirement to purchase as well as maintain the underlying infrastructure hardware (which includes servers, storage, and networks) and related software (like operating systems and virtualization technologies) to make application development and deployment dependable, safe, and scalable (Nasr & Ouf, 2012). IaaS offers adaptable infrastructure capabilities tailored to specific needs, including virtual computing, storage, and networking resources. Service Level Agreements (SLAs) are taken into consideration to guarantee that providers fulfill consumer requirements (Buyya et al., 2010)

21.2.1 Virtualization in e-Learning

Virtualization (Kristianto, 2014) enables the creation of virtual instances of computing resources, including servers, desktops, and applications, abstracting them from the underlying physical hardware. It addresses the issue of physical obstacles that usually arise from the limited resources and infrastructure required to automate resource management as a unified entity utilizing hypervisor technologies like virtual machines (VM). Regarding e-Learning, virtualization facilitates the deployment of scalable and flexible infrastructure, enabling educational institutions to maximize the efficient use of resources, minimize expenses, and improve the availability of learning materials. Virtualization enables the simulation of real-world environments and scenarios, facilitating hands-on training and practical learning exercises in fields such as science, engineering, and healthcare. The two types of virtualization are desktop virtualization and server virtualization.

21.2.1.1 Server Virtualization

Server virtualization is a foundational technology in the field of cloud computing and data center management. It involves abstracting physical servers into virtual instances, permitting the operation of numerous virtual servers on a single physical hardware. Server virtualization is the process of converting physical servers into virtual instances, which enables several virtual servers to operate on a single physical machine. Regarding e-Learning, this technology enables educational institutions to maximize the efficient use of resources, reduce hardware costs, and enhance the scalability as well as flexibility of their infrastructure. Server virtualization reduces operating expenses and improves resource management by combining numerous virtual servers with fewer physical machines (Geetha et al., 2023). Additionally, virtualization facilitates workload migration and disaster recovery, ensuring seamless continuity of educational services and resources. Furthermore, server virtualization enables the creation of isolated testing and development environments, enhancing security and mitigating risks associated with software deployment.

21.2.1.2 Desktop Virtualization

The technique of developing virtual desktop instances that are hosted and managed centrally in the cloud is known as desktop virtualization. Because of this, users can use any internet-connected device to access their desktop environments and applications. Regarding e-Learning, this technology enables seamless access to educational content, software applications, and resources, regardless of the user's location or device capabilities. By centralizing desktop environments in the cloud, educational institutions can improve resource utilization, reduce hardware costs, and streamline desktop management and maintenance tasks (Al Bashaireh, 2022). Furthermore, desktop virtualization enhances security by centralizing data storage and access controls, mitigating risks associated with data loss, theft, or unauthorized access. Additionally, desktop virtualization supports collaborative learning and remote instruction by enabling real-time collaboration and communication tools within virtual desktop environments.

21.2.2 Scalability and Flexibility

Scalability and flexibility are primary factors that must be taken into consideration in the design as well as in the implementation of cloud-based e-Learning environments, where dynamic user demands, evolving technologies, and diverse educational needs necessitate adaptable infrastructures. Scalability ensures that e-Learning platforms can accommodate fluctuating user loads, whether during peak enrolment periods or sudden spikes in usage. Cloud-based solutions offer auto-scaling capabilities, allowing resources to be provisioned or de-provisioned dynamically in response to demand, thereby ensuring optimal performance and user experience. Flexibility in cloud-based e-Learning environments enables rapid adaptation to changing requirements, emerging technologies, and pedagogical approaches. Through the adoption of modular architectures, microservices, and containerization, e-Learning platforms can achieve greater agility and resilience, enabling seamless integration of new features, content types, and instructional methodologies. Cloud computing optimizes resource utilization by dynamically scaling down when the workload is light, resulting in reduced resource consumption and expenditure (Ali, 2022).

21.2.3 Elasticity in Cloud Resources

Elasticity is an intrinsic attribute of cloud computing that allows enterprises to effectively handle their computing resources in accordance with changing demand. With elasticity, cloud users can scale their infrastructure up during periods of high demand to ensure optimal performance and scalability, and scale it down during periods of low demand to minimize costs. Elasticity is the process of aligning the allocation of resources to a service with its real resource requirements, hence preventing both over-provisioning (allocating more resources than necessary) and under-provisioning (allocating fewer resources than necessary). Alternatively, if the service provider fails to do so, it may not deliver satisfactory services to its users (Zhang & Zhu, 2017).

21.2.4 Adapting to Variable Workloads in e-Learning

Adapting to variable workloads in e-Learning implies the ability of educational platforms to scale resources dynamically based on fluctuations in user demand, content consumption, and system requirements. Additionally, e-Learning platforms employ optimization strategies such as caching frequently accessed content, compressing data transmission, and prioritizing critical tasks to maximize resource utilization and minimize latency. These strategies help mitigate the impact of variable workloads on system performance and ensure a responsive and reliable learning environment for users. Continuous monitoring of system performance, resource utilization, and user activity enables e-Learning platforms to anticipate workload fluctuations and implement auto-scaling policies proactively. Automated scaling triggers can be based on predefined thresholds or performance metrics, enabling the platform to dynamically scale resources up or down in response to shifting demand trends. The increasing popularity of Content Delivery Networks (CDNs) can be attributed to the continuous advancement of the internet and its applications (Sasikumar et al., 2023). CDNs enhance the performance and reliability of e-Learning platforms by caching and delivering content from edge servers located closer to users. This reduces the duration of time required for data transmission and enhances the rate at which content is delivered, particularly for media content like videos, animations, and interactive simulations. This guarantees an effortless learning procedure.

21.3 INTEGRATION OF EMERGING TECHNOLOGIES

Within the field of education, the incorporation of new technologies into online learning platforms that are based on cloud computing has become a crucial approach for improving involvement, availability, and efficiency. E-Learning providers face both possibilities and challenges due to the rapid development of technology. Integrating digitalization, artificial intelligence (AI), blockchain, animation, virtual reality (VR), and robotics into the education system and classroom is a vital aspect of the fourth industrial revolution (IR 4.0). This provides a glimpse into the current and future prospects for acquiring valuable skills for the upcoming generation (Pandey, 2023).

21.3.1 Artificial Intelligence and Machine Learning

Analyzing learner data and behavior, AI algorithms customize educational content and recommendations to suit individual needs and preferences, thereby enhancing the experience of personalized learning. AI-powered intelligent tutoring systems can provide instantaneous feedback, adaptive learning paths, and personalized support to learners, enhancing their engagement and comprehension. AI-driven assessment tools can streamline the grading process, provide instant feedback to learners, and identify areas for improvement. AI facilitates personalized decision-making by utilizing data analytics, resulting in enhanced education for customized instruction and the optimization of the educational process (Arun Kumar et al., 2022). AI and machine learning (ML) algorithms have the capability to gather data about a learner from a range of sources, like digital resources, LMSs, examinations, and online platforms. Along with other appropriate information, they collect data regarding learning preferences, engagement patterns, performance indicators, and demographics. Data gathering can occur either in real time or asynchronously, allowing adaptive learning systems to consistently update and improve learner profiles. AI and ML approaches are highly proficient at processing extensive and intricate datasets. After being gathered, these algorithms analyze the data to reveal patterns, correlations, and trends. AI involves developing intelligent computers that can imitate human intellect to carry out tasks that usually need human capabilities, such as perception, thinking, and decision-making.

21.3.2 Virtual and Augmented Reality for Immersive Learning Experiences

With the continual evolution of cloud-based e-Learning, educators are now using advanced technologies like VR and augmented reality (AR) more often. These tools are being utilized to enhance the educational process and encourage students to interact with the content material more thoroughly. While AR superimposes digital content on the actual world, providing unique chances for interactive and experiential learning, VR immerses students in a computer-generated setting. VR and AR simulations enable learners to engage in hands-on activities and experiments that would be impractical or impossible in traditional educational settings. AR applications support remote collaboration and communication, allowing learners to collaborate on projects, share resources, and receive feedback from anywhere in the world. Integrating VR/AR into instructional design necessitates pedagogical innovation, teacher training, and alignment with educational objectives to maximize learning outcomes. AR has the potential to be utilized in diverse sectors like tourism, education, industry, and medicine. Multiple studies have affirmed the advantages of utilizing AR in the realm of education (Al-Jammaz et al., 2023; Mystakidis et al., 2022).

21.3.3 Internet of Things

The Internet of Things (IoT), marked by interconnected gadgets communicating in real-time, combined with the scalable and flexible infrastructure of cloud computing, offers novel opportunities for enhancing online education. The integration of IoT in cloud-based e-Learning has been shown to improve learning experiences through interactive and immersive educational tools. For instance, smart sensors and wearable devices can track student activities and provide instant feedback, while IoT-enabled laboratories allow remote access to experimental setups. IoT facilitates greater accessibility for students with disabilities by providing adaptive learning technologies and real-time assistance. Cloud integration ensures that educational resources are available anytime and anywhere, making learning more inclusive. The IoT can act as the foundation for a widespread learning environment and allow intelligent environments to identify items and access information from the internet to enhance their adaptive capabilities (Ajaz Moharkan et al., 2017). Implementing the IoT in educational settings enhances the quality of the learning process by facilitating rapid student learning and enabling teachers to do their duties more efficiently (Mohamed, 2018).

21.3.4 Blockchain Technologies

Blockchain technology has multiple applications in the education sector, including digital credentialing and verification, secure peer-to-peer transactions, and tasks related to educational administration. It emphasized the advantages of utilizing blockchain technology in smart learning environments, such as promoting collaborative learning, safeguarding privacy, and improving trust and transparency in educational transactions and data (Bidry et al., 2023). Decentralized learning environments are made possible by the implementation of blockchain technology. These platforms operate through consensus rather than by a singular entity. This dynamic technology facilitates a collaborative learning environment among peers (Zhao et al., 2023).

21.4 SECURITY AND COMPLIANCE

From protecting sensitive learner data to ensuring compliance with data privacy regulations, educators and administrators must navigate a complex landscape of risks and regulatory requirements. Security and compliance are foundational pillars of trust and integrity in cloud-based e-Learning environments. By addressing the complex challenges of data privacy regulations, cybersecurity threats, and best practices for safeguarding e-Learning data, stakeholders can foster a safe and conducive learning environment for educators and learners alike. Through proactive measures such as data encryption, access controls, employee training, incident response planning, and compliance monitoring, educators and administrators can mitigate risks, protect sensitive data, and uphold the highest standards of security and compliance in e-Learning. Security issues with cloud-based online computing environments include a Lightweight Intrusion Detection System (LIDS), Tenant Security Requirement Manager (TSRM), and Remote Advanced Attack Detection (RAAD). These security measures are present in the SaaS within the cloud computing environment (Malele, 2023).

21.5 ANTICIPATED INNOVATIONS IN CLOUD-BASED E-LEARNING

Utilizing data analytics, cloud-based platforms customize learning by providing recommendations, evaluations, and content that corresponds to each learner's preferences, performance, and learning style. It seamlessly integrates with LMSs, allowing institutions to manage course content, enrolments, assessments, and analytics from a centralized system, streamlining administrative tasks and enhancing instructor insights. Some of them leverage blockchain technology to secure and verify academic credentials and certifications, providing learners with tamper-proof records of their educational achievements. Cloud-based e-Learning platforms incorporate gamification elements and cloud gaming techniques to enhance learner engagement and motivation through features like badges, ledger boards, and rewards. Personalization relies on AI approaches to find suitable information for individual learners depending on their comprehension level and chosen learning methods (Murtaza et al., 2022).

21.5.1 Adaptive Learning Algorithms

Adaptive learning algorithms are essential in cloud-based e-Learning as they customize the learning experience for individual students. A range of adaptive learning algorithm approaches are employed by e-Learning platforms, such as learning analytics, individualized learning methods, and intelligent tutoring systems (Gligorea et al., 2023). These algorithms analyze student data, such as learning preferences, performance, and pace, to tailor the content and learning paths to match individual needs. This personalization enhances engagement and improves learning outcomes by providing relevant and targeted material to each learner. Adaptive learning systems can be utilized to deliver customized educational material to students according to their individual learning preferences, leading to enhanced academic success and satisfaction, as well as reduced learning time (Bernard et al., 2015).

21.5.2 Collaborative Learning Spaces

Collaborative learning spaces in cloud-based e-Learning environments facilitate dynamic interaction and knowledge exchange among learners. These virtual platforms enable real-time collaboration on projects, discussions, and assignments regardless of geographical constraints. Learners can engage in peer-to-peer interactions, share resources, and provide feedback, fostering a collaborative learning culture. Through interactive features like virtual classrooms and group collaboration tools, learners can actively participate in their own learning journey. Performance tracking and analytics tools allow instructors to monitor progress and provide personalized support. Overall, these environments enhance engagement, collaboration, and the efficacy of online education. Research has shown that "both collaborative learning and e-Learning" can improve critical thinking, problem-solving, communication, and teamwork abilities. These skills are crucial for achieving success in today's workforce (Wagino et al., 2023).

21.5.3 Edge Computing in e-Learning

Edge computing has been suggested as an internet-based distributed computing paradigm to enable mobile devices to offload work to nearby edge servers instead of transmitting it to distant cloud servers (Ma et al., 2024). Edge computing revolutionizes cloud-based e-Learning by bringing processing power closer to the user, minimizing latency, and optimizing bandwidth usage. Processing data on edge devices or nearby servers, enables real-time interactions, offline capabilities, and enhanced privacy and security. This transformative approach ensures smoother user experiences, particularly in applications such as video conferencing, virtual labs, and interactive simulations. Additionally, edge computing architectures offer scalability and resilience, handling fluctuations in demand and providing redundancy. Overall, the integration of edge computing in cloud-based e-Learning signifies a paradigm shift toward more efficient, responsive, and accessible online education.

21.6 COST CONSIDERATIONS AND ECONOMIC BENEFITS

The adoption of cloud-based e-Learning platforms has revolutionized the delivery of education as well as training, enabling educational institutions to overcome traditional barriers such as high infrastructure costs, limited scalability, and resource constraints. By leveraging cloud computing technologies, educational institutions can access scalable, on-demand resources for hosting, managing, and delivering educational content and services. By managing software upgrades, security patches, and infrastructure maintenance, cloud service providers lower the workload for IT staff and operational expenses. By shifting from capital-intensive on-premises models to Operating expense-based cloud solutions, institutions can realize significant cost savings, improve operational efficiencies, and gain strategic advantages in the rapidly evolving education landscape.

21.6.1 Cost Models in Cloud Computing

Because cloud-based learning eliminates the need for local data center capital expenditures, it lessens the financial strain on educational institutions. This also includes lowering the cost of replacing old technical hardware assets and data center maintenance as well as university data storage expenditures (Bora & Ahmed, 2013; Elmasry & Ibrahim, 2021). Cost models prevalent in cloud-based e-Learning environments, including subscription-based pricing, pay-per-use models, total cost of ownership (TCO), and return on investment (ROI), empower institutions to make informed decisions regarding resource allocation, budgeting, and cost optimization. Cloud-based e-Learning can yield significant cost savings compared to traditional on-premises solutions, due to factors such as reduced infrastructure investments, lower operational overheads, and economies of scale. Calculating ROI involves quantifying the financial benefits of cost savings and operational efficiencies gained from cloud adoption. Beyond cost savings, cloud-based e-Learning can generate value through enhanced scalability, accessibility, and innovation. Value-based metrics such as learner engagement, satisfaction, and learning outcomes can complement traditional ROI calculations and provide a holistic view of the advantages of cloud-based e-Learning.

21.6.2 Economic Advantages of Cloud-Based e-Learning

By comprehending and leveraging the economic benefits of cloud-based e-Learning, educators, administrators, and policymakers can unlock value and foster enduring growth within the digital education landscape. Cloud-based e-Learning fosters the necessity to minimize infrastructure expenses, thereby avoiding substantial investments in on-site infrastructure like servers, network devices, and data centers. Through the utilization of cloud computing resources, institutions can obtain flexible and readily available infrastructure without the need for initial capital outlays. Cloud-based e-Learning platforms streamline administrative tasks, automate processes, and optimize resource utilization, reducing operational overheads and labor costs. By offloading maintenance, updates, and support to cloud service providers, institutions can focus resources on core educational activities.

Beyond its educational benefits, cloud-based e-Learning also provides significant economic advantages to students. It often provides access to digital textbooks and educational resources at lower costs compared to traditional printed materials. By eliminating the need to purchase expensive textbooks, students can save money on course materials and resources. Cloud-based e-Learning reduces or eradicates the requirement for students to commute to campus by enabling them to attend classes remotely from any location that has access to the internet. Students benefit financially from this by saving money on transportation costs including petrol, parking, and public transportation fares.

Cloud-based e-Learning offers students flexibility in scheduling and accessing educational content, permitting individuals to manage their academic endeavors with work, family responsibilities, and other engagements. Because of its adaptability, students can pursue education without having to sacrifice income or employment opportunities.

Online learning is economically feasible because it eliminates the need for print materials, substitutes digital infrastructure for fixed infrastructure, and requires no transportation expenses. The field of education and learning through digital connections has expanded with the introduction of online education. The idea of e-Learning has gained popularity due to the removal of needless expenses and the simplicity of the educational process (Alam, 2022).

21.7 FUTURE TRENDS AND CHALLENGES

The advancement of AI and data analytics has resulted in a rise of personalized learning experiences, precisely customized to align with the unique preferences, strengths, and areas of improvement for each learner. The use of VR and AR in e-Learning will increase as they offer immersive learning experiences that mimic real-world settings and situations, improving student engagement and retention. Short, bite-sized learning modules will gain popularity, allowing learners to consume content in small increments, fitting learning activities into their busy schedules and improving knowledge retention.

Among the difficulties is the "digital divide," which results in differences in people's access to technology and internet connectivity. This may hinder the implementation and efficiency of cloud-based e-Learning, worsening educational inequality. Safeguarding sensitive learner data and ensuring the privacy of users in cloud-based e-Learning environments remain a significant challenge, particularly with the increasing prevalence of cyber threats and data breaches. Maintaining the quality of online educational content and ensuring its alignment with learning objectives and standards poses a challenge, particularly with the rapid proliferation of user-generated content and open educational resources. Keeping learners engaged and motivated in online courses can be challenging, as distractions abound and the absence of in-person communication can cause emotions of isolation and disinterest.

21.8 CONCLUSION

As we reflect on the multifaceted aspects of the cloud in e-Learning, it is evident that this innovative incorporation cloud in e-Learning approach holds immense promise for the future of education. By utilizing cloud computing, we may lead to a more successful, inclusive, and dynamic learning environment that encourages students to realize their ultimate capability and prepares them for life in a world that is becoming increasingly connected. It enhances accessibility by facilitating the immediate utilization of learning materials from anywhere, promoting a more accessible and globalized educational experience. Cloud-based applications, such as LMSs, MOOCs, and collaborative tools, streamline administrative processes and facilitate seamless communication, establishing a learning environment that is more dynamic and connected. Moreover, the cost-effectiveness of cloud solutions contributes to resource optimization, making high-quality education more affordable and sustainable for institutions worldwide. In simple terms, the function of the cloud in e-Learning is transformative, offering a dynamic and efficient approach to education delivery. Embracing this transformative technology holds the key to shaping a brighter, more equitable future where education knows no limits and every learner has the opportunity to succeed.

REFERENCES

Ajaz Moharkan, Z., Choudhury, T., Gupta, S. C., & Raj, G. (2017, February). Internet of Things and its applications in e-Learning. In *2017 3rd International Conference on Computational Intelligence & Communication Technology (CICT)* (pp. 1–5). IEEE.

Al Bashaireh, R. (2022, July). Cloud-based e-Learning: Concepts, and its beneficial role during the COVID-19 dilemma. In *Proceedings of Seventh International Congress on Information and Communication Technology: ICICT 2022, London, Volume 2* (pp. 491–505). Springer Nature.

Alam, A. (2022). Cloud-based e-Learning: Scaffolding the environment for adaptive e-Learning ecosystem based on cloud computing infrastructure. In *Computer Communication, Networking and IoT: Proceedings of 5th ICICC 2021, Volume 2* (pp. 1–9). Springer Nature.

Ali, A. (2022). An overview of cloud computing for the advancement of the e-Learning process. *Journal of Theoretical and Applied Information Technology*, *100*(3), 847–855.

Al-Jammaz, R. A., Rawash, U. A., Kashef, N. M., & Ibrahim, E. M. (2023). A framework for providing augmented reality as a service provided by cloud computing for e-Learning. *International Journal on Recent and Innovation Trends in Computing and Communication*, *11*(2s), 20–31.

Arun Kumar, U., Mahendran, G., & Gobhinath, S. (2022). A review on artificial intelligence based e-Learning system. *Pervasive Computing and Social Networking: Proceedings of ICPCSN*, *2022*, 659–671.

Bernard, J., Chang, T. W., Popescu, E., & Graf, S. (2015). Using artificial neural networks to identify learning styles. In *Artificial Intelligence in Education: 17th International Conference, AIED 2015, Madrid, Spain, June 22–26, 2015. Proceedings 17* (pp. 541–544). Springer International Publishing.

Bidry, M., Ouaguid, A., & Hanine, M. (2023). Enhancing e-Learning with blockchain: Characteristics, projects, and emerging trends. *Future Internet*, *15*(9), 293.

Bora, U. J., & Ahmed, M. (2013). E-Learning using cloud computing. *International Journal of Science and Modern Engineering*, *1*(2), 9–12.

Buyya, R., Broberg, J., & Goscinski, A. M. (Eds.). (2010). *Cloud Computing: Principles and Paradigms*. John Wiley & Sons.

Dong, B., Zheng, Q., Yang, J., Li, H., & Qiao, M. (2009, July). An e-Learning ecosystem based on cloud computing infrastructure. In *2009 Ninth IEEE International Conference on Advanced Learning Technologies* (pp. 125–127). IEEE.

Eljak, H., Ibrahim, A. O., Saeed, F., Hashem, I. A. T., Abdelmaboud, A., Syed, H. J., & Elsafi, A. (2023). E-Learning based cloud computing environment: A systematic review, challenges, and opportunities. *IEEE Access*, 12, 7329–7355.

Elmasry, M. A., & Ibrahim, M. H. (2021). Cloud computing for e-Learning: A proposed model for higher education institutions in developing countries. *Article in International Journal of Scientific & Technology Research*, *10*(4), 408–416.

Fithri, D. L., Utomo, A. P., & Nugraha, F. (2020). Implementation of SaaS cloud computing services on e-Learning applications (case study: PGRI foundation school). In *Journal of Physics: Conference Series* (Vol. 1430, No. 1, p. 012049). IOP Publishing.

Geetha, J., Jayalakshmi, D. S., Naresh, E., & Sreenivasa, N. (2023). Lightweight cloud-based solution for digital education and assessment. *Science & Technology Libraries*, *43*, 1–13. 10.1080/0194262X.2023.2247460

Gligorea, I., Cioca, M., Oancea, R., Gorski, A. T., Gorski, H., & Tudorache, P. (2023). Adaptive learning using artificial intelligence in e-Learning: A literature review. *Education Sciences*, *13*(12), 1216.

Kristianto, E. (2014, August). The performance of e-Learning website on open source virtualization. In *2014 International Conference of Advanced Informatics: Concept, Theory and Application (ICAICTA)* (pp. 109–112). IEEE.

Kumar, V., & Sharma, D. (2021). E-Learning theories, components, and cloud computing-based learning platforms. *International Journal of Web-Based Learning and Teaching Technologies (IJWLTT), 16*(3), 1–16.

Liu, M., & Yu, D. (2023). Towards intelligent e-Learning systems. *Education and Information Technologies, 28*(7), 7845–7876.

Ma, X., Zong, K., & Rezaeipanah, A. (2024). Auto-scaling and computation offloading in edge/cloud computing: A fuzzy Q-learning-based approach. *Wireless Networks, 30*(2), 637–648.

Malele, V. (2023). Cybersecurity cloud-based online learning: A literature review approach. *Journal of Information Systems and Informatics, 5*(4), 1623–1632.

Mohamed, E. R. (2018). *Internet of Things in Smart Education Environment: Supportive Framework in the Decision-making Process*. John Wiley & Sons, Ltd.

Murtaza, M., Ahmed, Y., Shamsi, J. A., Sherwani, F., & Usman, M. (2022). AI-based personalized e-Learning systems: Issues, challenges, and solutions. *IEEE Access, 10*, 81323–81342.

Mystakidis, S., Christopoulos, A., &Pellas, N. (2022). A systematic mapping review of augmented reality applications to support STEM learning in higher education. *Education and Information Technologies*, 27(2), 1883–1927.

Nasr, M., & Ouf, S. (2012). A proposed smart e-Learning system using cloud computing services: PAAS, IAAS and web 3.0. *International Journal of Emerging Technologies in Learning (IJET), 7*(3), 19–24.

Pandey, A. (2023, January). E-Learning and Education 4.0: Revolution in Education of 21st Century. In *International Conference on Digital Technologies and Applications* (pp. 431–438). Springer Nature.

Sasikumar, M., Jayarin, P. J., & Vinnarasi, F. S. F. (2023). A Hierarchical Optimized Resource Utilization based Content Placement (HORCP) model for cloud Content Delivery Networks (CDNs). *Journal of Cloud Computing, 12*(1), 139.

Scalera, M., Gentile, E., Plantamura, P., & Dimauro, G. (2020). A systematic mapping study in cloud for educational innovation. *Applied Sciences, 10*(13), 4531.

Wagino, W., Maksum, H., Purwanto, W., Krismadinata, K., Suhendar, S., & Koto, R. D. (2023). Exploring the full potential of collaborative learning and e-Learning environments in universities: A systematic review. *TEM Journal, 12*(3), 1772–1178.

Wu, W., & Plakhtii, A. (2021). E-Learning based on cloud computing. *International Journal of Emerging Technologies in Learning (IJET), 16*(10), 4–17.

Zhang, W., & Zhu, Y. (2017). A new e-Learning model based on elastic cloud computing for distance education. *Eurasia Journal of Mathematics, Science and Technology Education, 13*(12), 8393–8403.

Zhao, M., Liu, W., Saif, A. N. M., Wang, B., Rupa, R. A., Islam, K. A., ... & Rahman, M. A. (2023). Blockchain in online learning: A systematic review and bibliographic visualization. *Sustainability, 15*(2), 1470.

22 Cloud-Based Secured Examination System for Collaborative Learning

Shatakshi Kokate and Urmila Shrawankar

22.1 INTRODUCTION

In the ever-changing world of education, using the newest technologies has become really important to make things work better, safer, and to help people work together more easily (Al-Hawari, 2019). This chapter talks about how one can use three types of modern technology–blockchain, fog computing, and cloud computing–to make sure examination data such as question papers, question banks with answers for framing e-question papers, scanned answer sheets, results, etc. stay safe and can be moved around securely.

Blockchain technology enables the secure storage of information, rendering it exceedingly difficult to manipulate without detection by other users (Guo & Yu, 2022). Blockchain ensures the integrity and confidentiality of exam content (Gervasiet al., 2022). This quality positions blockchain as a promising solution for tackling assurance concerns related to the privacy and security of examination data. Utilizing blockchain, one can monitor examination data transactions, ensuring only authorized access while upholding confidentiality, integrity, and availability (Sattar, 2023). Functioning as a decentralized and trusted mechanism, blockchain addresses security challenges inherent in deploying a distributed database for examination records accessed by various stakeholders such as teachers, examination departments, and students. This fortified security framework not only safeguards data but also significantly diminishes opportunities for cheating or tampering.

Contrarily, fog computing involves situating fog nodes in close proximity to examination sites. This proximity facilitates the swift processing and storage of exam data, enhancing efficiency (Kokate & Shrawankar, 2023a). Real-time analysis of information streamlines the exam process. In the envisioned system, fog nodes are categorized into primary and backup nodes (Kausar et al., 2020). Primary nodes generate and validate examination data blocks using a consensus mechanism (Rani & Bhambay, 2022), while backup nodes verify and integrate new blocks into the existing blockchain.

DOI: 10.1201/9781003472537-26

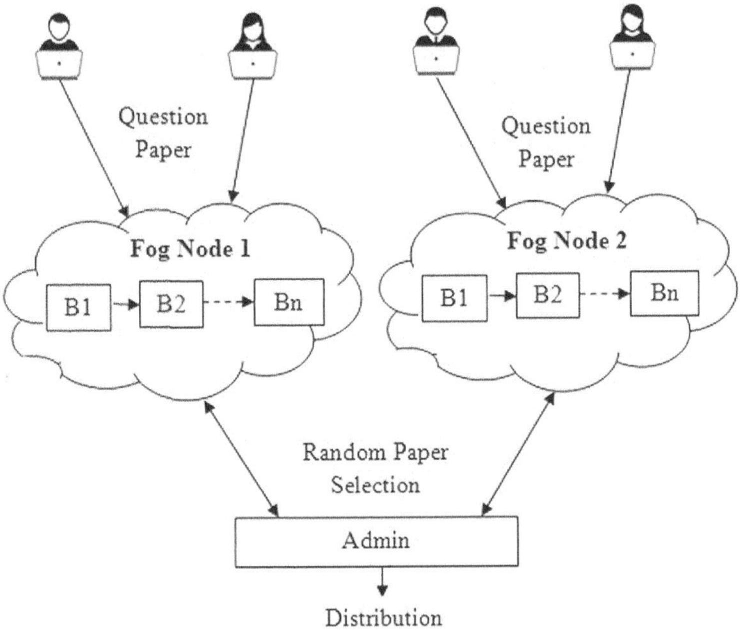

FIGURE 22.1 Securing Question Paper Using Fog and Blockchain.

Furthermore, ensuring the long-term security and accessibility of examination data is imperative for authorized personnel. Cloud computing plays a pivotal role in this endeavor, providing a secure means to store and access exam papers, answer sheets, and results (Kokate & Shrawankar, 2023b). Integration of the cloud with blockchain enhances the security and efficiency of data management in smart systems (Shrawankar, 2022). It can handle large amounts of data even when there are lots of exams happening at once.

Therefore, the objective of this chapter is to elucidate the collaborative functionality of these three technologies in ensuring the security and seamless operation of exams. Figure 22.1 illustrates an example of how fog and blockchain technologies collaborate to enhance the security of question papers set by multiple examiners. Question papers from diverse examiners are transmitted to the fog nodes, where they are compiled into blocks and integrated into the blockchain. During the examination, the Controller of Examination (Admin) randomly selects a question paper from the blockchain and distributes it to the students.

By exploring the synergies of these technologies, educational institutions can not only enhance the security and integrity of their assessment processes but also lay the foundation for smart education and collaborative learning environments.

22.2 LIMITATION OF EXISTING SYSTEM

While the existing systems for managing examination materials often serve their purpose adequately, they are not without their limitations. Some of the key limitations include:

1. **Security Vulnerabilities:** Traditional systems may be susceptible to security breaches, data manipulation, and unauthorized access. Without robust encryption and authentication mechanisms, sensitive examination materials could be compromised, leading to integrity issues and concerns regarding the fairness of assessments.
2. **Centralization Concerns:** Many existing systems rely on centralized servers for data storage and processing, which can pose risks in terms of single points of failure and potential bottlenecks. Centralization also makes systems more susceptible to targeted attacks or disruptions, impacting the reliability and availability of examination materials.
3. **Scalability Challenges:** As the volume of examination materials continues to grow, traditional systems may struggle to scale effectively to meet increasing demand. This could result in performance degradation, longer processing times, and potential delays in assessment workflows, especially during peak periods.
4. **Limited Transparency:** Without transparent and auditable processes, stakeholders such as students, educators, and administrators may lack visibility into the entire examination lifecycle. This could lead to distrust in the system and concerns about the fairness and validity of assessment outcomes.
5. **Infrastructure Dependency:** Existing systems often rely heavily on on-premises infrastructure, which can be costly to maintain and upgrade. Additionally, dependence on specific hardware and software configurations may limit flexibility and hinder the adoption of emerging technologies.
6. **Data Fragmentation:** Examination materials are typically stored in various formats and locations, leading to data fragmentation and potential inconsistencies. This fragmentation can make it challenging to maintain data integrity, track changes, and ensure seamless collaboration among stakeholders.
7. **Limited Interoperability:** Lack of standardized formats and protocols may hinder interoperability between different systems and platforms. This could lead to inefficiencies in data exchange, integration challenges, and barriers to seamless communication among disparate systems.

Addressing these limitations requires a holistic approach that leverages emerging technologies such as blockchain, fog computing, and cloud computing to create a more secure, scalable, and transparent framework for managing examination materials. By mitigating these limitations, educational institutions can enhance the integrity of their assessment processes and better support the needs of students, educators, and administrators alike.

22.3 SYSTEM ARCHITECTURE

Figure 22.2 depicts the system architecture of a secured examination system within the context of "Cloud Computing for Smart Education and Collaborative Learning." The architecture is structured into three distinct layers: the exam data preparation layer, the fog computing layer integrated with blockchain technology, and the cloud computing layer.

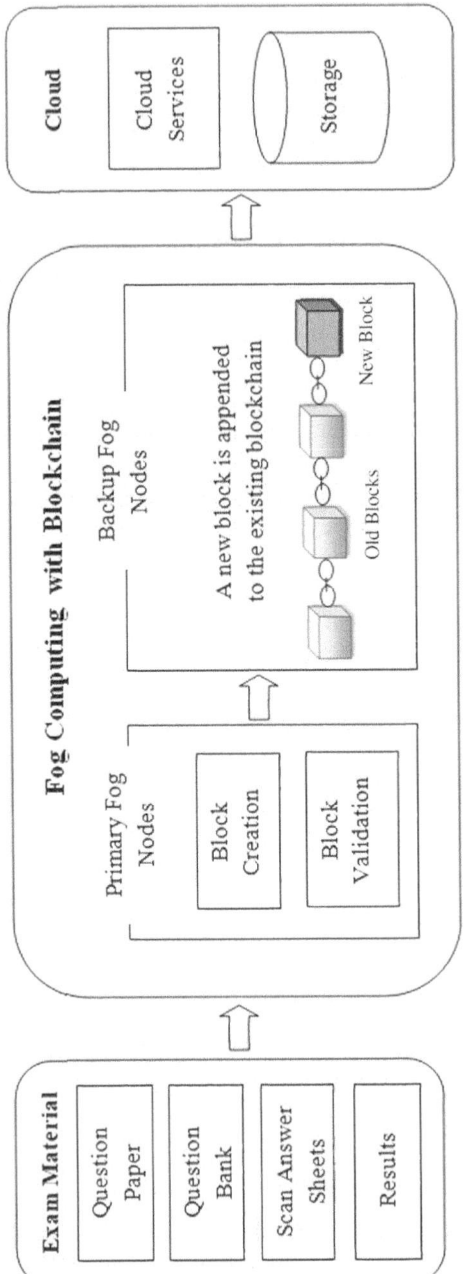

FIGURE 22.2 System Architecture of Proposed System.

Each layer plays a critical role in ensuring the security, integrity, and availability of examination data.

22.3.1 Exam Data Preparation Layer

The first layer is responsible for the preparation and initial handling of examination data. This includes:

- **Test Papers:** These are the structured documents containing the exam questions to be distributed to students.
- **Question Banks:** A repository of potential questions that can be dynamically selected and organized into test papers.
- **Scanned Answer Sheets:** Digital versions of students' handwritten responses, which are scanned and stored for further processing.
- **Results:** The processed scores and evaluations are based on the student's submitted answer sheets.

This data is initially prepared and then transmitted to the next layer for secure handling and processing.

22.3.2 Fog Computing Layer with Blockchain Integration

The second layer is the **Fog Computing Layer**, which incorporates blockchain technology to enhance security and reliability. This layer consists of multiple nodes, categorized as primary and backup nodes.

1. **Primary Fog Nodes:**
   - **Block Creation:** The primary node receives the prepared exam data from the previous layer.
   - **Validation:** The primary node constructs a new block with the received data and initiates a validation process using a consensus mechanism to ensure data integrity and authenticity.
2. **Backup Fog Nodes:**
   - **Blockchain Formation:** Once the block is validated by the primary node, it is forwarded to the backup nodes.
   - **Appending to Blockchain:** The backup nodes append the newly created block to the existing chain of blocks, thereby forming an immutable blockchain that records all transactions and modifications securely.

This decentralized approach ensures that even if one node fails, the system remains operational, and the data remains secure.

22.3.3 Cloud Computing Layer

The third layer is the Cloud Computing Layer, which is responsible for long-term data storage and additional processing capabilities. This layer receives the blockchain from the fog computing layer to ensure the persistence and availability of examination data. The cloud services offer scalable storage solutions and additional processing power, which can be utilized for various educational and administrative purposes.

- **Storage:** The entire blockchain, which includes all examination-related data, is securely stored in the cloud.
- **Cloud Services:** These services provide enhanced data retrieval, analytics, and reporting functionalities, which are crucial for managing large-scale educational environments.

In summary, this architecture ensures a secure, reliable, and efficient system for handling examination data within a smart education framework. By leveraging blockchain technology within a fog computing layer, the system achieves high levels of security and integrity, while the cloud computing layer provides scalability and long-term data retention. This integrated approach supports collaborative learning by ensuring that examination processes are transparent, secure, and accessible.

22.4 BLOCK CREATION

The steps involved in block creation in a blockchain are as follows:

1. **Data Collection:** Gather the data that needs to be stored in the blockchain. This could be any kind of information, such as transactions, records, or any other data.
2. **Block Formation:** Take the collected data and organize it into a block. A block typically consists of the data to be stored, a timestamp, and a hash of the previous block (except for the first block, which is called the genesis block).
3. **Hashing:** Apply a cryptographic hash function to the block. This function takes the data in the block and converts it into hash–a fixed-size string of characters that represent the block contents.
4. **Validation:** The block is legitimate and has not been tampered with. Validation is usually done through a consensus mechanism, where nodes in the network agree that the block is valid.
5. **Adding to the Chain:** After validation, the block is added to the blockchain. This involves linking the new block to the previous block in the chain using its hash. This linkage ensures the integrity and chronological order of the blocks in the blockchain.
6. **Broadcasting:** Once added to the blockchain, the new block is broadcasted to all nodes in the network so that they can update their copies of the blockchain.
7. **Confirmation:** Finally, the block is confirmed, meaning that it is considered a permanent part of the blockchain. Confirmation typically occurs after a certain number of subsequent blocks have been added to the chain, ensuring that the block is unlikely to be reversed or altered.

22.5 BLOCK VALIDATION

The steps involved in block validation using a consensus mechanism are as follows:

1. **Proposal:** The primary fog node proposes a new block containing examination data.
2. **Verification:** Other fog nodes (participants) in the network verify the proposed block to ensure it follows the rules of the network. They check things like whether the transactions are valid and whether the block was created by the right person.
3. **Agreement:** Participants come to an agreement about whether the proposed block is valid or not. This agreement is reached through a consensus mechanism, where everyone follows a set of rules to decide together.
4. **Consensus Reached:** Once a majority of participants agree that the block is valid, it is accepted into the blockchain. If there is disagreement, the process might continue until a consensus is reached or the block is rejected.
5. **Block Added:** The verified block is appended to the blockchain and becomes part of the ledger.
6. **Communication:** The decision about the validity of the block is communicated to all participants in the network so that they can update their copies of the blockchain accordingly.
7. **Continuation:** The process continues with the next proposed block, maintaining the integrity and security of the blockchain network.

22.6 RESULTS

The proposed framework operates within real-time scenarios where teachers construct question papers or question banks alongside answers. Furthermore, after examinations, teachers assess scanned answer sheets, with results being automatically generated thereafter. To ensure data integrity, the SHA256 algorithm is utilized for hash value creation, while the Proof of Sequential Work algorithm validates blocks. Implementation of the proposed system is carried out using the Java programming language.

In establishing the fog nodes, an open-source distributed event streaming platform, Apache Kafka, is employed. Additionally, the Kaleido platform is employedto streamline the deployment and management of blockchain networks. The system undergoes evaluation with various input data sizes, including 282 KB, 675 KB, 1338 KB, and 2589 KB. The outcomes of implementing the proposed system are summarized in Table 22.1, indicating that with an increase in data size, both throughput and accuracy experience enhancements.

22.7 ADVANTAGES OF THE PROPOSED SYSTEM

The advantages of the proposed secured examination system include:

1. **TamperResistance:** Blockchain technology ensures an immutable and transparent record of all transactions and interactions within the examination

TABLE 22.1
Outcomes of Proposed System

Data Size (KB)	Execution Time (msec)	Throughput (byte/msec)	Fog Processing Delay (msec)	Accuracy (%)	Data Size (KB)
282	12.38	22.19	6.25	85	282
675	18.73	35.64	7.81	88	675
1338	39.42	33.90	9.37	92	1338
2589	51.24	38.21	10.56	95	2589

process. This prevents unauthorized access and manipulation of examination materials, safeguarding the integrity of the assessment process.

2. **Data Integrity:** By leveraging blockchain's cryptographic features, the system guarantees the authenticity and integrity of examination materials, including question paper sets and answer sheets. This instills trust in the examination results and prevents any form of data tampering or alteration.
3. **Transparent Audit Trail:** The use of blockchain creates a transparent audit trail of all examination-related activities, from the creation of question papers to the assessment of answer sheets. This transparency enhances accountability and allows stakeholders to track the entire examination process in realtime.
4. **Increased Trust:** The implementation of a secured examination system instills confidence among stakeholders, including students, educators, and educational institutions. Knowing that examination materials are securely managed and protected against tampering builds trust in the fairness and reliability of the assessment process.
5. **Prevention of Cheating:** With enhanced security measures in place, such as encrypted storage and tamper-resistant records, the system reduces the likelihood of cheating or academic dishonesty during examinations. This upholds academic integrity and ensures that assessment outcomes accurately reflect students' knowledge and abilities.

Overall, the secured examination system not only protects sensitive examination data but also fosters trust, transparency, and fairness in the assessment process, ultimately contributing to the quality and credibility of education.

22.8 SUMMARY

This chapter investigates the pivotal role of blockchain, fog computing, and cloud computing in securely managing examination data for smart education and collaborative learning. Blockchain technology ensures an immutable and transparent record, fortifying content integrity and thwarting unauthorized access. Fog computing optimizes data processing and storage at the network's edge, facilitating real-time analysis and seamless data transfer. Cloud computing provides scalable and reliable storage solutions for examination data, ensuring accessibility and security. Together, these technologies enhance the efficiency, security, and integrity of the examination process. By integrating blockchain, fog computing, and cloud computing, educational institutions can establish a robust framework for securely managing examination materials, paving the way for smarter education and collaborative learning environments.

REFERENCES

Al-Hawari, Feras, et al. "Integrated and secure web-based examination management system." *Computer Applications in Engineering Education* 27, no. 4 (2019): 994–1014. https://doi.org/10.1002/cae.9.

Gervasi, Osvaldo,Damiano Perri, and Marco Simonetti. "Strategies and system implementations for secure electronic written exams." *IEEE Access* 10 (2022): 20559–20570. https://doi.org/10.1109/ACCESS.2022.3150860.

Guo, Huaqun, and Xingjie Yu. "A survey on blockchain technology and its security." *Blockchain: Research and Applications* 3, no. 2 (2022): 100067. https://doi.org/10.1016/j.bcra.2022.100067.

Kausar, Samina, et al. "Fog-assisted secure data exchange for examination and testing in E-learning system." *Mobile Networks and Applications* 28 (2020): 1–17. https://doi.org/10.1007/s11036-019-01429-x.

Kokate, Shatakshi, and Urmila Shrawankar. "An efficient approach for secured data transmission between IoT and cloud."*Research Reports on Computer Science* 2, no. 3(2023a): 35–44. https://doi.org/10.37256/rrcs.2320232628.

Kokate, Shatakshi, and Urmila Shrawankar. "Integration of the cloud with fog computing to secure data." In *Integration of Cloud Computing with Emerging Technologies: Issues, Challenges, and Practices.* Boca Raton, FL: CRC Press, 2023b, 83–92. https://doi.org/10.1201/9781003341437.

Rani, Poonam, and Rajul Bhambay. "A comparative survey of consensus algorithms based on proof of work." In *Emerging Technologies in Data Mining and Information Security: Proceedings of IEMIS 2022, Volume 1.* Singapore: Springer Nature Singapore, 2022. 261–268. https://doi.org/10.1007/978-981-19-4193-1_25.

Sattar, Md Rahat Ibne, et al. "An advanced and secure framework for conducting online examination using blockchain method." *Cyber Security and Applications* 1 (2023): 100005. https://doi.org/10.1016/j.csa.2022.100005.

Shrawankar, Chaitreya. *Blockchain for Smart Systems: Computing Technologies and Applications: BlockCloud: Blockchain as a Cloud Service.* Boca Raton, FL: Chapman and Hall/CRC, 2022.

23 Role of Educational Clouds in the Transformation of Higher Education

Bhargavi S. Chinchmalatpure and
Swati S. Sherekar

23.1 INTRODUCTION

With a diverse population and varied educational needs, the adoption of advanced cloud technologies becomes imperative for bridging gaps and providing quality learning experiences. The pandemic accelerated the adoption of cloud computing, marking it as a highly sought-after and rapidly advancing field within the modern IT landscape (Asadi Kostadinova, 2019). The integration of cloud technologies into education is gaining popularity and offers numerous benefits for educational institutions, teachers, and students.

These suites offer enterprise-grade solutions that are simple, easy to use, and employ a pay-as-you-grow model to help institutes achieve their business goals and facilitate growth. There has been a significant increase in the use of cloud communication platforms in the Indian EdTech ecosystem, transforming traditional classrooms into virtual learning environments (Joshi et al., 2024). Virtual classrooms foster collaborative learning experiences, promoting engagement and participation. To connect the country seamlessly, we use various platforms like Zoom, Microsoft Teams, Google Meet, etc. to facilitate real-time collaboration, enabling educators and students across the world. The scalability and cost-effectiveness of cloud communication infrastructure are particularly advantageous for Indian educational institutions that want to offer their services to students across geographies (Papadopoulou et al., 2022). Cloud-based platforms have shown tremendous promise to enhance the teaching process, allowing educators to create engaging content, conduct online tests, and communicate with students efficiently.

The educational cloud allows students and teachers to utilize learning resources at their convenience, eliminating geographical constraints (Mustafa et al., 2022). It provides automatic updates and facilitates seamless note-sharing, enhancing data safety and information exchange efficiency. The way forward is that cloud technologies are revolutionizing education, promoting competitiveness, and reducing both time and costs for all stakeholders. The education industry involves embracing the rising

 DOI: 10.1201/9781003472537-27

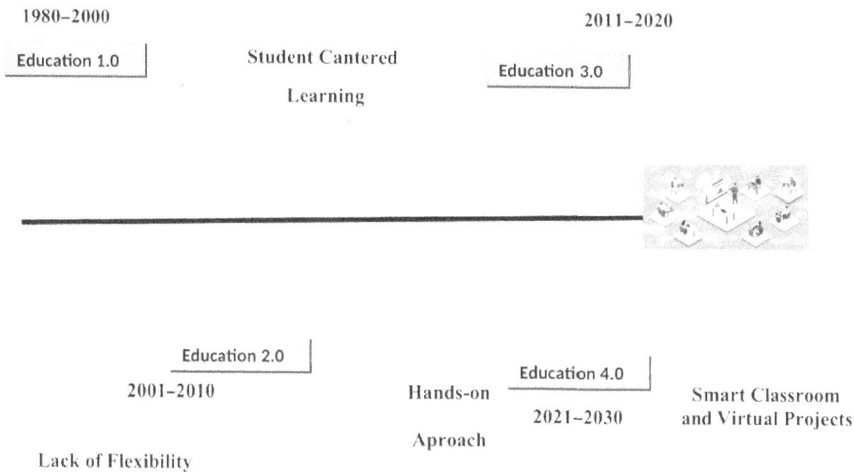

FIGURE 23.1 Classroom Revolution – Figure shows development of online study pattern using new technology with different years.

accessibility of the internet and adopting critical strategies. Cloud-based platforms simplify the admission process, enhancing transparency and creating a stress-free onboarding experience. Streamlining communication on exam schedules, homework, assignments, and progress updates is essential to optimize student engagement (Shi et al., 2022). Prioritizing cyber security and establishing strong security measures is vital to safeguard student data and maintain trust in the face of rising cyber threats. Collaboration and communication tools supported by robust network and cyber-security protocols are keys to creating a secure and connected campus. The future of cloud communication in the Indian EdTech sector is poised for continued growth and innovation.

In Figure 23.1, with the arrival of COVID-19 suddenly the classroom concept has been converted into an online pattern. When the study pattern came online, people adapted to the online system and used new technologies. Education has seen significant changes because of the combination of technology and the classroom (Muralidharan et al., 2022). Due to online patterns, student learning strategies have been totally changed so they may perform their task from anywhere without any dependence on teacher physical assistance in 2030. In cloud computing, access methods and the cost change as cloud is introduced in the infrastructure as compared to traditional educational structure. Cloud computing can be considered as a virtual hosting platform. Instead of expending capital on physical resources, all the servers, software, or networks can be hosted on the cloud to make the infrastructure less tedious.

23.2 CLOUD COMPUTING IN EDUCATION SECTOR

In the traditional education system, some problems happen, like a lack of teachers, lab facilities, latest books, infrastructure, etc. Because of these, cloud computing technology offers solutions for the above problems in the education system. It enables

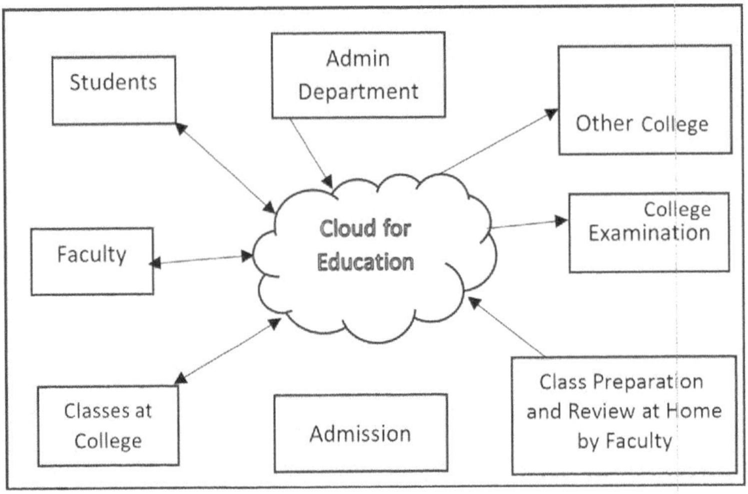

FIGURE 23.2 Implementation of Cloud Technology in Education – use of cloud technology in the educational field in different aspects.

users to control and access data via the internet. The main users of a typical higher education cloud include students, Faculty, Administrative department, Examination department, and Admission, as shown in Figure 23.2.

Cloud is connected to all the main users of the institution. Each and all users have a separate login for their respective work. Various class Tutorials, Assignments, Tests, Notes, and other Video lectures on the cloud server can be uploaded by their faculties, which can be accessed anywhere and at any time by the students. The education system will make it possible for faculties to identify problem areas in which students make mistakes by analyzing students' study records. So, faculties can improve teaching materials and methods. This will not only make it possible for students to use online teaching materials during class, but they will also be able to access these materials at home, using them to prepare for and review lessons (Venkatraman et al., 2022). Utilization of cloud computing systems in education will reduce the cost of operation because servers and learning materials are shared with another institute.

23.3 SMART CLASSROOMS: RECENT TRENDS IN THE EDUCATION SECTOR

A learning management system offers an online learning environment where students can study whenever and wherever they want without being constrained by time or location. Total duration started as the traditional era of teaching adopted with minor technologies from 1980 and placed with a new generation. Localization, transcription, text-to-speech, and personalization are increasing the impact and reach of online learning content (Yang et al., 2022). Table 23.1 shows how beneficial cloud computing is in higher education based on various parameters.

TABLE 23.1
Study of Cloud Technologies

Parameters	Monitoring	Communication unit	Technical unit
Institution	Monitoring unit deals with the course schedule.	Communication unit with answering students' questions	Technical unit explores digitizing course materials and supporting teachers in recording their video lectures.
Presidency	Monitoring explains the daily exchanges with the ministry.	Communication unit maintaining press release and coordination with the entire operation	Technical unit creates the academic address and monitors the quality of the network.
Others	Posting assignments	Posting lecture notes	Posting assessment marks and discussions with students

Many school districts employ cloud computing technologies to find more cost-effective methods to integrate technology in the classroom. The modern classroom has made cloud technology focus on professional development courses. Cloud-based computing in the smart classroom includes major terms like virtual classroom, secure data, collaboration, automation, speed of innovation, etc. Additionally, cloud computing provides software solutions to manage a number of the typical chores completed by instructors and school management, freeing up time for more imaginative activities. Apart from this, the architecture of cloud computing includes a couple of groups of Service Oriented Architecture (SOA) and Event Driven Architecture (EDA) (Kumari et al., 2024). To know the betterment of cloud technology, Figure 23.3 shows details about the scope of cloud computing in implementation and restriction in classroom architecture.

23.4 THE IMPACT OF CLOUD TECHNOLOGY IN HIGHER EDUCATION

There are various ways in which a cloud-based data management system and the technology as a whole are transforming the world of higher education. It explores the various benefits of migrating to the cloud and explains why it is slowly becoming the norm worldwide.

23.4.1 Cloud Technology Help to Use Resources More Efficiently

Cloud technologies provide computing power and data management tools on demand, which constitutes the most crucial benefit. Cloud technology is helping institutes to access research material, add, store, or manage data, etc., as well as assists operations a lot more efficiently. Cloud technology is thereby saving institutes a great deal of money and time.

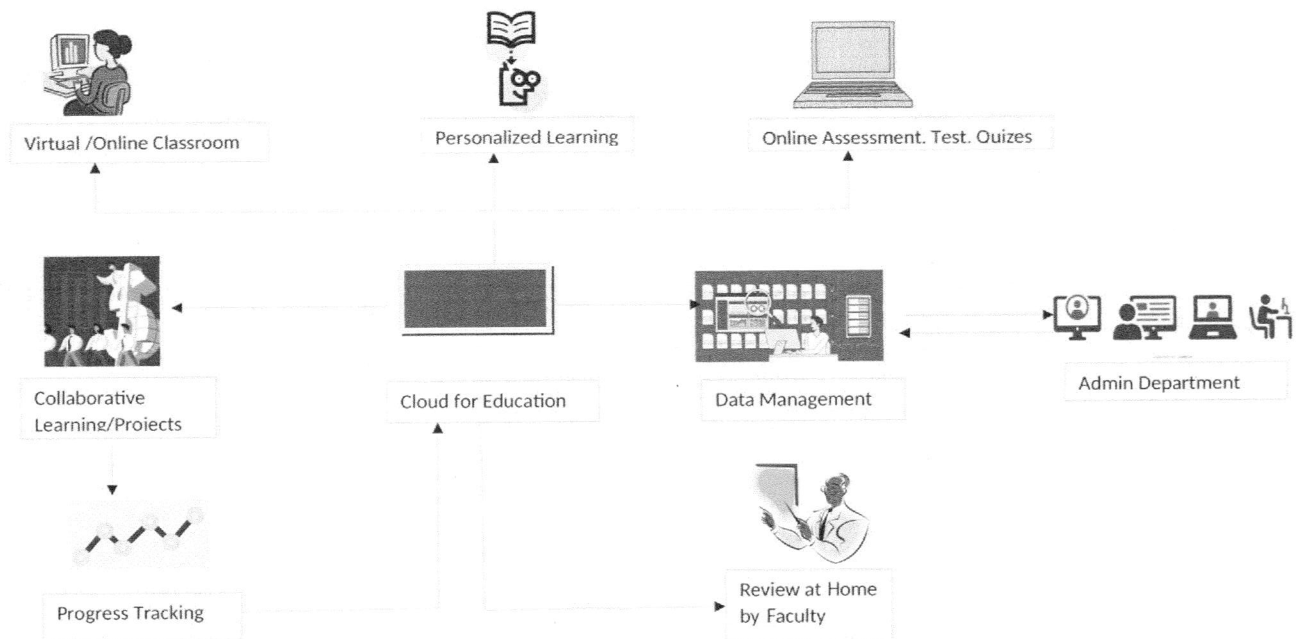

FIGURE 23.3 Cloud Computing in Classroom – various tasks done by technology in the education center.

23.4.2 Cloud Technology Helps Reduce IT Costs Overall

While institutes worldwide were adapting to electronic or digital means of streamlining their operations, the pandemic forced them into adopting cloud technology. This adoption of cloud computing might have been a sudden move for many, but it has the potential to help higher education institutes save considerable IT costs. Survey shows cloud technology can help companies save as much as 10% in IT costs, which adds up to a considerable amount. By eliminating personnel to maintain servers and hardware, repair, and purchase new equipment, cloud technology helps cut down on several such costs.

23.4.3 Cloud Transformation Can Help Improve Cyber-Security Mechanisms

One of the biggest concerns when storing large amounts of data electronically or digitally is that they can often be prone to cyber-security risks. With cybercrime rates rising over the past couple of years, cloud computing for education makes a whole lot of sense.

The cost of cybercrimes is estimated to reach $10.5 trillion by 2025, significantly higher than $6 trillion in 2022, making it ever so crucial to take the necessary measures to prevent such risks. The increasing risk of cyber-attacks is also pronounced in situations where higher education institutes do not receive adequate funding, which places them at greater risk and reduces their chances of a swift recovery if they are to be attacked.

23.4.4 Cloud Services Offer Immense Flexibility and Scalability

Another key benefit of cloud services for higher education is that they offer great flexibility and scalability. Unlike on-premises servers that can often find it tricky to keep up with a sudden influx of data, especially during registrations for new programs and so on, cloud systems handle these operations seamlessly. It helps save a great deal of infrastructural costs.

23.4.5 Cloud Transformation Allows Data To Be Accessed Anytime, Anywhere

With a cloud transformation strategy in place, the various stakeholders in higher education institutes benefit to a great degree from accessing information and data regardless of where they are. With individual login credentials, students, teachers, and administrative members can access logistical data, personal data, research material, and so on from anywhere in the world. It comes in handy, especially during times of crisis when people are forced to stay home but continue studying or working, such as during the recent pandemic.

23.4.6 Cloud Transformation Helps Prepare Students for the Workforce

Last but not least, a cloud-based learning management system helps prepare students pursuing their higher education for their careers in the workforce. With industries across the spectrum adopting technology like never before, it is becoming increasingly essential that individuals entering the workforce possess the skills to leverage this technology to produce the best results (Gharibvand et al., 2024).

23.5 TRANSFORMING EDUCATION USING CLOUD

> "As technology changes the way we communicate, connect, create, consume, and innovate, it is democratizing access to opportunity. Education is no exception."
>
> – Laura Andreessen

In the traditional approach, the organizations would go for an on-premises data center to host and access the various applications. Organizations would maintain the data center, including all the infrastructure and resources. Cloud is beneficial for moving all the applications and data from local servers to remote servers, which can be accessed using the internet. Because of this, it makes IT operations more agile and cost-effective.

Educational institutions are also gearing up for the adoption of the cloud. According to a paper published in the *Indian Journal of Science and Technology*, in North America, about 70% of higher educational institutions have adopted (or are adopting) their email frameworks to the cloud. Nearly 50% have taken up a cloud-based framework of collaboration to enhance the sharing of data across campuses.

There are multiple advantages of cloud adoption in education. Below are some key reasons why educational institutions are shifting gears toward cloud-based solutions:

23.5.1 Cost-Effectiveness and Scalability

In the cloud-based model, there are no heavy upfront investments in hardware and software licenses. Cloud services operate on a pay-as-you-go model, scaling resources up or down seamlessly to meet fluctuating needs. It offers cost savings and avoids the burden of over-provisioning on-premises infrastructure.

23.5.2 Enhanced Accessibility and Collaboration

Students and educators can access resources and collaborate in real time from anywhere, anytime, fostering remote learning opportunities. Google Docs and Microsoft Teams empower teamwork, while various cloud-based tools offer document sharing and seamless communication, creating a more connected learning environment.

23.5.3 Streamlined Operations and Management

Various operations such as server maintenance, backups, and upgrades, freeing up IT staff for strategic tasks, and improving operational efficiency are taken care of by cloud service providers. Automated processes like user provisioning and application deployment further streamline operations, minimizing errors and saving valuable time.

23.5.4 Advanced Technology and Innovation

The cloud opens doors to a plethora of innovative technologies like artificial intelligence (AI)-powered learning platforms, immersive virtual reality experiences, and data-driven analytics tools. These advancements personalize learning, enhance understanding, and provide valuable insights to inform data-driven decisions that optimize educational practices.

These advantages are leading to growth in the adoption of cloud computing. According to one website, the global cloud computing market is expected to grow from USD 626.4 billion in 2033 to USD 1266.4 billion in 2028 at a compound annual growth rate (CAGR) of 15.1% (Asadi et al., 2020). In a one-serve, the cloud computing market size in the education sector was valued at USD 23.81 billion in 2021 and is projected to reach USD 173.62 billion by 2030, growing at a CAGR of 24.70% from 2022 to 2030.

23.6 MIGRATING TO THE CLOUD

For migrating to the cloud and making it a successful implementation require planning, technology provider, change management, and training. It is not an easy and overnight task.

- **Planning:** Create a phased plan for migrating data, applications, and services to the cloud, considering security, training, and change management aspects. Start small and scale gradually to gain confidence and mitigate risks.
- **Choose the Right Partner**: Select a reputable cloud provider with a strong track record in education and the specific services required, such as robust security, compliance features, and data privacy protection.
- **Training and Support**: Equip faculty, staff, and students with the necessary skills and knowledge to utilize cloud-based tools effectively. This will ensure smooth adoption and maximize the benefits of the transition.
- **Monitor and Optimize:** Continuously monitor cloud usage and performance to identify areas for optimization and cost savings. Be open to adjusting strategy and adapting to new technologies as the cloud landscape evolves.

By migrating to the cloud, educational institutions can unlock a world of possibilities, creating a more accessible, collaborative, and innovative learning ecosystem for every student, educator, and administrator. It will lay the foundation for digital transformation, enabling Student Information Systems, Learning Management Systems, AI, Reporting, Analytics, etc.

23.7 CLOUD COMPUTING USED IN HIGHER EDUCATION

Cloud computing services are used in higher education to manage administrative, educational, and IT data and services. The education industry has trusted legacy on-premises data centers and servers. Cloud computing allows institutions to modernize their tech stack, improve efficiency, and earn long-term cost savings. In higher education, cloud services benefit students, faculty, and staff, in addition to streamlining IT processes and data management. Those institutions that invest in cloud computing education often see the benefits discussed below.

23.7.1 Cloud Improves IT Management and Efficiency

Managing and maintaining on-premises infrastructure leave IT professionals with little extra time. Cloud simplifies and streamlines IT management, freeing your team to focus on strategy rather than routine maintenance. Cloud providers use a shared responsibility model, which means they share security responsibilities with your internal team. Earn long-term cost-saving. On-site hardware and software expenses span everything from upfront costs to personnel maintenance fees, leases, and utilities. Unexpected issues like broken equipment can lead to additional costs. Additionally, if you need more data storage, you will likely need to buy more hardware as well. Because cloud applications can run on web browsers, users do not need to pay extra cash for specific devices to use them, either. For budget-conscious industries like higher education, this makes the cloud the most cost-effective choice in the long run.

23.7.2 Cloud Enhances Cyber Security and Business Continuity

The data stored by higher education institutions makes them prime targets for cyber-attacks. Storing all information on a hard drive leaves it vulnerable to theft and other disasters. On-premises data centers run into similar issues with data backups and disaster recovery. Storing data in the cloud, on the other hand, considerably reduces these risks. Most cloud vendors automatically perform data backups at least once per day and have robust disaster recovery plans. In the case of an incident, infrastructure and data recovery are faster, sometimes even instantaneous. As a result, organizations can quickly resume operations and keep data loss to a minimum.

23.7.3 Cloud Gains Scalability and Flexibility

Scaling on-premises servers can be costly and time-consuming. It is difficult for these systems to keep up with sudden changes, like a rush of demand during course registration. The cloud can automatically shrink or expand alongside your operational needs. Due to its elastic nature, cloud services give the higher education industry the ability to meet changing traffic or data storage needs. Also, as cloud services bill by usage, you only pay for what you need.

23.7.4 Cloud Computing Collaborates More Effectively

Cloud computing in education enables real-time communication and collaboration with students, faculty, and staff, facilitating collaboration with each other, even if they are spread across the globe, because data is stored in the cloud rather than on specific devices.

23.7.5 Cloud Computing Leverages Data to Drive Outcomes

Cloud computing collaborates with machine learning, AI, and predictive analytics to drive organizational goals. These can give you insights into student engagement and retention and ultimately allow you to deliver a personalized learning experience.

23.8 WHAT ARE THE BENEFITS OF CLOUD COMPUTING IN HIGHER EDUCATION FOR STUDENTS AND FACULTY?

Cloud services provide benefits to students and faculty administrators in the education field. Cloud provides various benefits in education, such as:

- **Accelerates academic research**
  Cloud computing in higher education has the power to process complex workloads and store large amounts of data. Researchers get more time to dedicate to research, speeding up innovation and time to insights.
- **Increases accessibility**
  Students and faculty can access digital resources through the cloud, which improves access to educational materials while reducing paper waste and eliminating the need for expensive physical textbooks. Cloud-based applications provide more affordable access with monthly subscriptions that students only need to pay for the duration of the course.
- **Powers virtual learning**
  Due to the pandemic, most universities now offer some form of virtual learning. As more students turn to e-learning, higher education needs to meet their needs. Higher education can shift to fully remote instruction and offer on-demand courses that let students study when it best suits their schedule only because of the cloud.
- **Augments learning experiences**
  Cloud learning platforms allow you to augment traditional education with the hottest topics and skill sets. This includes virtual computer labs, hands-on cloud sandboxes, and other experiences.
- **Requires minimal hardware**
  Once all the learning resources have moved to the cloud, educational institutions no longer have to maintain elaborate hardware on campus. All the hardware required to run the learning infrastructure is entirely managed by the cloud

service provider (CSP). This results in saving fixed, operational, and administrative costs. There is some degree of monotony to learning, which tends to reduce the motivation of students. Learning resources over the cloud can be diversified into multiple mediums, such as videos, quizzes, online assignments, and much more. This would make the learning process fun and more engaging for students over the long term.

- **Offers parental integration**
  With the availability of all learning resources over the cloud, the parents or guardians of students can be integrated with the student's progress. They can enjoy real-time access to the academic progress of their children and intervene if, when, and wherever required.
- **Helps in higher education**
  Most professionals fail to pursue higher education due to financial constraints and a growing compulsion to become financially self-sufficient. Education over the cloud infrastructure provides professionals to now enhance their academic and professional credentials by pursuing advanced-level studies, courses, training, and degree programs over the cloud. This will be a great value addition for ambitious professionals in various walks of life.

In cloud-based solutions, all hardware is the sole responsibility of the CSP. This relieves the deploying educational institution from procuring and maintaining expensive hardware in-house. In this way, such entities can focus more on their core domain of imparting knowledge (Singh, 2021). Cloud computing is transforming the education sector in several ways. The true results of a cloud-enabled learning environment will be possible once more educational institutions embrace the cloud.

23.9 CONCLUSION

The role of educational clouds in the transformation of higher education is undeniable, as they offer numerous benefits and opportunities for both educators and students. Through educational clouds, institutions can harness the power of cloud computing technology to enhance teaching and learning experiences, facilitate collaboration, and improve access to educational resources.

One of the key advantages of educational clouds is their ability to provide anytime, anywhere access to learning materials and tools, allowing students to engage in learning activities at their own pace and convenience. This flexibility is particularly beneficial for non-traditional students, such as working professionals or those with family commitments, who may not be able to attend traditional classes on campus.

Additionally, educational clouds enable educators to create and deliver innovative teaching materials, such as interactive multimedia content and virtual simulations, which enhance student engagement and comprehension. These resources can be easily shared and accessed across multiple devices, making it easier for students to collaborate with peers and participate in group projects. The cloud-based solutions are highly conducive for sectors such as education. Both the parties to this transaction, namely education providers and seekers, can hugely benefit from the cloud. It is imperative that more educational institutions migrate to the cloud and reap the benefits thereof.

Furthermore, educational clouds support data-driven decision-making by providing institutions with valuable insights into student learning behaviors and performance metrics. By analyzing this data, educators can identify areas for improvement and tailor instructional strategies to better meet the needs of individual students. Adopting cloud computing for education alone is not enough to ensure cyber security. Higher education also needs to invest time into maintaining security policies, creating their own data backup and disaster recovery plans, and implementing multi-factor authentication.

Overall, the transformational impact of educational clouds on higher education is profound, empowering institutions to deliver high-quality education that is accessible, engaging, and personalized to the needs of diverse learners. As technology continues to evolve, educational clouds will undoubtedly play an increasingly important role in shaping the future of higher education.

REFERENCES

Asadi, Z., Abdekhoda, M., and Nadrian, H., 2020, Jan., *"Cloud computing services adoption among higher education faculties: Development of a standardized questionnaire," Education and Information Technologies*, vol. 25, no. 1, page no. 175–191.

Gharibvand, V., Kolamroudi, M., Zeeshan, Q., Çınar, Z., Sahmani, S., Asmael, M., and Safaei, B., 2024, *"Cloud based manufacturing: A review of recent developments in architectures, technologies, infrastructures, platforms and associated challenges," The International Journal of Advanced Manufacturing Technology*, vol. 131, page no. 93–123. 10.1007/s00170-024-12989-y.

Joshi, Era Kapil, Rajesh Kumar, Salil Bharany, Dilip Kumar Jang Bahadur Saini, Rajiv Kumar, Ashraf Osman Ibrahim, Abdelzahir Abdelmaboud, Wamda Nagmeldin, and Mohammad Awad Medani, 2024, *"Exploring the connectivity between Education 4.0 and Classroom 4.0: Technologies, Student Perspectives, and Engagement in the Digital," IEEE*, vol. 12, page no. 24179–24204.

Kostadinova, Irina. 2019, *"Digital Models for Transformation of Corporate Social Responsibility Education,"* in *29th Annual Conference of the European Association for Education in Electrical and Information Engineering (EAEEIE)*, Page No. 1–5, 978-1-7281-3222-8.2019.

Muralidharan, K., K. Shanmugan, and Y. Klochkov, 2022, Jan., *"The new education policy 2020, digitalization and quality of life in India: Some reflections," Education Sciences*, vol. 12, no. 2, page no. 75.

Mustafa, D., I. G. Mustafa, S. Zriqat, and Q. Al Thebyan, *"Smart Assistive 3D Tool to Remedy Children's Learning Difficulties for Distance Education,"* in *Proceedings of the International Arab Conference on Information Technology (ACIT)*, page no. 1–5, Nov.979-8-3503-2024-4/22, IEEE, 2022.

Papadopoulou, K., N. Palaiologou, and Z. Karanikola, 2022, Jul., *"Insights into teachers intercultural and global competence within multicultural educational settings" Education Science*, vol. 12, no. 8, page no. 502.

Shi, Z Q. Liu, Z. Zhang, and T. Yue,, "Thermal comfort in the design classroom for architecture in the cold area of China", *Sustainability*, vol. 14, no. 14, page no. 8307, 2022, Jul.

Singh, Nivedita, *"Role of cloud computing on education system", The SAGE Journal of Innovative Research*, vol. 1, no. 1, page no. 138–146,2021, June.

Venkatraman, S. F. Benli, Y. Wei, and F. Wahr, *"Smart classroom teaching strategy to enhance higher order thinking skills (HOTS) – an agile approach for education 4.0", Future Internet*, vol. 14, no. 9, page no. 255, 2022.

Y.Yang, T., L. Zuo, X. Yang, and N. Liu, *"Target-oriented teaching path planning with deep reinforcement learning for cloud computing-assisted instructions",Applied Sciences*, vol. 12, no. 18, page no. 9376, 2022, Sep.

24 Leveraging Educational Clouds for Empowering Rural Education

Siddhivinayak Kulkarni and Sally Firmin

24.1 INTRODUCTION

Rural education systems face many challenges in providing good and quality education to students from rural areas. The term "education clouds" has been recently gaining popularity due to its usefulness in giving prominent solutions for students who are in remote areas. Opening an education institute in rural areas faces many challenges and issues due to limited resources of skilled personnel, hardware/software, proper infrastructure, and qualified technicians. Education clouds may help to overcome these challenges by providing a proper platform for students in rural areas. Digital resources would be used for delivering learning material contents and identifying collaborative learning.

By using educational clouds, there is no need to install costly hardware/software at each school, as well as providing applications on-demand by upgrading with the latest in technology. By using cloud-based services, teachers and students can have access to educational materials in an online mode, working with virtual laboratories, and collaborative tools with proper bandwidth without considering the location.

Intelligent techniques such as data analytics and machine learning models can also be used in support of educational clouds, benefiting teachers and students to gain more state-of-the-art knowledge. These techniques can also be used for getting feedback, and improvements in the delivery of materials and contents; they enhance the overall learning experience and ensure that no student is left behind. However, the successful implementation of educational clouds in rural areas requires addressing challenges such as limited internet connectivity, digital literacy gaps, and cultural barriers. Robust infrastructure can be built by taking the help of government, non-government agencies, academic institutes, and skilled and experienced professionals who are willing to have active participation in the design and development of this model. Leveraging educational clouds presents a promising opportunity to empower rural education by providing equitable access to quality educational resources, fostering collaborative learning environments, and enabling personalized and adaptive learning experiences. By addressing the unique challenges faced by rural communities and promoting digital inclusion, educational clouds can play a pivotal role in transforming rural education and unlocking the full potential of students in these regions.

DOI: 10.1201/9781003472537-28

24.2 LITERATURE REVIEW

Digital technologies have been used in most of the academic institutes these days due to availability of internet, communication networks, and availability of electronic devices. Due to the recent unfortunate event of the pandemic, lectures were conducted in an online mode for the benefit of the students and teachers, but it was not possible in many countries due to a lack of basic services (Jevsikova et al., 2021; Abdullayev, 2020). The emergence of digital technology in education has led to the development of numerous learning management systems (LMS). These platforms have facilitated the creation of virtual classrooms, enabling teachers to interact with students in live sessions, share educational materials, deliver lectures, evaluate student progress, collect feedback, and address their inquiries (Barakina et al., 2021). Understanding the issues in the progress of rural education and traditional forms of education, cloud computing provides better solution in the current scenario. It also disseminates the required information using basic education system and gives equal opportunities for the students in the rural areas (Peng et al., 2023).

Technologies try to increase students' knowledge, comprehension, and skills, ensuring that they prosper both individually and in a group. Instructors can foster student's curiosity by utilizing intriguing learning materials that can be used for improving overall achievement (Pinho et al., 2021; Tokareva et al., 2019). It is very important to have computer and mobile facilities for any academic institute to succeed in the competitive education market. These facilities are readily available using the internet and by deploying intelligent techniques. It is useful for individual learning approaches to understand and utilize the full intelligence and capacity of the students (Flavin, 2012). Researchers have proposed various strategies and frameworks to address these challenges. A collaborative model was suggested involving government agencies, educational institutions, and technology providers to develop sustainable solutions (Khanna and Ilavarasan, 2019). Additionally, authors proposed a cloud-based platform that leverages community resources and local knowledge to create contextually relevant educational content (Karan et al., 2021).

Leveraging educational clouds is crucial for empowering rural education by enhancing the level of education informatization, promoting balanced development, and sharing educational resources (Sinaga, 2022; Cai and Wang, 2022). Establishing unified and open education cloud platforms can address the lack of resources and talent in urban and rural education informatization, utilizing advanced technologies like cloud computing and mobile internet to support rural education (Wen and Zhao, 2022). Additionally, creating multi-organization, multi-tenant farmer learning service cloud platforms can connect farmers with learning service organizations, providing personalized learning services and breaking geographical barriers to support rural revitalization through "Internet + farmer education" initiatives (Shi et al., 2023). By implementing mobile educational resource-sharing platforms based on cloud technology, it is possible to overcome time and space limitations, enhance learning efficiency, and facilitate the sharing of excellent educational resources between urban and rural areas.

Overall, the literature underscores the potential of educational clouds to empower rural education by giving pathways to quality education, enabling significant learning,

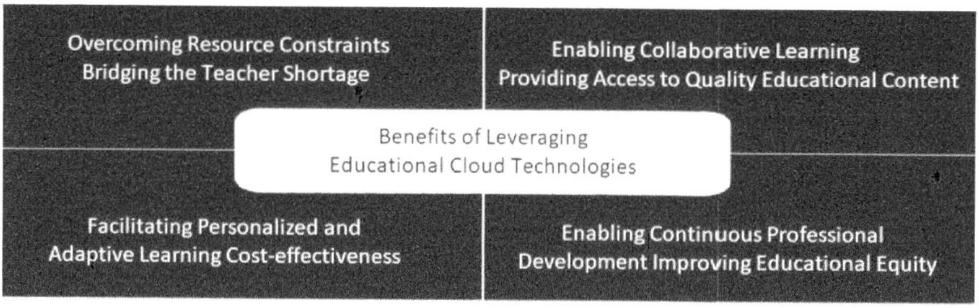

FIGURE 24.1 Benefits of Leveraging Educational Cloud Technologies.

and fostering association. However, successful implementation requires addressing infrastructural, technical, and socio-cultural barriers through collaborative efforts, capacity-building programs, and contextually relevant solutions.

Here are some key potential benefits of leveraging educational cloud technologies to address the challenges faced by rural education systems. Figure 24.1 summarizes the benefits of leveraging educational cloud technologies.

1. Overcoming Resource Constraints
Rural schools often lack access to essential educational resources, such as textbooks, laboratory equipment, and instructional materials. Educational clouds can provide a centralized platform for delivering digital content, virtual simulations, and online learning resources on demand, without the need for extensive physical infrastructure at each school.
2. Bridging the Teacher Shortage
Many rural areas face a shortage of qualified teachers, especially in specialized subjects. Cloud-based solutions can enable remote teaching and computer-generated schoolrooms, allowing learners to access expert instructors and school teaching material from beyond their local community.
3. Enabling Collaborative Learning
Educational clouds facilitate collaboration among students, teachers, and educational institutions across different locations. This can promote the sharing of best practices, peer-to-peer learning, and the development of online learning communities, which can be particularly valuable in isolated rural areas.
4. Providing Access to Quality Educational Content
Cloud-based platforms can aggregate and distribute high-quality educational content from various sources, making sure that all the students have the right study material from urban and rural areas.
5. Facilitating Personalized and Adaptive Learning
Using intelligent and hybrid techniques, facilities may be provided for improving individual learning by understanding students' capacity, by way of learning and evaluating their performance. This can be particularly beneficial in rural areas with diverse student populations and varying educational backgrounds.

6. Cost-Effectiveness
   Implementing educational cloud solutions can be more cost-effective than establishing physical infrastructure and maintaining traditional IT systems in each rural school. The scalability and pay-as-you-go models of cloud computing can help optimize resource utilization and reduce upfront capital investments.
7. Enabling Continuous Professional Development
   Along with the students, teachers from rural areas can also improve their technical and analytical skills and it helps them to gain up-to-date knowledge with the latest teaching and learning practice. They can also gain expertise in the subjects, and current educational technologies and make use of it for providing better education to the students from rural areas.
8. Improving Educational Equity
   By providing equitable access to educational resources and opportunities, educational clouds can help level the playing field for students in rural areas, addressing longstanding disparities in educational quality and outcomes.

Challenges such as internet connectivity, digital literacy, and cultural barriers required to provide significant advantages of educational cloud technologies make them a promising solution for empowering rural education and providing quality learning experiences to underserved communities.

24.3 EDUCATIONAL LANDSCAPE IN RURAL AREAS

Rural areas, characterized by their picturesque landscapes and close-knit communities, present a unique educational landscape shaped by geographical, socio-economic, and infrastructural factors. This section addresses the challenges faced and explains how to overcome these challenges beneficial to potential learners.

24.3.1 Challenges

Rural education faces a myriad of challenges that stem from geographical isolation, limited resources, and disparities in access to quality education. One of the primary challenges is the scarcity of educational infrastructure, including schools, libraries, and educational technology. Remote locations often lack adequate transportation networks, making it difficult for students to commute to schools, especially during inclement weather or rough terrain conditions.

Moreover, rural schools often grapple with shortages of qualified teachers and staff, exacerbating educational inequalities. Limited access to educational resources, including textbooks, technology, and extracurricular activities, further widens the gap between rural and urban education.

24.3.2 Impact on Students

The challenges of rural education have far-reaching implications for students, shaping their educational experiences and outcomes. Students in rural areas have issues with educational achievement due to lack of facilities, limited curriculum offerings, and a lack of opportunities for enrichment and extracurricular activities. Moreover, the scarcity of resources and qualified teachers may hinder students' access to personalized support and individualized learning experiences.

Socio-economic disparities, including poverty and unemployment, can impact students' access to resources, nutritional support, and healthcare services, further influencing their academic performance and overall well-being.

24.3.3 Opportunities and Innovations

Despite the challenges, rural education is not devoid of opportunities for growth and innovation. Educational stakeholders, including governments, educational institutions, and community organizations, are increasingly recognizing the importance of leveraging technology to bridge the gap and empower rural learners.

Initiatives such as educational clouds, digital learning platforms, and distance education programs hold promise for expanding access to quality education in rural areas. These technological innovations facilitate the delivery of educational content, resources, and support services to remote communities, overcoming geographical barriers, and enhancing learning opportunities for students.

24.4 CONCEPT OF EDUCATIONAL CLOUDS AND ITS BENEFITS

Educational clouds break the traditional classroom boundaries, by shifting a novel way of delivery of education. This section mainly deals with the concept of education clouds, its key features, benefits, and its use for future learning. This learning management system refers to a digital learning platform providing access to tools and services with the help of the internet. These platforms have ability to process, securely store, manage, govern, and disseminate all the related data and information among the users.

24.4.1 Features

Educational clouds offer a range of features designed to enhance teaching and learning experiences. Key features include:

1. Centralized Repository: Educational clouds serve as centralized repositories for educational materials, including textbooks, multimedia resources, and interactive learning modules.
2. Assessment and Analytics: Educational clouds often include assessment tools for creating quizzes, assignments, and exams, as well as analytics dashboards for tracking student progress and performance.
3. Accessibility: Cloud-based learning platforms are accessible anytime, anywhere, allowing students for getting academic materials and engage in interactions from any internet-enabled device.

4. Customization and Personalization: Educational clouds offer customization and personalization features that enable educators to tailor the educational abilities of each student's necessities and likings.

24.4.2 Benefits of Educational Clouds in Rural Education

Educational clouds offer a multitude of benefits for rural education systems, addressing longstanding challenges and unlocking new opportunities for learners and educators. This section explores the key advantages of leveraging educational clouds in rural education settings. Figure 24.2 elaborates the various features of educational clouds in enhancing teaching and learning.

1. Access to High-Quality Resources
   Educational clouds provide rural schools with access to a vast repository of high-quality educational resources, including digital textbooks, interactive multimedia content, and instructional materials. It provides the same access to students studying globally in rural or urban areas.
2. Flexibility and Adaptability
   Cloud-based educational platforms provide versatility and flexibility, enabling educators to tailor learning experiences according to the specific requirements and preferences of rural students. By accessing an extensive array of educational tools and applications, teachers can customize instruction to cater to various learning styles, paces, and abilities, thereby nurturing personalized learning environments for their students.
3. Cost-Effectiveness
   By appropriate deployment of educational clouds in rural schools, it eliminates the need for costly infrastructure, traditional textbooks, and other academic materials. It impacts highly on schools and students by reducing the costs and elaborating the educational access to the students.
4. Scalability and Resource Sharing
   Cloud-based learning platforms are highly scalable, enabling rural schools to expand their digital infrastructure and accommodate growing student populations without significant investments in hardware or software. Additionally, educational clouds facilitate resource sharing and collaboration

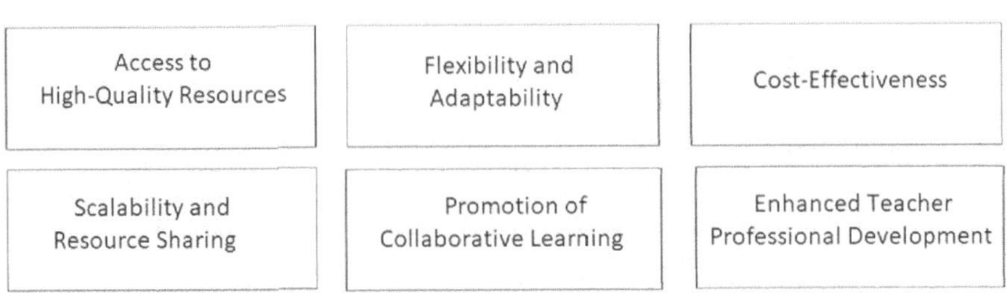

FIGURE 24.2 Educational Clouds Features to Enhance Teaching and Learning.

among schools and districts, allowing educators to pool resources, expertise, and best practices to enhance teaching and learning outcomes.

5. Promotion of Collaborative Learning
   Educational clouds foster collaborative learning environments, enabling students in rural areas to engage in collaborative projects, group discussions, and peer-to-peer learning activities. Through virtual classrooms, discussion forums, and collaborative tools, students can interact with their peers and educators, share ideas, and collaborate on projects irrespective of geographical barriers.
6. Enhanced Teacher Professional Development
   Educational clouds offer opportunities for teacher professional development and collaboration, enabling educators in rural areas to access training resources, participate in online courses, and collaborate with colleagues to enhance their education abilities. With the ease of professional development opportunities, educational clouds provide state-of-the-art abilities to have best practices in education.

The benefits of educational clouds in rural education are manifold, offering solutions to disclose the unique issues faced by schools and communities in rural areas. By providing admittance to a better teaching environment, promoting flexibility and adaptability, reducing costs, facilitating scalability and resource sharing, promoting collaborative learning, and enhancing teacher professional development, educational clouds have the potential to transform rural education systems and empower learners for success in the 21st century.

24.5 CHALLENGES AND MITIGATION STRATEGIES IN RURAL AREAS

When leveraging educational cloud technologies in rural areas, there are several challenges that are required to be analyzed by mitigation planning to ensure successful utilization besides adoption. Some key challenges and potential mitigation strategies are shown in Figure 24.3.

24.5.1 Inadequate Internet Connectivity

Challenge: Many rural areas lack reliable and high-speed networks, which is required for practicing internet-focused educational abilities and services.

Mitigation Strategies: Collaborate with internet service providers and government agencies to expand broadband infrastructure in rural regions.

Explore alternative connectivity solutions such as satellite internet or mobile broadband networks.

Implement local caching and offline access mechanisms to minimize bandwidth requirements.

FIGURE 24.3 Overview of Challenges and Mitigation Strategies in Rural Areas.

24.5.2 Limited Digital Literacy

Challenge: Rural communities often lack digital literacy skills, hindering their ability to effectively utilize cloud-based educational tools and resources.

Mitigation Strategies: Develop comprehensive digital literacy programs and training initiatives for students, teachers, and community members.

Incorporate user-friendly interfaces and localized content to facilitate adoption and ease of use.

Leverage community resources and local champions to promote digital literacy and address cultural barriers.

24.5.3 Lack of Technical Expertise

Challenge: Rural educational institutions may lack the technical expertise required to implement, maintain, and support cloud-based systems effectively.

Mitigation Strategies: Provide technical training and capacity-building programs for IT staff and teachers.

Establish partnerships with technology providers or educational institutions with expertise in cloud computing.

Leverage managed cloud services and support from cloud service providers.

24.5.4 Resistance to Change

Challenge: Adopting new technologies like educational clouds may face resistance from stakeholders accustomed to traditional teaching methods.

Mitigation Strategies: Conduct awareness campaigns and workshops to highlight the benefits of educational clouds.

Involve stakeholders in the planning and implementation process to foster buy-in and ownership.

Implement change management strategies and provide ongoing support and training.

24.5.5 Social and Language Issues

Challenge: Mainly people living in rural areas face issues with various ethnic educational characteristics, which may pose difficulties in accessing and utilizing educational cloud resources.

Mitigation Strategies: Develop localized and culturally relevant educational content and user interfaces.

Involve community members and local experts in content creation and translation efforts.

Leverage machine translation and language processing technologies to support multiple languages.

24.5.6 Sustainability and Scalability

Challenge: Due to limited resources, skilled manpower, and financial issues, it is very important to ensure the sustainability and continuous development in the deployment of educational clouds.

Mitigation Strategies: Develop sustainable funding models and partnerships with government agencies, non-governmental organizations (NGOs), and private sector entities.

Implement cost-effective and scalable cloud solutions that can grow with increasing demand.

Educational clouds can be leveraged efficiently and effectively to improve rural education and deliver better access to high-level learning opportunities.

24.6 EMPOWERING EDUCATORS THROUGH PROFESSIONAL DEVELOPMENT

It is very vital to have the current state of knowledge for the students by having excellent professional development to meet the needs of students from diverse backgrounds. This section briefly elaborates on the importance of professional development in enhancing teaching and learning outcomes.

1. Continuous Growth and Improvement
Continuous learning is one of the main basics for any educational institute. This professional development provides opportunities for growth and improvement in their careers. By involving actively in workshops, seminars, and faculty development programs, appropriate training sessions will provide best practices strategies, and methods to meet the better needs of the students.
2. Integrating Technology
These days technology plays an important role in every sector, preferably in education. These developments incorporate technologies, new methodologies, various educational software for improving students' learning outcomes, and finally knowledge. Technology also provides new learning preferences and styles to accommodate students from diverse backgrounds and learning experiences.
3. Supporting Social–Emotional Learning
Students' social–emotional developments emphasize the use of professional development programs by expanding positive relationships and addressing social and emotional needs. Use of integrating the social–emotional model in learning can create nurturing and supportive classroom environments for the overall growth of the students and academic success.
4. Strengthening Collaboration and Leadership
Professional development improves collaboration and active participation among the educators, working effectively with colleagues, partners, and stakeholders to improve student learning and their achievements.

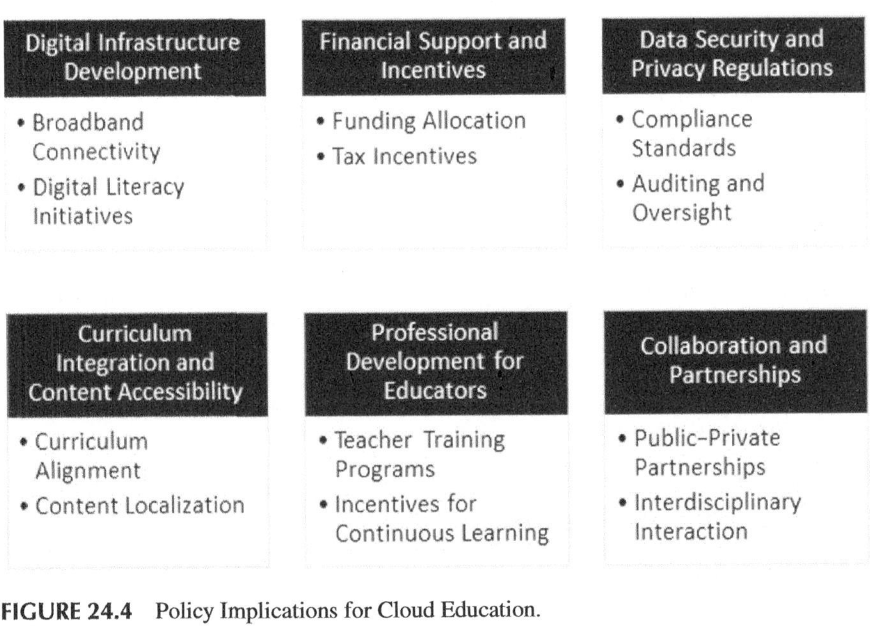

FIGURE 24.4 Policy Implications for Cloud Education.

24.7 POLICY IMPLICATIONS

The use of educational clouds in the rural education system has ability to improve students' knowledge, learning outcomes using digital resources. However, it requires strategic policy frameworks that identify the main challenges and accelerate sustainable implementation. This section describes the use of implementation of policy necessary for leveraging educational clouds to adopt rural education. Figure 24.4 depicts the various policy implications strategies.

24.7.1 Digital Infrastructure Development

Broadband Connectivity: The government should take a keen interest in expanding broadband wireless connectivity in rural areas to ensure reliable internet access. The government should make partnerships with internet service providers that will gain the appropriate bandwidth for teaching and learning.

Digital Literacy Initiatives: Policy frameworks should include provisions for digital literacy programs aimed at educators, students, and community members. These initiatives equip rural stakeholders with the skills necessary to navigate educational cloud platforms effectively.

24.7.2 Financial Support and Incentives

Funding Allocation: Governments and private companies should allocate budgets and provide funding for getting required resources, implementation, service, and maintenance of educational clouds. For these types of projects, continuous funding is required.

Tax Incentives: Policymakers can introduce tax incentives for technology providers and educational institutions investing in educational cloud solutions. These incentives encourage private sector involvement and innovation in the educational technology sector.

24.7.3 Data Security and Privacy Regulations

Compliance Standards: Policy frameworks must establish clear data security and privacy standards for educational cloud platforms. Regulations should mandate encryption protocols and data access controls.

Auditing and Oversight: Governments should implement mechanisms for auditing and oversight to ensure compliance with data security regulations. It is essential to have proper insight and monitoring to minimize any issues with data security and privacy.

24.7.4 Curriculum Integration and Content Accessibility

Curriculum Alignment: Policies should promote the integration of educational cloud resources into the national curriculum framework. Educational content hosted on cloud platforms should align with learning objectives and standards set by educational authorities.

Content Localization: Governments should support initiatives to develop and curate educational content tailored to the cultural and linguistic diversity of rural communities. Localized content enhances relevance and engagement among rural learners.

24.7.5 Professional Development for Educators

Teacher Training Programs: Policy frameworks should mandate ongoing professional development programs for educators focused on integrating educational cloud technologies into teaching practices. Training initiatives should cover both technical skills and pedagogical strategies.

Incentives for Continuous Learning: Governments can offer incentives such as certification programs or salary increments to educators who participate in professional development activities related to educational cloud usage. Incentives encourage lifelong learning and skill enhancement among teaching staff.

24.7.6 Collaboration and Partnerships

Public–Private Partnerships: Governments should foster collaboration between public education authorities, private technology firms, and non-profit organizations to leverage resources and expertise.

Interdisciplinary Interaction: Policymakers must help to provide interaction among the education area with appropriate stakeholders like telecommunications providers, community organizations, and civil society groups.

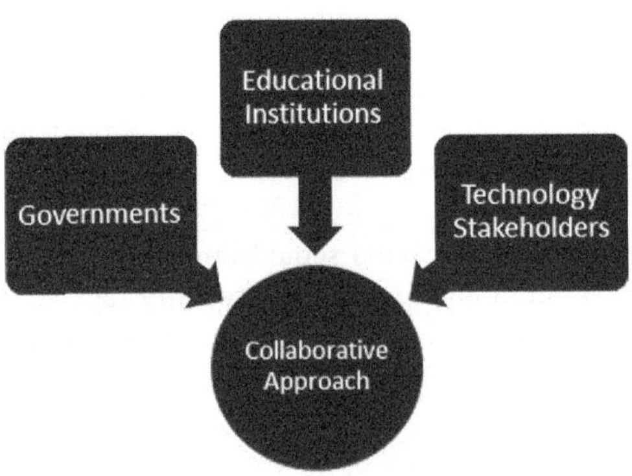

FIGURE 24.5 Collaborative Approach for Policy Implications.

Governments, educational institutions, and technology stakeholders should combine their efforts to create a platform that is appropriate for the adoption of educational clouds. For educational clouds to be successfully integrated into rural education systems, policies, support systems, and other infrastructure must be created. All of these players are essential to this process. We go into further detail about each stakeholder's individual function, as shown in Figure 24.5.

1. Governments
   Policy Formulation and Regulation: Governments are accountable for making rules and regulations to support the acceptance of educational clouds in rural education. This includes setting standards for data security and privacy, allocating funding for infrastructure development, and incentivizing the use of educational technology through tax breaks or subsidies.

   Structural Improvement: Governments play an important role in developing the necessary digital infrastructure to support educational cloud initiatives. This involves investing in broadband connectivity, ensuring reliable internet access in rural areas, and providing subsidies for technology procurement.

   Controlling and Assessment: There should be a system for controlling and assessing the use and benefits of educational cloud implementations. Part of it is to have monitoring and understanding the performance of the students, the use of teaching resources, and the ability of teachers to inform future policy decisions and strategic interventions.

   This includes collecting data on student outcomes, infrastructure utilization, and teacher satisfaction to inform future policy decisions and strategic interventions.
2. Educational Institutions
   Curriculum Integration: Educational institutions are responsible for integrating educational cloud resources into the curriculum in a meaningful and effective way. This involves aligning educational content hosted on cloud platforms with learning objectives and standards set by educational authorities.

   Infrastructure Management: Educational institutions are tasked with managing the infrastructure necessary to support educational cloud initiatives. This includes maintaining hardware, software, and network systems, as well as ensuring data security and privacy compliance.

   Community Engagement: Educational institutions should engage with local communities to garner support for educational cloud initiatives and solicit feedback on their utilization. It should encourage to have initiators meetings, forming senior member faculties, and collaborating through parents, students, and community leaders.
3. Technology Stakeholders
   Platform Development: Technology stakeholders such as software/hardware developers, and cloud/internet service providers are responsible for implementing and maintaining educational cloud platforms, incorporating new features to meet the needs of rural students.

Technical Support: Providing technical support and assistance is important for the smooth operation of providing and delivering content materials, offering online help, troubleshooting, software updates, training, and identifying and fixing problems.

Research and Development: Technology stakeholders should invest in research and development efforts to continuously improve educational cloud platforms. This may involve exploring new technologies, testing innovative features, and gathering feedback from users to enhance the functionality and effectiveness of educational cloud solutions.

By working together, governments, educational institutions, and technology stakeholders should build such a platform for the widespread adoption and sustainable use of educational clouds in rural education. Through collaborative efforts, these stakeholders can leverage the improvements for better education, and educational resources, as well as empower rural communities.

24.8 FUTURE DIRECTIONS AND SUSTAINABILITY

Considering the future of education in rural areas, the use of educational clouds holds immense capacity to enhance learning outcomes. In this section, future directions and strategic planning are discussed for a long-term approach and its usefulness to empower rural education.

1. Advancements in Technology
   Education sector needs continuous improvements, the use of new learning skills, technological advances in cloud computing, machine learning, artificial intelligence, and data analytics have the potential to further enhance the capabilities of educational clouds. Integrating new personalized algorithms, research in tele-education, and understanding the needs of future technology will provide a better platform for rural learners.
2. Community Engagement and Ownership
   Sustainability in educational cloud initiatives hinges on fostering community engagement and ownership. Empowering local communities to take ownership of educational accountability, resilience, etc. Governments as well as educational stakeholders should prioritize community participation in all aspects for development of educational cloud platforms. By involving local stakeholders in decision-making processes, educational initiatives can adopt the important aspects, cultural contexts, and needs of rural communities, thereby enhancing their sustainability and impact.
3. Lifelong Learning and Continuous Improvement
   The concept of education is evolving from a linear process to a lifelong journey. By providing authorization to a diverse academic environment, skill development programs, and professional development opportunities, educational clouds empower individuals of all ages to pursue continuous learning and personal growth. Governments and educational institutions should prioritize the integration of lifelong learning principles into educational cloud

initiatives, fostering a culture of curiosity, exploration, and self-improvement within rural communities.

4. Environmental Sustainability
   In addition to social and economic sustainability, environmental sustainability is an increasingly important consideration in educational cloud initiatives. To mitigate the impact of carbon emissions, governments and technology providers must help to build a system that consumes low energy and sustainable practices in the design and operation of educational cloud platforms.
5. Policy and Regulatory Frameworks
   Sustainability in leveraging educational clouds for empowering rural education requires supportive policy and regulatory frameworks. Governments should enact policies that incentivize investment in educational technology infrastructure, promote digital literacy and digital citizenship, and provide authentication for educational information to all the learners.
6. Continuous Evaluation and Adaptation
   Finally, ensuring the sustainability of educational cloud initiatives requires continuous evaluation, monitoring, and adaptation. Governments, educational institutions, and technology providers ensure effective monitoring, also evaluations to check the appropriate use of educational cloud programs. Feedback from students, educators, and community stakeholders should inform ongoing improvements and refinements to educational cloud platforms, ensuring their alignment with changing requirements, as well as priorities.
   The future of leveraging educational clouds for empowering rural education lies in embracing innovation, fostering community engagement, promoting lifelong learning, and prioritizing sustainability. By adopting a holistic and forward-thinking approach, stakeholders can ensure that educational cloud initiatives continue to make a meaningful and lasting impact in rural communities for generations to come.

24.9 CONCLUSION

The integration of educational clouds into rural education systems marks a significant milestone for the journey for equitable better education. Throughout the chapter, the transformative potential of leveraging educational clouds was explored to empower rural communities, address challenges, and foster inclusivity. As we conclude, it is evident that educational clouds offer a pathway to bridge the digital divide and unlock new opportunities for rural learners and educators alike.

Educational clouds serve as catalysts for change, providing centralized repositories of educational resources that transcend the constraints of physical infrastructure. By democratizing access to learning materials, these platforms empower students in rural areas to pursue their educational aspirations and unlock their full potential. Furthermore, educational clouds facilitate collaborative learning environments, enabling students to engage in shared educational experiences irrespective of geographical barriers. This collaborative ethos nurtures enriching their educational journey. This involves investing in digital infrastructure, providing financial support and incentives, and establishing regulations to ensure data security and privacy.

Moving forward, sustainability and scalability are paramount in understanding the utilization of educational clouds in rural education. By embracing innovation, collaboration, and a shared commitment to educational excellence, stakeholders should connect the utilization of educational clouds to look for novel ideas and empower rural communities for generations to come.

REFERENCES

Abdullayev, A. (2020). System of information and communication technologies in the education. *Science and World International Scientific Journal*, 2, pp. 19–21

Barakina, E.Y., Popova, A.V., Gorokhova, S.S., & Voskovskaya, A.S. (2021). Digital technologies and artificial intelligence technologies in education. *European Journal of Contemporary Education*, 10(2), pp. 285–296

Cai, B., & Wang, X. (2022). Design and Implementation of Educational Information System Based on Cloud Computing. In: Hung, J.C., Chang, J.W., Pei, Y., & Wu, W.C. (eds) *Innovative Computing. Lecture Notes in Electrical Engineering*, vol. 791. Springer, Singapore. https://doi.org/10.1007/978-981-16-4258-6_106

Flavin, M. (2012). Disruptive technologies in higher education. *Research in Learning Technology*, 20, pp. 102–111. https://doi.org/10.3402/rlt.v20i0.19184

Jevsikova, T., Stupurienė, G., Stumbrienė, D., Juškevičienė, A., & Dagienė, V. (2021). Acceptance of distance learning technologies by teachers: Determining factors and emergency state influence. *Informatica*, 32(3), pp. 517–542

Karan, A., Shankar, C., Mandal, S., & Ghosh, P. (2021). Rural Cloud: A cloud-based platform to bridge the digital divide in rural education. *IEEE Access*, 9, pp. 35335–35349

Khanna, A., & Ilavarasan, P.V. (2019). Cloud computing for sustainable rural development: A case study of a higher education ERP implementation in India. *Sustainability*, 11(23), p. 6637

Peng, G., Wu, M., Lin, C., Shi, X., He, N., & Sun, W. (2023). Regional Sharing Model of Information Education Resources in Rural Schools Based on Cloud Computing. In: Hung, J.C., Yen, N.Y., & Chang, J.W. (eds) *Frontier Computing. FC 2022. Lecture Notes in Electrical Engineering*, vol. 1031. Springer, Singapore. https://doi.org/10.1007/978-981-99-1428-9_127

Sinaga, G. (2023). Empowering rural area students through education: Youth in metaverse. *Dynamics of Dialogue, Cultural Development, and Peace in the Metaverse* doi: 10.4018/978-1-6684-5907-2.ch009, pp. 96–105

Pinho, C., Franco, M., & Mendes, L. (2021). Application of innovation diffusion theory to the E-learning process: Higher education context. *Education and Information Technologies*, 26(1), pp. 421–440

Shi, J., Zhang, J., Luan, Z., Lu, Q., & Li, J. (2023). "Research and design of professional farmer learning service platform based on cloud," *2023 IEEE 6th Information Technology, Networking, Electronic and Automation Control Conference (ITNEC)*, pp. 1321–1325. Chongqing, China, doi: 10.1109/ITNEC56291.2023.10082201

Tokareva, E.A., Smirnova, Y.V., & Orchakova, L.G. (2019). Innovation and communication technologies: Analysis of the effectiveness of their use and implementation in higher education. *Education and Information Technologies*, 24(5), pp. 3219–3234

Wen, J., & Zhao, Y.L. (2022). An urban and rural educational resource sharing and exchange platform based on cloud platform access technology. *Ingénierie des Systèmes d'Information*, 27(3), pp. 515–520 https://doi.org/10.18280/isi.270320

25 Building an Interactive Programming Learning Platform with MEAN Stack

Integrating Chatter Bots and Best Programming Practices

Baby Vadlana, N Venkata Sailaja, and D. N. Vasundhara

25.1 INTRODUCTION

Virtual programming environments (Czakóová 2023) offer availability from any place through an internet connection, are economical with no necessity for physical equipment, guarantee security, save time, and permit repeatable try-outs. They can put up several students, assimilate multimedia for improved learning, and deliver instant responses, making them appreciated means for engineering education.

Additionally, a survey found that 13% of students are reluctant to ask questions because they are afraid or have social anxiety, which makes them uncomfortable to ask doubts during the physical laboratory sessions. Therefore, students lose their grasp of the fundamentals, which according to the reverse Flynn Effect causes a decline in their intelligence quotient (IQ). An online survey form was created to perform a social experiment with 384 undergraduate computer science students to validate the research mentioned above. A few inquiries such as "Do you believe that online learning is beneficial?," "Do you comprehend the material being taught?," " Do you participate in lab sessions?," " Will you have all of your questions answered in online laboratories?" etc. were made to ascertain whether the students had a realistic grasp of their circumstances about online laboratories. The results showed that around 95% of the students expressed dissatisfaction with their educational experience, saying that it was merely a memory exercise for programming. It also showed that approximately 25% of students are asking for an automated online platform that helps them clear up their issues.

DOI: 10.1201/9781003472537-29

Online learning (Meng et al. 2024) is still widespread across the world. Thus, digital solutions are necessary for virtual learning platforms. To solve all of the aforementioned problems, it has been identified that virtual lab environments for computer programming can be created using the MEAN stack in conjunction with conversational chatbots (Sadhasivam et al. 2020), or "Chatter Robots," that can converse with students and answer any questions they may have about the language during online laboratory sessions. Additionally, the chatbots can identify a specific student's preferred method of programming and respond to them quickly and in an understandable manner.

This chapter concentrates on C Language, one of the most widely used programming languages. The rationale is that C is a fundamental programming language that all college students entering this cutthroat field of technology must know. Due to their limited practical programming experience, students also struggle to understand C language faults and come up with a work around. However, before delving into more advanced programming concepts like C++, Java, Python, etc., it is critical to solidify the understanding of the fundamentals. To support the students in clarifying their doubts while working with the programming methods, an effective and responsive chatterbot is incorporated by utilizing Amazon Web Services in place of conventional Natural Language Processing (NLP) systems. One of the most well-liked aspects of this system is that it was implemented using Angular framework-based online interface and a chatbot using Amazon Lex.

25.2 BACKGROUND SURVEY

To identify the barriers to online learning Viral Thakker et al. (2021) suggested a comprehensive strategy involving data analysis from a survey of 364 engineering students. The responses were graded from 2.81 to 3.46 on a 5-point Likert scale, which was used to define the metric. The results revealed that Microsoft Teams was the students' preferred platform, while Google Meet was the most popular platform. There are, however, some restrictions on this analysis. First, this idea was restricted to urban pupils, which is likely to introduce significant educational and geographic bias. The present study primarily centers on two domains: online education and online examination (Choubey et al. 2020). Studies on virtual learning indicate that these courses offer a number of benefits, including a vibrant online community where students can engage in discourse, the development of new technologies and well-organized course materials, regular and improved communication between teachers and students, and instructors who are genuinely supportive. Having said that, research indicates that college students in industrialized nations such as the United States are increasingly utilizing web-based learning environments.

Due to the many benefits of online learning, a small number of studies recommend the best methods for both teaching and learning on these platforms. A small number of studies have concluded that, in addition to its advantages, online learning (Naidu 2019) offers a strong means of connecting with professionals in the fields of ergonomics and human factors, and that, when compared to traditional classroom settings, students achieve better learning results. Online examinations have grown in popularity along with online education, and there are numerous studies on the subject. Online examinations save a great deal of human labor and yield more accurate results, according to one study. As online exams gained popularity, several sectors switched from offline to online hiring, using the exams to narrow down potential candidates for interviews. To identify potential applicants, most software businesses hold programming contests. To help with the online talent search, these companies have built integrated development environments (IDEs), which encourage candidates to think more logically than syntactically. Our development of this proposed work was made possible by our extensive study on online learning, online testing, and IDE development.

A conversational chatbot, created by Hariyadharshini et al. (2017), may converse with users by addressing their services, such as placing a pizza order. The bot is enhanced with setup so that it can understand the user's needs. The Lambda service was used to enable a serverless connection. In a similar vein, the system's backend database was constructed using the Amazon Relational Database Service (RDS). RDS offers a variety of database engines, including Microsoft SQL Server, Oracle, PostgreSQL, MariaDB, Amazon Aurora, and MySQL. This instance used the MySQL workbench. The database's virtual console aids in the administrators' effective database management. Through its responses to the user's irrelevant inquiries, the system has demonstrated its ability to handle errors.

A chatbot, created by Poongothai et al. (2021), is a personalized conversational assistant that may aid students with queries and clarifications regarding both completed and ongoing Internet of Things (IoT) projects. This system has a few advantages, such as auto scalability, real-time notifications, and quick response. Undergraduate students were surveyed by Chakraborty et al. (2021) regarding their views on online learning during the COVID-19 pandemic. After 358 students responded, it was found that they were more interested in learning through Massive Open Online Course (MOOC) platforms and in-person instruction than they were in online learning. However, the findings also show that the faculty members' methods of instructing students about online learning have improved.

To build a system that can span a wide range of spectrums, they applied ideas like text segmentation and custom labeling. A chatbot was used by Prashanth et al. (2020) to create a college management solution. The chatbot assists all users with their daily needs on campus, such as showing them where to go for libraries and other daily necessities. The use of AI chatbots to improve student learning in higher education was investigated by Sandu and Gide (2019). They discussed how a chatbot can be integrated as a learning platform and increase productivity, learning, assistance, and communication gaps. Rainer (Winkler and Söllner 2018) highlighted the influence of chatbots on the potential of students' learning. Tamayo et al. (2020) developed EconBot, a chatbot that serves as a support system for distance learning. They elucidated how a chatbot can function as a virtual teaching assistant for all college students enrolled in distance learning programs, enhancing their academic performance and assisting them with technical issues. In their discussion of chatbots as educational assistance systems Clarizia et al. (2018) emphasized the use of NLP techniques and the significance of providing students with the appropriate responses. The use of chatbots in formal education, evolution, their widespread use in business and educational institutions, and the advantages of doing so were discussed by Daniel et al. (2020) and Sreeharsha et al. (2022) who created a chatbot system that uses Facebook Messenger and Amazon Lex to assist users with hotel reservations. Here, the bot's utterance setting was done using Amazon Lex, and the responses were validated using the Lambda function. The real-time notification system and Facebook page login are two benefits of this technology.

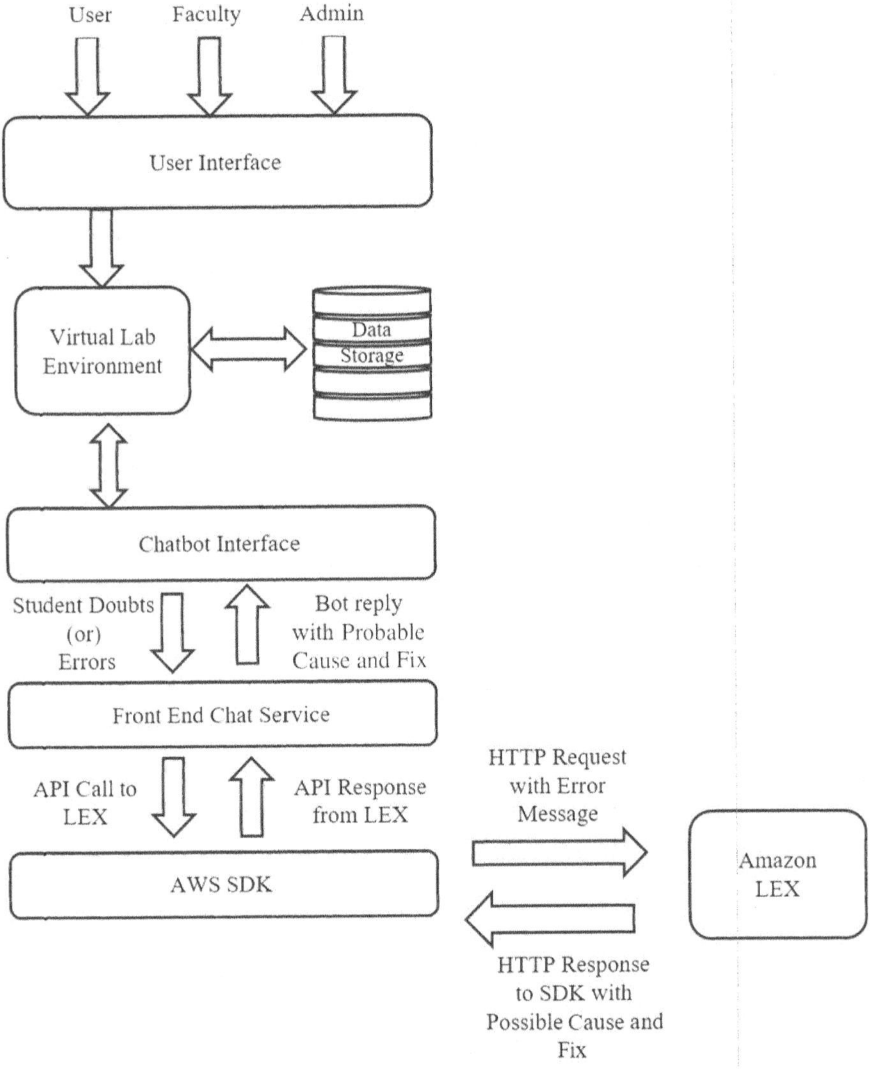

FIGURE 25.1 Architectural Design for Virtual Lab Environment Integrated with Chatbot Using Amazon Lex.

25.3 PROPOSED SYSTEM

The proposed system which serves as the virtual lab environment for "C programming" allows students to log in and view all the tasks to which they are assigned. Additionally, upon opening each lab, they are presented with a list of all the weekly tasks that need to be completed by the deadline. They will see the coding problems that need to be solved in that week when they open their respective weekly assignments. They are able to read the question, begin solving the problems, and able to write the solution code using the user-friendly IDE that is provided for each problem statement. Once they are satisfied with their solution, they can submit it, and the system will display the results right away, including the number of test cases that passed or failed, and the specific error for each test case.

If they encounter any issues or errors when coding, the IDE will display them. Using the discussion forum that is included, they can post the error information which can be answered by anyone, and can also interact with the chatbot for quick response. Due to the hands-on development, many questions come up in practically every lab session. Students are better able to understand the material and better retain it in their memory when these questions are answered. Anyone can gain a deeper understanding of a subject by making mistakes and learning from them. In a virtual environment, it is less common for a subject expert to assist them in resolving their problems.

As shown in Figure 25.1, the system was integrated with a chatbot which was developed by using deep learning engine-powered Amazon Lex and hosted NLP methods on Amazon Web Services. This will be protected from the intricacies of conventional NLP approaches by our usage of Amazon Web Services-hosted methodologies. By utilizing this capability, developers can communicate with the program in a manner like having a discussion with Amazon Alexa. It enables the creation, oversight, and management of chatbots utilizing natural language understanding (NLU) in both current and latest applications.

The environment helps to create new labs, change them, and manually enter the roll numbers of students who are part of that lab or provide a student details file. Faculty may quickly assess each student's and the class's progress and obtain the corresponding reports. Teachers find it easier to monitor each student's and the class's development through leaderboard.

25.4 METHODOLOGY

There are two modules that make up the system's architecture:

1. Module on virtual lab environment.
2. Module on chatbot.

25.4.1 Virtual Lab Environment Module

In this virtual lab environment, the front end is built using Angular. Angular is a JavaScript framework used to build single-page web applications. There are four modules in the front end, namely " App Module, Admin Module, Faculty Module, Student Module."

App module: App module is the first module that is executed when the user requests a web page. There are many components in the app module: the login component, register component, forget password component, home component, about component, and contact component. This module is divided into several smaller modules, such as the administration, faculty, and student modules, each of which is explained below.

Admin module: The administrator can add information about the students and faculty. Admin can also accept or reject applications from teachers and students who have self-registered.

Faculty module: Instructors can establish laboratories, add participants, amend difficulties, and design weekly assignments. By downloading the reports, they may see each student's and the class's development.

Student module: The students have access to all the laboratories they are enrolled in, as well as all the weekly assignments. They can also contribute solutions to the issues and ask questions in the discussion forum.

25.4.2 Chatbot Module

Chatbot features the subsequent following modules:

Bot Component: Encapsulates the features of the other user interface (UI) elements.

Session Component: Creates a session where users may ask questions and discuss errors with a chatbot.

Input Component: Receives the user's message and forwards it to the chatbot application programming interface (API).

Feed Component: Displays the chatbot API's response.

Message Service: In charge of sending the required hypertext transfer protocol (HTTP) requests to the chatbot API.

25.5 CONCLUSION

This work caters to the growing demand for online education by offering a digitalized lab environment. Key features include efficient handling of large student populations and time savings for both students and teachers. An interactive chatbot that provides personalized error correction and addresses foundational knowledge gaps in C programming. This online learning environment offers flexibility and accessibility, potentially improving student engagement through its interactive interface and quick response times. This work can be enhanced by creating a multi-language, interactive online learning environment. With real-time error correction and tailored learning support, we can address the broader needs of undergraduate computer science education.

REFERENCES

Chakraborty, Pinaki, Prabhat Mittal, Manu Sheel Gupta, Savita Yadav, and Anshika Arora. 2021. Opinion of Students on Online Education During the COVID-19 Pandemic, *Human Behavior and Emerging Technologies*, Vol. 3, pp. 357–365.

Choubey, Anjali, Avinash Kumar, Ayush Ranjan Behra, Anil Raj Kisku, Asha Rabidas, and Beas Bhadra. 2020. A Study on Web Based Online Examination System, *International Conference on Recent Trends in Artificial Intelligence, IOT, Smart Cities & Applications (ICAISC-2020)*.

Clarizia, Fabio, Francesco Colace, Marco Lombardi, Francesco Pascale, and Domenico Santaniello. 2018. Chatbot: An Education Support System for Student. In: Arcangelo Castiglione, Florin Pop, Massimo Ficco, Francesco Palmieri (eds.), *Cyberspace Safety and Security. CSS 2018. Lecture Notes in Computer Science*, Vol. 11161. Cham: Springer. https://doi.org/10.1007/978-3-030-01689-0_23.

Czakóová, Krisztina. 2023. Virtual Programming Environments and Simulations in Favor of Active Learning of Programming, *International Journal of Advanced Natural Sciences and Engineering Researches*, Vol. 7, pp. 105–109. https://doi.org/10.59287/ijanser.910.

Daniel, Gwendal, Jordi Cabot, Laurent Deruelle, and Mustapha Derras. 2020. Xatkit: A Multimodal Low-Code Chatbot Development Framework, *IEEE Access*, Vol. 8, pp. 15332–15346. https://doi.org/10.1109/ACCESS.2020.2966919.

Hariyadharshini, M., A. Selina, R. Subasurya, and Lina Dinesh. 2017. Conversational Interface Using Amazon LEX, *International Journal of Advanced Engineering and Recent Technology*, Vol. 18, No. 1, pp. 13–18.

Meng, Wentao, Lei Yu, Chen Liu, Nengchao Pan, Xiawen Pang, and Yunyun Zhu. 2024. A Systematic Review of the Effectiveness of Online Learning in Higher Education During the COVID-19 Pandemic Period, *Frontiers in Education* Vol. 8, p. 1334153. https://doi.org/10.3389/feduc.2023.1334153.

Naidu, Som. 2019. The Changing Narratives of Open, Flexible and Online Learning, Distance Education, Vol. 40, No. 2, pp. 149–152.

Poongothai, M., D. Diana Josephine, M. Gowtham, S. Jayanth, B. Sowmiah, and M. C. Uthra. 2021. Amazon LEX Based Personalized Chatbot for IOT Lab@CIT, *International Journal of Advance Scientific Research and Engineering Trends*, Vol. 6, No. 5, pp. 131–136.

Prashanth, S., N. Rakshith Gowda, Sourabh Kakade, Gouramma, and Vivek Sharma. 2020. Review of AI Chatbot, *International Research Journal of Engineering and Technology (IRJET)*, Vol. 7, No. 5, pp. 3965–3967.

Sadhasivam, Jayakumar, M. Ametwala, A. Mazumdar, A. Bhataiya, Balajee J.M, V. Kumar. 2020. Implementation of Chatbot That Teach Programming Language, *Journal of Xi'an University of Architecture & Technology*, Vol. XII, Issue III, pp. 1095–1101.

Sandu, Nitirajsingh, and Ergun Gide. 2019. Adoption of AI-Chatbots to Enhance Student Learning Experience in Higher Education in India, In *2019 18th International Conference on Information Technology Based Higher Education and Training (ITHET)*, Magdeburg, Germany, pp. 1–5. https://doi.org/10.1109/ITHET46829.2019.8937382.

Sreeharsha, A. S. S. K., Sai Mohan Kesapragada, and Sai Pratheek Chalamalasetty. 2022. Building Chatbot Using Amazon Lex and Integrating with a Chat Application, *International Journal of Scientific Research in Engineering and Management (IJSREM)*, Vol. 6, No. 4, pp. 1–6.

Tamayo, Pedro, Ana Herrero-Alcalde, Javier Martín-Román, Carolina Navarro, and José Tránchez. 2020. Design of a Chatbot as a Distance Learning Assistant, *Open Praxis*, Vol. 12. doi: 145.10.5944/openpraxis.12.1.1063.

Viral Thakker, Shivangi, Jayesh Parab, and Shubhankar Kaisare. 2021. Systematic Research of e-Learning Platforms for Solving Challenges Faced by Indian Engineering Students, *Asian Association of Open Universities Journal*, Vol. 16, No. 1, pp. 1–19.

Winkler, Rainer, and Matthias Söllner. 2018. Unleashing the Potential of Chatbots in Education: A State-of-the-Art Analysis, *Academy of Management Proceedings*. doi:15903.10.5465/AMBPP.2018.15903.

26 From Screens to Classrooms

A Comprehensive Study of E-Learning, M-Learning, and Face-to-Face Learning

Reena Thakur, Nishal Puri, and Parul Bhanarkar

26.1 INTRODUCTION

Students can access educational materials through e-learning even if they live far away from their teachers or other educators. E-learning makes use of technologies including computers, networking, the internet, and multimedia. The term "e-learning" has several definitions. Wentling et al. (2000) and Rosenberg (2001) both state that there are several ways to improve knowledge and performance through the use of internet technology for e-learning (Rosenberg, 2001; Wentling et al., 2000). Computers and communication technology are used to enhance and facilitate learning. According to Garisson and Anderson, e-learning is networked or online learning that occurs in a formally structured setting (Karim & Hashim, 2004).

The system is made up of software and electronic devices that can be used offline or online. Computer-based training or computer-enhanced learning is included in e-learning. According to Chan et al. (2007), computer-mediated learning includes e-learning. Other communication technologies, in addition to online lectures, tutorials, and learning support systems, can be employed to provide education. E-learning that is effective frequently combines several techniques.

Apart from Compact Disc Read-Only Memories (CD-ROMs) and satellite-based video conferencing, e-learning encompasses an array of software programs and procedures intended to provide education via electronic gadgets, furthermore covering computer-based training, web-based training, and online learning. Therefore, e-learning is utilizing technology, such as CD-ROMs, interactive multimedia, the internet, and other tools, to enhance classroom participation.

With the help of online tutorials, pupils can finish a task assigned to them on their own. This medium has the ability to pique students' interest in learning because of its interactive graphics, texts, sounds, videos, and collaborative sharing elements. We can access it from anywhere at any time as long as we have a computer and an internet connection.

DOI: 10.1201/9781003472537-30

Higher education institutions should preserve their competitive edge in this shifting market by utilizing e-learning to enhance education and training as well as the caliber of teaching and learning. As a result, IT is now fully utilized to enhance the teaching and learning process and provide educational courses to a larger number of students at a reduced cost. E-learning could thereby improve the standard of instruction and learning (Hsbullah & Idris, 2009; Martinez-Garcia et al., 2023).

Both benefits and drawbacks of e-learning are numerous. Previous studies have shown that switching from traditional to online learning can save learners both money and time. When they participate in online learning, students might be frugal. They may do other beneficial things in their free time. Furthermore, e-learning provides a great deal of freedom. With e-learning, students can attend classes at any time and from any location. Consequently, e-learning is accessible 7 days a week, 24 hours a day. Additionally, e-learning provides a range of learning strategies. Because they have access to so much interactive material, pupils are therefore unlikely to become bored while studying.

26.1.1 Definitions of E-learning

Internet-enabled learning is known as e-learning. A networked community of experts, content providers, and learners, as well as administration of the learning process, can all be considered components. Content delivery can take several forms. E-learning offers more accessibility to learning, quicker learning at lower costs and transparent accountability in the teaching–learning process for all participants. Organizations that use e-learning provide their workers the flexibility to use change to their advantage in the fast-paced culture of today. Online education offers opportunity, accountability, and accessibility. It makes it possible for individuals and institutions to stay informed about developments in the world economy that now take place online. The following are the challenges:

1. Nations need to educate their people
2. Businesses need to train their employees
3. Educational institutions need to provide cutting-edge curricula.

Because of e-learning, we can acquire more knowledge and skills, learn more quickly and for less money, and also handle the potential of knowledge and information. Increased profitability, increased productivity, and improved loyalty of employees are the outcomes of e-learning. All things considered, it offers information from a wider range of sources, better service quality, more knowledge accessible to life-long learners, and quick uptake of new data and initiatives. Based on earlier studies, we draw a broad architecture for contemporary e-learning systems in Figure 26.1, which essentially comprises three logical layers; (1) Presentation layer, (2) E-learning system layer, and (3) Data layer, all three together work to enhance the efficacy of teaching–learning.

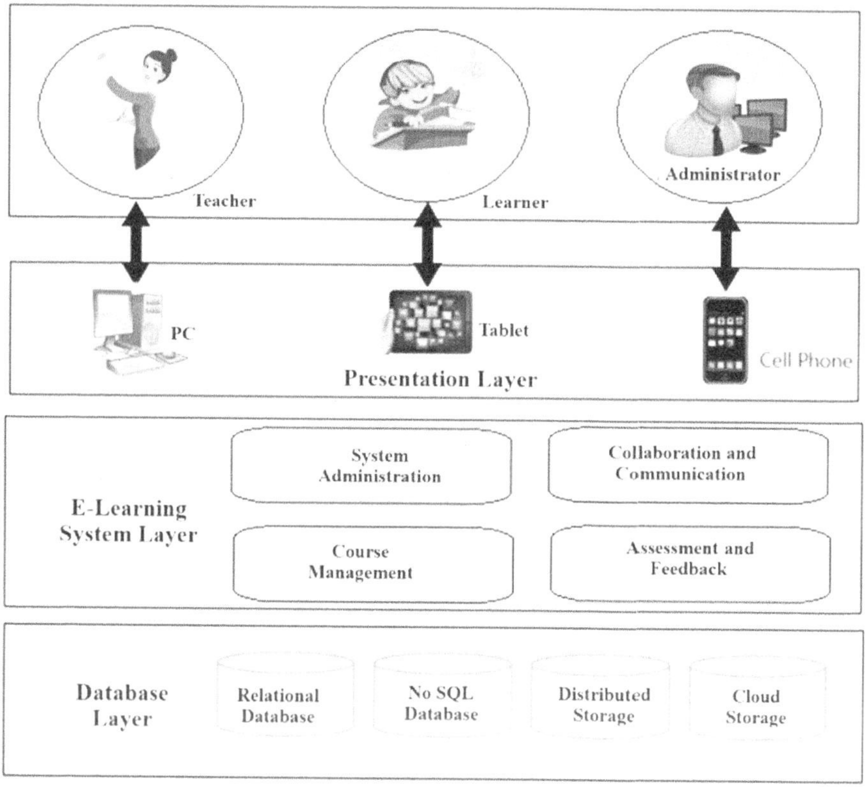

FIGURE 26.1 E-Learning System's General Framework.

26.1.2 Advantages of E-Learning for Students

1. Everyone's needs are accommodated in online learning
   For everyone, E-learning is the most suitable mode of instruction. The way that information is accessible, discussed, shared, and consumed has changed dramatically due to the digital revolution. Both housewives and office employees can register in online courses as per their convenience. Many people prefer to learn in the evenings or on weekends, depending on their convenience (Ahmad, 2023).
2. Lectures can be viewed infinite number of times
   Unlike classroom teaching, with E-learning the number of time that students can access the content is infinite. This plays an important role while revising during preparation for the test.
3. Access to updated content is offered
   Being able to keep up with up-to-date learners is one of the main benefits of E-learning. The learners will be updated whenever they would like.

4. Quick delivery of sessions
   Sessions may be provided fast with e-learning. This kind of instruction has relatively short delivery cycles compared to typical classroom methods. Hence, learning time is shortened by e-learning:
   - Sessions started and were completed in a single session. This makes it feasible for training to start in a few days or a few weeks.
   - Ideally learning at the group pace, learning pace can be set by learners on their own.
   - Student's traveling time is saved. You can study as per your convenience at home.
   - Focusing on every topic in the learning material, students can select to study only those that are concerned to them. For instance, they are free to exclude material in areas they choose not to learn.
5. Scalability
   New policies, concepts, training, and ideas can be created and conveyed with the help of E-learning. E-learning is a very quick way to study, even for formal education or leisure.
6. Consistency
   Instructors may reach a wider audience base using e-learning and provide the content more consistently. This guarantees that, when using this learning mode, every learner receives similar instruction.
7. Reduced costs
   E-learning is less expensive compared to traditional educational methods. E-learning can be quick and simple; hence, the price has been lowered. There is a considerably reduced amount of training time when it comes to course materials, travel, instructors, and lodging.
8. Effectiveness
   E-Learning has a kind of beneficial impact on the organization's gain. It makes it easier to understand the content and consume it:
   - This leads to tests, certifications, or other types of evaluation.
   - Improved results who achieve "pass" or mastery' level.
   - Improved ability to impart and learn new techniques or knowledge at the organization.
   - Helps in maintaining information for a longer time.
9. Environment friendly
   As e-learning is a paper-free and online way of learning, it helps to protect the environment to a great extent.

26.1.3 Disadvantages of E-learning

26.1.3.1 Lack of Self-Discipline

Lack of this will make someone unmotivated to study, which will result in delay. Rather traditional classroom instruction comes with ease because it allows you to be monitored if you are lagging behind in your coursework.

TABLE 26.1
Application of the Internet in E-Learning

Learning areas	E-learning strategies and technologies	Internet applications
Business	Online chat room, online news groups, email, WWW	Virtual online company tours, online group projects, online business courses,
Arts	Interactive and animated video on the WWW, email, online exchanging files	Online classes for vocabulary, language, and writing skills
Science	–	Online design of experiments, online virtual laboratory, online collaborative projects
Law and justice	–	Communication, practice of law online, simulation games
Engineering	WWW integrated CAD hyperlinks, email, and online 3D navigation	Engineering classes on online, virtual design, online team learning, online virtual vocabulary, and group projects
Law and justice	–	Online simulation games, online practice of law online, communication
Medicine	–	Online diagnosis, online simulation of surgical operations, chat room
Agriculture	–	Online training and education using WWW, treatment of crops from time to time

26.1.3.2 Health Problems

This is generally considered when someone spends more time on a computer or tablet, causing strain on eyes, blurry vision, and other issues. To avoid this, do periodic exercises like walking around, relax for at least every hour for 10 minutes, and also perform some wrist exercises.

26.1.3.3 Inability to Access Technology

People who wish to enroll in an online course but are unable to do so because they do not have access to a device with an internet connection, or rather, they do not live in a place where they can easily obtain an internet connection, encounter this issue. Table 26.1 shows the application of the internet in e-learning.

26.2 M-LEARNING – DEFINITION

The acronym for learning with portable devices is known as "M-learning" or mobile learning, because of which students can study while on the go or in varied settings rather than being confined to a desk or a classroom. Naturally, mobile learning is an electronic subset of e-learning, but it focuses more precisely on these portable gadgets and technology. The following are the functions of m-learning, as shown in Figure 26.2.

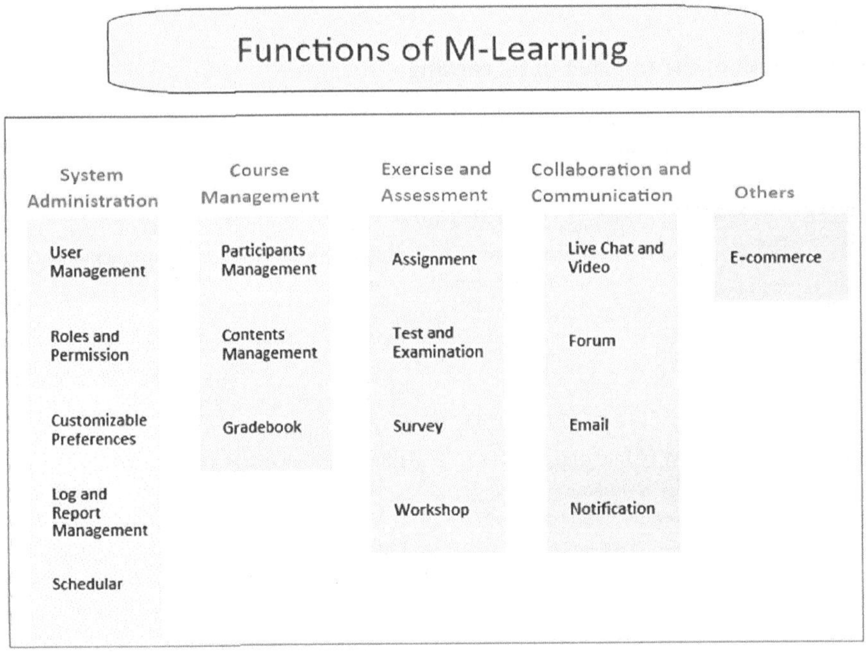

FIGURE 26.2 Functions of M-Learning.

26.2.1 Mobile Learning

By providing access to learning materials and enabling customized learning at any time and place, mobile learning, also known as nomadic learning, has improved and impacted e-learning. In the literature, m-learning is defined in various ways. Geddes defines it as the utilization of mobile technology to acquire knowledge and skills, anytime and anywhere, leading to a behavioral change. Other writers emphasize the importance of mobile devices and user mobility more than others. According to these scholars, m-learning takes place in casual learning environments as shown in Figure 26.3.

Students utilize their mobile devices to access the mobile learning system (refer to Figure 26.4). Through request messages (request profiles), the data and computational needs generated by the learners' devices are sent to the system's Multi-access Edge Computing (MEC) server. The MEC server performs tasks based on the request message profile (at the same level in the layer hierarchy) and verifies the learner's request message profile and computational requirements. Using the request result profile, the MEC server transmits the task execution outcomes. This process is repeated for each request message profile. If the request message profile requires more computational resources than the MEC server can handle, it is routed to nearby servers (edge cloud) within the same layer or a higher tier of the architecture hierarchy.

The Interactive m-Learning System block diagram shown in Figure 26.4 includes text, images, animations, and sound as input. Interactive questions, secure capture,

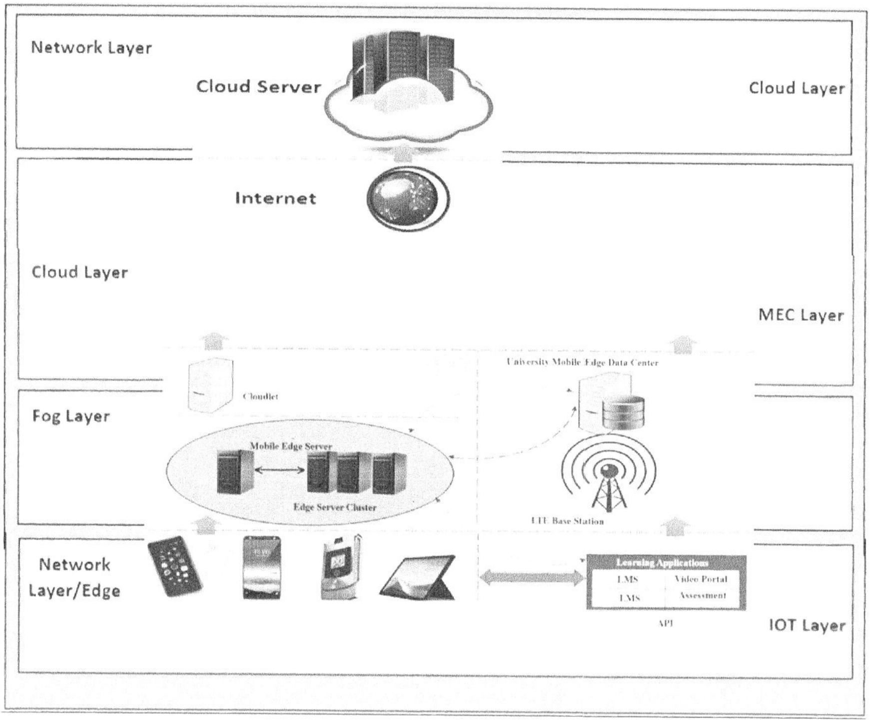

FIGURE 26.3 M-Learning Architecture.

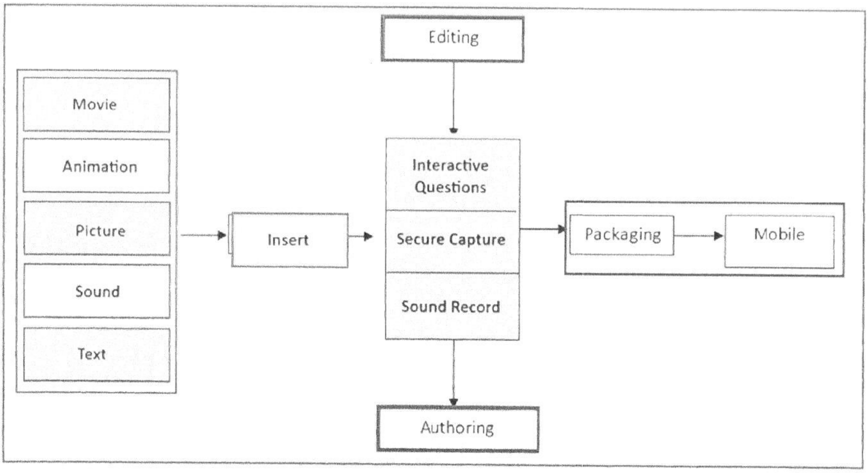

FIGURE 26.4 Diagram for Interactive M-Learning System.

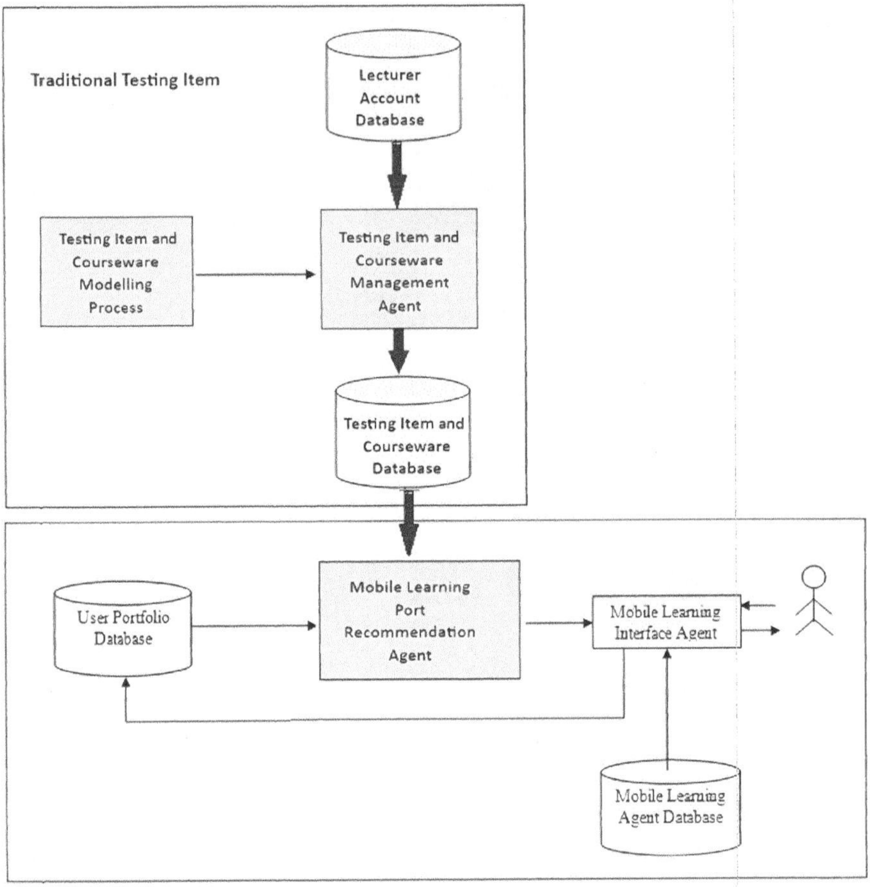

FIGURE 26.5 Mobile Learning Architecture (Offline to OnSine system).

and sound recording are included in the editing section, and the output is packaged and sent to a mobile device.

Figure 26.5 illustrates the complete architecture of mobile learning (offline to online system). The initial diagram encompasses the testing item and incorporates course details along with materials.

26.3 FACE-TO-FACE LEARNING DEFINITION

The term "face-to-face learning" explains the traditional approach of classroom teaching. Here, instructions are given face-to-face in the instructor's class. The teacher lays down the learning pace in this environment, while the students attend along at their own pace. The benefits of face-to-face learning between the teacher and students make in-person instruction considered beneficial. Figure 26.6 shows the face-to-face learning.

FIGURE 26.6 Face-to-Face Learning Model.

26.3.1 Benefits of Face-to-Face Learning

- **Social aspect.** As compared to online learning, peer learning in the same room encourages a sense of physical learning. All individuals in the group are learning at the same location and time.
- **Personalized learning.** Face-to-face instruction in individuals makes the teachers prepare personalized lesson plans and build relationships with individuals, which is not possible in online learning.
- **Discussion and collaboration.** The limitation of online forums lies in their inability to create the variation present in an in-person community.

26.4 THE DIFFERENCE BETWEEN E-LEARNING, M-LEARNING, AND FACE-TO-FACE LEARNING

Table 26.2 describes how they vary from each other.

26.5 RECENT ADVANCES IN E-LEARNING

Gamification is the integration of technology into education and learning. Internet of Things and blockchain are two emerging developments that are revolutionizing organizations that prioritize improving the learning experience (Raza, 2023). The main goal of gamification is to improve learning's capacity and effectiveness by incorporating game mechanics and concepts into educational and learning environments (Niromand et al., 2024). The process of gamification facilitates the transformation of tedious tasks into enjoyable learning opportunities. The gamification market is expected to grow from 15.9 billion dollars to around 48.9 billion dollars by 2028, according to observations. The most recent advancements in the gamification space are listed below, as shown in Figure 26.7.

TABLE 26.2
E-Learning vs M-learning vs Face-to-Face Learning

Key features	E-learning	M-learning	Face-to-face learning
Delivery of content	Using a desktop or laptop computer is the most common method of learning.	To learn, learners use wireless, lightweight devices that can be carried easily in their pockets, purses, or hands.	Face-to-face classroom lectures supported by tutorials, workshops, and independent studies for a large group of students.
Access	To complete the course, individuals should be seated comfortably.	Rather than being confined to a specific location, individuals can access knowledge or learning inputs wherever they are.	Group or individuals can access.
Screen size and navigation	The mouse pointer is smooth and the screens are larger. This enables visuals, graphics, and text to be effectively delivered.	Text and graphics are limited on mobile devices due to their small screens. Learners need larger buttons so they can easily use them with their fingers.	An interactive physical learning environment where students and teachers interact directly is known as face-to-face learning.
Content type	Content can be broad-based.	The content needs to be focused on a single concept.	The content needs to be focused on a single concept.
Context	It is necessary to establish context before adding it to the main module.	Spontaneous and contextual learning is facilitated by m-learning.	E-learning and remote teaching do not fully reflect face-to-face interaction and feedback.
Time	E-learning modules consist of 20–30 minutes, which allows them to gain a comprehensive understanding of the subject.	The length of an m-learning module should not exceed 5–7 minutes because learners have a difficult time focusing on anything longer.	Face-to-face learning does not depend on time.

26.6 PERSONALIZED LEARNING THROUGH ADAPTIVE TECHNOLOGY

The one-size-fits-all approach to education is recognized to be insufficient in assisting every student in realizing their full potential. It is evident that students have different learning styles, rates of acquisition, and skill levels. Because traditional education is

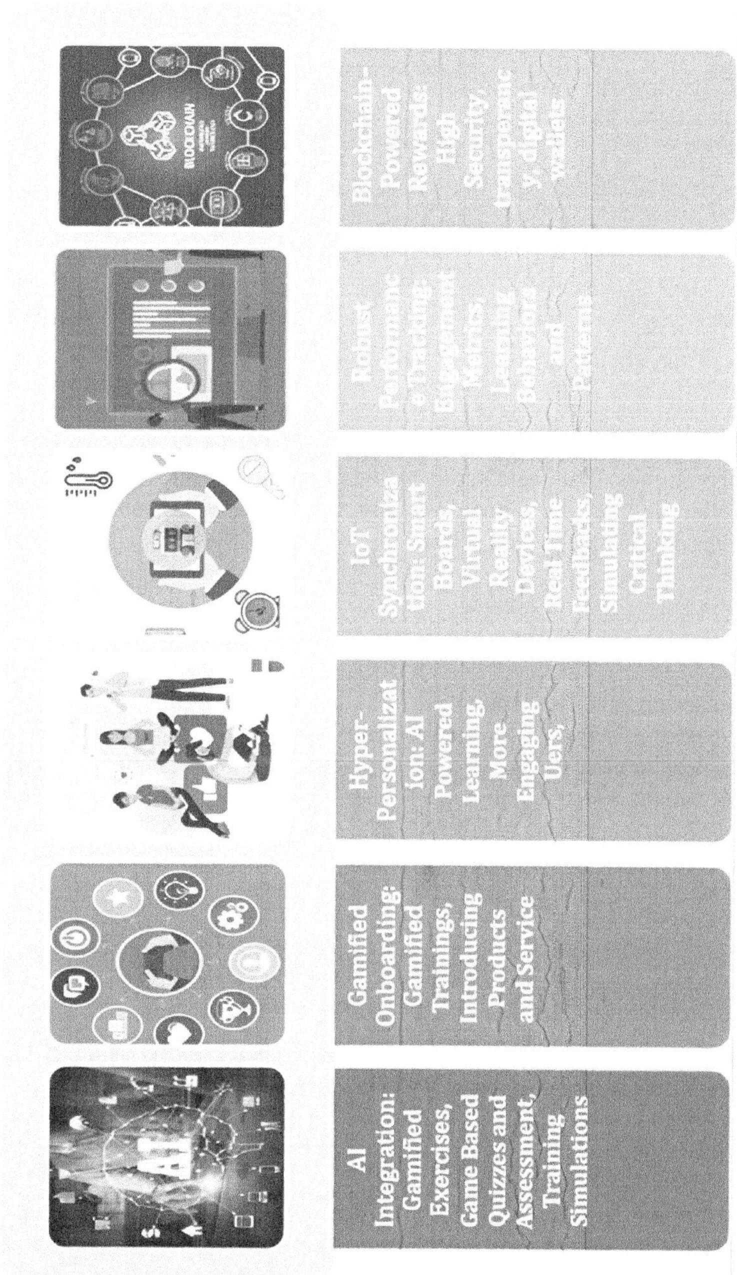

FIGURE 26.7 Latest Developments in Gamification.

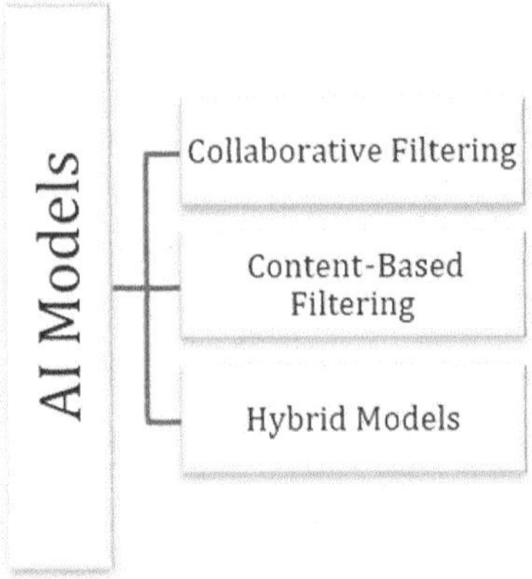

FIGURE 26.8 AI Models for Personalized Learning.

often unable to adapt to these variances, students suffer from disengagement and lose out on opportunities. The challenge is to figure out how artificial intelligence (AI) can more effectively provide tailored learning experiences and adaptive tests to better match the needs of every single student.

(1) AI in Personalized Learning:
(2) Virtual Reality (VR) and Augmented Reality (AR) in Education

When comparing VR-enhanced classes to traditional teaching techniques like watching movies and reading textbooks, recent research indicates that VR-supported courses can lead to more memorable and enjoyable learning experiences. Pre-service teacher who are interested in utilizing VR in the classroom may encounter difficulties because of worries regarding teachers' self-efficacy while utilizing the technology, safety issues with VR in the classroom, the requirement for technical support, and related costs, as shown in Figure 26.8.

26.7 CHALLENGES AND POTENTIAL LIMITATIONS OF ADOPTING THE ABOVE IN EDUCATION

Even though e-learning appears to have a bright future, issues and potential restrictions still need to be resolved. Infrastructure, training, and content creation will all come at a high cost when combining AI, gamification, adaptive technology, mobile learning, and VR/AR. In addition to established requirements for data security and privacy, there should also be ethical concerns. A lot of learner data is gathered by e-learning platforms, thus it is critical to make sure that data is handled securely. A digital divide may also result from different students' access to digital materials and technology. It is imperative to work toward closing this gap and giving every learner the same chances to gain from online education.

26.8 CONCLUSION

With E-learning, even the most occupied person may efficiently upgrade professionally and obtain new certificates by fitting learning around their schedules. Due to the internet, many noteworthy advancements in education have occurred. Today's students have no trouble enrolling in and administering an online course as they are used to using cell phones, messaging apps, and the internet. Due to the affordability of e-learning solutions and widespread internet access, education can now be conveniently accessed from virtually any location with the assistance of effective e-learning platforms. The objective of e-learning, mobile learning, and traditional in-person teaching is to enhance educational outcomes. It presents a promising path for education by offering flexibility, accessibility, and engagement that traditional approaches frequently do not. Time and location obstacles are eliminated for students by using smartphones, tablets, and other portable devices to access instructional information whenever and wherever they choose.

In conclusion, by meeting the various needs and preferences of contemporary learners, m-learning has the potential to completely transform the way we learn. However, in the end, careful planning, excellent writing, and continuous support are what make it effective. Using mobile-learning can result in more efficient, engaging, and personalized learning experiences for everyone as technology continues to develop and permeate into more aspects of our daily lives. In conclusion, while digital technologies offer innovative opportunities, face-to-face learning continues to play a vital role in education by providing a rich and dynamic environment for learning and growth. Its ability to facilitate real-time feedback, social interaction, and hands-on experiences contributes to a holistic and effective learning journey. As we navigate the continuous-evolving education landscape, it is important to recognize and leverage the enduring value of face-to-face learning alongside emerging digital modalities.

REFERENCES

Ahmad, S. (2023). E-learning and M-learning for English language teaching: Benefits, drawbacks and its pedagogical implications. *International Journal of Innovative Research in Technology (IJIRT)*, *9*(7), 732–738, ISSN: 2349-6002.

Chan, Y.F., Ranjit, K.S., Baba, J., & Parman, E. (2007). *Computer education for classroom teaching*. Malaysia: McGraw-Hill.

Hsbullah, H.M., & Idris, K.Md. (2009). E-learning adoption: The role of relative advantages, trialability and academic specialization. *Campus Wide Information System*, *26*(1), 54–70. Retrieved March 10, 2010, from www.123seminarsonly.com/Seminar-Reports/037/49532201-E-learning-adoption.pdf]

Karim, M.R.A., & Hashim, Y. (2004). The experience of the E-learning implementation at the Universiti Pendidikan Sultan Idris, Malaysia. *Malaysian Online Journal of Instructional Technology (MOJIT)*, *1*(1), 50–59. Retrieved March 10, 2010 from: http://pppjj.usm.my/mojit/articles/pdf/0804/The%20Experience%20of%20the%20E-Learning%20Implementation%20at%20UPSI.pdf

Martinez-Garcia, A., Horrach-Rosselló, P., & Mulet-Forteza, C. (2023). Evolution and current state of research into E-learning. *Heliyon*, 9(10), e21016.

Niromand, E., Mansoory, M.S., Ramezani, G., & Khazaei, M.R. (2024). Design, implementation and evaluation of e-learning program for common diseases to smartphone-based medical students: At a developing university. *BMC Medical Education, 24*, 52.

Raza, F. (2023). AI in education: Personalized learning and adaptive assessment. *Cosmic Bulletin of Business Management*, 2(1). https://doi.org/10.13140/RG.2.2.24796.77446.

Rosenberg, M.J. (2001). *E-Learning strategies for delivering knowledge in the digital age*. New York: McGraw-Hill.

Wentling, T.L., Waight, C., Gallaher, J., La Fleur, J., Wang, C., & Kanfer, A.G. (2000). E-learning: A review of literature. In: *Knowledge and Learning Systems Group*. USA: University of Illinois at Urbana-Champaign, pp. 1–73.

Index

A

Academic partnership survey, 237
Accessibility, 33–35, 37, 50
Accessible content, 51
Adaptive E-learning environment learning styles, 177, 180, 186
Adaptive learning, 203, 211, 321, 323
  systems, 72
AI and machine learning, 38
AI-chatbots, 338–341
AI-powered educational platforms, 211
Artificial intelligence (AI), 201, 229
Augmented reality (AR), 203
Authentication, 300
Automation, 229

B

Badges, 211
Blackboard, 199, 202, 206
Blended learning, 35
Blockchain, 203, 299–307
Block creation, 304, 305
Block validation, 305
Breakout rooms, 206
Broadband expansion, 209

C

Canvas, 199, 202, 206
Chat and messaging features, 206
Cloud-based learning, 278
  advantages and limitations, 277
  earning materials, 12
  environments cybersecurity, 145–147, 149
  management systems (LMS), 63
  multimedia learning, 284
  platforms, 283
Cloud-based LMS, 204, 206
Cloud computing, 14, 15, 17–29, 125, 128, 132, 199, 200, 202–205
  IT plans, 92
Cloud service models (IaaS, PaaS, SaaS), 62–63
Collaborative learning, 5–8, 299–302
  environments, 67
  modeling, 11
Collaborative tools, 205, 207, 212
Communication, 199–202, 204–207, 210
  protocols, 210
Content management, 202–207
Correspondence courses, 200–201
Critical thinking, 207–211

D

Data analysis, 233
Data fragmentation, 303
Data integrity, 306
Data manipulation, 301
Data privacy and ownership, 147
Data privacy concerns, 39
Data security, 34, 37, 39, 331, 333, 335
  advocating, 139–140
Digital divide, 33, 35, 209
Digital learning, 202–203
  technologies, 179, 187
Document collaboration, 199, 205–208, 212
Document interpretation system, 278, 280, 283
Document region detection, 280

E

EdTech, 120, 121
Educational access, 200
Educational cloud, 30, 31, 321–327, 329, 331, 333–336
Educational resources, 202, 207, 210
Educator training, 209
Elasticity in E-learning, 61, 71
E-learning, 3, 4, 6, 7, 11, 61, 275–278, 282–284
  architecture, interaction design, cloud layer, physical design, 95, 98
  cloud environment, 175–176
Empowering rural education, 335
Encryption, 300, 303, 305
  techniques, 129
Enhanced student support, 100
Evaluating learning outcomes, 130
Examination materials, 299, 301, 303, 306

F

File sharing, 205, 207–208

G

Gamification, 211–212
  and simulations, 72
Geographical constraints, 204

H

Hybrid learning environments, 206

I

Infrastructure as a Service (IaaS), 15, 19, 22
Integration hurdles, 33
Intelligent tutoring systems, 203, 211
Interactive Chatbot, 342
Interactive content, 209

L

Learning analytics, 173–179, 186
Learning environment, 107–109, 116, 120
Learning management systems (LMS), 125, 199

M

Machine learning, 233
Moodle, 199, 202, 206
Multimedia content, 127
Multimodal learning, 9

N

National Agency for Higher Education
(NAHE), 282
NLP, 238

O

Online courses, 202–203, 206, 209, 211
Online examinations, 339
Online learning, 338, 339, 342
Online pedagogy, 209
Online practice of law online, 349
Online teaching, 210
Open-source LMS, 206

P

Pedagogical innovations, 71
Personalized education, 53
Personalized learning, 30, 31, 35, 36, 39, 203, 211
  experiences, 72
Privacy and security, 127
Privacy controls, 206
Productivity tools, 206–208

R

Real-time collaboration, 204
  tools, 66
Recommender systems, 177–180, 186–187

S

Scalability, 37, 204
Security and privacy concerns, 31
Security considerations, 124, 131
Security challenges, 146–148
Smart document learning, 275
Smart Education, 3, 299–303, 306
  environment, 10
  framework, 8
Social learning platforms, 66
Student-centered learning, 209
Student engagement, 205, 209
Synchronous learning, 202

T

Tailored learning paths, 205
Teaching–learning paradigms, 275
Teaching–learning process, 282

V

Virtual backgrounds, 206
Virtual learning, 338
  environments, 203, 207–208, 212
Virtual programming, 337
Virtual reality (VR), 202–203

W

Workflow management, 208